NEW YORK IN LITERATURE

The Story Told in the Landmarks of
Town and Country

By

RUFUS ROCKWELL WILSON

Author of "New York Old and New" in Collaboration

with

OTILIE ERICKSON WILSON, M. A.

THE PRIMAVERA PRESS, INC.

ELMIRA, N. Y.

1947

Dedicated To

VIRGINIA STOUT

AIMS AND ACKNOWLEDGMENTS

An attempt is made in these pages to tell the story of New York in literature as reflected in the landmarks of town and country, thus dealing with a large section of our literary annals in a manner that blends recorded fact with intimate personal impression. The method of approach selected leads now and again to repetitions, but we are confident that these will be accepted by the reader as fresh emphasis given to significant facts. It is also hoped that, aside from its general appeal, the present volume will serve a needed purpose as supplementary reading in the literary courses of high schools and colleges.

The first eleven chapters have to with New York and Brooklyn, and the sites associated with more than two hundred writers of varying gifts and output, many of whom hold a permanent place in American letters—the chronicle ranging from the founders of New Amsterdam down to the Manhattan authors who only yesterday ceased from their labors. Three chapters are devoted to Long and Staten Islands, and a fourth to the Neutral Ground—presenting a gallery which includes such well-remembered figures as William Cullen Bryant and Margaret Fuller, Thomas Paine and James Fenimore Cooper.

Two other chapters record a leisurely pilgrimage along the east bank of the Hudson from Irving's Sleepy Hollow to Albany, and a like number deal with the authors of North and South Jersey, Walt Whitman among them, who also played their parts in the literary history of New York. In later chapters the authors describe journeys along the west bank of the Hudson and through the Catskills to the Finger Lakes Country. A final chapter deals with Mark Twain, and the days and labors in Elmira that made him, through the years, the most widely known American author of his period.

Thanks are due to our kinsman, Dr. Hiram Rockwell Bennett for assuring accuracy of detail to the chapters dealing with New York and Brooklyn. We have also had at every stage, cordial and effective aid from Mrs. Thelma R. King, reference librarian, Steele Memorial Library, Elmira.

Dr. and Mrs. Rufus Rockwell Wilson,

Elmira, N. Y., May 28, 1947.

TABLE OF CONTENTS

NEW YORK IN LITERATURE

CHAPTER I

THE BATTERY AND ITS NEIGHBORS

No matter how weighty the material task of each succeeding age, some part of the life of New York has always been touched to finer issues. Poet and story-teller from the first have had a part in the city's history, and memories of them lend interest to every corner of the older town. To begin where the town began, the Battery was a favorite loitering place of young Washington Irving when without set purpose he was making ready for his long career as America's foremost man of letters. A little later, James Fenimore Cooper, his love of the sea a deep and abiding one, frequently made his way to the Battery to watch the arrival of ships from far places. It had a place as a rule in the week-end rambles which cemented the friendship of Halleck and Drake, and it also knew in other days the footfalls of Morris and Willis. Howells gave the Battery a place in two of his novels; Taylor and Stedman celebrated it in verse; and it was while strolling on its seawall that Epes Sargent found inspiration for his song, *A Life on the Ocean Wave*.

Julia Ward Howe was born in one of the row of dwellings demolished many years ago to furnish a site for the present custom house. John Jay dwelt on the same spot, when, in an earlier time, it was occupied by a sightly mansion facing Bowling Green, and all the other streets adjacent to, or leading from the Battery are rich in literary associations. The hero of Bunner's *The Story of a New York House*, lived at 7 State Street, while ten doors removed once resided William Irving, elder brother of Washington and the Pindar Cockloft of *The Salmagundi Papers*. James Kirke Paulding was then a member of the Irving household, but afterwards dwelt for many years at 17 Whitehall Street, writing in the latter home the *Dutchman's Fireside* and other of his books.

Paulding was born at Tarrytown of sturdy Dutch ancestry, and when a lad with Washington Irving as an occasional companion hunted squirrels in Sleepy Hollow, or made pilgrimage to the places on the Hudson rich in history or fable, drinking in at first hand the legends of which as authors they were later to make satisfying use. Settled in New York at the age of nineteen Paulding made his way both as an author and in politics. He was Secretary of the Navy under Van Buren, and during thirty busy years he attempted almost every form of prose, among other things in 1819 after Irving's departure for Europe continuing *Salmagundi* in a second series. He is best remembered, however, for his *Letters from the South*, recording a journey made in 1816, which furnished understanding glimpses of an era and section soon to undergo great changes; and for the *Dutchman's Fireside*, which dealt with the Mohawk Valley in the days of the French and Indian War and of redoubtable Sir William Johnson—a simple yet charming tale which promptly passed through six editions and which in a later time saves its author's name from forgetfulness. It is also to be recorded to his credit that Paulding was one of the first among American critics to rightly estimate the rare gifts of Edgar Allan Poe, and to strive to help the latter on his troubled way.

It was at 2 Broad Street that Samuel Loudon, who had been a ship chandler before he became an editor, published the *American Magazine* in the closing years of the century before the last, the only periodical worthy of the name; and seven doors below the New York *American* had its office during the years that it was edited by Charles King, afterwards president of Columbia. Again, at 16 Broad Street, Laurence Oliphant had his office during one period of the varied career which, set in relief by unusual gifts, gave him a place among the most interesting of modern Englishmen. Oliphant was then manager of the American interests of the Direct Cable Company, serving the while as one of the editors of the *North American Review*. To this period also belonged his *Tender Recollections of Irene Macgillicuddy* and *Altiora Peto*, clever novels which embody many penetrating glimpses of American life and society.

An office building at 33 Broad Street covers the site of the house built by Nicasius de Sille—a house long remembered for its heavy plate, carved furniture and costly hangings—who had come from Holland in the service of the Dutch West India Company, and who in the intervals of his labors as a member of Stuyvesant's council in the last days of Dutch rule, found leisure to pen the verse which gives him a modest place on the roster of New York poets. But de Sille, being at bottom a practical man, ceased to write poems when success came to him as a merchant. And it was in Broad Street, between Water and Front that John Holt, a stout-hearted son of Virginia, for a number of years published the New York *Journal,* which, in the unquiet days preceding the Revolution, was the fearless organ of the Sons of Liberty. Holt was compelled to flee the town when the British entered it, but, taking his press with him, he continued to publish his newspaper at first one and than another of the towns on the Hudson under conditions that would have dismayed a less resolute man. He returned to New York upon the conclusion of peace, but died in 1784, and was buried in St. Paul's churchyard. An inscription on the stone which marks his grave pays moving tribute to his worth as a man. "To say," it runs, "that his family lament him is needless; that his friends bewail him is useless; that all regret him unnecessary; for that he merited every esteem is certain. The tongues of slander cannot say less, though justice might say more."

William Leete Stone lived at the corner of Bridge and State Streets in the early years of his career as editor of the *Commercial Advertiser,* a career of storm and stress and acid comment on men and events, which caused James Fenimore Cooper to sue him for libel and which ended only with his death in 1844 in his fifty-third year. Stone, however, is now best remembered for his Indian biographies, based on sound research, which included lives of Joseph Brant, Red Jacket and Uncas. In the third house from the head of Bridge Street Washington Irving dwelt with his brother, Eben, after his first return from Europe. It was also in Bridge Street, five doors from the home of Eben Irving, that, in the same period, James Cheetham published the New York *Citizen,* and waged the wars of words which made him the best known editor of his time. Cheetham was an English radical who fled from the Manchester riots of 1798, and found his way to New York with money enough in his purse to buy the newspaper which he made for a decade the leader of the Democratic press of the country. He was cut off, however, in his prime, dying in delirium, in the hot summer of 1809, with congestion of the brain. "Boys, study Bolingbroke for style, and Locke for sentiment!" are said to have been his last words to his sons.

Jacob Steendam, the Dutch verse-maker, was an early dweller in Stone Street, and there John Peter Zenger, an energetic young

German, had his home and shop, when, through the columns
of the *Weekly Journal,* he fought the battle for a free press,
which Gouverneur Morris acclaimed "the morning star of the
Revolution," while around the corner in Beaver Street, another
pioneer printer, James Parker, the friend and partner of Franklin, long plied his craft. Parker was a publisher as well as a
printer, and from his press issued the first American edition of
Richardson's *Pamela,* and other books now dear to the heart of
the collector.

In the early years of the last century, the site numbered 7
Beaver Street, was occupied by a school for boys, in which Henry
William Herbert, best remembered as Frank Forrester, long
taught Greek and Latin. Herman Melville was born at 6 Pearl
Street in 1819 the same year in which a few miles to the eastward Walt Whitman entered life—and on the opposite side of
that thoroughfare, between State and Whitehall Streets is the
site of the house which in 1791 was the birthplace of John
Howard Payne. Melville and Payne were to shape widely different careers, but a career in each instance charged with adventure of an unusual sort. Born of half Dutch, half English
parents, Melville grew with the years into a rugged, powerful,
broad-shouldered man destined by nature to make his own way
in the world. He went to school in Albany where his mother's
family, the Gansevoorts, were people of importance, and where
he read and was deeply moved by the sea tales of Cooper.

But it may have been Dana's *Two Years Before the Mast*
which caused Melville at the age of eighteen to voyage to the
South Seas on a whaler; to escape from its hardships and live
for a brief period among the cannibals in the Marquesas, and to
acquire by rough experiences the tragic sense of life that was to
remain with him until the end. There followed service in the
navy from which he was discharged in 1844 at Boston, to find a
wife in the daughter of Chief Justice Shaw of Massachusetts, and
to write within a half dozen years three remarkable books—*Typee,*
Omoo, and *Red Jacket,* the last of which by its moving account of the ill-treatment of enlisted men led to the abolition of
flogging in the navy.

During the acclaim which attended these books Melville was
a neighbor in the Berkshires of Nathaniel Hawthorne, the author
of his period whom he most admired; but after 1866 he was again
a resident of New York where, his popularity having deserted
him, he held for nearly a score of years a position in the custom
house. He was busy with his pen until shortly before his death

in 1891, but in his earlier books he had said all that the world care to read or remember, and the last days of a self-sought retirement were passed in almost complete obscurity—the record of which constitutes one of the strangest passages in the history of American letters.

The son of a roving schoolmaster, John Howard Payne, although born in New York, spent his infancy at East Hampton, Long Island, and at the age of five was taken by his father to Boston, where while still a lad, he worked on a magazine for children edited by Samuel Woodworth, who had been a printer's apprentice and who was shortly to win fame by his song *The Old Oaken Bucket*. Payne was born with a love for the stage, and, after brief interludes as clerk in a New York counting-house and as student at Union College, greatly to the disgust of a theatre-hating father, made his debut in Providence with a much-applauded recitation of *Ode to the Passions* by Collins. A quick turn of the wheel found young Payne on the Boston stage where he was warmly praised when he played Romeo to the Juliet of Elizabeth Arnold, an actress of charm who was about to become the mother of Edgar Allan Poe.

This was in 1809 and the same year brought Payne's successful appearance at the Park Theatre in New York, where he acted Young Norval in a tragedy called *Douglas*, and Edgar to the Lear of the veteran George Frederick Cooke, who pronounced him a "polite and sensible youth." Three years later he played Young Norval at Drury Lane in London, and then appeared at other English theatres, but only with moderate success, for he failed to mature as an actor as he passed from youth to manhood. So he turned to writing and adapting plays for Drury Lane. The tragedy of *Brutus* which he wrote when imprisoned for debt proved a great success and held the stage for fifty years; but most of his more than half a hundred other plays were flimsy affairs, which failed to survive a brief first production.

One of the few exceptions to this dismal order of things was *Clari, or the Maid of Milan,* in which the heroine, longing for her cottage in Italy, sang *Home, Sweet Home,* written by Payne in Paris and which won him a reputation that has survived the changing tastes of four generations of music lovers. Its author died in 1852 while serving as consul at Tunis, and thirty years later *Home, Sweet Home* was sung by a host of people gathered about the grave in a Washington cemetery where his body found its final resting-place. Payne was always in trouble, but he had also a genius for friendship, and one of those who remained faithful to him through good and evil report was Washington Irving, who in the principal character of *Buckthorne and His Friends*, painted a gentle and winning personality in an unforgetable way.

Returning to New York and to an earlier time, one finds at 81 Pearl Street the spot, where, in 1693, William Bradford, New York's first printer, set up his press and became, by appointment of the council, printer to the colony. Thereafter he was for nearly half a century, a useful and hard-working citizen of New York, the master and trainer of a generation of printers, including Parker and Zenger, and the founder, in 1725, of the New York *Gazette*, the first and for several years the only newspaper in the town. Bradford died in 1752, at the age of ninety, and the stone above his grave in Trinity burial ground tells the wayfarer that "he was printer to this government for upward of fifty years, and, being quite worn out with old age and labor, he left this mortal state in lively hopes of a blessed immortality."

The old Cotton Exchange covers the site of the building from which Bradford issued his *Gazette;* and close at hand, at the vanished sign of the Bible and Crown in Hanover Square, Hugh Gaine, another pioneer printer, for many years following 1752 issued his New York *Mercury*. This journal was originally edited in the interest of the Whigs, but, when the Revolution came and the British occupied New York, Gaine's prudence got the better of his convictions—if he had any—and he became a warm advocate of the royalist cause. True to his shifty nature, when the war ended he petitioned the Assembly to allow him to remain in the city and to continue his paper. His petition was granted, but the *Mercury* no longer found favor, and soon its existence came to an end. Thereafter Gaine devoted himself to general printing, and among the stream of pamphlets, almanacs and books that poured from his press was the first American edition of *Robinson Crusoe*. He died in 1807, at the age of eighty-one, and is buried in Trinity churchyard.

Philip Freneau, poet follower of Jefferson, in the birth years of the republic shaped at 131 Pearl Street the policy and utterances of the *Daily Advertiser*, making it a thorn in the side of the Federalists, and himself the editor most dreaded by Washington and his advisers. Folk of a later time value Freneau for other things than his education of the masses in public opinion. The son of a rich New York merchant of Huguenot descent, and the room-mate at Princeton of James Madison, he early produced a handful of lyrical and sea poems—*The Wild Honeysuckle* and

The Indian Burying Ground among them—which he printed on the press he had set up on his father's farm, and which for feeling and sheer loveliness were unequalled by those of any other verse-maker of his period.

Then Freneau became captain of a coastal vessel engaged in the West Indian trade, and during the Revolution, being an outspoken patriot and the commander of a privateer, was confined in a British prison-ship at New York, about which he wrote a lurid and bitter poem. Half a century later, with his career as shipmaster and editor a long way behind him, New York knew Freneau in neglected and lonely old age. He had freed his slaves; his holdings in New Jersey had dwindled to a few acres, and he had to mend clocks and work on the roads and at the printer's case to earn the small sums needed for taxes. Nevertheless when he came now and again to New York dressed in the small-clothes, buckled shoes and cocked hat of his youth, he was sure of a hearty welcome from Gulian Verplanck and other old friends who honored his past, and who sincerely mourned him when in the bleak winter of 1832 word came to them that he had been caught in a blizzard and picked up dying at the door of his New Jersey farmhouse.

Washington Irving was once in business with his brothers at 135 Pearl Street, and five doors northward on the other side of the way, Thomas Bailey Aldrich, before his early abandonment of business for letters, was for several years, a clerk in the counting-house of an uncle. Thence it is a short walk to the site of the warehouse at 84 South Street just below John, where, for a score of years, Fitz-Greene Halleck kept books for Jacob Barker, winning in his leisure hours fame as a maker of verse. It was also during his years in South Street that Halleck formed the friendship with Joseph Rodman Drake, which linked their names alike in life and death.

Born in 1790 at Guilford, Connecticut, then as now one of the loveliest of New England villages, Halleck had careful training there in the science of book-keeping and at the age of twenty-one made his modest entrance into the city which for nearly two score years was to be his home. When he quit the employ of Jacob Barker he entered that of John Jacob Astor, who at his death in 1848 left his secretary an annuity which enabled the latter to pass his last years in ease and comfort in his native town. Halleck had been only a short time in New York when he became the friend of Joseph Rodman Drake five years his junior and then a medical student. The son of a colonel in Washington's army and himself a man of charm and quality, Drake had been early left an orphan with a difficult path ahead of him, but while still in his teens had won praise as a facile and clever maker of verse. Halleck later described him as at this time "perhaps the handsomest man in New York—a face like an angel, a form like an Apollo."

The two men without delay became close friends, giving many of their leisure hours to long rambles in and around the growing town, and to boat trips up the Hudson and on the Sound. They also became literary partners and in March, 1819, using the signature Croakers to conceal their identity and taking *The Good-Natured Man* of Goldsmith as a model, contributed to *The Evening Post* a series of clever skits on men and manners which took the town by storm, winning an army of angry, puzzled or amused readers. Coleman, the editor of *The Evening Post* refused to disclose the names of his contributors, but Halleck did not conceal from intimate friends his delight in the commotion he and his partner had set afoot. "We have tasted all the pleasures and many of the pains of literary fame and notoriety," he wrote his sister. "We have had the consolation of seeing and hearing ourselves praised, puffed, eulogized, execrated, and threatened as much, I believe I can say with truth, as any writers since the days of Junius. The whole town has talked of nothing else for three weeks past, and every newspaper has done us the honor to mention us in some way, either of praise or censure but all uniting in owning our talents and genius."

It is clear from the foregoing that Halleck was not inclined to hide his light under a bushel, and, read in a later time, the Croaker rhymes, light in touch and charged with spirit and humor, afford diverting glimpses of the New York of the second decade of the last century. During the years which immediately followed their appearance their authors in individual effort did much of their best work as poets. Drake wrote and published *The Culprit Fay,* a charming flight of fancy, and his popular song *The American Flag,* and Halleck produced his *Fanny,* a satirical poem which passed through several editions, although much of his best verse, including the spirited lyric, *Marco Bozzaris,* which made him for a time the most widely quoted poet in the country, belong to later periods of his career.

Drake's untimely death in 1820 severed a rare friendship, but Halleck lived on in New York for nearly thirty years, his jaunty speech and carriage, and the out-of-the-common opinions to which it was his custom to give free expression making him a beguiling and unmistakable figure in the life of the town. Most of his friends were Henry Clay Whigs or Andrew Jackson Democrats, but he was wont to describe himself as a monarchist. Perhaps this was why he became the favorite comrade of Louis Napoleon when the future emperor of the French spent a few months in New York. Halleck, as already noted, retired to his native Guilford in 1848, but he never lost his love for the city which had given him rich friendships and moderate fame as a poet. Nor did New York forget him. He died at Guilford in 1867, and ten years later, with becoming ceremonies in which Bryant, had a part, a bronze statue of him was unveiled in Central Park.

Back again in New York's oldest thoroughfare, one finds at 326 Pearl Street the site of the Walton house, which, when it was still one of the lordly homes of the town, had pathetic association with Charlotte Temple's hapless romance. This romance, upon which Susanna Rowson based her *Tale of Truth*, had its beginning, if tradition can be trusted, in a house which stood aforetime in Art Street, now Astor Place, and it was when repulsed by her lover from the Walton house that, ill and despairing, she found refuge in a hovel in Pell Street, not far from the Bowery, where she died. She was buried in Trinity churchyard and her rightful name of Charlotte Stanley cut in her tombstone; but later the present name, Charlotte Temple, was carved in its place.

A little beyond, and across the way from the site of the Walton house, Pearl Street widens out into Franklin Square, where Lindley Murray once had his home, and where was for long the printing-house of the Harpers. Lindley Murray was, perhaps, America's first professional man of letters. He was born in Pennsylvania in 1745, but reared in New York, where his Quaker father made a fortune in the West Indian trade and gave the name of his family to Murray Hill. A friend and fellow student of John Jay, the younger Murray became a lawyer of parts; but a crippling illness early made him a lifelong invalid unable to leave his house or rise from his chair. True to his Quaker training he took no part in the Revolution. A man of large means, he removed to England in 1784 in the hope of improving his health and settled near York where he lived until death claimed him in his eighty-second year.

A devout and benevolent man, Murray, despite his physical handicap, became without delay, a recorded minister and leader of the Society of Friends in York, prompt to make the most of each new occasion for helpful service. His home for upward of three decades was a meeting place for like-minded people, and he tells in his memoirs of the never ending army of visitors, English and American, who found him in his snug sitting-room with portable writing-case and papers before him, busy with new plans to aid his fellows. He had been for long an earnest student of grammar, and it was for the pupils of a Quaker school for girls at York that in 1795 he wrote the *English Grammar* that remained for two generations a favorite textbook on both sides of the sea. He followed it with an *English Reader* and a *French Reader,* and all three met with such favor that within forty years more than a million and a half copies of them were sold, helping a host of boys and girls to correct reading and trained appreciation of the best in literature. His grave is in the Quaker burial ground at York, "hemmed in by walls and tufted with trees."

A dingy pile is the former home of the house of Harper, in Franklin Square, but richer in literary memories than any other structure in America. Time was when few American books were published that were not offered first to the Harpers, and their home in Franklin Square was the familiar haunt of three generations of bookmen. There George William Curtis long sat in his easy chair and edited *Harper's Weekly;* there Paul du Chaillu, the explorer, wrote the greater part of his book on Equatorial Africa; and there for many years William Mills Alden, editor, poet, and mystic in one, conducted *Harper's Magazine.* The guide and mentor of a long roll of literary beginners Alden gave more than friendship to some of those who came to him for aid. Another editor, unable to lend a helping hand to a young Southern widow who had come to New York in search of success as a writer, gave her a note of introduction to Alden. After a time the two editors met at dinner, and the question was asked: "Alden, what were you able to do for the young woman I sent you earlier in the year?" A moment of silence and then the quiet reply: "I married her."

The history of the house of Harper has been written with gusto and charm by J. Henry Harper, the grandson of one of its founders. He relates that the original Harper brothers—there were four of them—for many years had all things in common, each brother drawing from the firm's till whatever he needed without inquiry as to the size and number of the amounts taken by his associates. J. Henry Harper, who had piquant association with many of the authors at home and abroad whose books were published by his firm, recounts among a hundred interesting stories how Thomas Hardy conceived his best known romance, *Tess of the D'Urbervilles.* "Hardy told me," he writes, "that one day while he was out walking a farm wagon passed him, and sitting on the tailboard, her legs swinging, was a typical country lass. The hill was steep, and by the time he had reached the top this rural girl had become Tess and the theme of the story had developed in his mind."

At 97 Cliff Street, not far from the old home of the house of Harper, in the middle years of the last century was the printing office of Gray and Green, where in the summer of 1853 Samuel L. Clemens, then a lad of eighteen, worked as a compositor. A letter to his sister Pamela in St. Louis affords a diverting glimpse of the humorist at this period of his career. "I have been fooling myself," he writes, "with the idea that I was going to leave New York every day for the last two weeks. I have taken a liking to the abominable place, and every time I get ready to leave, I put it off a day or so. It is as hard on my conscience to leave New York, as it was easy to leave Hannibal . . . . If my letters do not come often, you need not bother yourself about me; for if you have a brother nearly eighteen years of age, who is not able to take care of himself a few miles from home, such a brother is not worth one's thought." Fourteen years later, much water in the meantime having gone under the bridge, Gray and Green set up and printed *The Jumping Frog,* the first book of their former compositor.

Memories of many an early author cling to the lower reaches of Broadway. William Smith, New York's first native historian, was born, and Cadwallader Colden, the town's most important literary figure in the first half of the eighteenth century, once dwelt in the block which faces Bowling Green from the west. Washington Irving lodged for a time at 16 Broadway and there prepared for the press a revision of his *Knickerbocker's History.* And at what was then 66 Broadway one finds the site of the boardinghouse where Alexis de Tocqueville and his friend Gustave de Beaumont lodged when in May, 1831, they began the New World sojourn which was to have splendid and enduring issue in the former's *Democracy in America.* The son of a Norman count of ancient and distinguished ancestry who after the fall of Napoleon had in turn ably served the Bourbons and the house of Orleans, Tocqueville was in his late twenties and already a magistrate when he crossed the Atlantic to study the American penal system, and, what was to prove more important, democratic processes at first hand. During a nine-months period he and his companion, after a brief stay in New York, journeyed to Buffalo and then through the Great Lakes region and Lower Canada to the Wisconsin wilderness. Later journeys took them to Boston, Philadelphia and Baltimore, and then down the Ohio to the Mississippi through Cincinnati and Memphis to New Orleans, whence they made their way northward by way of Mobile to Washington, and so back to New York.

Both Tocqueville and Beaumont had a gift for friendship and at every turn made cordial and informing contacts. John Quincy Adams, Daniel Webster, William Ellery Channing and Jared Sparks welcomed them to Boston, where they also found a truly helpful friend in Francis Lieber, a young man, who had lately fled his native Germany to begin a long career of light and leading in America, and who in due course was to translate into English their future Prison Report. Chancellor Kent called upon them during their early days in New York and later sent them a kindly letter accompanied by a copy of his *Commentaries,* a gift which later had an important part in shaping Tocqueville's *Democracy in America.* When they voyaged down the Mississippi they had Sam Houston for an unusual and perplexing fellow traveler and in Washington they were received with courtesy by Houston's friend and sage adviser, President Andrew Jackson.

This was in the last days of January, 1832, and a few weeks later Tocqueville and Beaumont went back to France with well-filled notebooks and minds charged with individual and arresting estimates of democracy in action. These, Tocqueville, when back in his native land, reexamined with patience and care wedded to great ability and then wrote his *Democracy in America,* which promptly translated into English was at once welcomed by students of the subject with which it dealt as a work of the first-rank in its field. And such, despite its defects, errors in observation and lack of perspective among them—many of the men whom its author met in America, and who helped to shape his views were Federalists pure and undefiled, held in contempt by such robust partisans as Thomas H. Benton—it has remained for upward of a century. Its author, who through his later years played an honorable and helpful part in French affairs, never returned to America, but than he no foreigner has more profoundly influenced the political thought of four generations, and for the originality and austere intelligence which found expression in his disinterested and always honest pages we are his continuing and weighty debtors. At 82 Broadway Edwin Lawrence Godkin in the decade preceding the Civil War was a student in the law office of David Dudley Field, and at 106 Broadway William Cullen Bryant began his long career in journalism as editor of the New York *Review and Athenaeum*. Godkin, then a young man of twenty-five, was the son of Irish Protestant parents and had studied at the University of Dublin. While reading for the bar he served also as correspondent of the London *Daily News*, but soon abandoned the law to become through the press, an effective shaper of public opinion. He had a strain of Swift in his mental makeup, and men now grown old recall his acid comments on men and measures, first as editor of *The Nation* and then of *The Evening Post*, as one of the enlivening experiences of their youth. In will and desire, however, he never became an integral part of the American scene, and, his labors as an editor behind him, recrossed the Atlantic to end his days in Ireland and England.

William Cullen Bryant, who preceded Godkin as editor of *The Evening Post*, had achieved a national reputation as a poet purely American in outlook and spirit, when in 1825 at the age of thirty-one, having met with meager success as a lawyer in his native Massachusetts, he sought a new field of effort in New York. He already had to his credit *Thanatopsis, Lines to a Waterfowl*, and other memorable poems, and so received a warm welcome from Cooper and Halleck and other well-known people in his new home. After a brief period of service on the New York *Review* at a salary of five hundred dollars a year, which made his financial position an uncertain one, he gladly accepted an invitation to join the editorial staff of *The Evening Post*. Four years later he succeeded William Coleman as chief editor and owner of that journal, a relation he was to maintain for nearly half a century.

And so in 1830 Bryant could inform his friend, the elder Richard Henry Dana, that he had made sure of a comfortable livelihood. "I do not like politics any better than you do," he wrote; "but they get only my mornings, and you know politics and a bellyful are better than poetry and starvation." Nevertheless, while *The Evening Post under* Bryant's control took high rank as an anti-slavery supporter of the Union, he did not cease to function with distinction as a poet, witness *A Forest Hymn, The Death of the Flowers* and *The Flood of Years;* and the complete translation of Homer which, seeking relief from loneliness, he made in old age.

At 111 Broadway long stood the Trinity Building where for years was the office of William Allen Butler, more widely known

as the witty author of *Nothing to Wear* than by the labors
which made him one of the leaders of the New York bar. The
site was occupied in an earlier time by a building in which Elam
Bliss had a book store, and there in 1832 Edgar Allan Poe, a
youth of twenty-three, prepared for the press his third volume
of verse, which included *To Helen* and *Israfel,* and one of
the few existing copies of which has sold in recent years for
more money than was ever earned by its author in any twelve-
month of his career. This was in the year following Poe's expulsion from West Point for absenting himself from roll call.
At this time a chance sojourner in New York, the town did not
know him as a permanent resident until a later period of his hapless career.

The corner of Broadway and Thames Street for half a century furnished a site for the City Hotel, where royal welcome
was extended to Irving upon his return in 1832 from extended
residence in Europe, and where a banquet, long remembered for
its brilliancy, was given to Charles Dickens, when, a decade later,
the latter made his first visit to America. Irving had sailed for
Liverpool in 1815, and he was quick on his return, after an
absence of seventeen years, to note great changes both in town
and people. He found New York fast out-growing the metes
and bounds of an earlier time; that the comrades of his youth
had passed into thoughtful middle age, and for members of his
craft a crowded field where there had once been a comfortable
absence of competition. "You young fellows" Irving later observed to George William Curtis, "have a harder time than we
old fellows had. You trip over each other's heels; there are so
many of you. We had it all our own way. But the account is
square, for you can make as much by a lecture as we made by
a book."

Charles Dickens had just turned thirty when he came for
the first time to America, but *Sketches by Boz,* the *Pickwick
Papers* and four of his full-length novels had already won him
a host of admirers on both sides of the Atlantic. Thus his reception in New York was of the heartiest sort. Irving presided
at a dinner at the City Hotel—breaking down, as he had predicted he would, from nervousness—and a ball in the novelist's
honor at the Park Theatre was noteworthy for its color and numbers. But the first visit of Dickens, which also carried him to the
South and West, had an unfortunate sequel. With no international copyright there was no American money for the British
novelist, and, failing to mend this condition of things, Dickens

on his return to England gave expression to his resentment in *American Notes* wherein he flayed his recent hosts for their alleged sins of omission and commission. Years were to pass before the latter again accorded him a full measure of his earlier popularity.

A boarding house on the east side of Broadway, two doors below Liberty Street, was the home of Halleck during his earlier years in New York, and at 161 Broadway was the office of the *Knickerbocker Magazine* when, under the editorship of Lewis Gaylord Clark, it held first place among American periodicals. At the same number the publishing house of Putnam had its headquarters during the earlier years of its long career. It was in 1829 that George Palmer Putnam, then a lad in his teens, enticed by a "Boy Wanted" sign in the window of George W. Bleecker's tiny bookshop on Broadway near Maiden Lane, applied for and secured the job. At the outset the reward for his services was his board and $25 a year, but from the first he forged steadily ahead in his chosen calling, and at the end of seven years set up for himself with results that are now a part of the history of publishing in America. Again, at the Fulton Street corner of Broadway was the home of the *Evening Post* when Bryant came to the end of his career as its editor. By the south window of an upper room which afforded a noble view of the lower city, he wrote and received visitors, and there he passed the morning of the day on which he was seized with his last illness.

Again, a boarding-house which flourished a century ago at the corner of Vesey and Church Streets was the first city home of Henry Jarvis Raymond when in 1841 he came to New York to serve as assistant to Horace Greeley, first on the *New Yorker* and then on the *Tribune* at a salary of eight dollars a week. The son of an up-state farmer, Raymond was then twenty-one years of age and a recent graduate from college intent upon getting on in the world. Many years later Greeley wrote of him that he had never known a person who "evinced so signal and such versatile ability in journalism," or who was "cleverer, readier, or more generally efficient." But in the matter of salaries the founder of the *Tribune* was rarely if ever a generous employer and Raymond ere long left him to become the right hand of James Watson Webb on the *Courier and Inquirer,* and in September, 1851, in association with George Jones, to found the New York *Times.*

It is interesting to recall that in sharp contrast to the $1,000. with which Greeley had established the *Tribune,* the *Times* was founded with a capital of $100,000. and that its success was never a matter of doubt. The rapid growth of New York had early convinced Raymond that there was room for a newspaper which, as Charles A. Dana later phrased it, would steer a "middle line between the mental eccentricity of the *Tribune* and the moral eccentricity of the *Herald*," and being a great admirer of the London *Times* as edited by Delane, he ably shaped the course and character of the New York *Times* on that journal. Raymond was also a man of the world whose political ambitions were of a controlling sort, and both of these qualities were manifest in the conduct of the *Times*. Perhaps the *Times* exercised less power than the *Herald* and *Tribune*, but its editorial and news pages were welcomed by men of moderate inclining and until Raymond's death in 1869 at the early age of forty-nine he remained an honored and restraining influence in the journalism of his period.

Returning once more to the Battery, the pilgrim finds, at 6 Greenwich Street, the site of the house in which, a helpless slave of drink, Stephen Collins Foster, the maker of songs, lodged during the last months of his life. A house on the opposite side of the way was for a time the home of Nathaniel Parker Willis, and in an earlier period, Irving had lodgings at 53 Greenwich Street, with Halleck for a neighbor. Charles Fenno Hoffman, who, after an early manhood of much promise, groped for half a century in mental darkness, was born at 68 Greenwich Street. The son of a well-known New York judge and a nephew of Gulian C. Verplanck, it was Hoffman's half-sister Matilda who had been engaged to Washington Irving. Perhaps the most popular member of the later Knickerbocker group, he was connected for a time with the New York *American* and in 1833 was one of the founders and the first editor of the *Knickerbocker Magazine*. Hoffman had also an unusual gift for song and verse-making—Griswold in his anthology accorded him more space than he gave any other poet—and although he had lost a leg when a boy, he toured the West on horseback, and his *Winter in the West*, made up of a series of letters, was one of the first volumes to report in a vivid way adventure and romance on the frontier. He also tried his hand at novel writing, and his *Greyslaer*, a tale in the manner of Cooper of the Mohawk Valley in Revoluntionary days, which had chief Joseph Brant for one of its heroes, still merits reading by those who honor America's past.

The birthplace of Hoffman became after October, 1823, the home of Chancellor Kent, lately retired from office, who there gave final form to his *Commentaries*. During the same period

Kent maintained an office in nearby Pine Street, and as a lawyer's lawyer, consulted in difficult cases alike by judges and eminent members of the bar, earned large fees; but it was in the main the returns from the sale of his *Commentaries* that assured him ease and comfort in his last years. This famous work, which when it appeared at once took rank with that of Blackstone, and has since been studied and held in reverent regard by four generations of lawyers, had its origin in a series of lectures which Kent delivered to the students of Columbia between 1824 and 1826.

In the latter year the first of them appeared in book form, and in 1830 the last of four volumes was given to the world. The product of great learning, set forth with rare charm and lucidity, the *Commentaries* commanded an immediate and continuing audience, and when the author died in 1847 the sixth edition was passing through the press. Kent told Philip Hone that the first edition yielded $5000. A dozen years later of the fifth edition. 3000 sets were sold at $10 a set, while a single volume edition which contained the author's exposition of the Constitutional law of the American Union when issued in 1838 became a college and university text-book, and thereafter passed every four years into the hands of a new and ever growing group of students, Robert E. Lee and other future generals of the Civil War being among those who studied it at West Point. All in all, Kent was the best paid author of his generation, and in the legal profession the favorite of later ones.

At 101 Greenwich Street in the closing days of 1819 a forward-looking publisher Van Winkle by name, printed the first American edition of *The Sketch Book,* and so helped Irving, then at work in England to renew his earlier successes at home. Horace Greeley met his future wife, Mary Cheney, a good-looking school teacher born in Cornwall, Connecticut, when they were boarders at 124 Greenwich Street where Dr. Sylvester Graham, a Presbyterian minister and deviser of the bread that bears his name, had set up a Graham boarding-house. That was in 1835, and twenty-four year old Greeley three years earlier had walked into town with all of his belongings in a bundle on his back, and had found work as a printer in one of the shops of that period Born in New Hampshire and reared in Vermont, the newcomer had left school at fourteen to learn the printer's trade and to complete his education by omnivrous reading. Settled in New York he soon became partner in a job printing office, and in 1834 at the age of twenty-three founded *The New Yorker,* a weekly journal which he edited for seven years and which helped in the shaping of his career as the best known editor of his era.

And it was to a house at 130 Greenwich Street that Edgar Allan Poe brought his girl wife, when in April, 1844, with a capital of four dollars, he came a second time to New York to put his doubtful fortunes to the test. Poe was then thirty-five years of age, and had behind him an orphaned boyhood at Richmond and in England; unhappy experiences at the University of Virginia, as a private soldier and as a cadet at West Point, and work as a poet, writer of tales and editor in Baltimore, Richmond and Philadelphia, work which had brought him fame but small returns in money. Before him lay five years of toil and privation in New York, which have now become an inseparable part of our literary history; loss of wife and failing health, and then a tragic death at the early age of forty.

CHAPTER II

THE TOWN OF WASHINGTON IRVING

William Irving and James Kirke Paulding lived at 287 Greenwich Street when with the former's brother Washington they projected the *Salmagundi Papers*. Announcements cleverly calculated to whet curiosity preceded the first number of *Salmagundi*, a thin pamphlet with a yellow cover which was published on January 24, 1807. Thereafter a number appeared every fortnight during the year, and it aroused such interest that eight hundred copies of one number were sold by its publisher, Longworth, in a single day. The three authors who painted themselves as a club of eccentrics, Evergreen, Langstaff, and Wizard by name, met to plan each number in the back parlor of Longworth's shop—styled by its proprietor the Sentimental Epicure's Ordinary—and writing in the manner, some degree removed, of Addison's *Spectator* their frank and amusing comments on the fashions and foibles of the time caught the fancy of the town.

Indeed, *Salmagundi* came to an untimely end in January, 1808, only because its high-spirited authors resented the arbitrary methods of their publisher. The younger Irving had no illusions as to the quality of the work in which he had had a part. In 1819 he wrote from England to his friend Brevoort that, while pardonable as a youthful production, it was full of faults and imperfections; and in a letter to Paulding he said: "I know you consider old Sal . . . . a saucy, flippant trollope, belonging to nobody and not worth fathering." But the staid *North American Review* described *Salmagundi* as a production of extraordinary merit, and the latter-day reader finds it, with its gaiety and self-confidence, a delectable first-hand record of old New York.

Resuming a ramble in the lower town one finds in Greenwich Street, three doors from the corner of Jay, the site of the house which was the home of James Fenimore Cooper in the early days of his success as a romancer. Again, nearer to the Battery, it was from a forbidding resort at the lower end of West Street that Stephen Collins Foster was borne to the hospital ward in which he died; and it was in a lodging house in the same thoroughfare that, in the autumn of 1879, Robert Louis Stevenson passed his first night in America.

The gifted Scotsman has partly described in the *Amateur Emigrant* the manner of his voyage to New York. Bound for California, limited means and a wish to husband them to the utmost, impelled him to make the entire journey in steerage and emigrant train. His friend Colvin adds that, besides these motives of economy, there was the underlying wish to learn at first-hand the discomforts of the unprivileged poor, and afterward to turn the whole experience to literary advantage by writing out the story of the journey. Thus it was that Stevenson crossed the Atlantic as a second-cabin passenger, and upon landing in New York, sought quarters at the Reunion House at 10 West Street, lodging there until he set out for California. That humble hostelry has now given way to a tall office building, but it still lives in Stevenson's delightful pages.

Again it was a second-story lodging house at what was then 168 West Street that youthful Horace Greeley first found quarters when in 1831 he came to New York to find work as a printer. He had only $10 in his pocket and carried his personal belongings in a bundle slung over his shoulder. "I realized then," he wrote later, "that the world was all before me." He paid one McGoldrick, keeper of the lodging-house, $2.50 a week for bed and board, and his uncouth appearance made the search for employment a long and hard one. But on a hot Sunday afternoon he was told by a fellow lodger of a vacancy in a printing shop at 85 Chatham Street, and, applying early next morning for the post, was finally told by a doubting foreman: "We will fix up a case for you and see what you can do." Given difficult copy to set the twenty-year old Greeley quickly proved himself a swift and capable craftsman, and thereafter and until the end of his days never again had to seek employment.

Jonathan Edwards once preached to a Presbyterian congregation housed at the lower end of Wall Street, and ever since his time the New World's most famous thoroughfare has played its part in the history of letters. The building at 2 Wall Street occupies the site of the meeting-place of the Ugly Club, which had Halleck for a directing spirit, while across the way, Washington Irving, during his brief excursion into the law, had his office in the house of his brother John, and there planned and partly executed his *Knickerbocker's History* which grew out of the *Salmagundi Papers*. Irving in executing his part of that venture discovered to his surprise that few of his readers were aware that their town had been once called New Amsterdam, and also that most of them were sadly ignorant of its Dutch governors and of their own Dutch ancestors. And so to recall a past in which he took honest pride, Irving shaped the history of Dietrich Knickerbocker, the appealing antiquarian whose thoughts and affections centered on odd things.

However, the author could not resist the temptation to make his narrative a humorous, mock heroic affair; and when his book appeared just before Christmas in 1809 its lively, diverting pages gave grave offense to those descendants of the old Dutch families who, strangers to a sense of the ridiculous, felt that their ancestors demanded more respectful treatment. But a larger audience read and laughed over it. "Looking at the simple and obvious meaning only," wrote Sir Walter Scott to Irving's friend Brevoort, "I have never read anything so closely resembling the style of Dean Swift as the annals of Dietrich Knickerbocker. I have employed these few evenings in reading them aloud to Mrs. S. and two ladies who are our guests, and our sides have been absolutely sore with laughing." And so passing quickly through the first and second of many editions this history of New York created the Knickerbocker Legend and both at home and abroad won for Irving recognition as the most gifted writer who up to that time had appeared in America.

Charles Wiley, who published Cooper's prose and Halleck's verse, for a number of years had his shop at what is now 9 Wall Street. He was the son of a successful merchant of the period and in 1807 at the age of twenty-five had set up as a bookseller in Reade Street. Travelling in up-state New York he made the acquaintance and won the friendship of Cooper, who had already published the first of his novels. Shortly thereafter Cooper brought Wiley the manuscript of the *Spy*. This Wiley published with great success, later issuing Cooper's *Pioneers,* the *Pilot* and *Lionel Lincoln*. It is recorded that the *Spy* was sold out in three months in the small edition then practicable and within the year there was a call for additional printings of 3,000 and 5,000 copies. This success made Wiley's bookstore the center of literary New York and a room in the rear called The Den became the meeting place for Cooper, Bryant, Halleck, Paulding, Verplanck and other choice and congenial spirits. The house of Wiley, devoted now to the field of science and engineering, still flourishes in another part of the town, headed by the great grandson of its founder.

Gulian Crommelin Verplanck, long the friend of Irving, whom he never quite forgave for holding up to ridicule the Dutch founders of the town, was born at 15 Wall Street. Verplanck's distaste for Irving's book may be accepted as proof that he was devoid of a keen sense of humor, but a ripe scholar and educator, he was also a fine type of the old-time gentleman of Dutch descent, and for half a century and in divers ways honorably served his city and period. Among other things he was a contributor to the *Talisman* with Bryant, and is remembered also for a scholarly edition of Shakespeare. Nearer to the East River the basement of a building which stood afortime at the corner of Wall and Nassau Streets was the first office of the New York *Herald*. Its founder was James Gordon Bennett, a restless, hardheaded Scotchman, who came to America in 1819 at the age of twenty-four, and for upward of a dozen years was a working journalist in New York and Washington, noted for his bold and trenchant comments on men and measures.

On May 6, 1835, with a total capital of $500—"One man in a cellar against the whole world" he proudly declared in after years —Bennett issued the first number of the *Herald,* a small penny sheet. The only furniture of his one-room office was a counter of two wide boards supported by a flour barrel at each end, and on that he wrote with untiring industry, at first doing all of the editorial work himself. But he possessed an instinct for news amounting to genius, and the success of his venture did not long remain in doubt. The *Herald's* treatment of local news was vivid and picturesque, and its editorials fearless and independent. Thus it never failed to interest a growing army of readers. Soon Bennett was able to employ capable assistants, and in 1836 he doubled the price of the paper with no loss of patrons. Thereafter the career of journal and owner, although the latter never won any measure of good-will, was a steadily prosperous one, and before the close of the *Herald's* first decade Bennett had fulfilled his promise to make it "the greatest, the best and the most profitable paper that ever appeared in this country."

The City Hall which for more than a century following 1700 stood at the northeast corner of Wall and Nassau Streets was the first home of the Society Library and of the New York Historical Society. Alexander Hamilton dwelt at what is now 33 Wall Street, when, aided by James Madison and John Jay, he wrote the *Federalist,* which Thomas Jefferson—Hamilton wrote fifty-one of the eighty-five papers making up the series—who had no liking for its chief author, declared "the best commentary on the principles of government ever written." Let it be added that it was not at his home in Wall Street but on a Hudson River sloop bound for Albany that Hamilton wrote the first number of the *Federalist* and so led in the task of securing New York's adoption of the Constitution.

A West Indian and born out of wedlock, Hamilton had then lately entered his thirty-third year, but already had behind him a record of brilliant service, a record that had made him a trusted confidant of Washington and the leader of the Federalists in New York. Before him lay a masterful part as secretary of the treasury in placing the infant republic on a firm foundation; his feud with Jefferson and undisputed mastery at the bar, and then at forty-seven his fatal duel with Burr. Hamilton had great ability and was in many ways a favorite child of Destiny, but he was also vain and unduly ambitious, a monarchist at heart and an admirer of Napoleon, whose influence, weighed across the years, had less of good than of evil in it.

Noah Webster for several years edited the *Minerva* at 37 Wall Street, writing his friends in Connecticut that great was his "admiration for New York's absence of affectation and social snobbery." There also was the law office of Josiah Ogden Hoffman when Irving was numbered among his students. The *Journal of Commerce* when Horace Bushnell was one of its editors, was at the corner of Wall and William Streets, and in the debenture room of the Custom House, which later occupied the same site Richard Henry Stoddard was employed during the years in which much of his best verse was given to the world. At 58 Wall Street, James Watson Webb long edited the *Courier and Inquirer* on which James Gordon Bennett was once employed as a reporter, gaining the mastery of his craft that enabled him a few years later to make a success of his own newspaper. Born in up-state New York in 1802, Webb in early manhood served seven years in the army. When in 1825 he became owner of the *Courier and Inquirer* an innate love of conflict remained strong within him, and for upward of a generation his career as an editor was a battle and a march. A man of imposing presence, Webb was always well dressed, perhaps in order, as enemies charged, to win favor with women, and when he had occasion to cross swords with Horace Greeley, proudly conscious of his own faultless garb, he made sneering reference to the editor of the *Tribune's* ill-worn clothes and shuffling gait.

It chanced that a short time before Webb had been indicted, convicted and sentenced to two years in Sing Sing for leaving the state to act as second to Henry Clay in a duel with Tom Marshall, but had been pardoned by William H. Seward, then governor, before he went behind the bars. Greeley in his prompt retort made effective use of this incident. He had worn, he declared, better clothing than Webb would wear if he paid his debts, adding: "That he ever affected eccentricity is most untrue; and certainly no costume he ever appeared in would create such a sensation in Broadway as that which James Watson Webb would have worn, but for the clemency of Governor Seward. We drop him." Webb did not again select Greeley as a target for his acid pen, but, it is a part of the record that he made his journal a militant organ of the Whig Party to which, tradition has it, he gave a name and later, as a reward for his championship of the Republican cause, Lincoln appointed him minister to Brazil, which post he held for eight years. His last days were passed in self-sought retirement in New York. The full length biography of Webb now in preparation should prove an informing and diverting volume.

The first home of the *Express*, founded by James and Erastus Brooks was at 67 Wall Street, and on the other side of the way, five doors below Pearl Street, James Rivington had his press before and during the Revolution. Rivington, who came from England to America in 1760, wielded the ablest pen of any New York editor of his period; but, following the break between the colonies and the mother country, he elected to support the royalist cause and made his *Gazetteer and Weekly Advertiser* most obnoxious to the Sons of Liberty. He was, however, a timeserver and trimmer, and, when persuaded that the colonies would win their independence, did not scruple to act as spy for Washington. This made it possible for him to remain in the town after its evacuation by the British, but he never prospered, and his last days were passed in obscurity.

A short walk from the head of Wall Street, past Trinity churchyard and the grave of Hamilton, brings one to the site of a small alehouse which long stood at the corner of Thames and Temple Streets. Six score years ago, the keeper of this resort was an Englishman, William Reynolds by name, who had the reputation of serving good ale, and his wife of knowing how to. cook a chop or steak. Halleck chanced upon the place one day, and delighted at what he found there, made its merits known to a group of kindred spirits. The semi-club thus formed, was kept up for many years, and to The Shades. as it was called, came of an afternoon almost every author and artist who lived in or visited New York. Reynolds made money as time went by, and finally retired to Fort Lee, where he was still visited by his literary friends and entertained them hospitably—Halleck being always sure of an especially cordial welcome—but gradually, by death or for other causes, The Shades lost favor, and, in the end, degenerated into a mere drinking shop. A generation ago it shared the fate of most old New York houses.

The Gillender Building at 1 Nassau Street covers the site of the structure from which Poe and Charles Frederick Briggs issued their short-lived *Broadway Journal*. Four doors removed on the same side of the street, the *Mirror* was founded by George P. Morris, who, as editor and author, was for more than forty years a leader in the literary life of New York. It was in 1823 that Morris, then one-and-twenty, in association with Samuel Woodworth established the *Mirror* which under a succession of names was to have a long and prosperous history. Woodworth soon withdrew from the venture, but in 1831 Morris was joined by Nathaniel Parker Willis, who, lately graduated at Yale, for two years had conducted a monthly magazine in Boston—not always to the liking of some of the staid citizens of that town—and the two men remained successful partners and devoted friends until death separated them. Morris, who died in 1864, knew how to command success, and as an author he duly placed to his credit a popular play and libretto, the former based on Revolutionary events, and anthologies of American song, prose and verse which had wide distribution; but he is now chiefly remembered as the author of *Woodman, Spare That Tree*, such power has a homely ballad to win and hold the hearts of men.

William Dunlap lived at 17 Nassau Street when manager first of the John Street and then of the Park Theatres, the latter built and opened in 1798, and there wrote or adapted many of the plays which made him the most prolific dramatist of his period. Born in 1766 at Perth Amboy, New Jersey, where in after years he often spent the summer months, Dunlap's father, when he was eighteen, sent him to London to study art under Benjamin West and after his return he was for a time a portrait painter in New York. However, when in London, he had seen all the current plays and had studied at first-hand stage life behind the scenes. And so ere long he gave up painting to become a dramatist, and following 1789 wrote or adapted some thirty plays of divers sorts and quality.

Dunlap's association with the theatre ended in disaster, but not before he had managed the American appearance of George Frederick Cooke, later writing a biography of that great eccentric, which, although a diffuse and rambling affair, by reason of its freshness and charm still commands delighted readers. His theatre days behind him he returned to portrait painting and travelled hither and yon in search of patrons. He also found time in old age to write histories of the stage and of the arts of design in America, books more highly prized by later students than they were by those who first read them. Poverty dogged this versatile man most of his days, but "industrious, active and poor," as he wrote Cooper in Paris, he faced hard conditions with a smile, and after his death in 1839 was long held in honored remembrance as a democrat of the strictest sort, as a devoted lover of Nature in all its phases, and as a talker whose gossip never failed to inform and amuse his friends.

It was at 19 Nassau Street that at one stage of his American sojourns William Cobbett, The Contentious Man of Bulwer's inimitable essay, and the wielder of the most vitriolic pen of his era, for a brief period sold seeds and plants in competition with Grant Thorburn, New York's first florist. Cobbett was one of those men who devoutly believe that they are born with a mission to set crooked things straight. He came into the world in 1763 on a farm in Surrey, England, ran away from home at the age of fourteen, and for several years was a soldier in the British army. Then he resigned, in order to expose the brutality and favoritism rampant in the military service of that day. But his single-handed task proved too much for him, and in 1792, to escape prosecution, he took ship for America, along with a young wife about to become a mother.

Cobbett brought with him a letter of introduction to Thomas Jefferson, but love for his native land, then at odds with France, quickly made him a champion of the Federalists, and settling in Philadelphia he wrote pamphlet after pamphlet savagely attacking the party of Jefferson and its friendship for the French. His attacks continued in a journal which he set up, giving it the name of *Porcupine's Gazette*—attacks which, witty, sarcastic, and violent in turn, never failed to miss their mark, made him the most feared and hated editor of his period, and did not a little during the uncertain first decade of the republic, to shape public opinion. But in 1799 Benjamin Rush, one of his victims, secured a crippling verdict against him for libel and caused his return to England. When after eighteen years and a memorable career in his native land Cobbett came again to America, having undergone a sea change, he brought with him a new and widely different set of opinions. But that is a story that belongs to another part of this chronicle.

The Society Library from 1795 to 1836 occupied the site of the Bank of Commerce Building at the corner of Cedar Street. At 54 Liberty Street, southwest corner of Nassau, Horace Greeley was first in business on his own account. That was in 1833 and Greeley was then twenty-two years old. He and his partner, also a printer, each invested $100 in the venture, and with type bought on credit, in their two-room, second-story plant they issued for a young physician fond of taking chances, one Dr. Horatio David Shepard, the *Morning Post,* the first low priced daily journal to come into being in New York. But just as the *Post* was gaining a foothold, Shepard's money gave out; his printers could not give him credit, and, as Greeley later recorded, "thus died the first cheap-for-cash daily in New York, perhaps in the world, and we printers were hard aground on a lee shore." A little later Greeley's partner was drowned in the East River, but the survivor, now confident of his powers, pushed resolutely ahead to the founding of a daily journal of his own—and a great future as the voice of forward-looking men and the champion of forward-looking causes.

An office structure at 64 Nassau Street covers the site of the city's second theatre, where Shakespeare's *Richard III, Othello, and King Lear* had their first recorded productions in New York, if not in America. A tavern bearing the name of the master dramatist stood for many years at the southwest corner of Nassau and Fulton Streets, with a bust of Shakespeare over its door. This hostelry was long a resort for the actors, writers and wits of the town, but was finally replaced by a building which from 1842 to 1868 furnished a home for the *Sun.* During the same period the *Herald* had its office upon the opposite corner, and for a part of it counted Mayne Reid as a member of its staff.

Reid and his tales merit more than passing mention. Born in the north of Ireland in 1818, the son of a Presbyterian clergyman who hoped that his son would follow in his footsteps, he ran away from home at the age of twenty to pursue in turn on this side of the sea the callings of hunter, actor, soldier and author. For five years he was a trader among the Indians of the Red River country, a part of the time having Audubon for a companion, and after that he was a contributor to the newspapers and magazines of New York and Philadelphia. When the Mexican War broke out he secured a lieutenant's commission in the army of General Winfield Scott and served with memorable gallantry at Vera Cruz, Churubusco and Chapultepec. The war ended he resumed his career as a writer for the *Herald,* but in 1849 sailed for Europe at the head of a company of volunteers he had organized to aid the Hungarians in their struggle for independence only to find, when he reached Paris, that they had been compelled to lay down their arms.

Dismissing his followers Captain Reid now took up his abode in London and devoted himself to story-writing, thereafter making only occasional visits to America. During the war between the States, however, he was a warm champion of the North at a time and in a place where the Union cause had sore need of friends. In 1850 appeared the *Rifle Rangers,* and this was followed the next year by the *Scalp Hunters,* in which Reid detailed his adventures in Mexico and the West. These titles met with immediate favor, and thereafter for thirty years one of their author's tales came from the presses every twelve-month to claim an army of delighted readers on both sides of the sea. Not a few of them were also translated into most of the languages of modern Europe. Reid died in London in 1883, having divided his last days between that city and a small sheep farm in Hertfordshire. His tales still find readers. To the boys of an earlier time the accounts they gave of moving incidents by flood and field were an ever renewing source of joy and exultant spirits, and there is more than one aging youngster who would welcome their reissue in the form in which they were first familiar to us, a form superior in all ways to the guise they have assumed in later years.

The *Mirror* was quartered at 107 Nassau Street, when Willis became one of its editors, and at 118 Nassau Street Henry Jarvis Raymond joined in the founding of the New York *Times.* Again it was at the same number that *Vanity Fair* was edited by Charles Farrar Browne, best remembered as Artemus Ward. Browne was born in 1834 at Waterford, Maine, where he now takes his rest beside his parents in the village cemetery; but, half-orphaned by the death of his father, he left the town while still a lad to become a printer, and later a writer for the press in Cleveland. There in 1858 under the name of Artemus Ward, an imaginary showman, he began the series of badly spelled skits, which soon brought him repute as a humorist. The part which Browne two years later played in the literary life of New York was that of a bird of passage, for he soon left to start upon the wanderings which finally led him to England to die of tuberculosis at the age of thirty-three. While he lived he was the delight of two nations, and a giving heart and gentle ways made him one of the best loved writers of his generation.

James C. Derby, who published the first books of Thomas Bailey Aldrich and other authors, was in business at 119 Nassau Street when across the way Robert Bonner, with growing profit to himself, was pushing the New York *Ledger* into favor with a unique and devoted constituency. Mary Rogers had her home at 126 Nassau Street when her mysterious slaying on the New Jersey side of the Hudson prompted Poe to make her the heroine of the stark tale to which he gave the title of *Marie Roget*. Horace Greeley for a time published the *New Yorker* and the *Log Cabin* at 127 Nassau Street, and one door above, on the other side of the way, was the birthplace of the *Nation*, in whose columns Edwin Lawrence Godkin began his noteworthy career as an editor.

And it was at 142 Nassau Street, not far from Printing House Square, that from 1841 to 1849 Lydia Maria Child, aided by her husband, David L. Child, edited the *Anti-Slavery Standard*, and by her fearless utterances helped to hasten the conflict which freed the bondsmen of the South. Mrs. Child's memorable editorship had a pleasant by-product—the letters she wrote to the Boston *Courier*, then under the direction of Joseph T. Buckingham. These *Letters from New York*, afterwards published in two volumes which ran through many editions, had the charm of intimacy and were heralds of the large place women presently were to fill in American journalism. "Their tone," writes a friend of the author, "did much to promote a fresh inquiry into the foundations of social science. Her rhapsodies about poetry and music were apt to end in some fervent appeal for an increase of harmony in daily life. She seemed always to be talking radicalism in a greenhouse; and there were many good people who held her all the more dangerous for her perfumes. There were young men and maidens, also who looked to her as a teacher, and were influenced for life, perhaps, by what she wrote." Her days as an editor behind her, Mrs. Childs with her husband retired to a cottage at Wayland, Massachusetts, bequeathed her by her baker father, but continued to write and preach the good life until in 1880 death came to her at the age of seventy-eight. One of her last efforts, *Looking Towards Sunset*, an admirably chosen anthology of prose and verse all bearing upon the aspects of old age, deserves a place on every shelf of bedside books.

The home of the *Sun* was at 170 Nassau Street for nearly half a century following 1868 during which period Charles Anderson Dana, witty, cynical and fearless, made it the journal most eagerly read by his fellow editors. Born in New Hampshire in 1819, Dana left Harvard to play for five years a part in the ill-starred history of the Brook Farm community. When that adventure in human uplift failed a mutual friend persuaded a reluctant Greeley to make a place for Dana on the staff of the *Tribune*. He began as a reader of exchanges at a salary of five dollars a week, and in 1849, at the end of his first six months of service, was made managing editor, a post he filled with great ability for thirteen years. But in 1862 his growing opposition to his chief's eccentric attitude toward the policy of Lincoln led to Dana's dismissal. Thereupon he became first an investigator for the War Department and then Assistant Secretary of War under Stanton, by his reports from Grant's headquarters, where he was stationed for a long period, doing much to confirm Lincoln's faith in the will and ability of that general to achieve results. As editor of the *Sun* Dana drew about him a brilliant and devoted staff which included such men as Amos Jay Cummings, John Swinton, Julian Ralph and Edward Page Mitchell, who was to succeed him. Aided by Ida Minerva Tarbell, he also found time shortly before his death in 1897 to put on paper his *Recollections of the Civil War,* which at once became a source book on a fateful period.

Starting again from Wall Street one finds at 43 William Street the site of the office of the Dutchess County Insurance Company which Halleck once served as secretary. Two doors above Mordecai Manual Noah, editor and playwright, for several years conducted one of the numerous periodicals which made him a colorful figure in the New York of his time, while, yet another door removed, was for a period the office of William Leggett, friend of Bryant and his early associate in the conduct of the *Evening Post*. Leggett, who had spent his earlier years in the navy, was a vigorous personality, not averse to a fight, and had a part in at least one duel at Weehawken, which, however, did not have the fatal issue of the meeting at the same place between Hamilton and Burr. A writer of trenchant prose, ever ready to defend his opinions, Leggett was also the author of a volume of verse which gave him a modest place among the poets of his period. And if his abrupt ways bred enemies his resolute integrity of purpose—he was one of the first to urge in print the abolition of slavery—also won him friends, and when he died in the summer of 1839, his passing brought from Bryant an impressive tribute to his worth, a tribute which Greeley reprinted in the *New Yorker*. It is only at rare intervals that a man appears of whom it can be justly said as Bryant said of Leggett, dead at the early age of thirty-eight:

His love of truth—too warm, too strong,

For Hope of Fear to chain or chill—

His hate of tyranny and wrong

Burn in the breasts he kindled still!

The office of the *Magazine of American History* was at 111 William Street during the span of years after 1878 when John Austin Stevens, its founder, also served as its editor. A keen and reverent student of the early history of the republic, Stevens was an author as well as editor, writing among other books a standard life of Albert Gallatin.

Lower New York has been thrice rebuilt in as many half centuries. Thus, a warehouse long ago replaced the two-story structure at 131 William Street in which Washington Irving was born; the house a door below on the opposite side of the way in which he grew to manhood has also disappeared, although a tablet now marks its site; and no trace remains of the antique dwelling at the corner of Ann and William Streets where he lived for several years with his widowed mother, and essayed his fledgling efforts as an author. The home of his youth had front and rear buildings with a narrow structure between, and it was from a sloping roof at the rear that young Irving descended, at the peril of life and limb, to enjoy on well-remembered evenings the forbidden but enticing delights of the John Street Theatre, where players of a sterling sort held the boards.

It was an easy twenty minutes walk from end to end of the New York of Irving's boyhood. He was an infant in arms when the British withdrew from it toward the end of 1783 leaving a half-ruined city behind them. A fire in September, 1776, had reduced much of the western section of the town to rubble and ashes. Samuel Breck returning in June, 1787, from a long sojourn in France, gives an arresting account of what confronted him. "I found it," he writes, "a neglected place, built chiefly of wood, and in a state of prostration and decay. A dozen vessels in port; Broadway from Trinity Church to the Battery in ruins, owing to the fire that had occurred when the city was occupied by the enemy, for although the war had ceased, and the enemy had departed, no attempt had been made to rebuild. In short, there was silence and inactivity everywhere."

Soon, however, began another period of enduring growth. Irving cherished until the end love for the associations of his youth, but as time passed he had also an aging man's aversion for unfamiliar things. "I often think what a strange place you would find yourself in if you could revisit your native place," he wrote in 1847 to his sister resident in England. "New York, as you knew it, was a mere corner of the present city; and that corner is all changed, pulled to pieces, burnt down and rebuilt—all but our little native nest in William Street, which still retains some of its old features, though these are daily altering. I can hardly realize that, within my term of life, this great, crowded metropolis, so full of life, bustle, noise, show and splendor, was a quiet little city . . . I dread the noise and turmoil of it and visit it but now and then, preferring the quiet of my country retreat, which shows that the bustling time of life is over with me, and that I am settling down into a sober, quiet, good-for-nothing old gentleman."

Bonner's *Ledger* was quartered at the corner of Spruce and William Streets during its most prosperous years. The office of the *Independent* when it had Henry Ward Beecher for its editor was at 201 William Street, and, a few rods away, a site now darkened by the shadows of the Brooklyn Bridge, was the birthplace of the New York *Sun*. This journal was founded in 1833 by Benjamin H. Day, a job printer located at 222 William Street, who designed it as a medium through which to advertise his business. It sold for a cent a copy, and its four pages of three columns each, offered a sharp contrast to the six-penny blanket sheets which up to that time had made the history of daily journalism in New York. Day wrote and edited the first number himself, and at the outset acted as his own editor, reporter, compositor, pressman, and delivery clerk. Still the *Sun* found readers from the first, and at the end of its second year could boast a circulation of 10,000 copies. Its founder at the same time worked a revolution in journalism. He made the *Sun* a good local newspaper, something no other editor was doing at the time, and thus sounded the knell of the ponderous journals that sorely taxed their readers and gave them little in return. These were distributed only to regular subscribers, but Day hired boys and sent them out to sell the *Sun* to anybody that wanted to buy it. Thus, he invented the newsboy, while the present system of delivery to the public from the urchin who sells ten copies to the great news company that handles 100,000 is the logical development of his idea of reaching the public.

Finally, it was at The Sign of the Lanthorne, back of an ironmonger's shop in William Street, that the Lantern Club for a few years at the turn of the century offered delightful hours to its members. One of these was Irving Bacheller, then manager of a newspaper syndicate, with his career as a maker of fiction still ahead of him. Many of its other members were newspaper workers of the period—the late Tom Masson and Edward Marshall among them—who in their spare hours contributed to the Bacheller syndicate. When they met at the club for lunch, they also read their short poems and stories to each other, for approval and criticism as the case might be, and it was there that Mr. Bacheller's first story found an admiring audience before it was published in the *Cosmopolitan,* then edited by Arthur Sherburne Hardy. Stephen Crane came now and again to the Lantern Club and it was the publication of the *Red Badge of Courage* through the Bacheller syndicate that confirmed his success as an author.

Other and older guests of the club in its palmy days included many of the best known writers of the period—Howells, Stoddard, and Stedman among them. When Mark Twain came one noonday to visit he found himself in such congenial company that he lingered from one until five o'clock, and finally took reluctant leave of his companions, with the remark: "Well, I have been here since one o'clock, and I have talked all the time, and I have enjoyed every damned word of it." So had those who listened to his humorous, drawling comment on men and things.

CHAPTER III

MORE WALKS IN THE OLDER CITY

A hundred and forty odd years ago, when Columbia College was growing into greatness, one of the professors in that institution was James Kent, who, in a later time, was to long serve the State of New York as its chancellor, and, following his retirement from the bench, write the *Commentaries* which by students of the law which, as elsewhere recorded, have ever since been classed with those of Blackstone. Kent's first New York home was at 17 Pine Street, just out of Broadway, and one of the neighbors with whom he delighted to pass a social hour was a young physician, Elihu Hubbard Smith, who dwelt a dozen doors away, near the corner of William Street, with Charles Brockden Brown, a member of his household. Brown and Smith became devoted friends while the latter was a student in Philadelphia. When Smith settled in New York, Brown followed him and in their common home wrote *Wieland, Ormond* and other strange and once widely read tales. Born in Philadelphia in 1771 Brown at the age of eleven read both Greek and Latin, and planned epic poems on Columbus, Pizarro and Cortes. He began his literary career as a translator of Volney's study of the soil and climate of the United States—Joel Barlow at Jefferson's suggestion had translated the same author's once popular *The Ruins*—but at the turn of the century became novelist and in quick succession wrote the romances charged with mystery and the foreboding of strange events that never happened, which influenced Shelley and Keats and were admired by Cooper, Hawthorne and Poe. Translated into French and German they found absorbed readers in Europe, who hailed them as harbingers of the new and original things America was to give the world; but, fantastic in conception and hastily written, men and women of a later time find them difficult reading. Silent with strangers but a rare comrade among friends of whom no man ever had truer ones, Brown, from the first of feeble make, died of consumption in 1810 in Philadelphia whence he had returned to end his days, and five years later the garrulous Dunlap wrote a book about him in two volumes. Dunlap's narrative is a prolix and dull one, but interspered with letters from and to Brown which throw revealing light on our literary beginnings.

The Pine Street home of Dr. Smith was also the meeting-place of the Friendly Club, a coterie of congenial folk, which, besides Smith, Brown and Dunlap, included Kent, who in his leisure hours read Defoe and Voltaire, and Joseph Dennie, author of the *Lay Preacher*. Dennie was only an occasional member of this circle, but no doubt always a welcome one, for, besides being a delightful companion, he was then the most widely read of New World authors. The Friendly Club, the members of which met to drink punch, sing hunting songs and play on the flute, then a favorite diversion, had only a brief existence. Smith, its founder, soon fell victim to yellow fever, and a few years later Dennie passed away in Philadelphia where in 1801 he had founded a weekly paper called the *Portfolio,* as a rival to Matthew Carey's *American Museum.*

The son of a Boston Loyalist who lost his wealth during the Revolution, Dennie was a figure strangely out of place in the land that gave him birth. Washington Irving with a large measure of truth had him in mind when he drew the character of Langstaff in *Salmagundi,* and there is little doubt that his chief regret all his life long was that he had not been born somewhere in England instead of Boston, for Dennie, like his father before him, could find nothing good in the American scene, and, an unregenerate Tory, was quick to oppose any man or measure conflicting with the interests of England.

Dennie passed his boyhood at Lexington, and when for ample cause, rusticated at Harvard set up as a lawyer in Walpole, New Hampshire. There he established a newspaper which he gave the name the *Farmer's Weekly Museum,* and to which under the pen name of The Lay Preacher he contributed a series of essays that duly collected in a book for a time won him a numerous audience. Then came Philadelphia and the *Portfolio* which he edited with acclaim until his death in 1815 at the age of forty-two. A dandy and a man of changing moods, Dennie had also a gift for friendship, being quick to praise talent wherever he found it; and, although he never got far below the surface of things, his urbane spirit and Addisonian periods made him for a score of years the author most admired by the Federalist rank and file.

When Smith and Brown still dwelt in Pine Street, just across the way from their abode the *Commercial Advertiser* was

published in a building which became, in 1801, the first home of
the *Evening Post*. The latter journal still occupied its birthplace
when William Cullen Bryant succeeded to its editorship. It did
not remove from Pine Street until 1849, and there the *Commercial
Advertiser* continued to be housed during the years that William
Leete Stone served as its editor. And a garret in William Street
just out of Pine at the turn of the centuries afforded an obscure
lodging place for Bilaud-Varenne, who, endowed with a gift for
lofty and compelling eloquence, on a September day in 1792 was
the first to proclaim the French Republic, but who, having plotted
in turn against Danton and Robespierre, was to end his days a
needy exile. The stroller also finds in Pine Street ten numbers
west of Pearl Street, the site of the office of the *Morning
Chronicle,* in whose columns in 1802 Washington Irving, then
a youth of nineteen, made his first appearance in print. His
elder brother Peter was owner and editor of the *Chronicle,* and
perhaps prompted the series of short papers to which the author
gave the title *Letters of Jonathan Oldstyle, Gent.* They dealt
in an amusing way with the fashions and foibles of the growing
town, and, while plainly the work of a beginner, their whimsical
humor was a herald of better things to come, for in a few years
Salmagundi grew out of *Oldstyle* and a little later bore fruit in
the *History of New York,* which gave the still youthful Irving
firm footing both at home and in England.

The building at 48 Cedar Street occupies the site of the
house where Noah Webster lodged before he quit journalism to
begin the dictionary which was to occupy the remainder of his
days. A little more than a block away, at 53 Liberty Street, the
Evening Post had its office for nearly three decades, being quartered there during the Civil War when Charles Nordhoff was
numbered among its editors, and helped by his fearless utterances
to keep the New York press firm in support of the Union. The
author of the Declaration of Independence lived at 57 Maiden
Lane when Secretary of State in Washington's cabinet, while
James Madison, when Congress sat in New York, boarded at
19 Maiden Lane, maintaining such friendly relations with his
landlady that, as he relates in one of his letters, "he was permitted to owe her part of his board when it was inconvenient
for him to pay it all, and even to borrow from her."

Just across the way, in 1783 St. John de Crevecoeur, author
of the *Letters of an American Farmer,* had his office and home
when serving as French consul in New York. One of the most

interesting of the many Frenchmen who have sojourned for longer or shorter periods in this country the story of Crevecoeur's earlier years in America and the writing of the book which saves his name from forgetfulness belongs to another part of the present chronicle; but here it is to be recorded that all his days this unusual man knew how to make friends, and in the America which followed the Revolution and preceded the birth of the republic counted many gifted men among his intimates, his correspondents and well-wishers ranging from President Stiles of Yale College to General Washington then in rewarding retirement at Mount Vernon and to stubborn Ethan Allen who for a time and for a variety of reasons kept his native Vermont from joining the Union, but as a token of regard for Crevecoeur gave the names of eminent Frenchmen to three of its towns.

Crossing to the westward side of Broadway, one finds at 18 Cortland Street, the site of the abode of Mrs. James Renwick —sister of Francis Jeffrey—a beauty of the Scottish lowlands transplanted to New World soil, whom Burns celebrated as the *Blue-eyed Lassie,* and who gave to Irving the ivy from Scott's Melrose which now covers the walls of his last home at Sunnyside. A dozen doors below, on the other side of the way, dwelt Major Fairlie in the years when Irving's first books were still the talk of the hour, and the Fairlie sisters, a trio of grace and beauty, were toasted and courted by the wits and beaux of the period. Mary Fairlie, the eldest of the three, was the Sophy Sparkle of the *Salmagundi Papers,* and Irving's friend and correspondent for many years. She married the tragedian Cooper, and from this union sprang a daughter, who became, in turn, the wife of John Tyler's son and mistress of the White House.

A narrow alley at 17 John Street, now obliterated, long marked the entrance to what for thirty years following 1767 was New York's only theatre. On its stage the elder Joseph Jefferson, Eliza Arnold, the mother of Poe, and John Hodgkinson, the prince of actors in his day, appeared for the first time in New York; there Shakespeare's *Cymbeline, Macbeth,* and *Merchant of Venice,* and his *Tempest, King John* and *As You Like it,* Milton's *Comus,* Goldsmith's *She Stoops to Conquer* and Sheridan's *Rivals* and *School for Scandal,* had their initial productions in New York; and there too, on April 16, 1787, was produced with great success Royall Tyler's comedy, *The Contrast,* the first play by an American brought out in New York. Tyler was perhaps the wittiest journalist of his day and in other ways a man of mark. Born in 1758, he left Harvard to serve in Washington's army and later had a hand in the suppression of Shay's rebellion. His fighting days ended, he studied and practiced law at Walpole, New Hampshire, where he helped Joseph Dennie make the *Farmer's Museum* for a time the most widely quoted journal in New England. There also he wrote and published the *Algerine Captive,* a novel of adventure which furnished exciting diversion to our great-grandfathers. Tyler's *The Contrast* had life and wit and the illusion of reality and it introduced the stage Yankee and other stock figures who ever since have held the boards. After 1790 its author was a resident of Vermont where he served for a number of years as chief justice of the State.

Dunlap's first comedy *The Father,* which trailed *The Contrast* at a distance, also had its initial production in John Street, and he was one of the theatre's managers in its last days. Andrew C. Wheeler who wrote under the pen name of Nym Crinkle, was born at 10 John Street, and at 42 John Street in 1867 was the office of the *Alta California* of San Francisco where Mark Twain made preparations for the trip to the Holy Land celebrated in *Innocents Abroad.* The *Home Journal,* the most successful of the joint ventures in journalism made by Morris and Willis, had its office for a dozen years at 107 Fulton Street, and from the same building the genial and witty John Brougham issued the short-lived comic weekly to which he gave the name of the *Lantern.* Brougham's good-will and diverting ways early won him an army of friends, but now and again his Irish wit bred for him determined and unrelenting enemies. The latter included William E. Burton, long first among the comedians of foreign birth who then graced the New York stage, and Augustus Maverick, a journalist of the period, chronicles an amusing passage at arms between the two men. "Brougham," writes Maverick, "on entering a restaurant found Burton and a companion sitting at a table. Burton replied to the question, 'Have you read the *Lantern* this week?' by saying, "No!' I never read the thing unless I'm drunk—unless I'm drunk—(repeating in a louder tone) unless I'm drunk." Brougham immediately rose from the table at which he was sitting; advanced, hat in hand, towards Burton, and making a bow in his grandest manner, observed: 'Then, Mr. Burton, I am sure of one constant reader!' Burton made no reply."

Until the middle years of the last century that part of Fulton Street which faces St. Paul's churchyard was devoted to residential uses and was a favorite abode of men of letters. Willis dwelt for a time at 184 Fulton Street; the house adjoining was in an earlier period the home of William Dunlap; and four doors further from Broadway, during his first days in America, lodged Lorenzo da Ponte, the Italian poet, an interesting and unusual figure in the New York of a century ago. Da Ponte had had an odd career filled with sharp turns before in 1805 he settled in this country. A Jew born in 1748, he had been in Venice the friend of Casanova, and in Vienna had written three librettos for Mozart. Then luckless turns of the wheel carried him first to London and later to America, where he set up as a grocer and distiller in Sunbury, Pennsylvania. Clement Clarke Moore, who was always seeking some one to aid and befriend, found him in that town by the Susquehanna and persuaded him to settle in New York.

Among Da Ponte's long list of pupils, when he yielded to Moore's urging, was Fitz-Greene Halleck and Julia Ward Howe. He also brought from Europe the Garcias and their children, one of whom was to become Madame Viardot, the mistress of Turgenev. During a period of two and thirty years, broken by occasional absences from the town, he filled a variety of posts in New York, but served longest as a professor in Columbia College. A handsome man, of winning personality, most of the scholars and authors of the period were numbered among his friends, and he kept until the last the vivacity of spirit and charm of manner which made him in youth the spoiled darling of the Venice salons. During his last days Da Ponte wrote his *Memoirs,* patterned after those of Cellini and Rousseau, as amusing and perhaps as truthful as those of his great forerunners. He died at the age of ninety, and was laid to rest in the old Catholic burial ground in Eleventh Street, between First and Second Avenues.

Ray Palmer, was a teacher in a girls' school in Fulton Street, hardby the whilom abode of Da Ponte, when he wrote his best known hymn, *My Faith Looks Up to Thee,* and the newsboys' lodging house which sixty years ago flourished in the same thoroughfare was long the New York headquarters of Horatio Alger, one of the most prolific authors of his period. Born in 1834 Alger was the son of a Unitarian minister of Chelsea, Massachusetts, studied for a time at Harvard, became a minister himself, and then, invited by William Taylor Adams, better known as Oliver Optic to write for a magazine called *Student and Schoolmate,* he began the first of his stories for boys, resigned his pulpit and removed to New York, establishing himself in the home for newsboys founded by Charles Loring Brace. That was in 1864 and before he died thirty-five years later he wrote in all one hundred and twenty tales which captured and held the boyhood of America for a full generation, besides a great number of magazine articles and poems. A lonely and somewhat pathetic figure, Alger never married, and instead used a large part of his generous earnings to aid homeless youngsters. Painfully crude as a writer there were few canons of taste which he did not persistently violate, but he pointed a great army the way to higher things, and so, despite his faults, is held in grateful memory by many a boy now grown old.

The city home of James Kirke Paulding was for a time at 43 Vesey Street, and Horace Greeley dwelt just across the way in the opening years of his career as editor of the *Tribune*. Two short blocks distant at 18 Ann Street the hard working Greeley had his printing shop on the second floor of a rear building when in 1834 he founded the *New Yorker,* a weekly journal in the conduct of which he proved himself a vigorous commentator on men and events and a keen and discriminating lover of good literature. In its pages appeared the first story by Charles Dickens, then an unknown author, ever published in this country. Greeley was also quick to recognize the talent of Edgar Allan Poe, loaning him money from a scanty purse and printing several of his compositions in the *New Yorker.* A few years later he reprinted *The Raven* in the *Tribune,* its first publication in a daily newspaper. But his memories of its author were not agreeable ones. "Poe," he declared later, "is a brilliant writer when neither too drunk nor too sober. He might be somebody if he were not an incorrigible rascal and vagabond."

Greeley still had his shop at 18 Ann Street when on a December day in 1837 he was called upon by Thurlow Weed, editor of the Albany *Evening Journal,* and Lewis Benedict, leaders of the lately born Whig Party. Climbing two steep flights of stairs they found him setting type for the *New Yorker,* and, Weed having been impressed by the vigor and quality of the editorials appearing in it, offered him the conduct of a campaign paper supporting William H. Seward for governor, to be published in Albany. Greeley at the end of a long talk accepted their offer of $1,000 and expenses, suggested *The Jeffersonian* as a name for the proposed journal, and from January until election day in 1838, journeying up and down by nightboat, he divided his time between *The Jeffersonian* in Albany and his own journal in New York.

It was a difficult and grinding schedule but Greeley met all of its demands, and in the process proved himself a writer and editor of a new and unusual sort. And in May, 1840, again prompted by Weed, he began to publish the *Log Cabin*, which helped not a little to the election of Harrison, and which continued to command a growing army of readers after the Whig triumph at the polls. Meanwhile, Greeley had moved his printing shop to the second floor and attic of a rear building at 30 Ann Street, and there on April 10, 1841, with $1,000 borrowed from a friend and type bought on credit, he put into effect a plan that had come to hold first place in his thoughts and issued the first number of the New York *Tribune* promising the readers of the new journal that no exertion would be "spared to render it worthy of the hearty approval of the virtuous and refined, and a welcome visitant at the family fireside."

This promise was kept in splendid fashion, and soon the *Tribune* had a broad and easy road stretching before it. A few months after the setting afoot of his larger venture Greeley discontinued the *New Yorker* and the *Log Cabin* and in their stead appeared the *Weekly Tribune*. The contents of the newcomer were made up with great care from the daily, and it soon found readers in every city, town and village in the country. In time the *Weekly Tribune* went to 300,000 subscribers, and no journal issued in America has ever equalled the influence which for half a century it held with the people.

The second home of the *Times*, abandoned at the turn of the century for quarters in another part of the town, was a building which filled the triangle formed by Park Row and Nassau and Beekman Streets. And Temple Court at the corner of the last two thoroughfares covers the site of the theatre where, in 1761, Shakespeare's *Hamlet* was first played in America, and of Clinton Hall, from which in a later time Poe issued the *Broadway Journal*, which he strove in vain to make the magazine of his dreams. Clinton Hall was also for nearly a quarter of a century the home of the Mercantile Library. This institution had its origin as a reading-room which some of the merchants of the city founded for their clerks. Two years later, the association thus created was duly incorporated, and in 1830, a building was erected for the growing collection of books, which was named Clinton Hall in honor of De Witt Clinton who had presented the first book to the library. A score of years later the growth of the town compelled it to seek new quarters, and in 1854 it established itself on the site of its present home in Astor Place. The Mercantile, as to the number of volumes on its shelves, now holds second place among the libraries of the city.

At 5 Beekman Street, was the office of the *Continental Monthly,* founded in 1862 by James R. Gilmore and edited by Charles Godfrey Leland, which during a brief but militant existence gave vigorous support to the acts and policies of President Lincoln. To its pages Leland contributed some of his best verse, and in its early numbers, signed by the pen name, Edmund Kirke, appeared the opening chapters of Gilmore's *Among the Pines,* a lively account of life in the South in the last days of slavery, which when gathered into a volume claimed a new army of delighted readers, as did a second volume, *My Southern Friends,* which also grew out of its author's contributions to his own magazine. In old age Gilmore wrote and published his recollections of the Civil War period, a book not always accurate as to facts but treasured by students for its intimate and revealing glimpses of Lincoln in critical hours.

Time was when the Astor House, which long faced Broadway between Vesey and Barclay Streets, was the rendezvous not only of merchants, politicians and travelers, but of all the literary men in the town. Irving, Hawthorne, and Willis were guests of its early days. The elder Henry James and his wife were lodged at the Astor House when their son William was born in 1842, while in later years Thomas Buchanan Read and Charles Graham Halpine were carried there to die. Walt Whitman delighted to bask on its steps and watch the omnibuses when, as Tuckerman phrases it, "you could walk from Barnum's to the Battery on their roofs," Poe went there for refreshment and for news, and there, during the Mary Rogers excitement, caught the idea which he embodied in the tale of *Marie Roget.* And it was in a room at the Astor House that, on a February afternoon in 1860, Abraham Lincoln gave the finishing touches to the great address which, delivered the following night at Cooper Institute, was declared by Horace Greeley the most convincing argument against the extension of slavery thus far offered by any shaper of public opinion. It also revealed Lincoln to the East as a man of light and leading, and helped to clear the way before the year's end for his election to the Presidency.

Another sequel to the Cooper Institute address often recalled by Amos Jay Cummings, who in 1860 was a proofreader on the

Tribune, is charged with rueful interest for every collector of rare manuscripts—either in act or desire. On his arrival in New York, Mr. Lincoln, who was never averse to publicity of the right sort, arranged for the publication of his address in the *Tribune.* Accordingly, the manuscript was duly turned over to the foreman of that journal, and it was arranged that after delivery he should call at the *Tribune* office for a reading of the proof slips. Thus Cummings had just begun comparing the galley proofs with the manuscript when Mr. Lincoln, after its delivery and lunch with a few friends, appeared and, drawing a chair to the table, sat down beside him, adjusted his glasses and read each galley with scrupulous care. The process completed he waited until the revised proofs were brought in, when these were in turn read and corrected. "After all the proofs were read," Cummings was wont to relate, "Mr. Lincoln had a few pleasant words with me and then went out alone, and passed through Printing House Square and City Hall Park to the Astor House where he was lodged." But as the proofs were read and revised, the manuscript had been tossed sheet by sheet into a convenient wastebasket to be claimed in due course by the junkman!

For twenty years following 1907 the office of the *Nation,* with Paul Elmer More as one of its editors, was at 20 Vesey Street. A store at 5 Barclay Street occupies the site of Frank's restaurant, once a favorite meeting-place of the wits of the town; and a fine house long gone from 235 Broadway was for a decade the home of Philip Hone, who from its windows witnessed the encounter between the rival editors, Bryant and Stone, of which he makes indignant record in his *Diary.* "While I was shaving this morning," he wrote on April 20, 1831, "I witnessed from the front window an encounter in the street nearly opposite between William C. Bryant and William L. Stone, the former one of the editors of the *Evening Post* and the latter editor of the *Commercial Advertiser.* The former commenced the attack by striking Stone over the head with a cowskin; after a few blows the men closed, and the whip was wrested from Bryant and carried off by Stone. A crowd soon closed in and separated the combatants." An unusual glimpse of a fighting Bryant whom folk of an aftertime were to know only as a serene and stately figure in the "white winter of his age."

Born in 1780, Hone at forty retired with an ample fortune made in trade to become mayor of his town and a leader in all measures for its welfare and upbuilding. He was also one of the organizers of the Whig Party and welcomed many of its leaders to his Broadway home. Thus in 1834 he was the host of Colonel David Crockett of Tennessee, a now legendary figure whose autobiography, not wholly ghost-written, he must have voted a most amusing book. And Crockett who, not long before, to the delight of the Whigs, had broken with Andrew Jackson, found much to admire in the former mayor of New York. "Philip Hone," he wrote, "I look upon as the politest man I ever did see, for when he asked me to take a drink at his own sideboard he turned his back upon me that I might'nt be ashamed to fill as much as I wanted. That was what I call doing the fair thing." Two years after his visit to New York Crockett fell at the Alamo, one of the heroes of an immortal defense. Hone died in 1851, and a generation later selections from his carefully kept, gossiping *Diary* were published in two goodly volumes which ever since have been held in high favor by those who find diversion in the small talk of history.

A door northward from the site of Hone's longtime home, William James Stillman began his journalistic career as one of the editors of the *Crayon*. Stillman's life of seventy-three years was marked by unusual experiences both in America and Europe as artist, journalist, revolutionist and friend and intimate of men and women of mark. Born in 1828 in Schenectady, he was graduated at Union College in his native town and later studied art in New York, London and Paris. It was during a first visit to Europe in 1849 that he made the acquaintance of Ruskin and Rossetti, and became a devoted member of the Preraphaelite Brotherhood, then in the first year of its existence. Returning to America about the time of Kossuth's visit to this country, he enlisted in the Magyar cause, and accepted a perilous mission to Vienna to carry off the crown jewels secreted by the exiled chief.

This venture had many thrilling moments, and in after days, Stillman used to relate how, when his task seemed a hopeless one and arrest at hand, he elected on a stormy night to commit his compromising credentials to the Danube. But barely had the boot that hid them in its heel splashed in the river when he was challenged by a guard who after a question or two permitted him to pass on to safety. And in relating this incident Stillman would usually add with a smile that when in 1894 he called on Kossuth in the latter's extreme old age he found that the great Magyar had completely forgotten the errand charged with danger and possible death with which in the long ago he had enlisted his young American follower.

After another sojourn in Paris Stillman came back to America and in 1855 with John Durand founded the *Crayon,* which, having its literary as well as its artistic side, presently brought him into intimate and delightful contact with Lowell and his circle at Cambridge, where from time to time he made extended sojourns. In this way he became a member of a group including Emerson, Lowell and Agassiz which in the summers of 1858 and 1859 made extended stays in the Adirondacks, the younger man serving as guide, philosopher and friend to his older companions, and making time also for some of his best work as a painter. The year 1860 found him again in London and Paris, among other things renewing and strengthening his association with Ruskin, for whom he named his first born.

Then the Civil War brought Stillman back to America and in 1861 Lincoln appointed him consul at Rome, where he remained several years. There followed extended service as consul to Crete, in the course of which he acquired a comprehensive knowledge of conditions in the Near East. This, following another brief stay in America, led to an association with the London *Times* which filled out the balance of his working days. The story goes that being in London in 1877 he called upon the editor of the *Times,* told him that trouble was about to break in the Balkans, and asked for the post of war correspondent. The editor refused to believe that trouble was brewing, and scouted the pressing need of a war correspondent.

"Very well," said Stillman, "I know there is no time to be lost; so I am off tonight for the Balkans. This will be my address. If you want a man on the ground telegraph me."

Stillman had barely reached his destination when events confirmed his predictions; the *Times* by telegraph engaged his services, and ere long he became its permanent representative in Italy and Greece with headquarters in Rome, an association which lasted until his retirement at the age of seventy, and, by the same token, made him one of the most influential journalists of his generation. Returning to England in 1898 Stillman passed the last three years of his life at Frimley Green, Surrey, where at the instance of a Boston publisher he wrote his *Autobiography of a Journalist,* a most interesting work which again and again gives proof of a striking gift for portraiture, and perhaps opens more vistas than are afforded by any other story of an American life put on paper during the last half century. All in all, Stillman was an unusual man, and in his career a shining example of what

American character can achieve under the quickening influences of cosmopolitan experience.

A century ago, the site at the southwest corner of Broadway and Park Place was occupied by Bixby's Hotel where Cooper and Irving often lodged in their last years, and which was the first New York home of Alice and Phoebe Cary. Four numbers removed on the opposite side of Park Place, George William Curtis, Parke Godwin, and Charles F. Briggs conducted *Putnam's Magazine*, while next door, James C. Derby was first in business as a publisher.

Later Derby and his partner Jackson were located at 498 Broadway and there gave favorable consideration to the proposed publication of a book by Charles Farrar Browne—Artemus Ward —when in 1861 the humorist came from Cleveland to New York and for a brief period served as editor of *Vanity Fair*. "Derby & Jackson, unquestionably the best house in the city," he wrote a Cleveland friend, "sent their agent to me almost as soon as I reached the city and today I had an interview with Mr. Derby. I have not closed with him but he speaks in the most encouraging manner of the enterprise and they all tell me he will make me a good offer. I am alright. Get along just as easily as rolling off a log. I dare not tell you all the fine things that have happened to me for fear you may think I blow but I certainly start out here under brilliant auspices." Derby appears, however, to have changed his mind and, as elsewhere recorded, the book which was to bring Browne money and added repute was issued by another publisher.

Park Place cuts through the plot bounded by Church and West and Barclay and Murray Streets which for nearly a hundred years after 1760 furnished a site for what was first called King's College and is now known as Columbia University. Some of the greatest men in American letters and public life knew as students the level spaces of College Green. John Jay, Alexander Hamilton, Robert R. Livingston, Gouverneur Morris and De Witt Clinton were among the college's early graduates. John Randolph of Roanoke was for a brief period numbered among its students, while, as had been noted in another place, James Kent was its first professor of law, and it was from his lectures as such that he later developed his famous *Commentaries*.

The office of *Hearth and Home*, when edited by Edward Eggleston and Frank Stockton, was at 245 Broadway, where they had a young woman of parts, Margaret Sangster by name, as their assistant. Three doors above the *Independent* had its office in 1890 when Bliss Carman, his repute as a poet still before him, was one of its assistant editors. George P. Morris dwelt for a time at 13 Murray Street, and a dozen doors removed on the same side of the way, was the home of Bayard Taylor, when he returned from early wanderings in Europe to become one of the editors of the *Tribune*. There Taylor had Charles Fenno Hoffman for a fellow-lodger and Richard Henry Stoddard for an associate, and must have often touched elbows with Seba Smith, whose home for a number of years was at 65 Murray Street. Smith was the first of a long line of humorists who have found our political life a congenial subject for their pens, and as Major Jack Downing wrote letters in Down East dialect which were a source of delight to thousands. While an editor at Portland, in his native state of Maine, he married Elizabeth Oakes Prince, a gifted and beautiful woman, who, after their removal to New York, won for herself a wide reputation as a maker of verse. She was also one of the first of her sex in this country to appear as a public lecturer, and among the first to speak from a pulpit. Three generations ago her popularity was at flood, and her *Sinless Child* was praised by Poe as one of the best American long poems. Men pass away, however, and their idols with them, and long before old age she had disappeared from public view. Her death in 1892 was chiefly noteworthy because it reminded a forgetful world that such a woman as Elizabeth Oakes Smith had ever lived.

The office of *Puck,* in the days when, with Henry Cuyler Bunner as its editor, it was growing in favor and influence, was at 23 Warren Street, and less than a block away, another once popular humorist was in business for a dozen years. This was Frederick Swartout Cozzens, who before and during the Civil War, conducted a wine cellar at 73 Warren Street, where he often gave welcome to Irving and Halleck and other bookmen. He also managed most successfully to mingle trade with letters, and his *Sparrowgrass Papers,* which whimsically describe a cockney residence in the country, passed through numerous editions, but now await the time when some enterprising publisher shall give them a new lease of life. Dr. John W. Francis, whom Cozzens made the central figure in another of his books, lived for many years at 149 Chambers Street, and in the same thoroughfare, one finds the site of Burton's Theatre, upon whose stage Samuel Lover appeared for the first time before an American audience.

City Hall Park was one of the places most frequented by McDonald Clarke, the hapless hero of Halleck's *Discarded* and himself the author of much tender and graceful verse. Clarke first appeared in New York when a youth of twenty-one, and he remained until his death a melancholy and unmistakable figure in the life of the town—made so by his poetic genius, his sharp wit and the vagaries of an unbalanced mind. Little was known of his antecedents or of his means of support, aside from the sale of his books of verse, but the sequel proved that he was often in need of both food and lodging. On a stormy night in March, 1842, a policeman came upon him wandering about the streets, and took him to the city prison for warmth and shelter. The following morning he was found dead, having drowned himself in his cell. Friends provided a tomb and burial, and he sleeps now on the margin of Sylvan Lake in Greenwood.

The shop of David Longworth, one of Irving's early publishers, was for a time at 11 Park Row facing City Hall Park. The same site was occupied a little later by the wine-cellar of Edward Windust, a nightly haunt of the authors, actors and artists who flourished in the first quarter of the last century. The son of a niece of Windust who knew his kinsman's establishment when a lad recalled in after years that port and Madeira were not the only appealing things served its patrons. "The whole house," he writes, "was heavy with the pungent aroma of turtle soup at all hours." Charles Delmonico long served Windust as head waiter and when his employer retired to a country home at Oak Nook on the shores of Oyster Bay, set up in business for himself with immediate and enduring success.

A door above the site of Windust's resort, where now is the Syndicate Building, then stood the Park Theatre, for fifty years the leading playhouse of the city. It was on the stage of the Park that John Howard Payne began his career as an actor, and there Sheridan Knowles was seen as Master Walter in his own play of the *Hunchback*. There too, Mary Duff, the early sweetheart of the poet Moore, and a wonder of genius and beauty, appeared for the first time on the New York stage.

Again, in Park Row a door below Beekman Street, is the site of the last home of Joseph Rodman Drake, whose gift of song and early death have led his career to be compared to that of John Keats. There he wrote his most widely known poem, the *American Flag,* and there, as elsewhere recorded, he died of tuberculosis at the age of twenty-five. "There will be less sunshine now that Joe is gone," said Halleck, returning from the burial of his friend, and the simple and feeling elegy in which he further voiced his sorrow has not been surpassed in our literature.

The first office of the *World* was at 35 Park Row. The publishing houses of Scribner and Dodd, Mead & Company had their beginnings in the chapel of the Brick Presbyterian Church, which in the earlier decades of the last century faced City Hall Park from Park Row and Spruce Street, while for eighty years the office of the *Tribune* was at the corner of Nassau and Spruce Streets. There Greeley had for associates such men as Bayard Taylor, George Ripley and Charles Anderson Dana. Later members of a brilliant staff were bearded Albert D. Richardson, a seeker of adventure in far places which he knew how to describe in an arresting way, and who for a decade was after his chief the most widely known writer for the *Tribune;* Whitelaw Reid, who, following its founder's death, was to be for forty years the journal's chief owner and directing spirit; John Hay, then just returned from abroad, whose *Pike County Ballads* and incisive editorials were warmly praised by an employer not given to praise, and William Winter, who for more than forty years served the *Tribune* as dramatic critic, being for the greater part of that period regarded as America's foremost authority on acting and the drama.

The building which housed the Tribune for a time was also the home of *Yankee Doodle,* a lively American counterpart of London *Punch.* A few doors distant, at 8 Spruce street ninety years ago was issued a book which won an army of readers on the eve of the Civil War and played a fateful part in hastening that struggle. Born in 1829 on a North Carolina farm, worked by his father's slaves, Hinton Rowan Helper early came to question the value of the slave system to the South, and after a sojourn in California returned to the East in 1855 to busy himself with the preparation of a book which should give telling expression to his views. He travelled about the country for two years; in 1857 completed the manuscript of his book in Baltimore, and, unable to find a publisher for it in that city, sought one in New York. After a series of refusals from leading publishers of the period, the firm of Burdick Brothers at 8 Spruce

Street told the author that they would publish his book if he would guarantee the cost of paper and printing.

Helper, resolved that an imperative message should go out to the world, agreed to this hard bargain, and his book, to which he gave the title *The Impending Crisis of the South: How to Meet It,* appeared late in 1857 and met with such instant demand that for several years thereafter Burdick Brothers were mainly occupied in the printing of successive editions of it. In his preface Helper expressed the hope that his friends and fellow citizens of the South would read what he had written and accept it in "a reasonable and friendly spirit." To the contrary the book, which argued that the South was left behind in a social and economic way by slavery, at once aroused angry dispute and discussion. John Sherman of Ohio was denied the speakership of the House because he had bought a copy of it, and a South Carolina minister found in possession of one had to flee to the North to escape prosecution; while in Arkansas three men were hanged by mobs for owning copies of it. All told, 100,000 copies of Helper's book were sold the first year and in 1859 millions of copies of a booklet which gave a digest of its contents were distributed as a campaign document by the Republican Party.

What most angered its Southern readers was its declaration that cotton was the curse of the South and of its non-slave holding whites. Although Southern attacks on the book were manifold and bitter ones, no one successfully attempted to refute the arguments of its author who became over night the "best known and worst hated man in America." When Lincoln took office as President he made Helper consul at Buenos Aires. His period of service in that post at an end, with money from his book royalties, he devoted his time and energy to the building of a railroad from Hudson's Bay to Patagonia. Nothing came of this undertaking and Helper's last days were passed in poverty in Washington. There towards the end he lived in a cheap hotel and there, it is to be recorded with regret, one night in 1909 he died by his own hand.

Again one finds at 109 Spruce Street the site of the building in which the Brook Farm Association once had an office, and from which for a number of years Henry Clapp issued the *Saturday Press,* a witty and vigorous journal which for a time enlisted a vast amount of talent. It also stands to its credit that it was the first to publish *The Jumping Frog* of Mark Twain. That was in November, 1865. A few months earlier Mark Twain, then employed on a San Francisco newspaper, had received from Artemus Ward a letter which was to have weighty issue. The two men had become friends when Ward visited Virginia City in the closing days of 1863, and he now asked Twain to contribute to a book he was about to publish in New York. So Twain wrote the story of the *Jumping Frog* and sent it to his friend. But the manuscript arrived in New York too late to claim a place in Ward's book. Ward having departed for England, Carlton, his publisher, handed the sketch to Clapp, who promptly published it and by so doing started its author on the way to worldwide fame as a humorist. The career of the *Saturday Press* had another and different ending. Had there been competent business management, it might have continued to flourish until the present day, but that element of success was wanting, and its existence ended with the terse announcement that it was discontinued for the want of funds, "which is," added the editor, "by a coincidence, precisely the same reason for which it was started." The last days of its gifted but wayward editor were grim ones. Clapp died under the saddest of circumstances on Blackwell's Island, and his funeral expenses were borne by men and women who admired his talent without joining in the excesses that hurried him to the grave.

The publications of Frank Leslie were long quartered at 12 Spruce Street, and there Thomas Nast began his career as an artist, while five doors removed, the *Sunday Mercury* had its office when its editor was Robert Henry Newell, who, during the Civil War period, under the pen name of Orpheus C. Kerr, won a national reputation as a humorist. Back again in City Hall Park, the stroller finds the northerly part of the old *Tribune* building, covering the site of the structure in which Walt Whitman, in his 'prentice days, edited the *Aurora,* while a walk northward through what was once Chatham Street brings one to 15 Bowery, where Stephen C. Foster lodged in his troubled later days. At what is now 85 Bowery Horace Greeley in 1831 was first employed as a printer in New York, while at 121 Bowery, the poet Drake had his office as a physician, and finished his *Culprit Fay.* Hard by, at 56 Division Street, Samuel Woodworth once had his home, and at 195 East Broadway, the building of the Educational Alliance replaces a house in which Poe dwelt with his ailing wife during his second sojourn in New York.

Again at 103 East Broadway in 1868 and after a boarding house long gratefully remembered by its guests from time to time furnished a first American home for Irish refugees driven into exile by the luckless and tragic outcome of the Fenian uprising of that time. Among them were Joseph I. C. Clarke, then twenty-two and a native of Kingstown, and Edmond and John Donovan, sons of John Donovan, the great Celtic scholar of Dublin. Clarke remained on in New York to perform outstanding service on the *Herald* and other journals, to win repute as a poet and to write that stirring bit of verse the *Fighting Race,* while John Donovan, learned in philosophy and the classics, after a time became a college professor and while still a young man was drowned in a lake near St. Louis where he was swimming with some of his students.

His brother was also to meet a tragic end. Returning soon to Europe, Edmond Donovan fought in the Foreign Legion of France and in 1876 became a correspondent of the London *News* in the Herzegovina campaign. A few years later he confirmed a growing reputation in his field by a daring and sensational ride to the Merv Oasis, where for a time he was held a prisoner, and out of which grew two brilliantly written and informing volumes on conditions in Mid-Asia. And in 1883, still seeking high adventure, Donovan joined the ill-starred expedition of Hicks Pasha against the Mahdists of the Soudan, there no doubt to meet death on the point of an African spear, for no word of him ever came back to his friends.

James Parton, during the first years of a career that was to win him high standing as the biographer of Andrew Jackson and other great Americans, lived at 20 Stanton Street, a few doors from the Bowery, and at 8 Hester Street was the early home of Robert Charles Sands, a man of uncommon talent and range, whose early death alone prevented him from winning a high place in letters, and who merits more than passing mention in this chronicle. Poet, journalist and kindly humorist, Sands was also the author of *Yamoden,* a lively narrative in verse of the wars of King Philip the Pequot, which in after days was to breed a long list of plays dealing with Indian characters and Indian themes. Graduated at Columbia he was likewise a master of Hebrew, Greek and Latin and a capable translator of Aeschylus and Euripides and of the Italian poet Politian. The friend of Paulding and Bryant, one of his last labors was to join them in editing the *Talisman,* a popular annual of the period. Ralph Hoyt, a contemporary of Sands, who in the intervals of his labors as an Episcopal clergyman, wrote wistful and pleasing verse

which still finds a place in the anthologies, lived for a time at
123 Henry Street, and seven doors removed, on the other side
of the way, Lewis Gaylord Clark, had his home, when editor
of the *Knickerbocker Magazine,* which for many years stood for
all that was best in native letters.

The reaches of Broadway lying north of City Hall Park
recall, at every turn, some well-remembered author of other days.
The Stewart building replaces Washington Hall in which were
held the meetings of the Bread and Cheese Club, founded by
Cooper, when in 1820 he settled in New York to be near his
publisher. Besides its founder, the membership of the club included Kent, Dunlap and Halleck and the painters Morse and
Durand, who met each fortnight for lunch and social converse.
As a maker of tales Cooper up to that time had produced only
Precaution and the *Spy,* but he was already widely known at
home and abroad, and the production during the next four years
of the *Pioneers,* the *Pilot* and the *Last of the Mohicans* confirmed this growing reputation. All of which, just before he
sailed in 1826 for a long stay in Europe, prompted the Bread
and Cheese Club to give him a dinner at the City Hotel at which
Chancellor Kent presided and DeWitt Clinton and General Winfield Scott praised the guest of the evening for the distinction
he had brought to his country and city. The story of what followed Cooper's return from abroad in 1833, as will presently
appear, is a drabber and less pleasing affair.

In theory the foe of privilege and power in every form, and
a thorough democrat, Cooper was also by inclination and practice an aristocrat intolerant of change and of unseemly standards.
Thus on his return after long absence abroad he found much in
the American scene to displease him, and in addition to his novels
there poured from his pen a steady stream of books and magazines in which in school-master fashion he called his countrymen
sharply to account for their short-comings. In response, his irri-
tating bluntness provoked to wrath editors of high and low degree
—Horace Greeley among them—and there followed a long series
of law suits which involved a heavy drain upon his purse and
popularity and which, until the New York Legislature effected a
more liberal interpretation of libel, made him the best abused
author of his period.

Meanwhile, Cooper bought back and remodeled the great
house at Cooperstown which after his mother's death had passed
into other hands, and there he dwelt for the rest of his days—a

writer of iron industry and prolific output; a devoted husband never touched by the breath of scandal, and the father of a brace of daughters who fondly regarded him as the center of their little word. At intervals the Cooper family journeyed to New York for the winter, and Donald Grant Mitchell in old age made graphic record of a youthful glimpse of the novelist strolling along Broadway between Cortlandt and Chambers Street—"a heavy, stalwart man, with a little of the sailor swing in his gait, and an unmistakable air of consequence as of one who had played his part, and a somewhat noisy and important part, in the game of life." Cooper died at Cooperstown in 1851 and a few months later a memorial meeting in recognition of his essential greatness was held in New York, at which stately Daniel Webster, who had read and loved his stirring tales of the sea, presided and his friend Bryant, now nearing old age, in an address of rare beauty and feeling, paid fittting tribute to his worth.

Just across the way from the site of the meeting place of the Bread and Cheese Club, two doors below Duane Street, John Townsend Trowbridge found lodgings, when at the age of nineteen he left his father's farm to seek success as an author in New York. Two blocks distant, at 342 Broadway, Lorenzo da Ponte, was once in business as a bookseller, while nearer to Leonard Street, in a still earlier time, stood the house wherein Irving courted lovely Matilda Hoffman, soon to be taken from him by death and to be mourned by him until his last hour. Here too, Irving met Rebecca Gratz, a beautiful Jewess who was the friend of his promised wife and her devoted nurse in her last illness. This lady sprang from an honorable Jewish family in Philadelphia, and when young, won the love of a man of character and wealth. His passion was returned, but difference in religious faith—the one a Christian and the other a disciple of the ancient creed of Israel—proved an insuperable obstacle to the union; and so, instead of knowing the joys of wife and mother, she made the spinsterhood to which conscience and duty impelled her "one long chain of golden deeds." Rebecca Gratz's friendship with Irving ended only with the latter's death, and when, in 1817, Irving was the guest of Scott at Abbotsford, the account he gave of her beauty and constancy caused the great romancer to make her the original of the loveliest of all his female characters—the Rebecca of *Ivanhoe*.

Dickens during his first visit to New York lodged at the Carlton House, which then stood at the northeast corner of

Leonard Street and Broadway. Four doors below Broome Street and on the same side of the way, was once the home of Isaac Lawrence, one of the merchant princes of his time, whose daughter was there wooed and wedded by the poet Hillhouse. The first home of the Century Club was at 495 Broadway; three doors above on the opposite side of the street the *Galaxy* had its office when Mark Twain, Justin McCarthy and Richard Grant White contributed to its pages; and in a Unitarian church long gone from 548 Broadway, Thackeray in 1852 delivered his lectures upon the English humorists. Cooper dwelt for a time on the east side of Broadway, a few doors from Prince Street, when just across the way at 585 Broadway was the home of John Jacob Astor, where Irving wrote a portion of his *Life of Washington*.

Two doors above the site of Astor's former dwelling was the birthplace of Robert Henry Newell, while the basement of a building at 647 Broadway not far from Bleecker Street, was, just before the Civil War, Charles Pfaff's beer-cellar, the chosen idling-place of the cleverest of New York's literary Bohemians. Henry Clapp chanced upon Pfaff's place one day in 1856, in company with Fitz-James O'Brien, and was so pleased with the coffee served him that he straightway sounded its praises among his comrades, who thereupon made it their habitual resort. A table was reserved for their use, and around it gathered almost nightly for several years such men as Clapp, O'Brien, Walt Whitman, George Arnold, Edward Wilkins, Charles Dawson Shanly and Charles Farrar Browne.

All of the group had ability, and not a few of them, genius; but strong drink and late hours were not the elements from which to expect enduring success; and soon the young men who drank so deeply and faced the world so joyously discovered their mistakes. Then the failure of the journals conducted by Clapp and Browne dissolved the chief links that held them together, and the Civil War scattered them far and wide. O'Brien, a handsome Irishman, who wrote with equal ease stirring virile poems, or weirdly powerful stories inferior only to those of Poe, volunteered in defense of the Union, and fell at Bloomery Gap. Wilkins, an admirable dramatic critic, died early; so did Arnold, whose verse still finds admiring readers, while Browne's career, as noted in another place, ended in England, when, at the age of thirty-three, he should have been preparing to do his strongest and best work.

Clapp's career was also one of few lights and many shadows. Born on the island of Nantucket he all his days gave the lie to his Puritan ancestry, for he was a Bohemian by instinct and with him instinct in the end always triumphed over convention. He went to sea in his youth and later was a merchant in the oil and candle line first in Boston and later in New Orleans. Then he became a reporter on a New Bedford newspaper, and after an interlude as champion of the causes of anti-drink and anti-slavery betook himself to London by way of Boston—as delegate to a world temperance convention. In London, however, his non-drinking views and habits fell away from him, and continuing on to Paris he began the career of bohemianism of which he was to become both an example and a warning.

Clapp found the atmosphere of Paris congenial to him, and, being a man of wit, whose talk in his best days had the brilliancy and sparkle of good champagne, he was soon on an intimate and friendly footing with the members of the group which saved the French capital from stodginess in the days of the third Napoleon. The story runs that he gained entrance to this circle through the elder Dumas to whom he wrote on his arrival in Paris, suggesting to the famous story-teller that he and Clapp should write a play in partnership. "Monsieur," Dumas replied, "you cannot find in Scripture or elsewhere an instance for hitching the ox and the ass together." And to this Clapp made instant reply: "Monsieur, by what authority do you call me an ox?" Whereupon Dumas sent for the young American, and though he did not write a play with him, they remained thereafter the best of friends.

Clapp wrote in Paris for one of the London journals and he also struck hands with Horace Greeley when the editor of the *Tribune* made his first visit to France. There resulted a bargain that Clapp should write letters from Paris and London alternately for the *Tribune,* nor did Clapp fail to persuade Greeley to give him an advance order on the *Tribune* for a part of his salary. This order he promptly cashed in London, but Greeley never received the letters in New York. Later, however, when a final turn of the wheel had landed Clapp in New York, he wrote articles for the *Tribune* to cancel the debt. In New York also he was employed by Albert Brisbane, disciple of Fourier and unusual father of a famous son, to translate socialistic books from the French; wrote off and on for the press—by fits and starts he was a hard worker—and founded with borrowed capital the *Saturday Press,* a clever paper which, as intimated elsewhere, ruined a lot of clever people. And then, last scene of all for Clapp, years of incurable poverty relieved by occasional gifts from old friends, commital to Blackwell's Island for vagrancy under an assumed name, and death and temporary burial there under grim conditions.

Yet more tragic was the fate of another member of the Pfaff crowd. Ada Clare was a beautiful Southern girl of birth and breeding, and had been carefully educated, but with the tastes that seemed born in her for an unconventional life, she drifted to New York, where she became a writer and actress, and queen of the brilliant circle which gathered around Pfaff's round table. "She was a great beauty in those days," William Winter once told the writer, "and poor old Clapp was hopelessly in love with her." But the last chapter in Ada Clare's career was a sorrowful one, for she outlived her beauty and most of her old companions to die of hydrophobia, the result of the bite of a pet dog.

In due course Plaff's cafe also became a thing of the past. "Years later," writes Don Carlos Seitz, who in the course of a busy and wide-ranging career was the author of many books, a biography of Artemus Ward among them, "647 Broadway became a loafing place of my own as a growing lad, for here James Miller, beloved of three generations of bookmen, then had a fine store, of which I had the run and where I spent many delightful hours. Pfaff's, of course, was gone, and Miller used the basement it had once occupied for storage and packing. Now and then I descended to its depths, but, alas, I did not know that once it had been Bohemia."

Another literary association with this part of the town demands a paragraph for at 713 Broadway, corner of Washington Place, was the second New York home of the publishing and book-selling house founded by Edward P. Dutton. It was in Boston in 1852, the year that *Uncle Tom's Cabin* came from the press, that Dutton began business. Coming to New York in 1868 he at first shared with another concern a store at 762 Broadway. At the end of a year his landlord decided that the man from Boston was prosperous and demanded a heavy increase in rent. Instead of paying it, Dutton moved his business a few hundred feet south to 713 Broadway, remaining there for thirteen years.

Dutton came to New York at the request of the General Protestant Sunday School Union and Church Society, to publish and distribute its books, but gradually widened the scope of his activities so that before he left Broadway for quarters farther north his list included works of weight and worth in widely separated fields. A noteworthy undertaking of his house in later years was publication of the first collected edition of the writings of Leonard Merrick with appreciative introductions by fellow novelists, whereby one of the most gifted and at the same time most neglected English writers of the last half century—an author's author in the best sense of the phrase—came finally and fully into the dignified repute that eminently belonged to him. Edward P. Dutton, a gentleman of the old school, had a useful and discriminating part in six decades of publishing history. He died in 1923 full of years and honors.

CHAPTER IV

NORTHWARD FROM THE COMMON

A goodly number of writers had their homes, in other days, in the thoroughfares lying between Broadway and the Bowery, now almost wholly given over to trade. One of these was Samuel Woodworth, author of the *Old Oaken Bucket*, who, when he wrote that song was living at 86 Duane Street. Woodworth's last home was at 457 Pearl Street, near to Elm, and there he died in 1842 after a long and wasting illness. His widow spent the remainder of her days at the home of a son in San Francisco. When she, too, passed away, the son had the remains of his father removed from New York and placed by her side in Laurel Hill Cemetery, San Francisco, so that in death they "might not be divided." In another burial-ground of that city sleeps the poet, Richard Realf, whose New York career is recalled by the Five Points House of Industry in Worth Street, where, during his first days in America, he was employed as a teacher.

Realf's career was an unusual one and it had a tragic ending. Born of humble parentage in Sussex, England, in 1834, he early gave proof of exceptional gifts and in his teens began to write and publish verse of an uncommon quality. Byron's widow was attracted by it, and she and some of her friends helped him to secure an education. Young Realf came to America in 1854, Lady Byron having given him money for the voyage, and taught for two years at the House of Industry. Then, fired by a desire to help preserve Kansas from slavery, he journeyed to that territory and there became a friend and follower of John Brown, but, at the end of a brief sojourn in England, he was in Texas at the time of the Harper's Ferry raid. Thus he had no direct part in that ill-fated affair, and although arrested and questioned was in due time released from custody.

Realf was in Columbus, Ohio, in the weeks of abeyance between Brown's capture and death, and William Dean Howells, then on the staff of one of the journals of that city, at a later time put on record appealing memories of the young Englishman. "He was a charming youth," writes Howells, "gentle mannered, sweet voiced, well dressed and girlishly beautiful. In the long walks and long talks we had together, when he cared more to speak of his literary than his military life, I cannot make out that he expected to help further in any attack upon the South. He did not appear to be afraid or anxious for himself as part of the scheme that had so bloodily failed. He was not keeping himself secret, and he went on to Canada as safely as he had come from Texas, if indeed he went to Canada."

Realf enlisted in 1862 in an Illinois regiment, was made an officer and served with gallantry until the close of the war between the sections. For six years following 1868 he was a writer for Pittsburgh newspapers. Then he fell ill, and friends raised a purse and sent him to the Pacific Coast. His relations with women had not been fortunate ones. Now his divorce from the second of his three wives was, on technical grounds, annulled by the courts, and, unable to care for his third wife and the children she had borne him, on an October night in 1878 he committed suicide in an Oakland hotel. Twenty years later his poems were collected and published by his friend Richard J. Hinton. They reveal a disordered and unhappy nature at war with fate, but some of them contain lines of great beauty which save their author's name from forgetfulness. Realf's grave is in Lone Mountain Cemetery overlooking San Francisco Bay.

Fitz-Greene Halleck lodged for a number of years at 25 Franklin Street, not far from Center, and at the southwest corner of Mulberry and Houston Streets, *Puck* had its office when Henry Cuyler Bunner's career as its editor came to an end. There also Harry Leon Wilson served as assistant to Bunner, later succeeding to his vacant chair which he filled for half a dozen years. Wilson, whose humor was individual and nearly of the first quality, was born in Illinois, in 1867, and in early manhood as a wandering stenographer knew mining camp life in the Rockies and the Sierras. While thus employed he began to write jokes and humorous bits which brought him the favorable attention of Eastern editors and a place on the staff of *Puck*. But he did not like the crowded life of a great center of population, and the story runs that he wrote his first novel, the *Spenders*, in order to escape from New York which he now and again declared the ugliest city in the world.

The success of the *Spenders* assured Wilson a summer in Colorado, and the returns from later novels enabled him to live for a longer period in or near Paris, where with Booth Tarkington he wrote the *Man from Home*, a play produced in Chicago in 1917 and which held the stage for half a dozen years. His early fondness for the West, however, persisted and after further wanderings he settled down in Carmel, California, where he lived until his death in 1939, and where as the years sped he wrote a long series of novels which proved him a diverting, sardonic and also veracious interpreter of the humorous side of an age and section now part of an irrecoverable past. An individualist of the robust sort he was at times an uncomfortable companion, but he had wit and insight, and was always the friend of the common man.

A house long gone from one of the Broadway corners of Bond Street was the last home of Dr. John W. Francis. Another house, which formerly occupied the site numbered 7 Bond Street, was once the abode of William North, author of the *Slave of the Lamp*, and other fantastic tales, who there died by his own hand. The dwelling of Henry Winter Bellows, one of the eloquent preachers of his period, was at the same time at 17 Bond Street, and seven doors removed on the other side of the way, Julia Ward Howe passed the last years of her girlhood. Maria Louise Shew, the good angel, of Poe and his wife, long lived in a house yet standing at 47 Bond Street, and here the poet, when a guest of the Shews, is said to have written the *Bells* in a room now used for factory purposes. Two doors nearer to Broadway stands a three-storied brick house in which Irving lived for several years when it was the home of his nephew.

Philip Hone died at 1 Great Jones Street. After his death, his home became a house of entertainment, and the last New York abode of Fitz-James O'Brien, who there wrote the *Lost Steamship*, and other of his verse. Just across the way, in the same period, stood the Jones House, a family hostelry of a now vanished type, which for a time was the home of Charles Farrar Browne when editor of *Vanity Fair*. Browne was given to late hours and an undue indulgence in drink, a manner of living confirmed by an amusing incident William Winter often recalled in his last years. Browne and Winter had been participants in a jolly gathering at Pfaff's which did not break up until the early morning hours. Then Winter kept Browne company to the Jones House, where the latter aroused the sleeping night clerk, and demanded an audience with the landlord. When a few minutes later that dignitary appeared half-dressed in the lobby, Browne huddled him into a corner and in earnest tones declared: "I have summoned you from bed at this unseemly hour to impress

upon your mind that eternal vigilance is the price of liberty."
Then he thrust his card into the landlord's hand and grasping
his companion's arm strode again into the street. Long after
Browne's death business one day took Winter to the Jones House,
and on the wall of the lobby he espied the card given to the landlord, which had been duly framed by its recipient.

The poet Duganne passed his closing years at 12 Lafayette
Place, and two doors northward on the other side of the street
was the home of John Reuben Thompson, when literary editor
of the *Evening Post*. The office of the *Magazine of American
History* when Martha J. Lamb was its editor was at 30 Lafayette
Place. John Jacob Astor's long life came to an end at 32 Lafayette Place, and four doors removed, flourished for half a century
the library which bore his name. A long line of famous scholars
and authors in the past made use of the Astor Library. Washington Irving drew from its shelves much of the material for
his *Life of Washington;* George Bancroft made constant use of
it when at work on the earlier volumes of his history, and when
Herman von Holst came from Germany to delve deeper into our
constitutional development than any alien before him had done,
he was for a time constantly in the library. Thackeray, during
his visits to America, also spent many hours in the alcoves of
the Astor.

Richard Henry Stoddard lived in Third Street near Second
Avenue when he wrote his *Songs of Summer,* and the home of
William James Stillman during his active years as an artist was
at 80 Seventh Street. Three blocks westward, at 8 Fourth Avenue, Mary Mapes Dodge passed a portion of her girlhood. Close
at hand at 743 Broadway, just below Astor Place, she first edited
St. Nicholas, having for an associate Frank R. Stockton, who
there began his career as a maker of odd and whimsical yet
wholly delightful fiction. There also was the first home of
Scribner's Magazine, when Josiah Gilbert Holland was its editor.

Charles Fenno Hoffman dwelt in Greenwich Street before
he passed into the mental gloom which shrouded his remaining
years; and a house yet standing at the corner of that thoroughfare and Third Street was the home of Edward Wilkins, in the
middle decades of the last century, perhaps the most gifted writer
in the service of the *Herald*. Stephen Collins Foster, when he
first came to New York in 1860, lodged with his family at 83
Greene Street, and less than a block away, at what is now 34 East
Eighth Street but was formerly Clinton Place, one finds the site

of the last home of William Leete Stone, who there completed
his memoirs of Brandt and Red Jacket. Four doors eastward
from Stone's dwelling was the home of the Century Club in the
days when Verplanck served as its president and Thackeray declared its spirit of good fellowship the most satisfying thing he
had found on this side of the sea. Two numbers nearer to University Place was for a quarter of a century the home of that
hard-working and many-sided man of letters, Evert Augustus
Duykinck, who in the years immediately preceding the Civil War
had Charles Anderson Dana for neighbor across the way. And
it was in the lodgings of his uncle Sam Ward at what was then
85 Clinton Place that Francis Marion Crawford wrote the opening chapters of his first novel, *Dr. Claudius*. Another of Crawford's novels, *Katherine Lauderdale,* was partly written in the
Sinclair House, which stood, until a recent time, at Broadway
and Eighth Street, and its scene is laid in the neighborhood.

One of the trim brick dwellings which formerly flanked the
part of Eighth Street lying between Third and Second Avenues
and known as St. Mark's Place, was, for several years, the winter
residence of Cooper, who there wrote the greater part of the
Monikins, and waged the war against his critics of the press
which, as noted elsewhere, helped to make him the best-abused
author of his generation. The whimsical Cozzens lived for a time
at 42 Stuyvesant Street, a door from the corner of Second Avenue. The home of Bryant's middle years was at 60 Ninth Street.
William James Linton, the English author and engraver, dwelt
during his first days in America at 210 East Ninth Street, and
on the same side of that thoroughfare, eleven numbers from
Fifth Avenue, was the last abode of Samuel Griswold Goodrich,
the Peter Parley whose juvenile fiction gave delight to the children
of two generations ago.

The last home of Sara Teasdale, a woman of rare and delicate fancy, who came from her native St. Louis to New York,
there to win a place quite her own among the verse makers of
her period, was at 1 Fifth Avenue. Bret Harte, when he returned to the East on the morrow of his success as a depicter
of the lives and deeds of the Argonauts, dwelt for a time with
a sister at 16 Fifth Avenue. Mark Twain, Harte's old comrade
of California days, who, when age and an ocean divided them,
was to grow to hate a former friend with unrelenting hatred,
resided for several years following 1904 at 21 Fifth Avenue, in
one of the few old houses which still resist the onslaught of the

remakers of a famous thoroughfare, and there planned with
Albert Bigelow Paine the writing of his biography. This house
was built in the middle decades of the last century by James
Renwick, whose mother was the Blue Eyed Lassie sung by
Burns, and who set aside a room in his new home for Washington Irving, his close friend for many years. Thus it has intimate
association with two of the most honored names in American
letters. A door northward was the passing abode of Clarence
King, a man of rich and varied gifts, whose the *Helmet of
Mambrino* is one of the most delicate and artless, as it is also
one of the most beautiful things in our literature. King's private
life offered weighty cause for censure, and his latter years were
shadowed ones; but he had a great gift for friendship and is
still held in tender memory by men once young and now old
who have long survived him.

At 46 East Tenth Street was for long the home of Steele
Mackaye. William Livingston Alden, when a member of the
staff of the *Times* and a writer of editorials which proved him
both a humorist and redresser of social abuses, lived in the same
thoroughfare, fifteen doors farther from Broadway, while at the
corner of Tenth Street and Fourth Avenue the poet Stoddard
and his wife had their home during their most productive period.
The home of John J. Johnston at 113 East Tenth Street claimed
Walt Whitman as a guest during his later visits to New York.
Across the way Edmund Clarence Stedman lived for a time, and
a brick house two doors nearer to Third Avenue was for a much
longer period the home of Richard Grant White, who there wrote
his *New Gospel of Peace,* the most telling satire evoked by the
Civil War, and did much work on the edition of Shakespeare
which, with his criticisms of the master dramatist, remains his
chief claim to remembrance. White, be it said, had also a love
for beautiful women which went out to those not always of his
own household, and this trait bequeathed to his gifted son Sanford led to the latter's slaying by a half-mad husband midway of
a brilliant career.

Herman Melville, when one of the most talked about of
native authors, lived at 103 Fourth Avenue. In an office he had
hired in the Bible House, yet standing at Fourth Avenue and
Eighth Street, Horace Greeley, urged to the task by a firm of
subscription book publishers, in 1864 began work on the *American Conflict,* the earliest exhaustive survey of the Civil War
period. "I proffer it," wrote Greeley, "as my contribution toward

a fuller realization of the truth that God governs the world by moral laws as active, immutable and all pervading as can be operative in any other."

In his Bible House retreat, the editor of the *Tribune* hid himself from all callers for at least half of each working day while he gave form to his two bulky volumes. To the relief of his publishers, for his script was the despair of most of those who attempted to decipher it, he dictated instead of writing, making use of a secretary for the first time. His output, nevertheless, was of the first order, and after four-score years the *American Conflict* as a source book retains its value for students of an eventful era. Upward of 150,000 copies of the first volume were sold, but when the second came out in 1867 its sales held sharp disappointment both for author and publisher.

Conflict ended, Greeley had been one of the first to urge generous treatment of the people of the South and their leaders, and, wedding action to word, in May, 1867, was one of a little group of Northern men who signed the $100,000 bond which released Jefferson Davis from his long imprisonment at Fortress Monroe, editor and Confederate leader meeting for the first and last time in the court-room where the bond was put into effect. Those were years of hatred and bitter prejudice, and Greeley's action aroused the wrath of a numerous element in the North. Members of the Union League Club of New York sought unsuccessfully to expel him, and thousands who had bought the first volume of the *American Conflict* refused to buy the second one. The bail-bond furor subsided after a time, and Greeley's *Recollections of a Busy Life* had a large sale when it came from the press in 1869; but during what remained of its founder's lifetime the *Weekly Tribune* never regained its former circulation and profits.

The New York Historical Society was located in other years at Second Avenue and Eleventh Street, and a brownstone mansion at the corner of the former thoroughfare and Fourteenth Street, was long the home of William Maxwell Evarts, who died there in 1901 in his eighty-fourth year. This unusual man's last days were passed in complete retirement, and going back in memory to a vanished time the writer of these lines recalls often seeing him seated at a second-story window fronting Second Avenue, a book or newspaper on his knees, and, lost in thought, apparently oblivious to what was passing about him. And how rich and rewarding must have been his recollections of the events in which he had played a part.

A master alike of the written and spoken word—in 1920 a dutiful son published his *Arguments and Speeches* in three stately volumes—Mr. Evarts early in his career became the rival of Charles O'Connor as leader of the New York bar and for two score years following 1860 he stood unrivaled among its members. His style as an advocate and speaker was his own, although an observer once declared that in method and manner he was more like Wendell Phillips than any other orator of his period. Based upon reason and ripe scholarship, his arguments before judge and jury were so effective that in his active years he had few equals as a trial lawyer.

Mr. Evarts also played a part, varied and weighty, in public affairs. He led in organizing the Republican Party in New York, and in the Chicago national convention of 1860, as a disappointed supporter of William H. Seward, moved the unanimous nomination of Abraham Lincoln for the Presidency. Eight years later he helped to save Andrew Johnson, Lincoln's successor, from impeachment and then served him as attorney-general during the remainder of his term. In 1876 he was leading counsel for the Republicans before the Electoral Commission, and when that body gave the disputed Presidency to Hayes the latter made him secretary of state. In 1885 he began a single term in the United States Senate which closed his public career.

This great lawyer, perhaps, is now best remembered for his apt and always telling wit. He was long in constant demand as a speaker at banquets and meetings of an impressive sort, and he was sure to give his hearers something unique and piquant to carry away with them. And he never failed to have ready the response demanded by a particular occasion. When the Chinese were refused admission to the United States and trouble occurred in Colorado in which a few of them were killed some one asked the Chinese minister at Washington: "What are you going to do with your surplus population if we exclude them and kill those who are here?" The minister confessed that he was at a loss for an answer. "Send them to Ireland," said Evarts. "That is the only country in the world that the Irish do not govern." Again he was asked whether he had told a visiting Englishman that Washington had been able to throw a dollar over the Natural Bridge in Virginia. "No," was the reply. "I have been misquoted. What I said to the Englishman was that Washington might readily have performed the feat, since he once threw a sovereign across the sea."

A house at 127 West Eighth Street, now in part surrendered to trade, was for a time the home of Anne Lynch Botta and the scene of the literary receptions that lady had begun in Waverly Place. Henry Jarvis Raymond dwelt during his closing years at 12 West Ninth Street. At 26 West Ninth Street was the last home of Alexander Black, novelist and journalist, whose fiction was praised by Howells, and who at the turn of the century originated and staged the picture plays from which sprang the motion picture. A few doors distant was the home of Elinor Wylie when death ended her labors, and in the same block once abode brilliant and beautiful Mary Duff, who in girlhood had been courted by the poet Moore and had inspired some of his sweetest songs. The home of William Dean Howells was at 48 West Ninth Street, when his *April Hopes* was given to the world. A vine-clad house fronted by a deep garden at 20 Seventh Avenue was the first New York home of Thomas A. Janvier. At 19 West Ninth Street aforetime flourished the Hotel Griffon, a resort noted for its comfort and good fare, which as the Casa Napoleon that writer celebrated in some of his most beguiling tales, and to which Howells sent the Marches in *A Hazard of New Fortunes*.

Richard Watson Gilder died at 9 West Ninth Street when a guest in the house of a friend. Mark Twain when in 1900 he returned from a trip around the world with all his debts paid lived for a time in a house selected for him by his publisher at 14 West Tenth Street, "Clemens is here," Howells wrote Aldrich, "looking younger and jollier than I have seen him in ten years. He says it is all Plassmon, a new German food-drug, he's been taking, but I think it's partly prosperity. He has distinctly the air of a man who has unloaded."

A room in the Studio Building at 15 West Tenth Street was for a decade the literary workshop of Henry Theodore Tuckerman, a native of Boston, pleasantly remembered for his books on early American art and artists. Before that he had spent long periods in Europe, and so was both a ripe scholar and a charming man of the world, popular alike in the social life of New York and Newport. A door westward on the other side of the way from the Studio Building lived and died Emma Lazarus, whose verse was praised by so keen a critic as Emerson, while nine numbers nearer to Sixth Avenue was long the home of Edwin

Laurence Godkin, who, his career as an editor behind him, chose to end his days in England. Edmund Lester Pearson lived at 44 West Tenth Street during some of his more active years.

Across the way at 51 West Tenth Street was for nearly a score of years the home and studio of Kahlil Gibran, equally gifted as man and artist. Born at Mount Lebanon in Syria Gibran came to New York in early manhood, and before his death in 1931, produced the masterly drawings and paintings most of which have now a final home in an old monastery at Becharre in his native Lebanon. He also wrote a handful of books, among them *Jesus, the Son of Mary,* whose teachings and the mystery of whose life always deeply moved him. These books have been translated into many languages, and their austere purity of thought and beauty of phrasing have influenced countless lives. It is altogether fitting that this unusual man who was a prophet before he was a poet should now take his rest "under grass as smooth as velvet," just outside the monastery which houses his life work and near a vineyard full of the olive trees which ever had a wistful place in his heart and thought.

Theodore Dreiser during his forty odd years in and near New York had many homes, some of them in his days of struggle of a drab sort; but he perhaps lived longest at 165 West Tenth Street in an apartment described by one who often visited it as having "two long rooms, tall windows from ceiling to floor, finely divided so that they offered the rare light of a century ago; a pair of marble fireplaces where coal burned; a bare gray floor wide-planked, again as of a century ago, and an air of order and space." In this apartment, presided over for a time by a woman of beauty and talent not his wife, Dreiser, his long fight for recognition successful, wrote *The Titan, A Hoosier Holiday,* and half a dozen other books. There also he gave a welcome to a motley throng of visitors, which included Edgar Lee Masters, who when a guest of the master accorded to a privileged group one of the first public readings of his *Spoon River Anthology,* and Henry L. Mencken, who first championed the cause of the author of *The Titan,* and then, for some unexplained reason fell away from him.

Dreiser was born in Terre Haute, Indiana in 1871, the eleventh in a German-Dutch family of thirteen children and a younger brother of the song writer who took the name of Paul Dresser. He passed his youth in Terre Haute, Evansville and Warsaw, and at sixteen found work as shipping clerk for a hardware house in Chicago. After that he underwent a strenuous apprenticeship as a newspaper reporter in various cities of the Middle West, and in 1894, having found a wife in his wanderings, took up his residence in New York, where for long his lot was mainly a stubborn fight against odds. It is a part of the record that Dreiser prospered mightily as an editor, but faced refusal and bitter opposition as a writer of novels in which he sought to portray life in a frank and unflinching way. He had passed the age of forty when recognition came to him, first in England and France, and then in America. Thereafter each new novel, *An American Tragedy* among them, prompted criticism but added steadily to the number of his readers who, despite their defects, proclaimed them masterly portrayals of the American scene. Their author, who until the end accepted stoically the bitter with the sweet, died in California in 1945 at the age of seventy-five.

It was the lot of the senior writer of these pages to watch from behind the scenes the shaping of the doubtful fortunes of Dreiser's first novel, *Sister Carrie*. The house of Doubleday and Page published but refused to circulate it, due to the opposition of Mrs. Doubleday, herself a writer of another and very different sort, who sternly objected to its blunt phrasing and sordid theme. A little later through the friendly offices of Benjamin W. Dodge, an amiable alcoholic who published the second edition of *Sister Carrie,* the writer came to know its author fairly well, and through the years had occasional meetings and talks with him. The impression of him that abides is of a man of burly figure and forthright speech, and of unbending will, ready at all times to disregard his own well-being and the wishes of friends in order to battle for what he regarded as the truth—a militant and not always agreeable fellow, but one well worth knowing.

One finds at 149 West Ninth Street the house where Lafcadio Hearn lodged with his friend, Joseph Tunison, in the days just preceding the pilgrimage to Japan from which he was never to return, and there translated Anatole France's the *Crime of Sylvestre Bonnard,* receiving, if tradition is to be believed, a hundred dollars for his labors. A recent student of his career has styled him an exotic non-conformist and the phrase is both a faithful and revealing one. Born in Greece and reared in Ireland, the son of a British soldier and a woman of Malta, moved by semi-blindness to shun the society to which he rightfully belonged, Hearn's career was one of the perverse romances of modern letters. Because of an inner disquiet, he rarely if ever knew happiness; and he was sure, sooner or later, to alienate the friends who sought to aid him. But out of the well of bitterness in which he buried himself—work, he declared, was with him a pain —came a style of writing that bespoke a mind at peace, and some of the loveliest books on Japan any author has given us.

William Starbuck Mayo whose tales of adventure call for reprinting died at 13 East Eleventh Street; across the way at 16 East Eleventh Street was the home of Lucy, daughter of Matthew Arnold, following her marriage in 1884 to Frederick Whitridge, who in his time played a noteworthy part in the business and professional life of New York, while a hotel which occupies the southeast corner of that thoroughfare and University Place, was at different times the winter home of Stockton and Howells and the last abode of Charles Taber Congdon, whose fine humor for a generation afforded delight to the readers of the *Tribune,* and at a later time of Arthur Warner, who had been a sailor in his youth and who as a lovable and witty writer for the *Nation* proved himself a radical whose cheerful pessimism was blended with commonsense. There Stevenson lodged during his second and final visit to America and there also in 1940 Thomas Beer came almost without warning to the end of a career of rare promise cut short by failing health. Another house of entertainment at the corner of Tenth Street and Broadway was the home of Justin McCarthy, the Irish author, during his brief excursion into New York journalism.

Paul Rosenfeld, author and literary critic and one of the leaders of a group the members of which gave a new trend to American letters during the second and third decades of the century, lived in turn at 15 and 270 West Eleventh Street. A native of New York and graduated at Yale, Rosenfeld proved his quality as a music and literary critic, and later was the unfailing friend and helper of writers, musicians and artists who still had their way to make in the world. He served in the First World War; gave aid and wise counsel to Sherwood Anderson and Alfred Stieglitz and was one of the founders and editors of the *Seven Arts,* a magazine which during its brief existence was diligent in its search for and effective in its promotion of new talent. His unexpected death at the age of fifty-six was mourned by a wide circle of friends and left unfinished much important work that called for the doing.

A triple balconied dwelling numbered 118 West Eleventh Street was the last New York residence of Orville Dewey. The

same house was afterward the girlhood home of Mabel Osgood
Wright, and there the latter's preacher father married Edwin
Booth to Mary Devlin, whose beauty and worth, when death
claimed her, moved the poet Parsons to one of his tenderest bits
of verse. Georges Clemenceau during a part of his sojourn in
America in 1870 lived at the corner of Seventh Avenue and
Twelfth Street, and in a house now replaced by the Sheridan
Square Theatre for a brief period practiced medicine. A bronze
tablet on the corner of the theatre erected by its manager and
unveiled a few years ago by the daughter of a French war veteran, now bears witness to this fact. The home of Thurlow
Weed, who would have found much to admire in Clemenceau's
career as editor and war premier, was after 1865 at 12 West
Twelfth Street, and there, when no longer active in politics and
journalism, he wrote the *Autobiography* which readers find remarkable for the things it fails to tell. The most interesting room
in his four-story house was his study with ivy-covered window
looking out across the property of the First Presbyterian Church
to the procession of horses and carriages moving steadily up and
down Fifth Avenue. There was an open fireplace with Weed's
desk at its left; book cases ranged in order from window to door,
and on the wall hung portraits of William H. Seward and other
friends of the master.

There also Weed's eldest daughter Harriet ministered with
unceasing care to her father's ease and comfort, and helped him
to receive and entertain visitors of all ages and conditions—a
service gratefully recalled by one who in turn now faces the sunset. In 1881 a youth of sixteen, employed in a country printing
office in Pennsylvania, made his first unaccompanied journey to
New York, resolved among other things to pay his respects to
Thurlow Weed, who held a premier place in his gallery of heroes.
Accordingly the visitor one morning made his way to the house
in Twelfth Street to be greeted by an imposing butler who made
inquiry as to whom he wished to see and the nature of his business. The reply was that the visitor wished to see Mr. Weed
but had no particular business with him; and the two were still
engaged in animated colloquy when Harriet Weed appeared in
the hallway. With a few tactful questions she learned the desires of the youth from Pennsylvania. "My father" she said, "is
an old man and a very busy one, but he always likes to meet

young men, and if you will come back at four o'clock this afternoon I am sure he will be glad to see you." The visitor returned
on the hour and, with the way cleared from him, had a lengthy
conversation with Thurlow Weed. One of the unusual things
the old man told his caller was how when a lad in Catskill with
other boys he had swum out to an island in the Hudson and from
that vantage point had watched the progress of Fulton's Clermont
up the river. Now after sixty-five years the visitor delights to
tell a younger generation how he once talked with a man who
had seen the first steamboat make its first trip. A house at 22 West
Twelfth Street, little changed by the years, was the birthplace
of Frederick Van Wyck, whose mellow *Recollections of an Old
New Yorker* has afforded pleasure and profit to many a student
of the city's past; and at 82 West Twelfth Street was long the
home of Florence Finch Kelly whose *Flowing Stream* written in
serene old age tells a life story of a varied and unusual sort.
General Winfield Scott for several years following 1852 occupied
a house in West Twelfth Street that had been presented to him
after his defeat for the Presidency by a group of wealthy admirers, there planning the *Memoirs* which now and again afford
diverting proof of the author's reverent and persistent regard
for his own merits as a soldier and leader of men. And the last
city residence of William Allen Butler whence he removed to
Yonkers was at 12 East Twelfth Street, in a house which later
became the home of Samuel Sullivan Cox, another author of
pleasant memory.

Close at hand at 1 University Place an apartment building
has replaced the house in which Elinor Wylie had her home when
she first came into notice as an acute and fastidious maker of
verse of an individual and uncommon sort. Those who were
fortunate enough to know her in the last years of a life of inner
conflict that was to have a tragic ending, tenderly recall the hint
of hauteur, the mocking wit, the keen, unfailing insight, and the
resolve that placed dignity on a level with courage and kindness,
which made her at home or abroad, a beguiling companion.
And her poetry, with at its best its inimitable fancy, its careful
shaping, its clarity and its subtlety, at once passionate and humble,
will long preserve her from the neglect that sooner or later overtakes all but the greatest names. Perhaps Elinor Wylie "should
have died hereafter," for her writing career was a brief one
reckoned in years, but hers now is the unfailing charm of youth.

Again at 8 University Place was the home of George Ripley during his most fruitful years as literary editor of the *Tribune*. Now half-forgotten, he was one of the writers of his generation who most deserves to be held in honored remembrance. Born in 1802 he was graduated at Harvard at twenty-one and three years later entered the Unitarian ministry. New methods of thought and a better lot for the average man were from the first Ripley's chief concerns. Thus he became a member of the group which included Emerson and Margaret Fuller; contributed to the short-lived *Dial*, organ of the group, and in 1841 quit his pulpit to lead in the founding of Brook Farm. When that widely discussed venture in social reform ended in disaster, Horace Greeley made a place for him on the staff of the *Tribune,* and until his death in 1880 he remained its shrewd yet kindly appraiser of books and their makers, helping many a beginner to the audience of which he or she stood in need.

Bayard Taylor also dwelt in University Place when he wrote his *Masque of the Gods,* which he accounted his chief claim to honor as a poet. And it is in University Place that the Society Library has had its home for more than sixty years. Wentworth Sanborn Butler, one of the most learned and kindly of men, was its librarian during the greater part of that period, and a source of light and leading to three generations of bookmen. In the block of Thirteenth Street lying between Third and Fourth Avenues was, just before the Civil War, the home of Stoddard and Taylor, the latter paying the rent because "he was the most prosperous," while Paul Du Chaillu had lodgings at 224 in the next block of Fourteenth Street when he wrote his *Land of the Midnight Sun.* John William Draper dwelt for a decade at 107 East Fourteenth Street, and one door eastward on the other side of the way was the first New York home of the poet Stedman and his wife. The abode of William Allen Butler when he wrote *Nothing to Wear* was at 38 East Fourteenth Street, and facing Union Square on the same side of the way, ten doors nearer to Fifth Avenue, was the last New York home of Frances Sargent Osgood. The career of this once famous woman proves how quick and complete is the oblivion which overtakes all but the greatest names. Ninety years ago her love lyrics were read, quoted, and widely praised, while her weekly receptions were thronged by the authors and artists of the city. Now few read her verse, and its author is remembered only because she was the devoted and helpful friend of Poe when he most sorely needed friends. Finally it was in Steinway Hall, also in East Fourteenth Street, and for a quarter of a century the musical center of New York City, that Charles Dickens gave readings during his last visit to America, and it was in a hall in the same thoroughfare that in the spring of 1879 Walt Whitman, urged thereto by friends, began his brief and doubtful efforts as a lecturer on Lincoln.

CHAPTER V

THE WAY TO GREENWICH VILLAGE

If the searcher after literary landmarks strolls northward from City Hall Park through the region lying west of Broadway, he will find at 50 Hudson Street the site of the house which for many years was the home of William Coleman, founder of the *Evening Post,* who there gave welcome to Halleck and Drake, when they came by night to confess to him the authorship of the *Croaker Papers.* Coleman had been a lawyer in Massachusetts before, at the instance of Alexander Hamilton, who needed a mouthpiece, he became a fighting editor in New York. He modeled his writings after the *Letters of Junius,* and his biting wit through the years, brought him many an ugly quarrel, one of which ended in a duel and the death of his antagonist. Thompson, harbor-master of the port of New York and a truculent Jeffersonian, in public places declared that although the Federalist editor was master of a sharp pen, he really had no fight in him, and that if slapped on one side of the face he could be counted on to offer the other for like treatment.

Coleman made sure that Thompson had used the language attributed to him, and then challenged him to a duel. The two men met at eleven o'clock on a winter night in 1804 in a field outside the town where now is Washington Square. Each had surgeons and seconds, and agreed, as snow was falling at the time, to fire at twelve yards, Thompson having named pistols as weapons. At the third exchange, the harbor master exclaimed in the darkness: "My God! I have got it," and fell dying into the snow. But he lived long enough to tell the friends who were with him that the duel had been of his own seeking and that he was sure Coleman had not intended to kill him.

The house in which Laurence Hutton passed the years described in *A Boy That I Knew* stood until a few years ago at 84 Hudson Street, and four doors above Bryant had his home when he succeeded Coleman as editor of the *Evening Post.* That was in 1829 and for nearly half a century he remained in that position championing needed reforms, political and social, and shaping, perhaps in fuller measure than any other man, the in-

tellectual life of the town. Nor did he ever lose the love of nature
he had brought with him from New England, and which in his
leisure hours took him to the New Jersey shore of the Hudson or,
crossing the East River, to the Dutch farms of Long Island; and
in these strolls he occasionally had for companion a younger
lover of groves and fields, Walt Whitman, then editing the
Brooklyn *Eagle*.

A decade earlier Horace Greeley lived at 123 Hudson Street.
The future founder of the *Tribune* was then only a few
years away from his arrival in New York a country printer
from Vermont, and like Abraham Lincoln in Illinois a follower
of Henry Clay. who had walked into town with all his belongings in a bundle on his back, but who was already joint owner
of a printing plant and editor of the *New Yorker*, a weekly
journal with a spread of essays and stories selected with care by
a lover of good writing which quickly won it an army of readers.
And it was while he lodged in Hudson Street that Greeley took
to wife Mary Cheney, a New England school teacher, intelligent,
good looking and with a mind of her own, but whose uncertain
temper too often was to make her husband's home life a battle
and a march.

William Dunlap lived at 55 Leonard Street when he wrote
his *History of the American Theatre,* in whose early making he
had played a conspicuous part; at 39 Walker Street was the home
of Charles Anderson Dana during his first years as managing
editor of the *Tribune,* and in North Moore Street, a few doors
from Hudson, Thomas Bailey Aldrich dwelt with a kinsman
during part of his boyhood. When nearby Beach Street, facing
vanished St. John's Park, was still a fashionable thoroughfare,
the novelist Cooper was one of its residents, and there, in a house
which stood not far from the corner of Hudson, wrote the *Pilot*
and *Lionel Lincoln.* Another lettered dweller by St. John's Park
in the opening years of the last century was William Ware,
author of *Zenobia* and *Aurelian,* who when pastor of a Unitarian
church in Chambers Street, lived at 17 Beach Street. A modest
red-brick structure yet standing at 67 Varick Street became the
home of Bryant when he removed from Hudson Street, and the
same house was the abode of John Howard Payne when in 1832,
after long absence in Europe, he returned to his native city.

The home of John James Audubon when he completed his
Birds of America was at 68 White Street. Elihu Vedder, gifted
alike as artist and writer and one of the great talkers of his gen-

eration, was born in Varick Street, and Charles Farrar Browne had lodgings in that thoroughfare—the house in which he roomed was the first to the right-hand from Canal Street—when George W. Carleton published *Artemus Ward: His Book,* to the great and unexpected profit of its author, whereby hangs an unusual tale that calls for retelling. It was soon after he withdrew from the editorship of *Vanity Fair* in 1861 that Browne bundled into a green-baize bag a motley collection of his scribblings for that and other journals and took them to Carleton, asking the latter to decide whether or not he would publish them in a book.

A generation later Carleton recalled with a laugh that the manuscript left with him was an almost illegible one, "blotted here and there, stuck with mucilage, and plastered with newspaper clippings." He added: "Ward looked to me then like a caricature of Uncle Sam, only he never wore his trousers quite so short. He appeared a serious man, and I wondered if there could possibly be any humor in him. I told him I would look over his stuff, and in due time decide what I could do with it. He said that time was no object and strode out. His manuscript was so mixed that it came near to giving me a nightmare, but it soon became clear to me that its author was much more than an ordinary humorist, and I decided to publish it. Even then it was a chore to whip the manuscript into shape for the printer. I had not only to edit, but to write a good deal; so that one day Artemus said to me that the next book he wrote he should get me to write for him."

Browne's book was finally published in May, 1862, and 40,000 copies of it quickly found buyers—a success without precedent in that period. The author was paid fifteen cents royalty on each copy. "He was living in cheap lodgings in St. John's Square," Mr. Carleton was wont to relate, "when I called on him to pay him $6,000—his share of the profits. I found him in a small hall room and paid him the money that set him on his feet in a financial way, and made easy the trip to England in 1866 from which he was not to return."

Lorenzo Da Ponte died at 91 Spring Street, just out of Broadway and at 148 Thompson Street was the birthplace of Fitzhugh Ludlow, eighty odd years ago an engaging if modest figure in the literary life of the town. Morris, before he found a final abiding-place at Cold Spring on the Hudson, lived for several years at 102 Prince Street, where Theodore Sedgwick Fay, his sometime associate on the *Mirror,* was a member of his household. Fay is now a fading memory, but his pen was long a busy one, and his story of New York entitled *Norman Leslie* gave delight to a generation, perhaps, more easily satisfied than our own.

Willis, the partner of Morris, when he first came from Boston to New York lodged at what is now 336 West Broadway. A later home of Willis was in that part of Houston Street then known as Ludlow Place, and close at hand at 102 Bleecker Street, John Lloyd Stephens, perhaps the greatest of American travel-writers, passed his last years. A graduate at Columbia, sprung from a well-to-do family in New Jersey, Stephens at the outset of his career studied and practiced law in New York, but was early mastered by a desire to visit and describe strange lands and out-of-the-way places. In 1834 and the years immediately following, he travelled through Egypt, Arabia Petra, the Holy Land and Russia, often with wild tribesmen as his only companions, and described his first experiences in vivid, moving magazine letters, later gathered into books which passed quickly through many editions and still find delighted readers although defter pens have since dealt with the same subjects.

Then between 1839 and 1841 while minister to Central America, Stephens explored the forests of Chiapas and Yucatan and the ruins of forgotten nations buried in them. These he also described in volumes which revealed a new world to their readers. He had imagination, insight and a brooding sense of the flight of time, and he wrote of what he saw and experienced with frankness and sincerity. A small man who made up in nervous energy what he lacked in stature, he loved the society of his fellows, if of a congenial kind, and his favorite resort when he lived in Bleecker Street was a bookshop in the Astor House, where men of like tastes gathered to hear him talk on whatever subject absorbed him at the moment. Stephens had a gift for affairs as well as for letters, and before his strenuous life ended at forty-seven directed the building of the railroad across the Isthmus of Panama over which passed multitudes bound for the gold districts of California.

Again at 144 Bleecker Street until a recent time flourished Mori's restaurant, long one of the literary landmarks of the town. Placido Mori and his wife Margherita came from Tuscany to New York in the closing decades of the last century, bringing with them a tradition of good eating, and set up a modest place in Bleecker Street, in the heart of Greenwich Village, which soon became known to and frequented by those who gave discriminating thought to the pleasures of the table. The late Minnie Maddern Fiske was one of the first to discover the high quality of the restaurant and sound its praises, and as the years passed actors, authors, painters and musicians became in increasing numbers its steady patrons. Placido Mori, graciously seconded by his wife, long remained its proprietor and when he died his sons carried on with the aid of their mother in an imposing establishment designed by Raymond Hood, an old friend of the family. In the end, however, a chain of untoward conditions brought bankruptcy to Mori's restaurant, and now it lives only in the memory of New Yorkers who love the past and its landmarks.

Thomas Paine ended his stormy career in this part of the town. The author of the *Rights of Man,* as will be set down in another place, passed his old age on a farm at New Rochelle voted him by the State of New York, but in 1808 failing health prompted his removal to New York where he took lodgings at what is now 293 Bleecker Street. Toward the end, in order to make him more comfortable than was possible in a lodging-house, his friend Madame Bonneville had him removed to a cottage, the site of which will be found at 59 Grove Street, and there Paine died in June, 1909. At the end, we are told, he had the "melancholy look of an old eagle moulting." Then as always he was a deeply religious man and a believer in God and immortality, but not in the minds of some of the preachers of his period, for when a youthful member of the choir of a Presbyterian church in New York dared to shake the hands of a great man fallen on evil days, he was suspended for it.

Madame Bonneville, whom Paine years before had rescued from danger in the Paris of the Revolution and brought to America, was the widow of the man who had printed the *Age of Reason* in France. One of her two sons later went to West Point and became the Captain Bonneville whose wanderings in the Farther West in due course furnished Washington Irving a subject and material for one of his most delightful books. The mother passed her later years in the St. Louis home of this son. The papers Paine had left to her care were kept in a storehouse in that city, and when the building burned there was destroyed with it not only the letters of Paine, but also, it is believed, the manuscript of the autobiography he had written—a loss mourned with good reason by students both of the American and the French Revolutions.

A house still standing at 85 West Third Street, until recent years in the shadow of the elevated railroad, was in the winter of 1845 and 1846 the home of Poe who there wrote the *Literati of New York* and the *Facts in the Case of M. Valdemar.* Frances Osgood Sargent tells of visiting the Poes at this place, and here Lowell called to find the author of *The Raven,* as he writes regretfully, "not himself that day." The West Third Street house is now occupied as an Italian hotel, but the writers when they visited it not long ago found the hall, stairway and upper rooms not unlike what their condition must have been in Poe's time. A block away at 87 Fourth Street was the last home of Rufus Wilmot Griswold, a Baptist minister and country editor of doubtful quality and caliber, whom Horace Greeley, a fellow Vermonter, induced to settle in New York, where he became a doer of literary odd jobs and one of the first in a long line of American anthologists. Griswold's *Poets and Poetry of America,* published in 1842 taught his countrymen that they had a literature of their own, and long enjoyed a full measure of popularity, with financial returns welcomed by its compiler; but he is now best remembered as Poe's first biographer, and a treacherous and heartless one—the source of a false myth of the career and character of the poet that persisted for three generations.

The home of Orville Dewey, when pastor of the Church of the Messiah and the friend and comrade of the choicest spirits of his era, was for long at 254 Mercer Street, and at 27 Fourth Street was for several years the abode of William Leggett— resolute champion of his own conceptions of social justice and a militant and unbending figure in an era of ferment and of uncertain cures for ancient evils. As elsewhere recorded, Leggett, a powerful writer described by Gideon Welles, as "the ablest editor in the Union," came first into notice as Bryant's assistant in the conduct of the *Evening Post,* but his radical utterances soon wrought havoc with the support of that journal and his personal income, and he was compelled to sell his interest in it to pay his own debts.

So Bryant and Leggett, although the best of friends, parted company and late in 1836 the latter, backed by Edwin Forrest, the actor, founded the *Plaindealer,* a weekly journal modeled on the London *Examiner.* Again Leggett's scornful assaults on those in high places whose acts and beliefs offended him alienated many at first inclined to support him, and within a year caused the suspension of the *Plaindealer..* But a persistent maker of enemies, Leggett also knew how to win and hold friends. When his health failed him Forrest, who loved money and had already lost large sums in his editorial ventures, nevertheless paid part of his debts, bought him a house in New Rochelle, and made generous provision for the support of the ailing man and his family, while early in 1839 President Van Buren, informed of Leggett's plight, ignored the bitter attacks the latter had made on him for his attitude toward slavery, and offered him the post of consul to Guatemala, in the hope that in a milder climate he might regain his health. But ebbing energies made Leggett unequal to the journey to Central America, and in May, 1839, he died at New Rochelle. Be it recorded that when he was gone Bryant in moving verse bore tribute to his worth, and Forrest provided for his widow by buying his library for $7,000.

One finds at 21 Washington Square South the last home of Frank O'Malley, long editor of the *Sun,* and at 61 Washington Square South the three-story brick house where for a full half a century before her death in 1937 Madame Catherine Blanchard, sprung of French and Swiss stock, and the widow of a colonel in the army of Maximilian, took lodgers, and now and again proved herself the good angel of talent in distress. Her tenants at various times included O. Henry, Theodore Dreiser, John Reed, Eugene O'Neill, Zona Gale, Oliver Herford, James Oppenheim and Gelett Burgess. The last named Madame Blanchard delighted to recall as a charming man who paid his rent promptly and entertained generously during a five-year residence.

Frank Norris was perhaps the best known of Madame's lodgers. He rented a front room from her in 1899, when reader for a publishing house, and there worked upon the first of the romances which remain his chief legacy to posterity. "I have the idea of a series of novels buzzing in my head these days," he wrote William Dean Howells from 61: "I think there is a chance for somebody to do some great work with the West and California as a background . . . My idea is to write three novels around the one subject of Wheat . . . and in each to keep the idea of this huge Niagara of wheat rolling from West to East . . . The idea is so big that it frightens me at times, but I have about made up my mind to have a try at it." An untimely death prevented Norris from completing his ambitious project, but he made a splendid beginning, and proved what he might have accomplished had length of days been granted him.

Stephen Crane in one of the early periods of his career had lodgings with Madame Blanchard, and in a later time Alan Seeger roomed with her, a plaque on the facade of the old house now bearing witness to the fact. And the Judson Hotel, also in Washington Square South, now become a dormitory for the students of New York University, was the home in an earlier time of Edwin Arlington Robinson, Ridgely Torrence, Frank Norris, Mary Watts and Florence, the daughter of Julia Ward Howe. Other guests of the Judson Hotel were Harriet Beecher Stowe's son, Lyman Beecher Stowe, and the latter's wife, daughter and son; and there father and son wrote a biography of their mother and grandmother. Again at the Pension Sands, also in Washington Square South, David Graham Phillips lived for a time and there wrote his first novel, the *Great God Success*.

Thence it is a short stroll to the apartment house at 107 Waverly Place which for several years in the opening decade of the century was the winter home of William Vaughn Moody and his gifted wife, Harriet Converse. After her husband's death in 1910, Mrs. Moody retained the Waverly Place apartment, and for an extended period made it a meeting-place for men and women of mark in letters and music, who found in their friend and hostess a kindly soul, and for beginners, one of the most helpful influences of her time. In an earlier day at 116 Waverly Place Anne Charlotte Lynch, before she became the wife of Vincenzo Botta, gave the receptions which Margaret Fuller frequented and Bayard Taylor praised in his novel, *John Godfrey's Fortunes*. Not far away, at 29 Macdougal Street, Taylor lived for several years and wrote many of his *Poems of the Orient*. The apartment house which has replaced his former dwelling was in a more recent time the home of George Parsons Lathrop and the latter's wife, Rose Hawthorne and of John Ames Mitchell, during his first years as editor of *Life*. Henry Clapp when king of the nightly revels at Pfaff's had lodgings in another block of Macdougal Street. A few rods distant at the corner of Waverly Place and Washington Square an office building holds the site of the gray and gloomy pile which for sixty years was the home of New York University and which when demolished in 1895 was as rich in piquant memories as any other building in the city. A part of it was given over to lodging purposes, and Theodore Winthrop abode there when he planned *Cecil Dreeme*, and other stories which, published after he fell in one of the opening skirmishes of the Civil War, proved how heavy a loss American letters suffered in his death. Christopher Pearce Cranch, who left the Unitarian ministry to become a painter and maker of verse, had chambers in the University building when a resident of New York, and it was also long the home of William Henry Hurlbert, who after noteworthy service on the *Times* was, for many years, editor of the *World*, and whom natural gifts, enhanced by an education of extraordinary fullness, made one of the most brilliant workers in the journalism of his generation. There were chapters in Hurlbert's career that are not pleasant reading, and his last years were solitary and shadowed ones, but had his integrity equalled his other gifts, he would have been a noteworthy figure in our history.

In his *Cheerful Yesterdays* Thomas Wentworth Higginson who companioned with Hurlbert at Harvard makes piquant reference to him. He writes of him, as in his youth "so handsome in his dark beauty that he seemed like a picturesque Oriental. Slender, keen-eyed, raven-haired he arrested the eye and heart like some fascinating girl. He was also the most variously gifted and accomplished man I have ever known, acquiring knowledge as if by magic." Another side of Hurlbert is revealed in a story which Thomas E. Willson, long a member of the staff of the New York *World*, used to relate with gusto. Hurlbert, when there was need for it, despatched Willson on a mission to Chicago. In the streets of that city the latter met Stephen Hurlbut, a brother of his employer and an uncommon man who also had the defects of his qualities. Hurlbut had studied law in South Carolina under James Louis Petigru and had then settled in Belvidere, Illinois, where he achieved prominence at the bar. He was long on intimate terms with Abraham Lincoln and during the Civil War served as a general in the Union Army. After greetings Willson and Hurlbut made their way to the nearest saloon and as they sipped their cocktails the older man inquired as to the welfare of his brother.

"Mr. Hurlbert was very well when I left New York," was the reply.

"Willson, a remarkable man that brother of mine," said the General, after an instant's silence, "a man of extraordinary gifts. He could have been anything he aspired to if he was not such an infernal thief."

Willson on his return to New York reported the details of his mission to his chief and then added that he had met General Hurlbut while in Chicago. "I as glad you found Stephen well," said Hurlbert. "A remarkable man that brother of mine—a man of extraordinary gifts. He could have been anything he aspired to if he were not such an infernal liar."

And Willson in telling this story always ended it with the terse comment: "They knew each other."

The elder Henry James, one of the most acute and virile intellects of his time, dwelt for a number of years at 2 Washington Place, and there his son and namesake was born in a house now replaced by a loft building devoted to trades having to do with hats. The house numbered 23 Waverly Place was occupied in early life by William Allen Butler, and two doors westward on the same side of the way was the home in youth of George William Curtis. The last home of William Sydney Porter better known as O. Henry, was at 88 Washington Place, and thence on a winter day in 1910 he was carried to a hospital to die untimely at the age of forty-eight. The story of his unusual career is a familiar but not wholly pleasant one. An editor once asked him where he got his education. "In the school of good books and in the university of hard knocks," was his reply. But the university of hard knocks did not prevent him from becoming an amiable opportunist who won repute as a teller of tales of an uncommon sort, as he had earned a term in prison, by putting off his obligations until forced to hectic effort. And so during his years in New York Henry burned the candle at both ends and died broken in spirit. But love of the whimsical remained with him until the end, for his last words to a friend at his bedside and to the nurse attending him were: "Put the pillows up higher and turn up the lights. I don't want to go home in the dark."

Judge Charles P. Daly long resided at 22 West Eighth Street, and there gave welcome to his friend, Paul Du Chaillu, when the famous traveler came for the last time to America. In a dwelling at 31 West Eighth Street, now occupied by tradesmen, Thomas Bailey Aldrich lived for a time with a kinsman and there produced a number of his poems, including *Baby Bell* and *Judith,* and there also, as a passing guest, Fitz-James O'Brien wrote the *Story of the Diamond Lens.*

Across the way at the corner of Eighth Street and Macdougal Alley at the turn of the century was the Hotel Gonfarone, operated by a widow of that name. One hot summer day Anacleto Sermolino a lately landed Italian emigrant and a man of slender build, who, to assure a liveliihood for himself and his runaway bride, had secured a job as delivery man for a wine merchant, staggered under the load of a huge jug and its contents into the Hotel Gonfarone, and aroused the sympathies of its owner, who learning that he was good at figures, offered him a job as cashier. At the end of a year during which Sermolino devoted himself with success to the restaurant end of the business, Madame Gonfarone took him into partnership, and later he bought out her interest.

It was Sermolino who for the first time taught New Yorkers in a large way the meaning of an Italian table d'hote dinner, and with such success that soon the clientele of the Hotel Gonfarone overflowed the original premises, and forced its owner to break down the walls of adjacent buildings until finally the tables marched in unbroken array through five houses, three in West Eighth Street and two in Macdougal Alley. Here assembled nightly lovers of good food drawn from all parts of the town to feast among other things on incredible quantities of spaghetti and generous servings of red wine. And not content merely with feeding his patrons the proprietor would lead them from table to table introducing them to other guests. Thus more than one understanding and enduring friendship had its beginning in the Hotel Gonfarone.

Moreover, two or three favored ones, were always invited to the family table in the basement. O. Henry in his last days, was one of these, and Sermolino among the few who knew how to overcome the shyness of the famous story teller. Arnold Daly also partook frequently of the private Sermolino fare, as did Margaret Anglin and Enrico Caruso. The coming of prohibition put an end to the Hotel Gonfarone, but Sermolino had wisely invested the profits of its palmy days in Greenwich Village real estate, and his last years were years of comfort and peace of mind. It should be noted in passing that many of his daughter's fellow students in the Pulitzer School of Journalism, class of 1917, are now prominent in the world of letters.

Southward and westward of the region just traversed lies what was once Greenwich Village. The lanes which grew into roads and then into streets when Greenwich was yet a village, still follow their ancient course, bidding defiance to the rectangular lines of the City Plan, and by their twists and turns recalling the loose and easy ways of an earlier day. Brick and wooden cottages are to be found in nearly all of them, and it is easy for the stroller to call to life the staid folk who trod their paves when

Greenwich Village was an entity and not a tradition. One of these was William Dunlap. A century ago the present Greenwich Avenue was Greenwich Lane, a by-road leading from the Bowery toward the Hudson. At what is now 16 Greenwich Avenue, Dunlap, who just before that had been domiciled at 64 Sixth Avenue, took up his residence in 1835, moving at the end of two years to a house five doors above on the other side of the way where he died in the fall of 1839 at the age of seventy-three. A member of the Dunlap household when it was quartered in Greenwich Avenue was Samuel F. B. Morse, now remembered as the inventor of the telegraph, but then known only as a painter of skill and promise. Artists of that day commanded small returns for their labors, and Morse took pupils to eke out a scanty income. One of these was a young Virginian, David Henry Strother by name, who later studied in Europe, and after that, under the pen name of Porte Crayon, was long a contributor to *Harper's Magazine* of writings and drawings which depicted Southern life and scenes with spirit and humor.

The site of the Columbian Gardens, a modest resort which until 1927 flourished at 5 Greenwich Avenue, also has interest for the seeker after literary landmarks, for there, in 1896, John Masefield, a runaway sailor, found employment and friends at a time when he had urgent need for both of them. Masefield was then penniless, sleeping where he could at night and wandering where he would in the daytime, and it was the generous free lunch waiting on the purchase of a five-cent glass of beer that took him again and again to the Columbian Gardens. One day the proprietor, Luke O'Connor, a kindly Irishman long since gone to his rest, asked him if he wanted a job. He replied that he did, was given a dollar for a haircut, and went to work as general utility man at ten dollars a month, with board and lodging. The hours were long, and he has since recalled that when his labors ended usually after midnight he would climb to his garret room and until he fell asleep read Malory's *Morte d'Arthur*, his only book.

Masefield remained with O'Connor for several months. Then he found a place in a Yonkers carpet factory, and while thus employed read a cheap edition of Chaucer and resolved to become a poet. He returned ere long to England, but it was ten years before he published his first volume of verse, and as many more before he paid another visit to America. When he did he made haste to seek out Luke O'Connor as a friend held in grateful remembrance, and on later journeys to America, as long as O'Connor lived, he never failed to visit and talk with his former employer about old times. John Masefield is a true democrat as well as first among his country's living poets.

Poe was also a dweller in Greenwich during his first protracted sojourn in New York. In 1837, after he retired from the editorship of the *Southern Literary Messenger,* the poet and his girl wife removed from Richmond to New York. The wife's mother, then and always Poe's best friend, kept them company, and when the husband failed to mend his fortunes by the change, in order to furnish support for the family, she opened a boarding-house at what was then 13½ Carmine Street. Thence at the end of a few months the trio removed to rooms in a building which stood within a recent period in Sixth Avenue, not far from Waverly Place, where they remained until Poe secured a post on the staff of the *Gentleman's Magazine* in Philadelphia. It was during the months Poe spent in Greenwich that he completed the *Narrative of Arthur Gordon Pym, Ligeia,* and the *Fall of the House of Usher,* in which his romantic genius reached its finest expression.

Another poet dweller in Greenwich was Bryant, who, during his early years on the *Evening Post,* lived in turn at 12 Carmine Street and at 147 West Fourth Street. The home of Willis, just before he removed to Cornwall-on-the-Hudson, was a house which still stands in its original condition at 198 West Fourth Street. The home of Clement Clark Moore, after unsought fame had come to him as the author of *A Visit from St. Nicholas,* was at the corner of Charlton and Macdougal Streets, while Epes Sargent lived and Mordecai M. Noah died in Bank Street. At 45 Rose Street was the last home of Daniel De Leon, one of the stormiest figures in the radical labor movement of half a century ago, and perhaps the ablest American exponent both with tongue and pen of the teachings of Carl Marx, giving to Lenin, who found it in one of his pamphlets, the plan of the Soviet system that now rules Russia.

Kathleen Millay, talented sister of a more amply endowed maker of verse, lived during her last years at 65 Bedford Street, and at 52 Jane Street was the home in turn of William Mac-Donald, teacher of history and journalist of distinction, and of Stuart Pratt Sherman, whose accidental death by drowning in 1826 cut short at forty-five a career of substantial achievement and signal promise. Sherman left a college chair in 1924 to become literary editor of the New York *Herald-Tribune,* and had length of days been granted him would have left a wide and deep mark in his chosen field. Victor Francis Calverton, born George Goetz, lived at 16 St. Luke's Place when in 1940 the end also came to him in mid-career. It may fairly be said of him that he took all knowledge for his province, and alike by word and printed page was a stimulating influence on many lives. It was a motley group that used to gather of evenings in Calverton's apartment, but its members came first of all to listen to the talk of their host, and most of them cherish grateful memories of the wealth of ideas on everything under the sun which they brought away with them.

A man of like caliber was Randolph Bourne who three days before Christmas in 1916 at the age of thirty, died of pneumonia in a Greenwich Village rooming house, and was duly borne to his grave from the Presbyterian Church at the corner of Seventh Avenue and Spring Street. Born in Bloomfield, New Jersey, a hunchback with a twisted face, Bourne, his unhappy school days in his own town behind him, contrived at twenty-three and in the face of ugly handicaps, to obtain a scholarship that assured him four years at Columbia University. Another scholarship made it possible for him to travel and study in Europe, where, as at Columbia, he found understanding and helpful friends, George Bernard Shaw among them.

Before Bourne left for Europe, conversation in the basement of the New York Public Library with a legless cripple who wheeled himself about in a chair, had made him a socialist. He returned to America in 1914 a hater of war and a radical without alloy. Herbert Croly chose him as one of the first contributors to the *New Republic,* and in articles for that and other liberal journals he preached the faith that was in him with a poignant and deeply moving beauty of expression commanded by no other writer of his group. But soon his drastic views and acid comments on men given to other ways of thinking caused the *New Republic* to dispense with his services. Other journals refused to publish his articles, and how to secure lodging, food and clothing, presented for him an ever present and pressing problem. Then came the end. Except for those yet surviving who had familiar contact with him and thus knew at first hand the hard conditions under which he labored, Bourne is now a fading memory, but he loved his fellows and his misshapen body housed a great heart and a great soul. A collection of his best papers would make a volume sure to be read and cherished by like minds in many lands As it is his *The History of a Literary Radical*, published after his death, is one of the books to which the forward looking instinctively turn in moments of doubt and hesitation.

Mary Hunter Austin, during one of her lengthier sojourns in New York, lived at 10 Barrow Street, and at 15 Gay Street was the last home of William Griffith, editor and verse-maker. Finally, what is now the parish house of St. Luke's Church, at 477 Hudson Street, between Barrow and Grove, was the early home of Bret Harte, who was a school-boy in Greenwich Village when his first bit of verse found its way into print. While yet a lad Harte drifted with many another youthful adventurer to California, where he dipped into mining, tried his hand at school-teaching, type-setting, and frontier journalism, and at last found his place as editor of the *Overland Monthly,* and as author of the *Luck of Roaring Camp,* first of the long line of stories in which his genius clothed with undying romance the New World Argonauts of which he was himself a winning and unforgetable type.

CHAPTER VI

The Middle Reaches of Manhattan

On the morrow of the Civil War the restaurant first set up by the Delmonico brothers in 1831 at 23 William Street, after divers removals by younger members of the family, prompted by the northward growth of the town, was located at one of the corners of Fifth Avenue and Fourteenth Street, and in 1868 furnished a setting for an unusual tribute by one gifted man to another, the story of which merits a place in these pages. The previous year, Charles Dickens had come for a second time to America to give a series of readings from his works, in order, as it came out later, to mend an exchequer that had been too heavily drawn upon. These readings, from first to last, were an uncommon success. Great crowds greeted him at every stage of his progress, and not less cordial were the personal welcomes—welcomes which reached a fitting climax in a dinner given to him at Delmonico's on the night of April 18, 1868.

This represented authorship and journalism from Maine to Texas and over the West to California. It was a noble gathering —ten score guests from the four quarters of the Union, and all men of authority and renown. Horace Greeley, presided, and opened the speaking in an address of persuasive eloquence and humor. He began by telling how more than thirty years before, as set forth in an earlier chapter, he had founded a journal called the *New Yorker*. "In looking about," said he, "for matter to fill my literary department I ran against some sketches from a cheap English periodical which I at once transferred to my paper. These sketches were by a then unknown author who wrote under the name of Boz. So I think I can claim to be the first who introduced Mr. Dickens to this country." Then, in his quaint way he told how he had tried in a Florentine inn to read *David Copperfield* in Italian, ending in a toast that made every glass ring: "Health and happiness, honor and generous because just recompense to our friend and guest, Charles Dickens."

When the cheering died away Dickens arose to reply, his remarks commanding close attention and at times enraptured applause. There was a figure at the end of his speech—that it was better for America and England to go back to the ice age than to fight each other—that brought every guest to his feet, and as he sat down in a burst of cheers the band played *God Save the Queen.* Four days later Dickens sailed for home. "Come to England when the roses are in bloom, and report at Gadshill," he said to a friend at the steamer's side. A short two years later his friend voyaged to England, and found the hedges in bloom, but—no master at Gadshill. Dickens had died a few days before, and the American who had planned to be his guest was only in time to find the flowers still fresh on the slab above his grave in Westminster Abbey.

The elder Henry James lived for several years at 58 West Fourteenth Street, where his son and namesake passed the childhood which lives again in the delectable pages of *A Small Boy and Others;* and at 24 West Sixteenth Street long resided Edward Livingston Youmans, who, compelled nearly all his days to contend with total or partial blindness, yet managed to give himself an education which few university men have gained, and then, as writer and lecturer, made effective use of his hard-won acquisitions by awakening his countrymen to the significance of the great scientific discoveries of his age. Above all other men, Youmans was for many years the American apostle and expounder of evolution, and when his useful life ended in 1887, at the age of sixty-six, it was well said of him that among the agencies which during the previous half century had opened the American mind to scientific truth, few had been so potent as his own gentle but persuasive work.

Rossiter Johnson and Moses Coit Tyler, who afterwards was to write an admirable history of early American literature, lodged at 27 West Eighteenth Street when members of the staff of the *Christian Union,* under Henry Ward Beecher. One of the later homes of George Ripley was at 37 West Nineteenth Street, and a block distant at 53 West Twentieth Street for more than a decade dwelt William Augustine Muhlenberg, whose life of good deeds wedded to reverent thought found fit expression in the hymn, *I Would Not Live Always,* while another house in the latter thoroughfare, two blocks nearer the Hudson, was the last home of Oliver Bell Bunce, who in early life headed a publishing house of his own, and afterward served until his death as literary adviser to the house of Appleton. Bunce's niche in the temple of letters is a modest one, but he was quick to discover talent in others, and many a beginner found the upward path smoothed by his counsel and helping hand. At 155 West Twentieth Street Edwin Markham in his last days was often the guest of his son. Again at 346 West Twentieth Street the Protestant Episcopal Church of St. Peter helps to keep green the memory of Clement Clarke Moore, churchman, student and poet. Moore led in the organization of the church in 1820, and eleven years later contributed generously to the building of the chapel which now serves St. Peter's as a rectory. The cornerstone of the present church was laid in 1836.

In the opening years of the last century the middle reaches of Manhattan Island were given over to farms and the country seats of wealthy dwellers in the still distant town. The seat of George Clinton lay just north of Greenwich Village, while farther afield the country house of Henry Eckford, a wealthy shipbuilder of the period, faced Love Lane, a shaded by-road which ran from what is now Broadway to the Hudson on the line of the present Twenty-first Street. The Eckford home was a favorite resort of the poet Drake, who often went there with his friend, Halleck, and who, in 1816 found a wife in one of the daughters of the house. Less than four years later the poet died, but the wife, who was his tender and devoted nurse in his last illness, made herself the guardian of his fame, and until the end of her days reverently cherished his memory.

The growing town in due time, claimed Love Lane and its shaded places for its own, and there, following its surrender to the City Plan, George Bancroft for many years had his home. During the year 1849 he was domiciled at No. 32, but thereafter, until 1867, the directory placed him at 17 West Twenty-first Street. In the third story of this house he placed the literary gatherings of many years, and there wrought upon the imposing history which furnishes his strongest claim to remembrance. Llewellyn Powys during his first days in New York lodged with his brother John in West Twenty-first Street. One also finds at 240 West Twenty-first Street, the last home of John Flavel Mines, who, under the pen name of Felix Oldboy, painted for a later generation the New York he had known in his youth.

Speaking portraits of many a dead-and-gone worthy fill the pages of Oldboy's rambling and delightful chronicle, but over no name does his pen linger more lovingly than that of Clement Clarke Moore, who was born and passed nearly all his days in this quarter of the town. Moore was descended from Captain Thomas Clarke, a veteran of the old French war, who about 1750 bought an estate on the shores of the Hudson to which he gave the name of Chelsea. The home built by the captain was burned during his last illness, but later his widow built another and larger house on the crest of a low hill not far from the river and on the southern line of the present Twenty-third Street. When she died in 1802, at a ripe old age, the greater part of her estate passed, with the homestead, to Bishop Benjamin Moore, who had married her daughter, and from him it descended in 1813, to Clement C. Moore, his only son. The younger Moore added another story to the old house, whose terraced grounds were shaded by oaks and elms, and it stood, until its demolition in 1853, a picturesque survival of the past.

Clement C. Moore was trained for the ministry after being graduated from Columbia in 1798, but he never took orders, and, devoting himself instead to oriental and classical studies, from 1821 until his death filled a chair in the General Theological Seminary of the Episcopal Church. Mines, speaking with the authority of long friendship, describes him as the kindliest of scholars, the most assiduous of bookworms, a writer whose works were held in high regard by the learned men of his day. Yet he is known to posterity by none of these things. It was his custom to employ his leisure in writing verse, not for profit or publication, but as relief from severer labors; and it was *A Visit From St. Nicholas*, penned solely to amuse his children, that made his name a household word. This nursery rhyme, written in 1822, a young woman visiting the family copied into her album and sent it, unknown to Dr. Moore, to the editor of the Troy *Sentinel*, who printed it at Christmas time of the following year. Thence it found its way into the school-readers, and by this modest pathway its author mounted to fame. The last home of Dr. Moore was at 400 West Twenty-third Street.

John Russell Young during his most active years as a New York editor lived at 214 West Twenty-second Street, and thence departed to accompany General Grant in the latter's trip around the world and to chronicle the events of a memorable journey in a portly volume that still affords good reading. Nearer to the Hudson at 422 West Twenty-second Street was the last home of Paxton Hibben, who has been aptly described as a "dissentient afflicted with the malady of thought," and with no fear of the opinions of the herd. Hibben was also a writer of insight and capacity who had been educated at Princeton and at the Harvard Law School, and who after a brief period in the diplomatic service held the rank of captain in the first World War, later serving as correspondent for American journals in Moscow and other European capitals. He also found time to write an outstanding biography of Henry Ward Beecher, and was at work on another of William Jennings Bryan when he died in 1928 at the age of forty-eight years. But Paxton is now best remembered as a stout champion of the Russian Revolution and its aims when both stood in need of champions, and after his death, in accord with his wish to be laid near his friend, John Reed, whose career had been very like his own, his ashes were taken to Russia and buried in the north Kremlin wall in Moscow.

An aged brownstone house at 421 West Twenty-first Street served as office of the *New Republic* when Herbert Croly was its editor and Randolph Bourne a member of its staff. The son of an immigrant Irish newspaperman and the first child adopted by the Ethical Culture Society of New York, Croly was a scholar and gentleman, and he also possessed many of the qualities of a great editor. In his quiet way he dominated the incongruous and often irreconcilable people who in the first years of the journal he had founded came from all quarters to take counsel with him, and by the books and editorials he wrote helped to shape liberal opinion in the opening decades of the century. His all too early death in 1930 is still deeply regretted by men who hold that only spiritual forces of the first order can remake and bring abiding cure to a troubled world.

Edith Wharton was born at 14 West Twenty-third Street, when that thoroughfare was still in one of the fashionable quarters of the town, and one of her first memories, recalled in age, was of prim walks up Fifth Avenue past rows of brownstone mansions. The publishing house of Dutton for a generation following 1882 was located at 31 West Twenty-third Street. Two blocks westward the Chelsea apartment house, standing on what was formerly a part of the Moore estate, was, at different periods, the home of Edward Eggleston; of Jane Cunningham Croly best known as Jennie June, and of George H. Hepworth, who dwelt there when he died, as did Thomas Wolfe in a later time. Stephen Crane had lodgings during a portion of his pathetically brief career at 165 West Twenty-third Street and the writer of this paragraph vividly recalls from first-hand knowledge the conditions under which his first book found its way into notice. Unknown to editors and without influential friends, young Crane was finding food and bed pressing problems when by happy chance his path crossed that of Hamlin Garland, alert to discover new talent. There was now delivered to the elder man the first half of a manuscript the younger had lately brought to completion. It was a candid tale of slum life, and its author had given it the title *Maggie: A Girl of the Streets.*

When, moved by the evidences of an unusual gift for arresting and realistic narrative afforded in the pages submitted to him, Garland asked for the second half of the manuscript he was told that it was being held by a typist for her unpaid bill. The small sum needed to redeem it was promptly supplied, and a little later ways were found to print the tale in modest form for private distribution. One of the slim volumes thus brought into being fell into the hands of William Dean Howells, who, having read it, praised it in the right quarters; and thereafter Crane did not have to seek for a publisher. In 1896 appeared his best known work, the *Red Badge of Courage,* a moving story of the Civil War, and the record of what he did or failed to do during the four years of life that remained to him—he died at twenty-nine— has to do with fatal excesses, and a career that was never more than a promise.

Edwin Arlington Robinson lived at 450 West Twenty-third Street when he wrote *Captain Craig* in which, with an ingratiating hero taken from real life, he made one of his happiest excursions into narrative verse. The first home of the Authors Club was at 19 West Twenty-fourth Street. Morgan Dix long dwelt at 27 West Twenty-fifth Street, and Sydney Porter better known as O. Henry once had quarters in the Caledonia, a seven-story apartment house at 28 West Twenty-sixth Street. O.Henry's apartment was on the second floor, and there at a white pine table now owned by one of his friends, using invariably a yellow pad and a supply of short, stubby pencils, he wrote many of the stories of his latter years. A decade ago the name of Caledonia was changed to the O. Henry, and a plaque recording his residence there attached to the front of the building.

Douglas Campbell, whose untimely death, it is believed by many, robbed him of a noteworthy place among American historians, lived for several years at 222 West Twenty-seventh Street, and two numbers removed was once the home of Edgar Fawcett, who after writing a long list of novels filled with sharp-edged comment on the social life of his native city, elected to end his days in England.

The house numbered 317 West Twenty-ninth Street deserves a place all its own in any account of the literary landmarks of New York, for during the first three decades of the century its ground floor, and in summer its rear yard, furnished quarters for the Maison Petitpas, a French table d'hote conducted by three sisters from Brittany and long the vogue with a goodly part of the literary and art circles of the period, while in a back room on the third floor for a dozen years preceding his death lodged John Butler Yeats, gifted father of a more gifted son, William Butler Yeats. In 1910 the elder Yeats, born and trained in Ireland, was an aging portrait painter of rank and quality in London, widely known as a sound craftsman and brilliant conversationalist, his studio a meeting place for all the talents.

When early in the year just named an exhibition of Irish arts and crafts, in which the work of John Butler Yeats was represented, was held in New York, John Quin, one of its projectors, persuaded the old painter to cross the Atlantic to attend it; and what he had planned as a brief visit ended only with his death. Guided by Quin he found congenial quarters at the Maison Petitpas, and instantly and by right took his place at the head of a great table around which gathered nightly artists and writers, Robert Henri, George Bellows, Jack London, and Van Wyck Brooks among them, who found his sparkling and wide ranging talk a treat of the rarest sort. Here, wholly content with his new surroundings, he talked and painted and wrote letters to his son which published a few years ago in London afford a superb self-portrait of their author. "It is easier," he declared in one of them, "to write poetry that is far away from life, but it is infinitely more exciting to write the poetry of life"; and there came a time when the younger Yeats gave belated heed to this advice. The father grew to be a very old man as he put off from year to year his return to England, but his interest in his fellows and his zest for life remained with him until the end. That came in February, 1922, when, after a sudden cold, his heart failed and death claimed him. His funeral from a church a block from his last home was attended by nearly every one who had come to know the diverting and lovable old man.

The last home of Mayo Williamson Hazletine, who as literary editor of the *Sun*, long performed for New York a service in range and quality very like that given by Ste. Beuve to the Paris of an earlier time, was the Burlington at 10 West Thirtieth Street. This remarkable man was born in Boston and graduated in 1865 at Harvard, after which he spent sometime in further study at Oxford and on the Continent. Returning to Boston he studied law and was admitted to the bar; but he had a strong urge to another calling and in 1878 began thirty years of service as book reviewer and editorial writer for the *Sun*. He had industry and genius wedded to a store of learning almost incredible in its volume and exactness, and he wrote superbly and at great length of the books that claimed his attention. He was also quick to recognize and welcome talented newcomers, and was perhaps the first to introduce the sea tales of Joseph Conrad to readers for whom that great writer was then an unknown quantity. It was well said of Hazletine when he died in 1909 that he had been the educator of thousands.

William Dean Howells at various times between 1905 and 1911 also had quarters in the Burlington. "After long toil," the novelist, following a summer at Kittery Point, wrote Thomas Sergeant Perry in December, 1905, "we found this red brick refuge behind the Holland House, where we have five rooms and our meals (they might be better) served in our apartment. It is very, very quiet, and I can work mornings in the parlor as if I were in my own barnbury at Kittery Point. That is, I could if I had anything to say; but as poor G. P. Lathrop used to express it I seem to be lying fallow at present." Nevertheless at the Burlington Howells finished *New Leaf Mills* and worked upon *Familiar Spanish Travels*.

The working days of John Ames Mitchell came to an end at 17 West Thirty-first Street, and at the corner of that thoroughfare and Broadway stands the Grand Hotel first stopping place in New York of Oscar Wilde when in 1882 he came to America to preach a new aesthetic gospel, and incidentally to put needed dollars into his pocket. Carl Schurz had quarters at 40 West Thirty-second Street when in 1876 he aided by voice and pen in the election of Hayes, and as a reward for his labors was given a place in the new President's cabinet. Richard Hildreth lived at 210 West Thirty-third Street, then Boorman Place, when he finished his *History of the United States*. At 229 West Thirty-fourth Street, was for many years the home of Laurence Hutton, and McCreary's store, also in West Thirty-fourth Street, occupies the site of the birthplace of Clement C. Moore.

The last home of Vincenzo and Anne Lynch Botta was an English basement house at 25 West Thirty-seventh Street. "The quaint, old-fashioned parlor," writes a former guest of the Bottas, "formed a pleasant background for some of the most delightful gatherings it has ever been my privilege to attend. Every notability to set foot in New York came armed with a letter to them, for not to be seen at their receptions was to proclaim oneself either a nobody or a pariah." Amelia Edith Barr lived in another block of West Thirty-seventh Street when she achieved her first success in letters, and General James Watson Webb, whose wars of words more often than not were bloodless ones, passed his last years and died at 14 West Thirty-eighth Street. Across the way and a short block westward Harriet Beecher Stowe was often the guest of Dr. George H. Taylor and his family, and there in 1869 wrote a part of her hasty and ill-considered *Lady Byron Vindicated* in which, to the deep regret of many of her friends, she appeared as little better than a scandal monger and breaker of confidences.

At the turn of the century what then was a new studio building at the corner of Sixth Avenue and Fortieth Street facing Bryant Park was the home of Ernest Thompson Seton, British born and Canadian trained nature writer and artist, who lived there on the morrow of the publication of his best known book, *Wild Animals I Have Known,* a book which, by its free and easy treatment of mooted subjects, aroused the abiding wrath of John Burroughs, but prompted Rudyard Kipling to write his *Jungle Tales;* also winning for its author an army of delighted readers who did not fail to buy and enjoy the forty odd volumes which he wrote and illustrated before his busy life ended in 1946 in his eighty-seventh year. Seton also found time through the years to deliver more than 3000 lectures, and, when he died, with a zest and energy that never failed him, was making plans for another and final platform tour which was to have involved 10,000 miles of travel. He passed his last days in a village named for him a few miles south of Santa Fe, and two generations of boys and girls who grew up on his books hold him in loving memory.

The office of George Washburn Smalley during his final sojourn in New York was at 2 West Forty-third Street; Arthur Richmond Marsh, another master of trenchant English, who left a college chair to become a broker in Wall Street died at 44 West Forty-fourth Street; and not far away at 532 Fifth Avenue was the last American home of Manton Marble, during the Civil War and Reconstruction periods the plain-speaking and fight-loving editor of the *World.* Marble was one of those who most effectively served the cause of Samuel J. Tilden in 1876, and it is a part of the small talk of history that had his advice been followed in the closing days of that eventful year Tilden and not Hayes would have succeeded Grant in the Presidency. The Hotel Algonquin at 59 West Forty-fourth Street was for a time the New York home of Richard Harding Davis, and has long been a favorite resort for writers and stage folk. There in 1937 Rollo Ogden ended a career which constituted one of the longest chapters in the history of the American newspaper. Born in upstate New York, and educated at Williams and Andover, Ogden left the Presbyterian ministry at the age of thirty-one to become for four years a literary freelance in New York. In 1891 he joined the staff of the *Evening Post* and in 1903 succeeded Godkin as its editor, holding that post for seventeen years. In 1920 he became associated with the *Times* and from 1922 until his death served as its editor—the honored dean in New York of a great profession. One of the most self-effacing of men he was also a writer of rare capacity whose every effort bore the impress of encyclopedic knowledge and a catholic mind. Again the Hotel Langwell, at 123 West Forty-fourth Street, was the last home of William James Henderson, for half a century as music critic first of the *Times* and then of the *Sun,* like Ogden a giant living on from the great days of old, was an inspiring example to younger members of his calling. Mrs. Jefferson Davis was also and often a guest at the Langwell in the years when with her pen she was stoutly defending her husband's career as leader of the Confederacy.

Park Benjamin, vigorous editor of various literary periodicals, and a writer of narrative verse which still lives in the anthologies, dwelt, during his closing years, at 75 West Forty-fifth Street, while on the other side of the same thoroughfare and nearer Fifth Avenue was the last home of Hjalmar Hjorth Boyesen, a son of the Northland, who early sought a home in America, and both in prose and verse made vigorous contribution to the literature of his adopted country. A few blocks away, at 441 West Forty-seventh Street, William Dean Howells lodged with a kinsman, during his first excursion into New York journalism as one of the editors of the *Nation,* just after the Civil War and the termination of his Venice consulship. "Today," Howells wrote his wife on December 17, 1865, "Mr. Godkin engaged me to write for the *Nation* at a salary of $40 a week. This leaves me free to write for all other papers except the *Round Table;* and does not include articles on Italian subjects, and poems, which will be paid for extra." Two short months later, however, came an offer and acceptance of the assistant editorship of the *Atlantic Monthly* and thereafter for more than a score of years New York knew Howells only as an occasional visitor.

Samuel Austin Allibone lived at 146 West Forty-eighth Street when he brought his monumental *Dictionary of Authors* to a conclusion. Marie Van Vorst, author of many novels widely read in the opening years of the century was born at 22 West Forty-ninth Street and Horace Liveright died at 33 West Fifty-first Street. A publisher of vision and courage, Liveright, in the opening decades of the century, helped to secure an audience for more than one author of merit and promise, but conditions for which he was only in part responsible, made his last days drab and shadowed ones.

At 62 West Fifty-second Street was the last home of Richard R. Bowker, long editor of the *Publishers' Weekly,* and an author of prose and verse held in high regard by the men and women of his time, and a boardinghouse at 53 West Fifty-third Street numbered Clyde Fitch among its guests when in 1886 at the age of twenty-one he settled in New York to put his literary qualities to the test, at the outset writing short stories and sketches to meet the weekly demands for room-rent and meals.

Joseph Bucklin Bishop, the biographer of Roosevelt, died at 1 West Fifty-fourth Street, and in the home of Isaac Henderson, eight doors westward, on the opposite side of the way, tenderly cared for by his friend and host, the Southern poet, John R. Thompson suffered his last illness. And at 109 West Fifty-fourth Street was the home when he came to New York of William James Lampton, wise and witty commentator on men and events.

Andrew Carnegie lived for years in West Fifty-fifth Street in a house where three rooms thrown into one on the second floor afforded scant room for the owner's library. Here he wrote the *Gospel of Wealth* and planned the wide-ranging gifts which made him one of the great benefactors of men and women who love books but lack money to buy them.

Clyde Fitch occupied a modest apartment in the Sherwood Studios in West Fifty-seventh Street, where he had Carroll Beckwith and other arists for friends and neighbors, when in 1890 he wrote *Beau Brummel* for Richard Mansfield and at twenty-five found himself unexpectedly launched on the career which overnight was to make him the most popular playright of his period. During the years that remained to him—he died in 1909 at the age of forty-four—he wrote sixty-one plays, thirty-five of his own devising and twenty-six adaptations, and nearly all of them from a box-office standpoint were manifest successes. He had easy command both of dialogue and action, and his appeal to the playgoer was nearly always an unfailing one. Fitch was also born with a unique gift for winning and holding friends, and he was widely and sincerely mourned on both sides of the sea, when, burning the candles at both ends, death claimed him.

The Hotel Buckingham at 101 West Fifty-seventh Street was the home of Damon Runyan during the months that preceded his death last year. Born in Manhattan, Kansas, in 1884, the son of a printer father given to founding newspapers in short-lived boom towns, Runyon, after a roving youth and service with a Minnesota regiment in the Philippines, had lively and varied training as a reporter in Pueblo, Denver and San Francisco, before in 1911 he settled in New York as a sports writer, first for the Hearst journals and then for different newspaper syndicates. Soon he won repute and favor as the author of short stories which dealt in the main with the night life of New York, and, in addition to being fables and fairy tales of a diverting sort, were couched in a slang which gave them a novelty and raciness all their own. During his last dozen years Runyon published nearly as many collections of his diverting tales along with two volumes of verse, and he also wrote acceptably for the stage and screen, although until the end he preferred to be known as a faithful reporter of the human scene. Those who touched elbows with him knew him as a delightful companion, and one who rarely missed an opportunity to help and encourage younger workers.

William Dean Howells lived, during his closing years and died at 120 West Fifty-seventh Street, in a cooperative studio apartment which he bought in 1909, and to which Hamlin Garland makes reference in his diary. "Howells," writes Garland, "is in his new apartment and greatly pleased with it. When I bantered him on its splendor he replied, 'It *is* more than I can afford; but I am luxuriating in it—while my conscience is cajoled'." At 152 West Fifty-seventh Street was the home in his latter days of Junius Henry Browne, a native of Central New York who joined the staff of the *Tribune* under Greeley when it included more outstanding editors and reporters than any newspaper in America, and who while still under thirty as one of that journal's correspondents, with the Union armies during the Civil

War was made a prisoner by the Confederates and confined for a time in a stockade at Salisbury, North Carolina. Then he escaped with one of his fellow correspondents, and after long and perilous wandering in the mountains reached safety and wrote about his adventures in a book, *Four Years in Secessia*, which still finds readers.

Browne's old employer, Horace Greeley and the wife who sorely tried his love and patience were the guests of friends at 323 West Fifty-seventh Street when the great editor's contest for the Presidency came to an ill-starred end. There Mrs. Greeley, after wasting illness, died just before election day, tenderly cared for by her husband and daughters. "I am not dead, but I wish I were," Greeley wrote a friend. "My house is desolate, my future dark, my heart is a stone. I could not shed tears; they would not come; they would bring relief." A few weeks later he was still a guest at 323 when, facing in turn what was to prove a fatal illness, on November 7, 1872, he wrote the last words from his pen ever to appear in the *Tribune*. A little more than three weeks later he died and was laid to rest in Greenwood Cemetery, Brooklyn.

It is to be recorded that the house in which Mrs. Greeley died became in a later time the home of John W. Burgess, the historian, while Charles Henry Webb dwelt for many years just across the way at 328 West Fifty-seventh Street. Although he, in a measure, outlived the fame he had won under the pen name of John Paul, Webb was long an attractive figure in the literary life of his time, and his half-dozen volumes of prose and verse could ill be spared from our literature. He was also the friend of some of the most gifted men of an exceptional era, and it was he who, when others refused it, published Mark Twain's first volume, at his own expense, and in so doing launched its author upon a career unique in literary annals.

CHAPTER VII

MEMBERS OF A GOODLY COMPANY

The last homes of Dion Boucicault and Isaac Hill Bromley were in the same block of West Fifty-eighth Street near to Sixth Avenue. That of Virginia Terhune Vandewater, gifted member of a family of varied talents, was at 68, while Bronson Howard lived for a long period at 117 in the same thoroughfare. Howard was a still youthful member of the staff of the *Tribune* when in 1870 the production of his *Saratoga*, a wholly delightful play which still holds the stage, won him repute and a premier place among American dramatists, who up to that time had been few in number and of uncertain quality. Later plays destined to long life on the stage—*The Henrietta* and *Shenandoah* among them—assured him a devoted following until the end of his days. One of the writers of these lines recalls Howard who died in 1908 as a man of good-will whose outlook on life remained a wholesome and sunny one, and who was ever ready to give sound advice and a helping hand to beginners in a crowded field.

Kate Douglas Wiggin and her broker husband during their final years in New York had an apartment at 145 West Fifty-eighth Street, which they at the same time made a pleasant gathering place for literary workers. Hamlin Garland records in his diary for 1903 a New Year call at their home. "Our lovely, blue-eyed, blond hostess," he writes, "was in the full enjoyment of a wide acclaim. Kate Douglas, as her friends called her, was a popular hostess, and at her teas one might meet Howells and Gilder, or Geraldine Farrar and Edward McDowell. None of the critics," Garland adds with the note of condescension which was a part of that unusual man, "took her writing seriously, and she made no pretense to greatness, but her novels were delightfully humorous and colorful." He might have added that she was a born story-teller who knew how to please readers of all ages. Let the belief be recorded that her *My Garden of Memory* is one of the delightful autobiographies of the last half century.

An apartment house at 200 West Fifty-eighth Street was the last home of Lawrence Gilman, who for sixteen years prior to his death in 1839 as music critic of the New York *Herald-*

Tribune sat in judgment on most of the music, new and old, heard in New York. For Gilman music had a varied and urgent appeal matched by no other art. He had also an inquiring mind, and a gift of expression that gave him a place among the masters of a stately prose always adapted to the subject in hand. Gilman was a native of Flushing, Long Island, and had been a student of painting under William Merritt Chase before at the age of nineteen he began forty years of labor as a writer for the press. He was a witty and gentle man, with a rare gift for friendship which helped Edward MacDowell to a leading place among American composers.

And at 200 West Fifty-eighth Street was also the last New York home of Robert Hobart Davis than whom no editor of his generation did more to direct and help young writers. Indeed the names of the successful men and women who owed their start to Davis would make a long and moving list. And his help was of a many-sided-kind, for in addition to wise counsel at the right moment, he fed them when they were hungry, and loaned them money when they were in need of it. The son of a pioneer preacher, born in Nebraska and reared in Nevada, Davis was a reporter and editor in San Francisco before in 1895 he drifted to New York to become ere long Sunday editor of the *World*. and in 1904 the assistant editor of the magazine to which Frank Munsey, a man of untiring industry and a consuming ambition rarely balked by obstacles, had given his name, and in due course to aid his chief in launching seven other magazines, of each of which he was the first managing editor.

Thus Davis became the guide and almoner of an ever growing company of literary beginners, many of whom survive to revere his memory. Before that while Sunday editor of the *World* he had been the first to seek out and recognize the ability of O. Henry, whom he found in cheap quarters on the top floor of a rooming house and helped to instant success as a teller of tales. Later during a manuscript hunt in London he read and persuaded Joseph Conrad to revise his *Victory* which he purchased for *Munsey's* and which was the first of the gifted Pole's tales to command a wide sale when published as a book.

Following the death of Munsey in 1925 and the dispersal of his properties Davis became a roving reporter for the New York *Sun,* and held that post until his own death in Montreal in 1942, traveling now and again to all parts of the world, and making up from the accounts of his journeys which ran into millions of words more than a dozen books, charged with alert and unfailing interest in his fellow humans.

An apartment in the Carnegie Studio Building in West Fifty-ninth Street was for four years following 1893 the home of Clyde Fitch, who, working "day and night, and often far into the next day," there wrote some of his best known plays, among them *Nathan Hale* and *The Climbers,* and partly completed *Major Andre* not produced until 1903 when, in the opinion of critics and playgoers, it added greatly to its author's stature. Fitch wrote a friend that *Major Andre* lay closer to his heart than any other of his plays, and the care and labor he gave to its composition throw welcome light on his methods as a playmaker. Not only in its preparation did he read widely and deeply in books dealing with the Revolution, but he also made repeated visits to the scenes associated with Andre's tragic last days. "I again saw," he writes in one of his letters, "the spot where Andre was captured, the prison where he spent his last night, and the stone that marks the place where he was hung—the latter on a hill with the setting sun behind it, and the moon already risen in front. It was a beautiful sight and full of romance and feeling."

It is a short walk from the Carnegie Studio Building to the former site at 880 Seventh Avenue of the Hotel Grenoble where in 1899 Rudyard Kipling lodged during one of his last visits to America, and there suffered an illness which brought his near to death. It was just before this illness that Hamlin Garland conducted Izrael Zangwill to a first meeting with the great story teller of which he gives an account in his *Roadside Meetings.* "We spent a lively hour with him," writes Garland, and he "gave us a brilliant statement of his merciless philosophy, qualifying it by reference to 'the white man's burden,' and declaring 'I am for the white man and the English race.' At the end Zangwill remarked with reproachful but humorous surprise, 'Why, Kipling, you are almost Hebraic!' That was precisely the situation— Zangwill the Jew, the disciple of Christ; Kipling, the Christian, a follower of Gideon and the God of Battle. As we came away Zangwill could talk of nothing else but Kipling's resemblance to the chieftains of David's time, the men who believed in smiting their enemies root and branch. I was opposed to Kipling's philosophy, and so was Howells, with whom I discussed it, but I am not sure that his view was not honester and more consistent than ours."

At 48 West Fifty-ninth Street was the abode in his later years of William Crary Brownell, who for more than a generation served as literary adviser to the house of Scribner, and who for a period equally long, held a high place, perhaps the highest, among American critics. Mary Mapes Dodge once had her home in the Navarro flats in West Fifty-ninth Street, and at different times between 1892 and 1905 Howells had an apartment at 48 West Fifty-ninth Street, writing there the *Coast of Bohemia, My Literary Passions* and *Literary Friends and Acquaintances.* The last home of Thomas A. Janvier, delightful historian of old New York, was at 225 West Fifty-ninth Street.

The home of Ella Wheeler Wilcox when she was one of the town's most talked about writers of verse was at 41 West Sixtieth Street. Bayard Taylor lived for a time at 31 West Sixty-first Street and it was at a hotel located at the corner of that thoroughfare and Central Park West, that Ernest Toller, the German poet and dramatist, died by his own hand. Toller's career was typical of his class and period. Born near Bromberg, then a part of Germany but now in Poland, the son of Jewish parents, he cut short a university career to serve as a private in the German army during the opening months of the First World War. Then illness led to his discharge, contact with the revolutionary movement in Bavaria, and five years in prison, during which he wrote several of the plays, which were to win him world acclaim. It was at that time also that, inspired by sight of the nests swallows had built outside his cell windows, he wrote his tender and moving *Book of Swallows.*

The advent of Hitler and Nazis deprived Toller of his citizenship and confiscated his property, the fact that he was at the time in Switzerland alone saving him from a concentration camp. When able to do so he fled to England and became a British subject. There followed many visits to the United States on lecture tours; an appeal in person to the democracies of the world for food and medical aid for the starving children of Spain, and finally, residence in New York. All of these facts are set forth in the arresting autobiography, *I Was a German*, which Toller wrote and published two years before his death at the age of forty-six years—the story of a heroic and selfless spirit which in the end proved unequal to the conditions a brutal age had put upon it.

One finds at 1 West Sixty-fourth Street the apartment house that was the last home of Alexander Dana Noyes, for half a century prior to his death in 1944 the financial editor in turn of the *Evening Post* and the *Times*. A master craftsman in his chosen field, Mr. Noyes always spoke with precision and authority. A generation of younger writers owed their success to his considerate yet diligent and rigid training, and the volumes on our financial history that he found time to write have been long used as source books by students of economics. And he was ever a steadying influence in a period of hasty and too often mistaken judgments. "Form your opinion on the facts, and then stick to it," was his shrewd and unvarying advice to younger men. "If some one proves that you have been wrong admit it. You will then be wrong only once, but if you keep changing your mind you can be wrong a dozen times."

Carolyn Wells, a woman of wit and sound sense, whose lively pages will long provide a welcome uplift for lowered spirits, dwelt at the end of her career at 1 West Sixty-seventh Street, and that also was the address in his latter years of Frederick S. Dellenbaugh, who kept Major John W. Powell company in the latter's second trip through the Grand Canyon, and whose *Breaking the Wilderness* is one of the books most often in the hands of students of the making of the West. During the same period another apartment house just across the way had for one of its tenants James Stetson Metcalfe who joined in the founding of the periodical *Life* and for upward of thirty years in its columns wrote of the stage and its people with vigor, distinction and a careful measuring of individual worth, and who early in his career took to wife Elizabeth Tyree, a Southern girl whose gifts and charm as an actress are gracious memories with many an old playgoer.

At 27 West Sixty-seventh Street was the abode for a long period of Edward Augustus Dithmar for more than forty years a member of the editorial staff of the *Times* and during the first half of that time its dramatic critic. Dithmar had a sense of values in the actor's art that was at once just and true. He was also prompt to discover the dramatic gifts of newcomers, persuading Richard Mansfield to employ Clyde Fitch to write *Beau Brummel,* one of the actor's outstanding successes and the start, as elsewhere recorded, of an exceptional and all too brief career for its author. And as an editorial writer, the chief occupation of his later years, Dithmar had sound judgment wedded to an admirable style and a philosophy of life in which humor and a breath of outlook rarely failed to find a place; and many a worthy cause owed no small part of its success to the fact that he fought and wrought for it in the *Times*.

The last home of Horace White, friend of Lincoln, and long a leader among the makers of the American press, was at 18 West Sixty-ninth Street, and that of Emanuel Hertz, Lincoln biographer and collector, at 17 West Seventy-first Street, while at 171 West Seventy-first Street before his retirement and removal to Scarsdale resided William Fayal Clarke in turn assistant to Mary Mapes Dodge and then her successor as editor of *St. Nicholas*. During more than forty years of devoted service Clarke helped to make that magazine a model in its field and the beloved companion of successive generations of boys and girls, and at the same time the way to profitable labor and growing repute an easy one for some of the best known writers of his period. A modest man of kindly impulses Clarke was also a master of the epistolary art, and could a volume of his letters be brought together they would rival those of Lamb and Fitzgerald.

The home in his last years of Adrian H. Joline, who in a busy lawyer's hours of diversion collected autographs and wrote about them in a beguiling way, was at 1 West Seventy-second Street. Ethel Watts Mumford, a writer of varied range and gifts, died at 22 West Seventy-fourth Street, and 317 West Seventy-fourth was the last New York home of Richard Aldrich, for more than a generation a member in turn of the staffs of the *Tribune* and the *Times*, and during that period a clarifying and informing force in the musical life of the nation. May Riley Smith, whose verse is cherished by many grateful readers, died at 151 Central Park West, and the last home of Willard Huntington Wright was at 241 in the same thoroughfare. Wright may now be a fading memory, but his career was an unusual and in some ways dramatic one. A brilliant reporter at twenty-two on the Los Angeles *Times*, a splitting headache forced him to quit work early on a fateful night. A short quarter hour after he left the *Times* building the McNamaras blew it up, killing twenty-one men. A little later he journeyed East, found employment on the *Smart Set* and becoming its editor made it what Burton Rascoe has styled "the most memorable, the most audacious, the best edited, and the best remembered of any magazine ever published in America"—a magazine which attracted and helped to recognition a full score of talented young men and women, who still had the future before them.

By the time he was thirty-five Wright had published nine scholarly books and worked himself into a nervous breakdown, which compelled him to spend two years in bed, with detective stories the only literary fare allowed him by his doctor. These, however, he read and analyzed to such good purpose that when his health returned to him he also as Philo Vance became a writer of detective fiction which quickly won a growing army of readers ignorant of their author's real name and past. Assured in this unexpected way of financial ease Wright was looking forward to a resumption of his scholarly pursuits when heart failure intervened and at fifty-one death put an end to a singular career.

Edmund Clarence Stedman had his residence at 137 West Seventy-eighth Street just before he removed to Bronxville, and at 166 in the same thoroughfare James Lane Allen lived and did his last work as a sensitive interpreter of life in the Blue Grass region of Kentucky as he had known and observed it in early manhood. Again at 324 West Seventy-eighth Street Charles Haynes Haswell in 1907 came to the end of his long life of ninety-eight years in the course of which he had watched his native town grow to be one of the great cities of the world, as an engineer had had a noteworthy part in that growth, and had written about it with loving regard for men and places in a book still read and prized by every student for whom the New York of an earlier time has charm and meaning.

The abode in old age of James Grant Wilson, who had known and written about American men of mark in three generations, was at 143 West Seventy-ninth Street. The home of Harry Thurston Peck, Columbia professor and brilliant and many-sided man of letters, just before he died by his own hand was at 219 West Eightieth Street. Sara Teasdale, much of whose verse will long escape the winnowing hand of time, lived during a part of her shadowed last days at 1 West Eighty-first Street. Benjamin B. Vallentine, author of the *Fitznoddle Papers* and for a number of years editor of *Puck*, died at 56 West Eighty-second Street, and at 325 in the same thoroughfare was long the city home of John Jay Chapman, outspoken essayist and uncompromising reformer.

Two blocks northward at 206 West Eighty-fourth Street, the pilgrim finds the site of the house in which Poe wrote *The Raven*, and the *Imp of the Preverse*. A century ago, where are now long rows of brownstone dwellings, lay the farm of Patrick

Brennan, and in the latter's home, which overlooked the Hudson from the site indicated, Poe and his wife boarded during the summer and fall of 1844 and a part of the following year. The poet's room was on the second floor, and its front windows afforded a noble view of the river and the more distant Palisades. Above the door of the room, resting on the ledge of a semi-circular fanlight, was the bust of Pallas, mentioned in *The Raven*. The bust was stolen by a relic-hunter when the house was vacant in later years. The house itself, a rambling wooden structure, was torn down in 1893, but the mantelpiece from the room in which *The Raven* was written passed into the ownership of a wealthy resident of Brooklyn who had read and cherished the work of its author.

The last New York home of Edith Wharton, who died in France in 1937 after long and self-imposed exile from her native land, was at 131 West Eighty-fifth Street. Three years earlier she had published her autobiography, *A Backward Glance* which, among other things, reveals her as a shrewd observer but rarely a part of the American scene of her time. "When I was young," she confesses in the pages of that book, "it used to seem to me that the group in which I grew up was like an empty vessel into which no new wine would ever again be poured. Now I see that one of its uses lay in preserving a few drops of an old vintage too rare to be savored by a youthful palate; and I should like to atone for my unappreciativeness by trying to revive that faint fragrance."

Thanks to her early mastery of the writing craft, none of Mrs. Wharton's long array of novels and short stories lacks in varying measure the pathos of distance and the charm of the past, if a faded one. But it would not be safe to predict a long future for them, as one hesitates to forecast a permanent appeal for those of another self-exile, Mrs. Wharton's close friend, Henry James, who is portrayed in her volume of recollections as more or less of a fuss-budget, ready to give or lend money to needed friends, and also to bore them with prolix discussion of matters of little concern. It may not be out of place to here record that a vivid memory of other days has to do with the sight of Mrs. Wharton and Henry James emerging from the bookstore of the Brentanos then in Union Square, and regarding with manifest distaste the elbowing crowd in the street of which they were about to become a part.

An early city home of Mrs. Frances Hodgson Burnett was at 44 West Eighty-seventh Street, and two doors removed on the same side of the way was the last abode of Richard Walton Tully, author of the *Bird of Paradise* and other popular plays. Henry Edward Krehbiel lived at 66 West Eighty-eighth Street during some of his most active years as musical editor of the *Tribune*. Able to write with authority and in a trenchant way on every phase of a great art, Krehbiel was also a man of unfailing goodwill. Among those who had reason to give thanks for his aid was Lafcadio Hearn whom, both in his native Cincinnati and later in New York, he strove to advance on a troubled way —not always with satisfying results. When occasion demanded Krehbiel had ready command of sharply phrased invective, and one recalls vivid, first-hand memories of his robust and clearly rewarding survey of Hearn's sins both of omission and commission when their friendship had reached a final and irrevocable end, and the offender had begun the long sojourn in Japan which was to produce his greatest books. And there is little doubt that could Hearn been spared defective vision and the ills that kept it company his lot would have been a less preverse and solitary one.

Brander Matthews, Columbia professor, and pleasant if often acute commentator on the lives of greater men, died at 337 West Eighty-ninth Street, and four doors removed on the other side of the way was for many years the home of Emma Wottan De Long, widow of George Washington De Long, whose tragic fate as commander of the *Jeanette* Arctic expedition she movingly recorded in her memoirs, *Explorer's Wife,* which she wrote and published in extreme old age. Dr. Charles A. Briggs lived during most of the years of his professorship at Union Theological Seminary at 120 West Ninety-third Street, and at 80 Claremont Avenue was long the home of Arthur C. McGiffert, who also knew how to give attractive expression to the fruits of profound and comprehensive scholarship. The poet Stedman was living at 2643 Broadway when in 1908 death came to him, as he had often voiced the wish that it should, suddenly and without warning. Not far away, in West Ninety-fourth Street, was the home of Thomas Dixon when in 1902 he left a Baptist pulpit to write the *Leopard's Spots,* and the *Clansman,* later made into the film the *Birth of a Nation.* These were the first of a score of novels in which he dealt with his native South in the years following the Civil War in a narrow and biased spirit which could see no good in the drab days which followed a great period, but which brought their author a fortune later wasted in real estate ventures in the mountains of his native North Carolina.

A block distant at 159 West Ninety-fifth Street was the last home of Joseph I. C. Clarke, gifted journalist, poet and man of affairs whose autobiography, *My Life and Memories* tells of close and friendly contacts with an army of men and women of real distinction ranging from the younger Bennett to Henry Irving and Mary Baker Eddy. A Dublin Irishman of the finest type, ruled always by tactful good-will for his fellows, Clarke kept until old age the enthusiasms of his youth and unfaltering faith in his own ability to command results. "Know your own limitations?" he once replied to the self-deprecations of a friend. "My boy, never admit even to yourself that you have limitations."

Six doors removed on the same side of the way from Clarke's last home was that of George Cary Eggleston, who, after gallant service in the Confederate Army, where he fought under Stuart, was for more than a generation a hard working editor and author in New York. Eggleston's *Recollections of a Varied Life*, published near the close of his career, is a gallery rich in portraits of men and women who have now become part of a past in which its author was ever a picturesque and individual figure. One of the later homes of Marian Harland was at 311 West Ninety-fifth Street, and Julius Chambers died at 255 West Ninety-seventh Street, putting on paper just before the end the story of a varied life which had included discovery of the sources of the Mississippi, editorship in turn of the *Herald* and *World*, and brilliant service as a correspondent in many lands. Chambers had also a gift for helpful friendship and many a younger man has reason to remember aid of the right sort given when he had real and urgent need for it.

George Alfred Townsend, reporter of Civil War battles and thereafter for nearly half a century an individual and outstanding commentator on men and events, finding time also for a number of historical novels, passed his old age in comfortable retirement at 318 West One Hundred and Sixth Street, and just across the was was the last home of Harold M. Anderson, who had his training on the *Sun* when Charles A. Dana was its editor, and who for upward of forty years was one of the ablest writers of good English enlisted in the service of that journal.

Hamlin Garland in the years preceding his removal to California lived at 307 Cathedral Parkway and in a fifth story apartment, secure from the noises of the street, gave final form to some of the volumes of recollections which when published assured him a full purse and ease of mind at the end of a career attended in some of its stages by trial and disappointment. Frank Jenners Wilstach, an author of another and very different sort— manager of actors and actresses, biographer of Wild Bill Hickok and zealous maker of a dictionary of similes which will long remain an authority in its field—lived at 220 Manhattan Avenue when death put an end to his wide-ranging labors. The last home of Edward L. Burlingame, earliest and best remembered of the editors of *Scribner's Magazine,* was at 440 West End Avenue. and that of Henry Mills Alden at 521 West One Hundred and Twelfth Street.

Three blocks northward at 411 West One Hundred and Fifteenth Street, Thomas S. Jones, Jr., author of sonnets and lyrics read and cherished by lovers of what is finest and best in modern poetry, long shared the home of devoted friends. The last home of John Bates Clark, author and economist and long a member of the faculty of Columbia University, was at 420 Riverside Drive, and at 445 in the same thoroughfare for a time dwelt James Moffett, perhaps the most learned of a little group of great scholars who when the century was young came from Scotland to teach in America, and, who eminent as a translator of the Bible, sought with unusual success to couch its books in the language of today.

A few blocks away at 600 West End Avenue was the last city home of Channing Pollock, playwright and many-sided man of affairs. Born in Washington in 1880 Pollock was early left an orphan and while still in his teens found employment as a reporter for the *Post* of that city becoming at the end of two years its dramatic critic. Before he was twenty-one seeking a wider field he made his way to New York with three dollars in his pocket, and until he found a congenial post worked as a stevedore. His first play was produced in 1901, and before his death in 1946 he turned out more than thirty others, not a few of them proving popular successes. A man of untiring energy, Pollock between his plays found time to serve as press agent and dramatic critic, to publish worthwhile books, and as writer and lecturer to champion worthy causes in need of advocates of the right sort, towards the end telling the story of his activities in a delightful volume, the *Adventures of a Happy Man.* All in all his was a crowded and happy, and also a useful career.

Edgar Saltus had his home during his closing years at 508 West One Hundred and Fourteenth Street, while at 423 West One Hundred and Seventeenth Street was the last abode of Talcott Williams, one of the most richly endowed journalists of his time and in turn the trainer of two generations of workers for the press. Edward Waterman Townsend, whose *Chimmie Fadden* stories—told by a Bowery boy who mingled an uncouth philosophy with bizarre anecdote and humor of a bitter sort—enlivened the pages of the *Sun* and amused an army of readers at the turn of the century, died at 343 West One Hundred Twentieth Street in 1942 at the age of eighty-seven years. Like many other able newspaper workers, Townsend, when still a young man came to New York from California by way of Washington, and in the course of his long life played many parts, serving in Congress and as postmaster of a New Jersey town, and writing a work on the Constitution which was adopted for use as a textbook in a number of colleges. But men who were young half a century ago prefer to remember him as the creator of the Bowery roughneck who had a mind of his own and gave a new and diverting turn to American dialect. And while Townsend was ending his days within a stone's throw of Columbia University at 187 West One Hundred and Thirty-fifth Street was the home of James Weldon Johnson, poet, editor and stout champion of his race, during the most fruitful years of an exceptional career through a tragic mishap brought to an untimely end.

In the opening decades of the last century, what is now the Boulevard was a country road which ran northward from the present Union Square to the village of Bloomingdale, and then, skirting the foot of the hill where Manhattanville nestled, joined the Kingsbridge Road at the intersection of One Hundred and Forty-seventh Street and Ninth Avenue. A daily traveler over the Bloomingdale Road in a still earlier period, was Alexander Hamilton, who, when his public career was ended, built a house near its northern end. Hamilton Grange, as it was called, stood until a few years ago, at the corner of Tenth Avenue and One Hundred and Forty-second Street, but now adjoins St. Luke's Protestant Episcopal Church in Convent Avenue of which it is the parish school. Its original site, when bought by Hamilton, was eight miles from the center of the city, and the author of the *Federalist* chose it mainly for its quiet and seclusion.

Here, when the home was finished in 1802, he brought his wife and children, and here, no doubt, for he was then but forty-five and in the prime of his powers, he hoped to pass many happy and useful years. Sad and sudden was the ending of this pleasant dream. On the morning of July 11, 1804, he rode forth to face the pistol of an adversary, and at Weehawken, Burr's bullet laid him low. Hamilton Grange is a square wooden structure having two stories and a basement. There are verandahs on the west and east sides, and the main entrance is also fronted by a porch, where Mrs. Hamilton, the daughter of Philip Schuyler, used to wait for her husband, when on summer afternoons he came galloping up from his office in the distant town. The front door of the house opens into a small hallway, and to the right is a spacious room which was used by Hamilton as a study, but which in its altered condition serves to mock the irony of human hopes and ambitions.

Alfred Henry Lewis died at 457 West One Hundred and Forty-eighth Street, and ten blocks northward at 524 West One Hundred and Fifty-eighth Street was the home three score years ago of William Henry Bishop, an alert descendant of the Puritans who was by turns college professor, diplomat and author of a score of novels and travel books which still claim readers. Thence a short walk takes one to Aubudon Lane, a narrow road which leads out of West One Hundred and Fifty-eighth Street, just east of the Hudson. John James Audubon, the ornithologist, bought the property hereabouts in 1841, and built thereon the house which he named Minniesland in honor of his devoted wife whom he called Minnie, an old Scotch term for mother, and which was his home during the last years of his life. The house passed in 1864 from the possession of his family, but standing as it did well out of the beaten track, remained until its demolition in 1932 a picturesque reminder of the time when a home at the far end of Manhattan was almost as remote from the city and as difficult of access as a present day lodge in the Catskills.

A spacious house now gone from the corner of West One Hundred and Fifty-seventh Street and Eleventh Avenue was the home in early manhood and until late middle life of George Bird Grinnell, author, naturalist and explorer, organizer also of the first Audubon Society and long regarded by many as Audubon's successor as the outstanding defender of wild life in America. Descended from Betty Alden, the first white woman born in New England, and from no less than five colonial governors, ample means enabled him after his graduation at Yale in 1870 to turn to the pusuits that most appealed to him.

Thus Grinnell made repeated exploring trips to and through the Far West; after a buffalo hunt with the Pawnees passed many summers among the Plains and Rocky Mountain Indians; wrote more than thirty scholarly and informing volumes, among them the *Fighting Cheyennes* and the *Story of the Indian,* and for thirty-five years following 1876 edited and partly owned *Forest and Stream,* a weekly periodical devoted to outdoor life and filled in fuller measure than any of its successors with information of abiding value in the field of natural history. In 1887 with Theodore Roosevelt he founded the Boone and Crockett Club, and to his effort was mainly due the creation in 1910 of Glacier National Park, a reserve of a million acres of mountain country in Northwestern Montana, no doubt his most enduring monument.

Along with the will and ability to carry a good cause to a successful conclusion, Dr. Grinnell had a genius for friendship, and one of the admiring group he drew about him hastened to record an account of the first of many visits to his home in Audubon Park. "His house is a joy," he wrote. "Just the sort of a homestead for a family reunion—the kind of mansion to date from. Its dusky, wide mysterious rooms are such as a child would remember with shuddering delight—savage weapons on the walls, wolf and bear skins on the floor, and in the corner bookshelves volumes filled with pictures of red men and animals." And it may be added that the master of this house, a lean, brown, strong faced man, had the never-failing dignity of his friends of the Plains. To meet and clasp hands with him, and to listen to his talk was to be made to feel that here was a figure from the antique world.

There is no record that they met, but if they had Dr. Grinnell would have found Morgan Robertson, teller of sea tales, in some ways a man after his own heart. Robertson, who lived in his last days at 500 West One Hundred and Sixty-sixth Street, was born in 1861 on the shores of Lake Ontario, at sixteen ran away to sea as cabin-boy on a square-rigged vessel that sailed around the world and at twenty-one became a mate and pilot. Then he left the sea and mastered the trade of watchmaker and diamond-setter. In 1894, his sight failing him, he turned to authorship as a means of support, and before his death in 1915 wrote and sold several hundred stories, most of them based upon his experiences as a sailor. He found his path, however, a thorny one, and poverty, often of the grimmest sort, pursued him until the end of his days.

Among Robertson's effects when he died was a notebook filled with the names of those from whom he had borrowed in varying amounts between the sale of one and the marketing of another story. A change of luck had come to him at the very last, and from royalties his widow set up a fund from which his creditors were to be paid in full. But many refused what was due them, and the money went back into the fund to be used, in Robertson's words, "to take care of writing fellows who go on the rocks." In 1926, eleven years after his death, Robertson's stories were collected in eight volumes. Here one will find much hasty and ill-considered work, but also a goodly sifting of tales of the first-class. Perhaps in future years belated fame will come to their author as it did to Herman Melville. Members of the now thinning group who knew and companioned with him cherish his memory as that of a sturdy and resolute spirit who never railed at ill-luck.

From the last home of Robertson it is a short walk northward to Trinity Cemetery opened in 1843 where Clement Clarke Moore and many another worthy of the New York of an earlier time take their rest. There also is the grave of Madame Jumel, second wife of Aaron Burr, whose last days contrasting strangely with her youth and middle age will some day afford an appealing theme to a writer of fiction based upon fact. If the tale is well told it will be sure to find delighted readers.

Finally an apartment at 854 West One Hundred and Eighty-first Street was the last New York home of Morris Raphael Cohen, for more than twenty years prior to 1938 professor of philosophy at the City College of New York, and also one of the most penetrating and creative minds of his generation, whose books and essays covering a wide range have profoundly influenced thinkers in many fields. Born in Russia in 1880 and brought to America when a lad of twelve, Dr. Cohen's earlier years, the story of which is modestly set forth in his autobiography *A Dreamer's Journey,* were a struggle with conditions that would have dismayed a less resolute man. He worked in a poolroom and as a private tutor to put himself through City College. Later a scholarship enabled him to secure a degree at Harvard, where he had Felix Frankfurter for a room-mate, and in 1912 he became a teacher of philosophy at City College and an inspiring influence with successive generations of students.

Through the years Dr. Cohen also made leisure to write his *Reason and Nature, Preface to Logic, Faith of a Liberal* and other widely read books which dealt with a life of reason in a liberal world in a brilliant and individual way. A reporter once asked him what he would do to stamp out radicalism in American colleges. "I wouldn't do anything," was the reply. "I am a radical myself." And this militant spirit found expression in all of his writings. Dr. Cohen's last days were passed in Washington, in order that, now a widower, he might be near his children leading useful lives in that city. There in January, 1947, death claimed him. Despite crippling illness until the end he kept two secretaries busy with dictation, and in two years wrote five books now in course of publication. Than he no man did more to prompt to clear thinking the men and women of a troubled period.

CHAPTER VIII

Strolls Through the Upper East Side

Henry George died in an upper room of a hostelry which faces Union Square at Fifteenth Street and at 26 Union Square was the last home of Chancellor James Kent. Dion Boucicault in the heyday of his career as dramatist and actor had lodgings in a house now gone from 20 East Fifteenth Street, and at the same number long flourished Pinard's restaurant, a favorite resort of blithe and clever folk. Sixty odd years ago a large residence on the northeast corner of Fourth Avenue and Fifteenth Street was replaced by a business structure. The stable in the rear was transformed by Stanford White into a unique and attractive dwelling, the stable yard in front becoming a garden, and here Richard Watson Gilder and his wife, Helena De Kay, on the morrow of their marriage set up a home still remembered as a gathering place of writers and bookmen. The Century Club was also quartered for nearly four decades in East Fifteenth Street, two doors farther from Fourth Avenue, and in the same thoroughfare were the last homes of Henry Winter Bellows and of George Bird Grinnell.

Again, at 329 East Fifteenth Street, just beyond Stuyvesant Square, was, for nearly a score of years, the abode of Richard Henry Stoddard and his gifted wife Elizabeth Barstow. A front room on the second floor of a cheerful seeming brick house, demolished some years ago, was the poet's study, and housed a rare collection of books, manuscripts and autographs, the sifted treasures of a lifetime, so rich in association and pedigrees that a hundred Immortals seemed in turn to be leaning over the visitor's shoulder and inviting him to intimacy, and many were those famous in letters who found their way to this upper room there to spend delightful and beguiling hours. There too, alas, blindness and failing powers crept upon the poet, and later death came to make his path a yet more shadowed one. First the son who was the pride of his old age, and then his wife were summoned hence. Mrs. Stoddard died in 1902 and within the year the husband followed her into the long silence.

That sturdy descendant of the Knickerbockers, Gulian C. Verplanck, died at 12 East Sixteenth Street, and adjoining the College of St. Francis Xavier, less than a block distant, is the brownstone house which was the home of Bryant in the "white winter of his age." Again at 115 East Sixteenth Street Howells lodged for a time in 1900 and 1901. "I see a great deal of Mark Twain nowadays," he wrote his sister from this address, "and we have good times denouncing everything. We are old fellows, and it is pleasant to find the world so much worse than it was when we were young." And William S. Rainsford's home was at 209 East Sixteenth Street in the years when he was finding zest and profit in the labors later recorded in the *Story of a Varied Life.* George E. Woodberry, when a professor at Columbia, had bachelor apartments at 5 East Seventeenth Street This was on the morrow of the writing and publication of the life of Poe for which he is now best remembered, and which summed up that poet's shortcomings with a severity still disputed by students of a troubled career. A three-story structure of red brick at 66 East Seventeenth Street was for a number of years the home of Edgar, nephew of Washington Irving, and an occasional sojourn of the gentle humorist when in old age he came from Sunnyside for a few days' visit to the city; and the last home of Jeannette L. Gilder, long editor of the *Critic* and an arresting, if some times amusing, figure in the literary life of the town a generation ago, was at 100 East Seventeenth Street.

At 23 Irving Place in the middle years of the last century dwelt Isaac C. Pray, brother of the gifted Malvina Pray and himself an author, actor and playwright of parts, who there wrote a biography of the elder Bennett, founder of the *Herald*, and welcomed Charles Dickens as friend and guest when in 1842 the latter visited America for the first time. Eleven numbers northward on the same side of Irving Place, still stands an old-fashioned house which was the last home of Caroline Matilda Kirkland, whose sketches of Western life, published under the pen name of Mary Clevers, gave her a secure if modest place in the literary circles of her period. At 57 Irving Place was long the home of William Conant Church, editor of the *Army and Navy Journal,* who there wrote his life of Ericsson and other books Two doors removed on the same side of the way William Sidney Porter had his lodgings during his most productive years as an author, finding in the neighborhood the background for some of his most diverting tales.

Howells lived at 241 East Seventeenth Street during his brief period of service as editor of the *Cosmopolitan Magazine,* and Richard Grant White died at 330 East Seventeenth Street in an apartment house which in other years furnished a home for Howells and Henry Cuyler Bunner. There the novelist began *A Hazard of New Fortunes* and the poet gave form to many of his *Airs of Arcady.* Frederick Van Wyck and Oliver Herford died and Bayard Taylor and Elinor Wylie lived at 142 East Eighteenth Street, one of New York's oldest apartment houses. There Taylor wrote his *Prince Deukalion,* thence departing upon the mission from which he was not to return. A shaded house twenty doors to the eastward and on the same side of the way was the abode of James Parton during and after the Civil War, and there he did much of his best work, including his lives of Burr and Franklin. The last home of John R. G. Hassard was at 218 East Eighteenth Street, and that gifted man's friend and comrade William Winter, dwelt just across the way during the years when he was ripening into fame as a poet and as the most brilliant writer of his era about the stage and its people.

A block eastward at 308 Second Avenue, stands a still stately house which had intimate and delightful association with the American visits of Thackeray. Four score and odd years ago the lower reaches of Second Avenue were a choice residential section and at one of the corners of that thoroughfare and Eighteenth Street dwelt George Baxter, in his time a man of large affairs. Merchant and novelist became friends during the former's first lecture tour in America, and the Brown House, as Thackeray called the home of the Baxters, soon grew to be his favorite resort in New York. "He came to us whenever he could," writes a daughter of the household, "and his place at my mother's right at table, with the claret pitcher ready for him, was an established arrangement before a lecture. We saw only," she adds, "the loving side of his great nature. It was always impossible for us to feel afraid of his cynicism, his sharp criticism, of which others speak. He could not help seeing the weakness of human nature, but he did the fullest justice to whatever was fine or noble in man or woman." Thackeray's friendship for the Baxter family, kept warm by letters long afterward given to the world, lasted until the end of his life, and when the shock of his sudden death saddened for many the Christmas of 1863, nowhere was he more sincerely mourned than in the Brown House in Second Avenue.

Nearer to the East River, Christodora House, a settlement house at 147 Avenue B, has intimate association with Anna Hempstead Branch, verse maker and playwright, who passed several winters there in the last years of her life. Sprung of Puritan anecstry, and claiming as her home Hempstead House, at New London, one of the oldest houses in New England, this unusual woman united a superior poetic gift to a strong urge for social service, and so was moved to become one of the founders of the Poet's Guild of Christodora House through which continuing effort was made to bring poetry into the lives of under-priviliged children and their parents. To this effort Miss Branch gave the best that was in her, and her classes at Christodora House remained her chief concern until her death in 1937 after long illness. Serenity cloistered her, and all her days her life was one of sunny and cheerful selflessness.

The city home of Horace Greeley for more than a score of years was at 35 East Nineteenth Street, and during a part of that time he had William Allen Butler for a next-door neighbor. The houses in which editor and poet dwelt are now given over to business purposes, and a woman's tailor plies his trade in the room in which the founder of the *Tribune* labored over his *Recollections of a Busy Life* and the final chapters of *What I Know About Farming*. Butler found Greeley an unusual and now and then disturbing neighbor. "During a part of our residence in Nineteenth Street," he writes, "our next door neighbor was Horace Greeley, who carried his personal eccentricities to some extent into his domestic arrangements. He kept a goat in his backyard, and appealed, when necessity required, to his neighbors to aid him in looking after his gas meter when the lights went out. As the houses in our row were identical in appearance, it was not strange that Mr. Greeley, with his mind intent on great affairs, should mistake one of the others for his own. Returning home one time carrying a box of tea, he made an ineffectual effort to enter our house. My wife, hearing some one at the front door, opened it rather suddenly and the founder of the New York *Tribune* was precipitated, tea chest and all, into our front hall."

In truth's behalf be it recorded that Butler was wrong as to the number of goats. Sometimes there were three of them, kept by Mrs. Greeley, not her husband, for the amusement of their children, crowding the family backyard, and lending it the shantytown appearance then common to many parts of New York.

And Greeley was quick to successfully defend his neighbor from an absurd charge of plagarism that kept company with the popularity of Butler's *Nothing to Wear,* which had been published without its author's name in *Harper's Weekly,* and which some school girl, with small regard for morals, foolishly claimed for her own.

The apartment house numbered 119 East Nineteenth Street, was the home of the novelist, David Graham Phillips at the time of his tragic death—struck down by a madman to whom he had done no wrong; and across the way at 120 East Nineteenth Street, Ida Minerva Tarbell for many years had her office, there giving final form to *In the Footsteps of 'the Lincolns* and other of her later works best deserving remembrance.   The last New York home of Ernest Boyd was an apartment at 151 East Nineteenth Street where he died alone in the last days of 1946 while at work on a volume of memories.   Boyd deserves mention in this chronicle, for he had no mean part in the American literary renaissance of the first decades of the century.   He invariably dressed in brown and that, with his copper-red beard, long made him an unusual figure at gatherings of his fellow authors.   Born in Dublin in 1887, he served for a period on the staff of the *Irish Times,* and then came to America residing first in Baltimore, but later and until the end in New York.   The master of half a dozen languages, Boyd translated and edited an edition in many volumes of the works of Guy de Maupassant, while half a dozen books of his own proved him a critic with views rarely shared by the majority, but to which he gave individual and always arresting expression.   Due to ill-health his latter years were in the main silent ones.

A short walk to the eastward one finds at 327 East Nineteenth Street the last New York abode of Henry George, who there began what he planned should be his master-work—the treatise on political economy which still engaged him when death halted his labors.   George's former dwelling was razed some years ago, and its site now serves as entrance to a factory; but the destroying hand has thus far spared the house at 53 East Twentieth Street which was long the home of Alice and Phoebe Cary.   The poet sisters, in whom exceptional mental gifts were united to rare loveliness of spirit, came to New York from Ohio about 1852, soon after their first joint volume of verse issued from the press.   Horace Greeley had met them while on a lecture trip, and convinced them that in New York they would command more ample reward for their talents than in their native village.

The story of the success that attended their modest venture was in due course set forth by the editor of the *Tribune* in his *Recollections of a Busy Life*. "Gradually signs of thrift appeared," writes Greeley, "and eventually they lived in a house of their own, paid for by the labor of their hands. Here they received weekly, without ostentation, literary and artistic guests, and dispensed a quiet, inexpensive hospitality. The literary persons or artists who met at their informal invitation to discuss with them a cup of tea, and the newest books, poems, and events, might have found many more pretentious, but few more enjoyable gatherings." The receptions recalled by Mr. Greeley were for nearly a score of years a pleasant feature of the city's artistic and literary life. The former home of the Carys has changed but little since it passed into other hands. Phoebe Cary's study was directly above a small bay-windowed parlor on the ground floor, and in an adjoining room Alice wrote some of her best verse, and there laid down her pen for the last time.

Henry Cuyler Bunner, during his first days as editor of *Puck,* had lodgings in East Twentieth Street, near Fourth Avenue, and a loft building at 45 East Twentieth Street occupies the site of Gramercy Park Place, a family hotel where in 1879 Gilbert and Sullivan put on paper the *Pirates of Penzance,* and in so-doing added an unusual chapter to the annals of comic opera on this side of the Atlantic. Lyrist and composer, whose fruitful association brought them multiplying returns in the later decades of the last century, came to America when they learned that eight companies were producing their opera *Pinafore* at a profit, but giving no thought to rightful royalties to its authors. Arrived in New York, they made haste, after fruitless negotiations, to organize a company of their own, and when the venture prospered wrote a new opera to enlarge its repertoire, with satisfying results.

Henry Winter Bellows in his years of greatest fame and influence lived at the corner of Twentieth Street and Fourth Avenue, and a four-story house which stood formerly at 39 East Twenty-first Street was for a considerable period the home of John Treat Irving, favorite nephew of the author, who was often a visitor there in his last days, and in a third story front room reserved for his use, with his books and papers about him, wrote a portion of his *History of Mahomet.*

The National Arts Club at 15 Gramercy Park was the last home of Arthur Goodrich, novelist and playwright, while the Players Club at 16 Gramercy Park recalls pleasant memories of Edwin Booth, its actor founder, and of Mark Twain, Oliver Herford, Albert Bigelow Paine, Hamlin Garland and other wits and authors for whom it was a favorite meeting-place in its first years. The Players Club was also the last home of Robert Cortes Holliday who early in 1947 was carried thence to die in a nearby hospital. Holliday was born in Indianapolis and there passed a youth which he often declared as very like that described by Booth Tarkington in *Penrod* and *Seventeen*. He left school at an early age to come to New York where through the years he followed a variety of callings, but will be best remembered for his labors as a contributor to or editor of magazines, and as the author of *Walking Stick Papers, Broome Street Straws* and other whimsical and wholly delightful books which through the years ahead are fairly sure to find readers. Holliday was also the friend and literary executor of Joyce Kilmer whose verse he prepared for the press.

John Bigelow died at 21 Gramercy Park. Three doors removed was the last city home of Richard Watson Gilder, and that of Art Young was the Hotel Irving at 26 Gramercy Park. Convivial, gregarious, lovable and a lover of all sorts, and conditions of men, mourned by uncounted numbers when in 1943 he passed from life, Young was also one of the finest cartoonists of his period, and a writer and talker of initimable and unfailing charm. Born in Illinois in 1866, and reared in Wisconsin, where he grew up in and around his father's general store, from boyhood he drew pictures on any surface at hand, and his parents approved when, still in his teens, he departed for Chicago to study at the Art Institute.

Young as a student sold cartoons to *Judge, Life* and *Puck*, and from his earnings saved money which enabled him to study for a time at the Academie Julien in Paris. Then he returned to Chicago and quickly won favor as a political cartoonist for the *Inter-Ocean* and other journals. The turn of the century found him in New York, and, assured from the first of profitable employment as a free lance, during the remainder of his days he never moved far from it. In 1911, with Max Eastman and others, he founded the *Masses*, a leftist and pacifist magazine which during the First World War brought him and his associates into conflict with the law, but with no loss of friends, for while in his crusading he was an unyielding advocate of what he regarded as right and justice, his selfless sincerity was always in evidence and disarmed opposition.

Through the years Young wrote and illustrated half a dozen volumes, among them an autobiography of a beguiling sort, and he was still busy with pencil and pen when in 1943 without warning death claimed him. In fulfilment of his wishes his remains were cremated and buried at Bethel, Connecticut, where for a time he had had a small country place and a one-man art gallery. There his ashes rest under an apple tree in whose shade he had in an earlier time delighted to "lie as nearly naked as possible and enjoy life." Before his last days on Gramercy Park Young lived for twenty years at 9 East Seventeenth Street in Greenwich Village, and there after the First World War for a time produced a one-man magazine, *Good Morning* which his friends in the village published "almost every week."

Ripley Hitchcock, long literary adviser to the house of Appleton died at 34 Gramercy Park, and Honore Willsie Morrow, a daughter of the Middle West, had her home in the same apartment house when merited repute came to her as a writer of historical romances, the result of long and painstaking labor, which deal in a spirited way with the Colonial, Revolutionary and Civil War periods. Next door, at 36 Gramercy Park, was the last home of Elizabeth Jordan, another woman of mark who for a full half century had a varied and wide-ranging part in the literary life of New York. It was in 1890 that Miss Jordan came from her native Milwaukee to seek and find a place as a reporter on the *World*. She was associated with that journal for a decade, and then for a much longer period was an editor and literary adviser to the house of Harper. Meanwhile, she wrote scores of short stories, some of which found a place in her *Tales of a City Room*, and more than thirty novels and other books, including an autobiography published in 1938 under the title of *Three Rousing Cheers*. Miss Jordan always had something worthwhile to say; but, a woman of goodwill, she was also quick to recognize talent in others, and when she died early in 1947 it was recalled to her credit that she had had a helpful part in the discovery and acclaim, among others of such authors as Sinclair Lewis, Zona Gale and Dorothy Canfield.

Again one finds set in the walls of the hotel known as 82 Gramercy Park a tablet which reads: "On this site was the home of Robert G. Ingersoll. He knew no fear except the fear of doing wrong." The famous orator and lawyer lived on Gramercy Park during a part of his last years, and here gave welcome to Mark Twain, John Burroughs, James Whitcomb Riiley and other guests whose names have not yet passed into forgetfulness. Stephen Crane once had lodgings at 33 East Twenty-second Street. On the other side of the same thoroughfare a dozen doors nearer to Fourth Avenue, was the final abode of Francis Lister Hawks, the friend of Irving and Bryant and long a pulpit orator of earnestness and power.

John Huston Finley during most of the twenty years of a memorable association with the *Times* which ended in 1940 lived at 1 Lexington Avenue. Finley's career as educator, author and editor was one of successful achievement and devoted human service. A native of Illinois and president of Knox College at twenty-eight, he was later professor of politics at Princeton, head of City College in New York and commissioner of education for the State of New York. His association with the *Times* began in 1921 and in 1937 he succeeded Rollo Ogden as its editor. Dr. Finley was an active and vigorous thinker and wrote with lucidity and force on a wide range of subjects. The making of the West especially appealed to him, and his *French in the Heart of America* is, perhaps, without a superior in its field. No man of his period had a larger army of friends, or strove more effectively for the welfare of his fellows.

Parke Godwin, when Bryant's chief lieutenant on the *Evening Post,* lived at 53 Lexington Avenue. Stephen Crane before success came to him had modest quarters at 143 Each Twenty-third Street. Charles de Kay, grandson of the poet Drake and himself a verse-maker of quality, lived in his last years at 128 East Twenty-fourth Street. At 32 East Twenty-fifth Street was the home in old age of Daniel T. Valentine, whose quaint history of New York is a source of delight to every student of the city's past, and at 111 East Twenty-fifth Street John Hay had lodgings when as a writer for the *Tribune* he won praise from Horace Greeley, an editor usually slow to acknowledge the merits of his fellow workers.

Edmund Clarence Stedman was living at 44 East Twenty-sixth Street when he brought to a conclusion his many-volumed *Library of American Literature,* and eight doors removed on the same side of the way was for a decade after the Civil War the home of Herman Melville. A son of New York, the death of Melville's father compelled him while still a growing lad to

make his own way in the world. He was master for a time of
a country school, but soon left that post to ship before the mast
on the Pacific whaler Acushnet, and in 1841, at the age of
twenty-two, sailed from New Bedford on the voyage which was
to give him material for his chief books. The Acushnet, after a
year and a half's cruising, reached the Marquesas Islands, and
there Melville, weary of poor fare and harsh treatment, escaped
from the whaler, only to lose his way in a forest on the Island
of Nukahiva, the home of the Typee cannibals, with whom he
spent several months in virtual but friendly captivity.

Melville was finally rescued by the captain of an Australian
whaler, and shipping as one of her sailors, he in due time reached
Tahiti in the Society Islands. Thence he made his way to Hono-
lulu, where he joined the crew of an American frigate, and in
the fall of 1844, landed in Boston. Two years later he published
Typee, describing his experiences among the Nukahiva cannibals,
and this was followed in 1849 by *Omoo*—two books which caught
and reflected the glamor and mystery of the South Sea and its
islands as never before, and brought instant fame to their author,
whose career for several years thereafter was as brilliant as that
of any prose writer then living and at work. The romance of
White Jacket, based on his life aboard a man-of-war was published in 1850, and in 1851 he gave the world *Moby Dick, or
the White Whale,* an account of the whaler's life which so capable
a judge as Clark Russell placed first among his books, and in a
class by itself.

The completion of *Moby Dick,* however, marked the end of
Melville's important literary work. Henceforth, he had nothing
to say which the world cared to hear, and though he wrote and
published other books, all his later writings were a puzzling mixture of philosophy and fantasy. He married in 1847 and resided
on a farm in the Berkshire Hills until 1863, when he returned
to his native city, where his closing years were passed in a self-
sought seclusion, which made room only for his books, his family
and a few old friends. Melville's last home was a house at 104
East Twenty-sixth Street, long since replaced by flats; and
one who in his youth had found delight in *Omoo* and *Typee,*
recalls occasional sight of him out for a stroll in this part of
the town—a white-haired stalwart indifferent to his surroundings
and manifestly content with his own thoughts for compaions.

Henry Loomis Nelson, editor of *Harper's Weekly* and later
professor of political science at Williams, died at 69 Madison

Avenue, and at 131 Madison Avenue was the last home of Arthur Guiterman, dean when he died of American light verse writers, and one of the few poets of his generation who managed to make a comfortable income from his calling.

The office of the New York *Evangelist* when Henry Martyn Field served it during a part of his forty-four years as editor was at 156 Fifth Avenue. The youngest but by no means the least gifted of a group of brothers of varied and exceptional achievement—David Dudley Field was chief author of civil and criminal codes adopted by New York and a number of states; Stephen Johnson Field served for thirty-four years as a justice of the federal Supreme Court, while Cyrus West Field led in the laying of the first Atlantic cable—Henry Field was also a man of mark in allied callings, by turns preacher and journalist, but taking time for biographies of his brothers David and Cyrus and for journeys to far places which he described in a long list of entertaining books read with zest and profit by many a stay-at-home traveler, dividing favor with those of Bayard Taylor.

The most talked about event in the younger Field's life, however, was his marriage to a gracious and gifted French woman who had been a central figure in a murder trial which startled and mystified the Paris of the third Napoleon. When in 1850 a French duke was arrested for the slaying of his wife it was charged that he had been moved to the crime by his love for a younger woman, Henrietta de Partes, governess of his children and a member of his household. The nobleman after a long and stubborn contest in the courts was found guilty and sent to the guillotine, but the young woman was cleared of all blame in the affair, and presently sought refuge from the curious in New York where she became a teacher of French in a school for girls. Then it was that she met and won the heart of Henry Field who married her without delay. Under these changed conditions Mrs. Field not only made her husband's life a happy one, but also proved a gracious hostess to his friends, and until her death in 1875 welcome to their home was counted a privilege by alert and understanding guests.

The last home of Frank Irving Cobb, for a dozen years editor of the *World*, and during the same period perhaps the strongest writer associated with the New York press, was at 247 Fifth Avenue. Frederick Van Rensselaer Day, creator of Nick Carter, and author of more than a thousand tales, died by his own hand when a lodger in 1922 at 3 East Twenty-seventh Street.

The home in his last days of William Henry Jackson, who in his long life of more than ninety years played many parts, and of Michael Monahan, quick champion of struggling causes was the Latham, 4 East Twenty-eighth Street. In an earlier time, Charles Farrar Browne, when serving as editor of *Vanity Fair,* lodged at 28 East Twenty-eighth Street, sharing quarters with the publisher of that journal. "We have a parlor, bathroom," he wrote a Cleveland friend "and breakfast sent to our room for four dollars a week each. Our dinners we get downtown, a shilling getting a beefsteak pie or a piece of baked beef. I mention these things so that if you come on here by and by you will come to the office and go home with me. I can keep you like a fighting cock for a few shillings a day. Such beef as we get at Crook & Duff's you never saw since God made you."

Again at 119 East Twenty-eighth Street once dwelt Wolcott Balestier, the brother-in-law and literary partner of Rudyard Kipling, who, dying before he was thirty, left behind him a record of achievement that would have done credit to a man twice his years. A native of Rochester, Balestier studied at Cornell University but left without graduating, and after serving as a reporter in his native city and as an assistant in the Astor Library, was, for a time, editor of a short-lived humorous journal in New York. His 'prentice efforts in journalism were broken by two long journeys to the Southwest and Mexico, and in 1888, as the representative of a firm of publishers, he settled in England where, during the next three years, his rare qualities of head and heart won him a wider circle of friends among English authors than was enjoyed by any other American of his time, one of these being Rudyard Kipling, whose gifts he was among the first to recognize and acclaim.

Balestier began to write tales and essays while still a schoolboy, and before he left America, he had published three novels and numerous short stories of mark and promise. In England he joined with Kipling, who declared him "a collaborator after my own heart," in writing the *Naulahka,* and there also he produced his own *Benefits Forgot,* a penetrating study of life in the West, not issued until after his death. That event, the result of a swift fever, occurred in Dresden in 1891, and his grave is in the American cemetery of that city. What he might have done, had length of days been granted him, is melancholy and regretful conjecture, but men who knew and loved him, cherish the memory of his eager and generous spirit as one of the inspiring influences of a youth that has now become a part of the vanished past.

Allen Thorndike Rice lived for a number of years at 12 East Twenty-ninth Street, just across the way from the Little Church Around the Corner. There Laurence Oliphant was for a time a member of his household and aided him in editing the *North American Review*. And the home at the turn of the century of Mrs. Burton Harrison, who was born Constance Cary, of an ancient Virginia family of that name, was at 43 East Twenty-ninth Street. Earlier New York homes of Mrs. Harrison were at 142 East Seventeenth Street and 83 Irving Place, not far from Gramercy Park. The life of this gifted woman was one of sharp contrasts. Her father, Archibald Cary, an editor in the mountain town of Cumberland, died in early manhood, and his widow, Monimia Fairfax and their three children went to live at Vaucluse, one of the Fairfax estates on the Virginia side of the Potomac, a few miles from Washington. There as a girl she poured over the English and French classics and made sound preparation for her future career as an author.

Then came the Civil War period with its strains and losses, and after that brief residence of the mother and daughter in Paris, where they saw the Empire in all the glitter of the third Napoleon's reign. In 1867 they returned to America, and the daughter was married to Burton Norvell Harrison, who had served as secretary to Jefferson Davis, and had studied law during the long imprisonment which he shared with his chief. Thereafter and until her husband's death in 1904 Mrs. Harrison lived in New York. Her literary career began in 1876 with contributions to the magazines, and included before her death in 1920 a goodly number of novels and plays, and a delightful volume of memories. Her touch was a light and graceful one, and all that she wrote had distinction and charm. She was also a woman of rare social graces and each of her New York homes a center of refined and winning hospitality

The last home of Henry Theodore Tuckerman was at 220 Madison Avenue, and four doors removed on the opposite side of the way long lived General Horace Porter, one of Grant's numerous biographers and the last survivor of his staff. Porter was also one of the wittiest of after-dinner speakers, held in grateful memory by many a veteran reporter forced in his time to listen to a seemingly endless flow of oratory of the dull and commonplace order.

At 46 East Thirtieth Street was the last abode of Francis Pharcellus Church, who helped to found the *Galaxy Magazine,* and afterward, for nearly a third of a century, was one of the most vigorous and original writers in the service of the New York *Sun.* Edward Henry Chapin, eloquent preacher of the Unitarian creed, died at 14 East Thirty-fourth Street, while a block to the east, at 48 East Thirty-fourth Street, was the home for a number of years of Francis Lieber, a noteworthy and inspiring figure in the group of gifted men which Germany, in the early decades of the last century, gave to the New World. Born in Berlin in 1800, the youth of Lieber was passed in the turmoil that followed Napoleon's onslaught on Prussia, and he imbibed as a child the intense hatred of tyranny and despotism, and the passionate faith in personal and political liberty, which were ever afterward the mainsprings of his life.

After Waterloo came a period of political reaction in Germany, and Lieber, who sang and talked too much of freedom, was imprisoned, forbidden to study in the universities, and finally compelled to flee his native land. During the next ten years he was a refugee in Greece, in Rome, and in London, whence, at the age of twenty-seven he sailed for America. He was for a time a teacher of gymnastics in Boston, but soon proposed and found a publisher for the *Encyclopedia Americana* which he edited, largely wrote, and carried to a success, which long made it the most authoritative American work of reference. This task ended another opportunity opened to him in his election to the chair of political history and economics in the South Carolina State College at Columbia, a position which he filled for twenty years, and which gave him, though regarded by him as an intellectual exile, leisure and opportunity to write the books on government which brought him fame.

For fifteen years, from 1857 Lieber was a member of the faculty of Columbia College, honored and beloved by successive generations of students. He was, at the same time, a distinguished figure in the social life of the town, and his home in East Thirty-fourth Street was a meeting-place for men and women who found inspiration in the extent and depth of their host's knowledge and his broad and virile way of applying it. "He looked the great man he was," writes a friend, "and there was something majestic about his way of discussing great topics. Thoroughly conversant with the best thoughts of other writers on political subjects, he was as independent in his thinking as any wise man is likely to be. Most political writers have looked at political life from a single point of view—that of their own times. Lieber looked at it from the viewpoint of every period presented in the successive cycles of human progress, and not only appreciated the results of the workings of various institutions at particular epochs, but noted the growth and mutation of those institutions from age to age." Lieber died in 1872, and his grave should be a place of pilgrimage for all who believe in the future of government for and by the people.

A house at 150 East Thirty-fourth Street long distinguished from its fellows by a studio window rising above its roof, was for upward of a generation the home of Francis Hopkinson Smith, an engineer skilled in the construction of lighthouses and, as a diversion, a painter in oils and water colors and a writer of books of travel which he also illustrated, who after he was fifty won gratifying and abundant success as a novelist. Among his tales which still claim readers were *Tom Grogan, Caleb West, Master Diver* and *Colonel Carter of Cartersville*, the last duly turned into a play which had a long and profitable career. Named for one of the signers of the Declaration of Independence and born in Baltimore, Smith had the ways and restless energy of a native of New England, but he always found time for leisure hours with friends, and for helpful service to beginners in art and letters held in grateful memory by men and women now grown old. Best of all he never lost his love for the picturesque in nature and life. In his last years arriving by night at Cold Spring Harbor for a sketching holiday a companion took him on the water by moonlight. At the end of a happy half hour he stood up in the boat, and with fervor announced to land and water: "I will let you know I am here in the morning." And there is little doubt that he kept his word.

John Swinton, whose trenchant gift of expression and individual point of view contributed for a generation to the influence and prestige of the New York *Sun,* once resided at 134 East Thirty-fourth Street, and four doors westward on the same side of the way William Peterfield Trent lived during his early years as professor of English literature at Columbia, years in which he produced his history of American letters, and other of his best work as author and as editor of the writings of Milton and Defoe. Miriam Coles Harris, author of *Rutledge,* and a dozen other widely read novels, lived for many years at 125 East Thirty-fifth Street. Four doors eastward was the abode of

Charles Henry Parkhurst during the years when as the militant pastor of the Madison Avenue Church he was one of the great pulpit orators of New York. Robert Underwood Johnson, who served under and then succeeded Gilder as editor of the *Century Magazine,* lived for many years at 327 Lexington Avenue. Johnson's experiences as editor and poet, and later as minister to Italy are set forth with insight and unfailing good humor in his *Remembered Yesterdays,* published in 1923 in which one finds faithfully pictured the literary New York of half a century and more ago. He was one of the first to discover the story-telling gifts of Frank Stockton and George W. Cable, of John Luther Long and Thomas Nelson Page; and in other ways he served generously and well his period and fellow craftsmen.

Again, the career of Willa Cather as a writer of masterly fiction came to an end at 570 Park Avenue where she died in late April, 1947, a few months past her seventieth birthday. Born in Virginia and reared on a Nebraska farm where in girlhood she had intimate contact with a generation of sturdy pioneers of alien birth, Miss Cather arrived at the vocation of novelist by way of the teacher and the editor's desk. And she wrote with direct and resolute vision of the life she had known in her youth. Thus in *O Pioneers, My Antonia, One of Ours* and the tales that followed them she recalled and gave life to the farm women she had known as a girl, and to the wind, the dust and the far horizons that environed them. Sparing of detail she made that environment emerge through her tales. Perhaps in fuller measure than any other woman writer of her time she helped to mould what is now styled the "American tradition."

CHAPTER IX

BELOW AND BEYOND THE HARLEM

Samuel L. Clemens was buried from the Brick Presbyterian Church at Fifth Avenue and Thirty-seventh Street. Charles Anthon died at 12 East Thirty-seventh Street, and four doors eastward on the other side of the way was the home after 1870 of Parke Godwin, son-in-law and biographer of Bryant, and long his associate in the editorship of the *Evening Post*. A block distant an apartment house at the corner of Lexington Avenue and Thirty-seventh Street was the last home of Irvin Shrewsbury Cobb, fellow of infinite jest and so diligent a laborer in divers fields of literary endeavour that few writers of any age or country have excelled him in productivity. Cobb began his career as a newspaper writer in his native Kentucky at the age of sixteen and for more than half a century, mainly in New York, he worked for the pleasure of his countrymen, his books when he ceased from labor numbering more than three score titles. A robust American, never afraid to speak his piece, he lived to see himself become a tradition. Perhaps now and again he offended good taste, but his irony and humor, which found happiest expression in his sketches celebrating Judge Priest, amused and refreshed a great army of readers. And Cobb had also a gift for friendship which caused him to be best liked by those who knew him best.

The last home of Josiah Gilbert Holland, two generations ago a dominant force in the literary life of New York, was at 46 Park Avenue. Dr. Holland was born in Belchertown, Massachusetts, in 1819, and after a struggling youth passed mainly in Northampton, was graduated in 1844 from the Berkshire Medical College. He practiced for a time in Springfield, but literature was the calling to which his taste and powers attracted him, and in 1849 he abandoned medicine for the assistant editorship of the Springfield *Republican,* becoming at the end of two years a part owner of the paper. He had found his true vocation, and in the editorial columns of the *Republican* soon proved himself an effective preacher of social and domestic moralities. His articles more often than not were short and pithy lay sermons, dealing in a practical way with questions of conduct and character, and they found instant favor with readers who took life as a serious and earnest affair.

In 1858 some of the best of them were published in book form under the title of *Timothy Titcomb's Letters,* and this was the first of a series of books, including a number of tales in prose and verse, which reached a total sale of more than a half million copies, making Dr. Holland one of the most successful, as he was one of the most popular, of American authors. He remained in the office of the *Republican* until 1857, and for seven years more was a constant contributor to its columns; a little later he sold his interest in the establishment, and in 1868 went to Europe. There he remained two years, and there with his friend Roswell Smith, a man who combined rare business ability with a love of letters, he planned the founding of the periodical known first as *Scribner's Monthly,* and later as the *Century Magazine.* He edited the *Century* until his death in 1881, and it long remained a monument to his memory.

George Arthur Plimpton, publisher and diligent searcher after rare books, lived for many years at 61 Park Avenue, and there brought together what was accounted when he died in his eighty-first year the world's largest collection of precious and costly volumes and manuscripts dealing with educational matters from the earliest times, the last of the former to come into his hands, it is good to recall by one who was his occasional guest, dealing with the education of Chaucer. Five doors removed on the same side of the way was the home for many years of Elizabeth Bacon Custer, who died there in her ninety-first year. This gifted woman, widow of the gallant soldier who fell on the Little Big Horn in 1876 in a memorable battle with the Sioux, was in turn the author of a series of delightful books on the life of the regular army's mounted men in the old days of Indian warfare and remote frontier posts sure to find delighted readers through the long future. And at 343 Madison Avenue was the site of Barnard College when Alice Duer Miller and Virginia Gildersleeve were numbered among its pupils.

Robert G. Ingersoll lived at 400 Fifth Avenue during his final years in New York, and at 108 East Thirty-eighth Street was the last home of Louis Joseph Vance, who as a writer of mystery fiction, to the number of upward of thirty volumes, for a quarter of a century enjoyed a devoted following. The home of Henry Van Dyke, when he quit the pulpit to become a professor at Princeton, was at 105 East Thirty-ninth Street. Clyde Fitch, the dramatist, lived for several years at 113 East Fortieth Street, and there wrote *The Girl and the Judge* and other of his strongest and most compelling plays. His study, his biographer tells us, was on the second floor with books covering the walls and its general color a warm green. The owner's desk was its keynote, and "on the latter there was brief space left to write so crowded was it with framed photographs, unanswered letters, scissors, paper-knife, cigarette-box, a bunch of violets, a long blue pencil, address-book and never idle telephone. The address-book might have struck because of overwork for everyone seemed to be in it. Fitch liked a great many people; he loved few, and even claimed a few bores among his acquaintances, for as he said: 'Everyone has his own bores; it's only other people's bores we can't stand'."

The first New York home of John Hay and his wife was at 11 East Forty-second Street, and the winter abode of Edwin Arlington Robinson at 328 in the same thoroughfare, where in keeping with the tastes that governed his recluse ways of living, he occupied an upper room in the house of his sculptor friend, James E. Fraser. The few intimates who were permitted to visit him in his attic sanctuary took care not to make known his address lest he be troubled by calls from curious strangers. The walls of the room were bare except for a photograph of Emerson and a sombre landscape in oil painted by a friend of the poet. Here Robinson received his friends; read Shakespeare, Cervantes, the Bible and other books in which he found renewing delight, those of Melville, Dickens and Hardy among them, and meditated and put on paper his last efforts as a poet. And from this room, when stricken by what proved a mortal illness in the spring of 1934, he was taken to the hospital ward where he passed from life.

Philip Schaff, during his latter years, lived at 15 East Forty-third Street, and there brought to a conclusion his imposing *History of the Christian Church*. An office building at 571 Fifth Avenue now occupies the site of the Windsor Hotel, long the winter home of Josh Billings, and the Lotos Club for many years prior to 1908 was located at 558 Fifth Avenue. Another building at the corner of Fifth Avenue and Forty-fourth Street covers the site of the Church of the Divine Paternity where during the later decades of the last century Edward Hubbell Chapin, burly and huge headed and one of the great pulpit orators of his generation, preached to intent congregations which often included Horace Greeley and Phineas Taylor Barnum.

It was from Chapin's church that on a gray December day in 1872 Greeley dead was carried to his long rest in Greenwood; and thence a short walk eastward carries one to another part of the town which once had intimate association with the editor of the *Tribune*. A century ago this part of Manhattan was known as Turtle Bay and given over in the main to open fields. Only a few scattered houses flecked the bank of the East River, and one of these, set down at the foot of Forty-ninth Street, following the spring of 1845 was for a time the country home of Greeley. The house occupied by the editor of the *Tribune* was a rambling wooden structure, set down in a ten-acre plot, with ample shrubbery and shade, and reached, as Greeley tells us, by a long lane from the Boston Road, while the only regular communication with town was by an hourly stage on Third Avenue. It was there that he began the tree chopping that thereafter was to be his favorite exercise. "I am a poor tree chopper," he said of himself. "Yet the ax is my doctor and my delight. Its use gives the mind just enough occupation to prevent its falling into reveries and absorbing trains of thought, while every muscle of the body receives sufficient yet not exhausting exercise. If every youth and man from fifteen to fifty years old could or would wield an ax two hours a day dyspepsia would vanish from the earth and rheumatism become scarce. I wish all boys would learn to love an ax."

Margaret Fuller was then a writer for the *Tribune* and remained a member of the Turtle Bay household until in August, 1846, she sailed for Europe—Mrs. Greeley had met her in Boston or at Brook Farm and persuaded an at first reluctant husband to give her employment—and her letters testify to the delight she found in this suburban retreat—the wide hall and the piazza, the garden and the trees, the rocks and the gliding sails. "I have never been so well situated," she writes to her brother in New Orleans. "As to a home—the place where we live is old and dilapidated, but in a situation of great natural loveliness. When there I am perfectly secluded, yet every one I wish to see comes to see me, and I can get to the center of the city in half an hour. The house is kept in a Castle Rackrent style, but there is all affection for me and desire to make me feel at home; and I do feel so, which could scarcely have been expected from such an arrangement. My room is delightful; how I wish you could sit at its window with me and see the sails glide by! As to the public part, that is entirely satisfactory. I do just as I please, and the editors express themselves perfectly satisfied; and others say my pieces tell to a degree I could not expect. I think, too, I shall do better and better. I am truly interested in the great field which opens before me, and it is pleasant to be sure of a chance at half a hundred thousand readers. Mr. Greeley I like—nay, more, love. He is in his habits a plebeian, in his heart a nobleman. His abilities in his own way are great. He believes in mine to a surprising extent. We are true friends."

Richard Washburn Child, journalist, author and lawyer, whose helpful part in the nomination and election of Warren Harding led to his appointment as ambassador to Italy came to the end of restless and crowded days at 277 Park Avenue, and at 340 Park Avenue was the winter home of Frances Hodgson Burnett, during her last years of success and large returns as an author and of unfailing helpfulness to less fortunate friends.

The house numbered 35 Beekman Place, a secluded and picturesque thoroughfare which fronts the East River between Forty-ninth and Fifty-first Streets, was the home of Henry Harland, when he wrote *As It Was Written,* the *Yoke of Thorah,* and other well remembered stories of Jewish life in New York. Harland was then in his early twenties, and a clerk in the office of the local surrogate, but the success of his first books decided his career and after 1886 he devoted himself wholly to literary labors. In 1889 he settled in London and there and in Paris he made his home until an attack of consumption drove him to San Remo where he died in 1905 at the age of forty-two. Harland developed with the years into a maker of such dainty and polished stories as the *Cardinal's Snuffbox,* and *My Friend Prospero.* He had style and imagination and by those to whom his books had given delight his early death was mourned as a genuine loss to literature.

George Ripley, social reformer and wise shaper of public taste, died at 661 Fifth Avenue, and at 21 East Fifty-second Street was long the New York home of Peter Finley Dunne, creator of Mr. Dooley, a character once as famous at home and abroad as William J. Bryan or Theodore Roosevelt. Dunne well deserves an understanding biographer. A native of Chicago he left one of the high schools of that city to become a reporter as soon as he could find a city editor who would employ him. This was at the age of eighteen. He worked first for the *Evening Post,* then was city editor of the *Times* and after that editorial writer on the *Times-Herald.* One James McGarry, a saloon-

keeper in Dearborn Street, had a happy way of commenting on
men and current events. Dunne listening to McGarry's observations on the death and burial of Jay Gould, voted them so amusing that he wrote them out with slight changes and alterations,
and his article when it appeared met with such a hearty reception
that it was promptly followed by other reports of McGarry's
humorous sayings. Thus came into being that far-famed individual, Mr. Dooley of Archey Road.

Then the Spanish-American War gave Dooley and his interpreter their opportunity and a diverting sketch, *Uncle George
Dewey,* caught the country, Dewey himself advising the author
that he liked it better than anything else that had been written
about him. Practically in a day, as it were, Dunne's reputation
became a national one. His shrewd, diverting articles when first
published caused an army of readers to burst into laughter, and
later gathered into books brought wider fame and added profit
to their author—his first collection, *Mr. Dooley in Peace and
War,* selling ten thousand copies a month for many months.
Dunne knew how to wed wit and humor so that his articles
always left with the reader an impression of fundamental truth.
And they had a versatility and a lasting quality which gave them
point and freshness for a later circle of readers. Dunne fell on
silence while his rare and individual gift was still functioning in
an effective way. A New York admirer had placed a generous
annuity at his disposal, and his last days were leisurely and comfortable but unproductive ones.

Major George Haven Putnam, soldier, reformer, author and
publisher, who during eighty-six years of life played many parts
and was ever an embodiment of physical and intellectual vigor,
ended his days at 1 Sutton Place South. The home of Alice
Duer Miller when she died in 1942 was at 450 East Fifty-second
Street. Few writers of the last half century have left behind
them more gracious memories than did this gifted woman, born
and reared in New York. There was order and charm in all
that she wrote; several of her plays, if not classics, added to the
enjoyment of countless men and women; but her first and inmost
love was the writing of poetry, and she will be long and best
remembered for her brief tale in verse, the *White Cliffs of
Dover* written two years before her death which tells in unfor-
gettable lines of an American girl who wed an Englishman, lost
him in the First World War, and then faced the prospect of sending his son off to face death in the second one—a slim volume

of which many thousand copies were sold during its early months in print. Mrs. Miller may not have been a great poet, but she moved the popular heart when it needed stirring and so achieved the results all true poets strive for.

Francis Lewis Wellman, one of the great trial lawyers of his period, lived at 667 Madison Avenue when in ripe old age he wrote the last of the informing volumes, notably the *Art of Cross Examination,* which were the rich by-product of his lengthy labors at the bar; and not far away at 555 Park Avenue was the last New York abode of Frederick Peterson, long one of America's outstanding neurologists, and also a poet of quality and the writer of songs which still enjoy wide favor. The last home of Ralph Hoyt, an earlier poet of pleasant memory, was at 230 East Fifty-fourth Street. That of Alexander Woollcott was in an apartment house at the corner of Fifth Avenue and Fifty-fifth Street. A genial middleman of the arts, who began his career as a reporter and ended it as a town crier against untoward things, this unusual man was always at his best in the baroque and often exasperating role of Alexander Woollcott, and if now and then he appeared to find delight in making enemies he was also given to helpful and unworldly gestures. Another hand must pen the final estimate of him. Horace White, editor and shrewd measurer of his contemporaries, Abraham Lincoln and Lyman Trumbull among them, lived for years at 51 East Fifty-sixth Street, and at 140 East Fifty-sixth Street was the last abode of Joseph Benson Gilder, editor and author and not least gifted member of a gifted family. Frank Moore Colby, one of the wisest and wittiest writers of his period, did his last work at 326 East Fifty-seventh Street, and William Dean Howells lived at different periods of his old age at 12 and 50 East Fifty-eighth Street.

A block northward at 117 East Fifty-ninth Street, Myra Kelly dwelt with her parents when the first of her tales of child life were given to the world. This rarely gifted woman was born in Dublin, Ireland, but in childhood came with her parents to America. She was educated in New York, and at an early age became a primary teacher in an East Side public school. Her pupils were mainly Jewish children from the tenements, and from them, aided by an understanding mind and sympathetic heart, she gained the material of which she first made use in stories told to friends. These stories, based on incidents in the lives and clothed in the dialect of her pupils, won the fancy of her hearers, who urged her to try something with the magazines.

Accordingly, she wrote a *Christmas Present to a Lady,* her first story. Tradition has it that Miss Kelly manifolded it and sent it to two magazines, not expecting either to take it. Both did, and it was with some difficulty that the claims of the two editors were adjusted by a tactful friend. Recognition of her rare talent followed at once, and the stories she wrote, grew, as time went on, into books, which, blending drollery, pathos and tenderness, gave delight to jaded readers and influenced for good the methods of many of the societies and organizations which seek to make worthy citizens of the children of the Ghetto. Length of days, however, was denied their author. She died in 1910, at the end of a vain search for health, which had carried her across seas, and the Devon hills guard her grave at Torquay.

For four years following 1873 the father, mother and four small boys of whose doings Clarence Day was to make himself the droll and diverting chronicler lived at 251 Madison Avenue, but in 1877 they moved to 420 Madison Avenue then a quieter neighborhood, where were enacted the scenes and incidents, transformed into a droll classic in *Life With Father.* There, parents and red-headed children lived through most of the experiences which wait upon an average American family—ailments, broken legs, days in school, fights with neighboring toughs and paternal fretfulness and impatience. Nothing out of the ordinary happened to them, but the eldest of the four boys stored up in memory, item by item, the details of their life, that of a quarrelsome but affectionate and lovable family, and long afterward, in days of hopeless and helpless invalidism, recorded them with inimitable yet veracious joyousness of spirit in *Life With Father,* a book which, translated into various languages, has been read and eagerly reread by hundreds of thousands of people. The last home of Clarence Day was at 139 East End Avenue.

An old mansion which overlooks the East River from a high terrace at the foot of Sixty-first Street claims a modest place in the literary annals of New York. The house in question was built in 1799 by Colonel William S. Smith, who had married the only daughter of President John Adams. Smith had acquired wealth in trade and designed the house as a present for his wife. No expense was spared in the building, but when the walls were up and the roof on, Smith failed and the house which thereafter was known as Smith's Folly, passed to a new owner who com-

pleted it and opened it as a roadhouse. There in 1833 James
Stuart had lodgings and wrote the great part of his *Three Years
in America.* Stuart was a choleric Scotsman, who, having slain
in a duel Sir Alexander Boswell, elder son of Johnson's biographer, found temporary refuge in the United States, and on
his return to Edinburgh published his impressions of the New
World. Stuart's book shows clear insight into our political institutions, but its strictures on our social short-comings proved
at the time as salt and vinegar to a thin-skinned people. Smith's
Folly which, when Stuart lodged there, must have been one of the
show places of the town, consists of two wings and a connecting
hall, and is quaint to an unusual degree. Heavy columns support
the second, which is also the main story, and you enter by a doorway flanked on either side by windows whose tiny panes light
a hallway that might have been modeled from sketches by Pyle
and Parsons. Among those who visited Smith's Folly in its roadhouse days, was Jermial Towle, who attracted by its architecture,
bought it and made it his home. This was in 1834 and it long
remained in the possession of the family.

George Michael Cohan, who began his career as a comedian
of the boisterous sort and ended it as a writer of plays in which
his acting gave delight to a multitude of playgoers, passed his
painful last years at 993 Fifth Avenue, and at 1136 Fifth Avenue
was long the home of Mrs. William Bourke Cockran, born Anna
Louise Ide—by native endowment a woman of personality and
charm, and by fortunate gift the holder of a unique place in
literary annals. In 1891 when her father Henry Clay Ide was
United States Land Commissioner of Samoa and the future Mrs.
Cockran a girl of fifteen, Robert Louis Stevenson, then a resident
of Samoa with only three more years to live, learning that her
birthday fell on Christmas Day, and that she was thus "denied
the consolation and profit of a proper birthday" declared that he
would give her a birthday at another place in the calendar. Accordingly he deeded to her his birthday, November 13, stipulating
that it be used "with moderation and humanity," and also enjoin-
ing that it should be observed with "the sporting of fine raiment,
eating of rich meats and receipts of gifts, compliments and copies
of verses according to the manner of our ancestors." Thence-
forward the recipient of this rare gift observed November 13 as
her birthday. On one of the last of them Mrs. Cockran gave a
dinner to a few old friends, some of them going back to her girlhood days in the South Seas, and then went with her guests to a

theater to witness the performance of a George Cohan play.

Joseph Choate, lawyer, orator and sterling American, ended his days at 8 East Sixty-third Street. The home of Edward Sanford Martin during the latter years of his life in New York was at 179 East Sixty-fourth Street and there he died in 1939 at the age of eighty-three. Born in upstate New York and a graduate of Harvard, Martin was co-founder and first editor of the humorous weekly, *Life,* and until 1928, a period of more than two score years, wrote its editorial page. He also for a considerable time contributed editorials to *Harper's Weekly,* and, by eminent fitness for the place, filled the Editor's Easy Chair of *Harper's Magazine* as the successor of Curtis and Howells. Self-effacing modesty was part of the man, but he was also an unyielding, if gentle, champion of old-fashioned liberalism in a changing world. Martin's terse but keenly sagacious comments on the social and political problems of the nation, clothed in easy, graceful English, more often than not sparkled with wit and humor. His was an ideal style for an essayist, and this delightful fact had fresh and more enduring proof when he gathered the best of his writings into a group of volumes which began with *Windfalls of Observation* and ended with *Unrest of Women*—these pleasantly interspersed with volumes of verse which helped to win their author a devoted following. Like Lamb before him, no one enjoyed in fuller measure the love and esteem of the writers of his own generation, and no one more richly deserved them.

A brownstone house which until 1928 stood at 3 East Sixty-sixth Street, was the last home of General Ulysses S. Grant. It was bought by friends and presented to Mrs. Grant in 1879, soon after their return from Europe. Here occurred the most heroic struggle of the General's life. The failure of the firm of Grant & Ward, in which he was special partner, left him in the spring of 1884 with hardly a dollar he could call his own. Soon his health failed and he was told that his span of life must be a brief one. Then it was that, gazing as it were into the open grave, he nerved himself for his last battle. He had begun his *Personal Memoirs,* upon whose sale he counted for the future support of his family, but the monetary value of the book would be greatly depreciated if it should be completed by any hand but his own. This thought gave the stricken man courage to hold death at bay until he could secure a competence to his loved ones.

Well has it been said by his friend, Adam Badeau, that "the spectacle of the hero who had earned and worn the highest earthly honors, working amid the miseries of a sick-chamber to glean the gains he knew he could never enjoy—the fainting warrior, propped up to stammer out utterances to sell for the benefit of his children—can find no parallel." Strength of will sustained him through a task that might fairly have occupied a well man trained to literary effort for several years. Every line was either written by General Grant or dictated by him. And he won in the race with death, completing the last chapter on July 19, 1885. His task accomplished, will and strength alike failed, and on the twenty-third of the same month the end came. But his last battle was a triumphant one, for no book ever written in America by a single hand has returned a large reward. More sufficing, however, is the thought that the unselfish labor which brought this reward made Grant's last days the greatest of a great career.

Many of the books which won Henry Osborn Taylor a foremost place among the historians of civilization were written at 135 East Sixty-sixth Street. A native of New York and a graduate at Harvard and the Columbia Law School, Dr. Taylor began as a writer of legal treatises but soon turned to "the study of what other men deemed best and had striven to attain in thought and work and conduct." He gave ten years of study and labor to his *Ancient Ideals* published in 1896; like time and effort were devoted to his masterpiece, the *Medieval Mind,* and he was still occupied with his favorite pursuits when death claimed him at the age of eighty-four. Few men have made so splendid and wide-ranging a contribution to American scholarship.

The last home of Clarence Clough Buel, long one of the editors of the *Century Magazine* and author and conductor of some of that periodical's most important undertakings, was at 180 East Sixty-seventh Street. That of Stephen Vincent Benet at a later time was at 215 East Sixty-eighth Street, and there, a writer of rare gifts and extraordinary vigor of thought, he died in 1942, almost without warning at the age of forty-four. Born and reared in a family of writers, Benet came first into notice in 1928 when he won the Pulitzer Prize for his *John Brown's Body,* a poem of 10,000 lines which told a swiftly-moving story of the Civil War in all its aspects, and of which more than half a million copies are now in American homes. Benet's later output included the *Devil and Daniel Webster,* in which Beelzebub is argued out of his just dues by the great advocate, and when he died he was at work on another long poem, *Western Star* in which he purposed, in the tradition of *John Brown's Body,* to depict the sweep of American civilization. Recognition came to him in full and rounded measure, but he was never other than the modest workman, the understanding and gentle companion.

Herbert Croly, before he started on the long search for health from which he was not to return, lived at 255 East Seventy-first Street. Two blocks away at 57 East Seventy-second Street was the abode during the same period of Henry Holt, publisher, editor and author, who there wrote, when in the shadow of his eighty-fifth year, his lively yet mellow and tolerant *Garrulities of an Octogenarian.* When he died in 1923 Holt, who entered business in 1866, had been for long the dean of American publishers. Mystic and man of action in one, he remained in extreme old age a majestic, stalwart figure, vigorous in thought and action and with a kindly courtliness of manner which recalled an earlier time—a gallant fighter with a youthful spirit which persisted unabated until the very end.

The home of William Dean Howells for a brief period at the opening of the century was at 38 East Seventy-third Street; there he began the *Kentons* and finished his *Heroines of Fiction.* A short block distant, at 113 East Seventy-third Street, was during his last years the city home of Arthur Charles Train, lawyer, novelist and creator of Ephraim Tutt, a fictional character whose reality was taken for granted by countless numbers of readers. Born and reared in Boston and there admitted to the bar, Train settled in New York at the turn of the century, and, after brilliant service as a prosecutor, retired from practice to devote himself to writing, a vocation at which he had early tried his hand. In 1905 appeared the first of the fourteen volumes in which, to the delight of an ever growing clientele, he set forth the legal acumen of Ephraim Tutt, who wandered in and out of courts "inventing legal strategems for saving the technically guilty but morally innocent from the toils of the law." Indeed Tutt's exploits were described with such wealth of convincing detail that much of the time of his creator had to be devoted to answering letters of those ready on generous retainers to employ th lanky legal friend of the widow, orphan and service man. And now and again he found it difficult to convince his correspondents that Tutt had existence only in a story teller's fertile imagination. Be it noted in passing that Lawyer Train like Lawyer Tutt was prompt to guard the deserving from sharp practices. Thus in 1911 he helped to organize the Authors League of

America to protect writers from unscrupulous publishers and later served as its president.

The abode of Edward J. Wheeler during his last days as editor and helpful friend of writers struggling for a foothold in New York was at 55 East Seventy-sixth Street. And the home of Joel Elias Spingarn, when in 1939 death came to him, was at 110 East Seventy-eighth Street. Spingarn, although never as widely known as he should have been, was during most of his mature years one of the most interesting men in American life. Dismissed in 1911 from his post as head of the department of comparative literature at Columbia, in the main because of his stout championship of a fellow professor sorely in need of friends, in 1915, although a lover of peace, he gave up a literary career to bear his part, as a soldier, in the First World War. He came back from France a lieutenant-colonel, and mustered out of service resumed his lifelong labors for people handicapped by race or condition. A scholar who wrote with grace and precision, Joel Spingarn was first of all a lover of his country, and a shining exemplar of the patriotism we owe and must continue to owe to the Jews among us. He could not have earned higher honors had a greater length of strenuous days been granted him.

The house numbered 37 East Seventy-ninth Street recalls the tragic passing of Paul Leicester Ford, who was there done to death by a half-mad brother. Born in 1865, the son of a man of fortune who gathered about him one of the great private libraries of his period, all of Ford's mature years were given to scholarly pursuits. The father's collection of books, bequeathed in due time to the son, concerned itself particularly with American origins. Thus it was that the younger Ford, prompted in his choice of tasks by the materials at his command, came first into notice as the editor of many-volumed editions of the writings of Jefferson and Dickinson, and as the author of pamphlets and brochures dealing with historical subjects. He soon turned, however, to the making of fiction, and is best remembered as the author of *Janice Meredith* and other novels of original merit which enjoyed wide popularity when they first came from the press, and after the lapse of years still find readers. Yet more worthy of recollection is the fact that, a cripple and invalid from birth, success was won by Ford in the face of constant and heavy handicaps—handicaps met by him with a quiet heroism which added pathos to his untimely death.

Lucy Arnold Whitridge, the daughter of Matthew Arnold,

died at 39 East Seventy-ninth Street, and seven numbers eastward on the same side of the way is the present home of the Society Library. Robert William Chambers, for upward of a generation one of America's most popular novelists had his home during his middle period, at 43 West Eighty-third Street, and Edward Brewster Sheldon lived for a score of years and died at 35 East Eighty-fourth Street. Sheldon's career was a tragic yet inspiring one. Born in Chicago, in 1886 while still a student at Harvard he wrote his first play *Salvation Nell* in which Minnie Maddern Fiske assumed the title role. Five years later *Romance,* his most popular play, gave him first place among American dramatists, and thereafter until 1923 hardly a theatrical season went by without one or more Sheldon openings.

Then at thirty-seven Sheldon fell victim to a strange and shattering ailment. He became slowly paralyzed and for the rest of his life was forced to remain immobile in his bed. Moreover, in 1929 his sight also failed him, and only his hearing and his uncommon talent for the stage were left to him. But during the fifteen years that remained to him he did not lose touch with his chosen calling. The major figures of the stage found their way to his bedside and read him parts before accepting them. Managers sought his advice and until 1930 in collaboration with others he continued to produce successful plays. And when he died in 1944 it was said of him that "he was not of the theater. Instead his life was the theater."

Frank Crane, preacher of the commonplace, lived at 3 West Eighty-fifth Street when in 1928 failing health impelled him to cross the seas to end his days in the south of France. Thence a stroll eastward and then northward along Central Park brings one to 1215 Fifth Avenue, the palatial last home of Arthur Brisbane, another preacher of the commonplace, but over a longer period and to a wider audience. Gifted with indefatigable energy, a keen sense of the accurate word and the timely theme, Brisbane was from early manhood to old age the best paid writer for the American press; but he was always the ready defender of the established order, and, speaking the language of those who read as they run, rarely if ever got far below the surface of things—perhaps a harsh verdict, but of the sort his reformer father, if permitted to do so, doubtless would have recorded against him.

At 1309 Fifth Avenue, a house that was then the home of Walt Whitman's friend John H. Johnston, was the scene of a poignant incident in the life of the poet. It is a familiar story of how Anne Gilchrist, a woman of rare gifts of mind and heart, was one of the first to champion in England the cause of the author of *Leaves of Grass,* and of how after long correspondence, a widow with two grown children, she came to America intent upon becoming the wife of Whitman's old age. But in the gentlest way it was quickly made clear to her that the ailing and enfeebled poet had no thought of marriage. Thus a deep and sincere friendship was the only issue of a woman's odd adventure, and after brief sojourns, first in Philadelphia and then in New England and New York, Mrs. Gilchrist returned to end her days in England.

On the eve of their departure in early June of 1879 she and her son and daughter were entertained by the Johnston family in Fifth Avenue and Whitman, who had frequently been their guest in Philadelphia and elsewhere, came from Camden to bid them farewell. One of Whitman's biographers devotes a feeling paragraph to his last hours with Mrs. Gilchrist. The day before she sailed, we are told, "the two friends held a long conference in the Johnston parlor. Both were deeply moved on rejoining the family. It was their real farewell."

The last home of James C. Grey, following 1918 literary editor of the New York *Sun,* was at 11 East Eighty-seventh Street, and that of Henry Bellamann at 2 East Eighty-seventh Street. Bellamann, a man of varied gifts, who turned to writing after a career in music which included service as dean of the Curtis Institute in Philadelphia, scored instant success in 1940 with his *Kings Row,* an arresting story of a small city in the Middle West, aloof from the Main Stream, and the people young and old who shaped its life. Six hundred thousand copies of this book were sold during a five-year period, and its author was at work on a sequel to it when he died in 1945 at the age of sixty-three. Bellamann came of a Missouri family of German descent which included Henry Edward Krebhiel, as recorded elsewhere, helpful early friend of Lafcadio Hearn and long music critic of the New York *Tribune.* His other books included several lesser novels and translations into English of the songs of Brahms and Dante's *Divine Comedy.*

At 24 East Ninety-first Street was the home in old age of Carl Schurz, friend of Lincoln and first among the men of foreign birth who have contributed to the greatness of America. Driven from his native Germany by the failure of the revolution in 1848, in which he took an active part, Schurz came to America in 1852, abode for a time in Philadelphia, and in 1858 began the practice of law in Milwaukee. Meanwhile he had mastered English, and developing without delay a large capacity for leadership, was one of the directing minds in the formation of the Republican Party; the breadth and force of his arguments against slavery convincing thousands who up to that time had held aloof from the great issue of the period. Lincoln appointed him minister to Spain, but he soon resigned that post to become a general in the Union Army, serving until the end of the war. Then he assumed the editorship of a German paper in St. Louis, and in 1869 was chosen a senator from Missouri. In 1877 he entered the cabinet of Hayes as Secretary of the Interior, and while holding that office led in the work of making the merit system an integral part of the public service.

The last twenty-five years of Schurz's life were passed in and near New York, and, though during that time he held no public office, his large and eager nature made him, until the end, the ready champion of pure purposes in affairs of government, and a brilliant and uncommon figure in business and social life. Few moderns have surpassed him in kindling, effective use of the spoken word, while his admirable exercise of the lucid English style early acquired by him, gave him with the passage of years, a secure place among American authors. His life of Henry Clay is the best account we have of the career of that statesman, and the *Reminiscenes of a Long Life*, which he did not live to complete, written with a simple frankness that is full of charm, are also a noteworthy contribution to American history. He died in 1906 at the age of seventy-seven, and now that passions once hot have been cooled by time the memory of him that endures is of a man of high and austere ideals who through nearly sixty years strove without faltering for the truth as he saw it.

Again one finds at 71 East Ninety-second Street the site of an apartment house which for nine years following 1916 was the home of Hamlin Garland. There much of Garland's *Middle Border* chronicle took shape, and there welcome was once and again given to Henry B. Fuller, a rarely gifted man whose patiently meditated and finely wrought tales call for reprinting. "Next to Howells," Garland wrote of Fuller after the latter's death in 1929, "he was my most trusted literary adviser, his judgments always ready, incisive and just. Wise, witty, humorous . . . his merry laugh was evidence of an essential optimism, although he held and often voiced a despairing concept of human life. He is worthy of a volume. He should be treated like a character in fiction with fullest detail, and with the understanding humor which he himself would employ."

Lyman Abbott's long and useful life came to an end in 1922 at 1184 Lexington Avenue, and at 625 Park Avenue in the same part of the town was the home of Charles Ransom Miller during his final years of service as editor of the *Times*. Miller was born in 1849 at Hanover, New Hampshire; was graduated at Dartmouth in the class of 1872, the members of which persuaded Walt Whitman to read to them from his works on Commencement Day; and had his first training in journalism on the Springfield *Republican* under Samuel Bowles. In 1875 he journeyed to New York to join in a modest capacity the staff of the *Times*, and, rising steadily in the service of that journal, was its editor from 1883 until his death in 1922. Than Miller no journalist of his generation in the shaping of American thought and discussion rendered weightier service over a longer period. His personality he never thrust forward, but he knew all sorts and conditions of men; was a scholar with an extraordinary range of interest and information, and he wielded a trained and ready pen which, enforced by calm and disciplined judgment, gave effective service to every worthy cause. One of the writers of these pages counts an occasional hour with him at a time when great issues were taking final shape among the cherished and uplifting memories of other years.

North of the Harlem are three shrines which have abiding interest for the literary pilgrim—the old burial ground at Hunt's Point, where sleeps the poet Drake, and the cottage at Fordham, which has pathetic association with Poe, and not far removed the last home of Francis Carlin, the Irish poet. The tiny God's acre in which Drake was buried in 1820, lies on the left-hand side of the ancient Hunt's Point Road, in the Borough of the Bronx, a little less than a mile from the Hunt's Point railway station, as one goes eastward from the station to the point. It was formerly the burial-ground of the Hunt and Leggett families, who between them for generations owned much of the adjacent country, but since 1910 it has been a city park, bearing the name of the poet. Drake was distantly related to the Hunts; some of the happiest days of his boyhood were passed in the home of the family which overlooked the Sound at the extreme end of the point, and at his own request he was buried on their lands. His grave is marked by a marble shaft, inscribed with the lines in which Halleck bore loving witness to the beauty of his character, and it is good to know that, after years of neglect, it is now assured of reverent care through the long future.

Poe moved to Fordham in the spring of 1846, because doctors told him that his wife, who had been made an invalid through the bursting of a blood vessel, needed country air. The cottage which for the next three years was his home, still stands beside the Kingsbridge Road on the crest of Fordham Hill, at what is now One Hundred and Ninety-fourth Street. A story and a half structure with shingled sides and roof, a narrow portico, its roof supported by short wooden pillars, runs along the south side. A living-room and kitchen occupy what was originally the ground floor, and above stairs, under the low hipped roof is the room which was used by Poe as a study, and a box of a bed-room. Here, as elsewhere, poverty was the grim companion of the Poes. The husband's writings brought small returns in money, and they were often in want of food and fuel, nor was it long before it became clear that the wife's last illness was upon her. Mrs. Gove, who visited the cottage in the autumn of 1846, has left a touching description of the suffering which it housed. "I saw her (Poe's wife) in her bed-chamber," she writes. "There was no clothing on the bed—which was only straw—but a snow white counterpane and sheets. The weather was cold and the sick lady had the dreadful chills that accompany the hectic fever of consumption. She lay on the straw bed wrapped in her husband's great coat, with a large tortoise-shell cat on her bosom. The wonderful cat seemed conscious of her great usefulness. The coat and the cat were the sufferer's only means of warmth, except as her husband held her hands, and her mother, her feet."

Virginia Poe died in January, 1847, and was buried in the old Dutch cemetery in Fordham, but in 1878 her remains were removed to Baltimore and laid beside those of her husband. Poe remained a resident of Fordham for two years following his wife's death, with his mother-in-law, Mrs. Clemm, for a comrade, and during this period gave form to *Annabel Lee, Ulalume, For Annie,* the *Cask of Amontillado,* the *Domain of Arnheim,* and his fantastic and ambitious philosophical work, *Eureka.* Some of these efforts represented the finest flowering of his genius, but the sequel proved that they were written within the shadow. Their author left Fordham for the last time in June, 1848, and a few weeks later in Baltimore death put an end to his wanderings.

The cottage on Fordham Hill has twice changed its location since Poe's time. When Kingsbridge Road was widened a few years ago, it was moved further back, and its original site is now traversed by the broader thoroughfare. In 1913 possession of the cottage was acquired by the City of New York, and it was moved from the southeast corner of One Hundred and Ninety-fourth Street, across Kingsbridge Road to a tiny park which takes its name from the poet. It has been carefully restored and a basement added for the use of its present tenants, who have charge of a scant collection of Poe relics housed on the ground floor. Close to the original site of the cottage and shadowed by a tall apartment house which bears Poe's name, flourished until a few years ago, some of the cherry trees which once gave delight to the poet and his wife. In the rear the ground formerly sloped away to a grassy hollow, ending in a ledge of rocks which over-looked the valley below, and to the east the view stretched into Connecticut and over the Sound to the Long Island hills.

James Francis Carlin MacDonnell, known in literary circles as Francis Carlin, a poet of Irish ancestry who shaped for himself a singular career, lived during his last years at 660 East One Hundred and Eighty-third Street, the Bronx. Born at Bay Shore, Long Island, MacDonnell received his only formal education in a parochial school at Norwalk, Connecticut, and was a floorwalker at Macy's in New York when in 1918 he published his first volume of poems, *My Ireland,* under the pen name of Francis Carlin, in honor of a grandfather of that name, a weaver in County Tyrone, and a great story teller held in high regard by his descendant. The book won praise from lovers of good poetry, and so in 1920 did a second one the *Cairns of Stars.*

Then suddenly the poet dropped out of sight, and his where-abouts remained a mystery until in 1939 he was found going from one city employment agency to another searching for a job as a dishwasher or night watchman. Now white haired and sparing of speech, he explained to old friends that he had withdrawn from the world in order to think and to pursue undisturbed his most cherished pastime—the construction of the Bible, and that he had finally sought a job because he had spent his savings and had debts which troubled him. Again he secured employment, and his poems, charged always with a mystical quality, found favor with editors, but they failed to advance his earlier reputation, and his last days were unrecorded and uneventful ones.

Felix Adler, who began his career as a tutor of German

princes and ended it as an American educator and author of wide ranging activities, dwelt during his last years at 3902 Spuyten Duyvil Parkway. Edgehill Inn, a family hotel in the same section of the Bronx, was the last home of Ernest Sutherland Bates, author and critic, who there worked upon his somewhat cynical studies of Mary Baker Eddy and William Randolph Hearst; the history of American religious belief, which he finished just before his sudden death in 1939, and the editorial undertaking by which the public knows him best, the *Bible Designed to be Read as Living Literature,* which, widely circulated, has done for a later generation of students what the *Modern Readers' Bible* did for an earlier one. Trained as a theologian and philosopher, Bates was something more than a scholarly popularizer. He was also and always an eager, questing student of whatever concerned his fellowmen and could he have carried out any or all of the ambitious projects he had in mind when the end came almost without warning his place in the history of American thought might have been an outstanding one.

Perhaps Edmund Clarence Stedman's most satisfying years were passed in the plain but roomy cottage the pilgrim finds in one of the shaded streets of Lawrence Park, in another part of the Bronx—the poet's home at the turn of the century. "In his study, its walls stocked with volumes of poetry from all lands and all ages," writes a visitor, "he was wholly admirable. One honored him as a scholarly and charming man of letters as he sat behind his desk surrounded by treasured portraits, manuscripts, and letters. He was especially hospitable to young poets and, although many of his supposed swans proved to be geese, his influence was altogether helpful to authorship. Like Howells he stood for plain living and high thinking as distinctly as Emerson and Lowell had done in their time."

A bit farther afield at 31 Pondfield Road in Bronxville one finds the last home of Felix Riesenberg, belated yet masterly teller of tales of the sea. The son of a shipmaster father, Riesenberg was born in Milwaukee in 1879 and educated in part in the public schools of that city. When he was seventeen the sea called him, and during the next dozen years he made voyages, both in sail and steam, to many parts of the world, first as a sailor before the mast and later as an officer of the Coast and Geodetic Survey. In 1906 he was a member of the Wellman polar expedition. Five years later he received from Columbia a degree in civil engineering, and for the remainder of his days followed that vocation as a means of support. Riesenberg published his first book, *Under Sail,* in 1915 when he was thirty-six, to meet with immediate acclaim from a steadily enlarging circle of readers, and before his death in 1939 nearly a score of novels, sketches and recollections came from his pen, among them such outstanding volumes as *Log of the Sea* and *Endless River.* He had keenly enjoyed his days at sea, and he wrote of them with the zest and gusto of the born story-teller. When working under the spell of a deep emotion he rarely failed to move and hold his readers, and Cooper or Dana would have been glad to claim Riesenberg's arresting account of his ship, when the Straits of Magellan were impassable, finding shelter in a night of snow. He was also a great talker in a period which could boast few great talkers and rare hours of food and speech are abiding memories for those privileged to know and companion with him.

Finally, a spacious house overlooking the Hudson and the Palisades at Riverdale has poignant association with one of the closing chapters in the life of Mark Twain. In the fall of 1901 the uncertain health of Mrs. Clemens prompted the family's removal from the city to a home in the country. "They decided," writes Albert Bigelow Paine, "that they must have easy access to the New York center, but they wished also to have the advantage of space and spreading lawn and trees, large rooms and light." After due consideration it was decided that the Appleton homestead at Riverdale assured all of these things. Built in the last century by a member of the historic Morris family, it later passed into the possession of the founder of the publishing house of Appleton, who enlarged and beautified it and named it Holbrook Hall.

There were pleasant neighbors at Riverdale, and except for the illness of the wife and mother, the Clemens family found life there an agreeable one. Many old friends made their way to Riverdale, not least among them William Dean Howells. "Clemens has got so far from town as Spuyten Duyvil," Howells wrote Aldrich in November, 1901, "and is beyond the reach of all the dinners he does not want to accept. I was at his house one afternoon, and saw his Hudson and his Palisades, and some of the steamboats he delights in more. He is the only tie that binds me here, to the old times (they *were* good, weren't they?) and I'm sorry he's got a time-table's length away." And Howells writes in another place: "They kept no carriage, and there was a snowy night when I drove up to their handsome old mansion in the station carryall, which was crusted with mud, as from the going down of the Deluge after transporting Noah and his family from the Ark to whatever point they decided to settle provisionally. But the good talk, the rich talk, the talk that could never suffer poverty of mind or soul was there, and we jubilantly found ourselves in our middle youth."

One of the present writers recalls across the years a visit to Riverdale in the late spring of 1903, a visit prompted by a pardonable desire on the part of the visitor to renew a pleasant association between the most widely known writer of his era and a youthful newspaper laborer begun in an earlier time at Elmira. The visitor's welcome was a kindly one, and, except for an occasional question, Mark Twain did all of the talking. It was the wise and whimsical talk which was part of the man, and it was with keen regret that the caller at the end of an hour bade what proved a final farewell to his host. The Clemenses were then preparing to take up residence in Florence, and early in the following October they departed on the voyage from which Mrs. Clemens was not to return.

And at 968 Kelly Street, the Bronx, one finds the apartment house which was the last home of Solom Aleichem, the Jewish humorist born Solomon Rabinowitch, whom Mark Twain was one of the first to welcome when in 1914 at the age of fifty-five he crossed the Atlantic to end his days in America. "I wanted to meet you," was Mark Twain's greeting, "for I am told that I am the American Solom Aleichem." The newcomer's reply has not been preserved, but had he not been a modest as well as rarely gifted man he could have said that he was the voice of Russian Jewry as his visitor was of the American West of his youth.

Born of middle class parentage at Pereyeslav in the Ukraine, Rabinowitch became an author at twenty-four when, without set purpose and as brief relief from distracting worry, he put on paper some fantasies of his childhood. These the editor of a Yiddish journal printed, demanding more of the same sort, and taking as a pen name Solom Aleichem, two words which freely translated into English mean, Good morning! their author began a career of such range and purpose that his collected works run to thirty volumes made up of more than three hundred stories, five novels and many plays—all set off by a style those competent to pass judgment declare the most impressive Yiddish of his era.

In measured degrees the spiritual heir not only of Rabelais and Cervantes, but also of Heine and Dickens, Solom Aleichem, humorous, whimsical and tolerant, was in the end and always his inimitable self—a simple and candid genius who knew how in his writings, which no doubt lose much in translation, to artlessly yet perfectly express his people, "their mind, heart, wit, wisdom, and above all their perfect idiom." He left his native land to escape what seemed to him the endless tyranny of the Romanoffs, but could length of days been granted him it would no doubt have greatly surprised this gentle soul to have found himself the best beloved and most widely read author in the Russia ruled by Stalin and his fellows.

Instead, after long and wasting illness, he died in his Kelly Street apartment in May, 1916, for his race the darkest hours of the First World War. Three bearded and aging Jews from his native Pereyeslav, devoutly observant of the last rites of an ancient faith performed them for him, and unnumbered thousands gathered to mourn his passing or to witness the progress of his funeral procession through crowded streets. But after the cremation there was long and sharp dispute among his kinsfolk and friends as to choice of an appropriate resting-place for the ashes of Solom Aleichem. "Let me be buried among the poor," he had written, "that their graves may shine on mine, and mine on theirs"; and at long last a grave was made for him in the Workmen's Circle Cemetery, Cypress Hills, Brooklyn. Only a tall black shaft distinguishes it from those around it, but it has become a shrine to which each returning year thousands, not all of them Jews, make reverent pilgrimage.

CHAPTER X

The name of Walt Whitman heads a goodly roll of authors who in other days dwelt in the old town of Brooklyn, now a part of the greater city. The poet, whom growing numbers regard as one of the elemental forces in America life and thought, passed many years in Brooklyn, and it holds more than one reminder in brick and mortar of his picturesque career. Born at West Hills in 1819, of mingled New England and Dutch stock, Whitman was a child of four years when his parents moved to Brooklyn and took up their residence in Front Street. Two years later the elder Whitman, who was a carpenter, built and occupied a house in Cranberry Street, opposite the rear of Plymouth Church, and this structure stood until a few years ago, when it was demolished, nothing now remaining but the foundation.

A third removal in 1826 took the Whitmans to a house at 251 Adams Street, then in the outskirts of the town. This house, which was the home of young Walter during the years when he was attending the schools of the neighborhood, still stands, but with its lower part converted into a store. The growing lad left school at thirteen to enter as errand boy the law office of William Clarke, on Fulton Street, near to Orange. Meanwhile he had become a subscriber to the Mercantile Library, then housed in Montague Street, and most of his leisure hours were devoted to reading, in which the Bible and Shakespeare, we are told, played a major part. When he was fourteen he entered as printer's apprentice the office of the *Long Island Patriot,* on Fulton Street near Concord, passing at the end of four years to the service of the *Long Island Star,* which had its office at the corner of Orange and Fulton Streets.

By this time Whitman had become a master printer, and a contributor to the newspapers and magazines of the period. Love of the open however, was from the first a dominant passion with him, and in due time, drew him from the town to school teaching in the country. When he was twenty he was editing a paper at Huntingdon. The venture did not prosper, and the year 1840 found him once more in Brooklyn. During his absence his father had moved to 106 Myrtle Avenue, where he had built a substantial frame house, with a store on the ground floor, which stood until 1927, in a fair state of preservation, but with the number changed to 106. Here the son took up his abode when he returned to the city, and here for a brief period he published a weekly paper called the *Salesman and Travelers' Director for Long Island,* conducting at the same time a general printing business.

Another turn of the wheel furnished Whitman employment as a printer and newspaper writer in the city across the river, and while thus engaged during the next half dozen years, he gave his leisure to cordial intercourse with all sorts and conditions of men, thus securing the friendly and intimate knowledge of the life of the masses, of which he was in due time to make compelling use as a poet. In 1840 he became editor of the Brooklyn *Eagle,* which then had its office at 30 Fulton Street, but quit that post in 1848 for a leisurely tour through the Southwest, joining at its close the staff of the New Orleans *Crescent.* A journey through the Northwest, during which, as in New Orleans, he studied American life at its sources, brought him back in 1850 to Brooklyn, and to the editorship of the *Freeman,* a short-lived daily and weekly publication which championed the Free-Soil cause.

Soon after Whitman's return from the South his family moved to Cumberland Street, near Atlantic, but the year 1855 found them in a new home, this time at 142 Skillman Street, near Myrtle Avenue. Before this removal Walt had quit journalism to become a builder and seller of houses in the outer reaches of the town, and it was in the leisure these new labors afforded him that he put on paper the poetic message which, born of years of sympathetic contact with his fellows, had long been taking shape in his mind. When he had finished *Leaves of Grass,* twelve poems setting forth in an unusual way the larger meaning life had come to hold for him, he set with his own hands, most of the type for the first edition, a thin volume of quarto size, which in 1855 issued from the press of Andrew and James Rome, at 98 Cranberry Street, corner of Fulton.

The reviewers saw little to commend in this bizarre and often grotesque book, but Whitman went his way undisturbed by their criticisms, and in the following year issued a second and expanded edition of *Leaves.* The poet was living at the time in Ryerson Street near Myrtle Avenue, and it was there that he

was visited by Alcott and Thoreau, who joined Emerson in a
heartening injunction to him "to go on with his poetic enterprise
in his own way and finish it as well as he could." Thoreau, moreover, was deeply impressed by Whitman's physical vigor, and
large and open ways, and described him in a letter to a friend
as "apparently the greatest democrat the world has seen." For
three years following 1857 Whitman lived in a house yet standing at 91½ Classon Avenue, there preparing an edition of his
poems published in 1860 in Boston, and his home was at 122
North Portland Avenue when the outbreak of the Civil War
gave him opportunity to write the most inspiring chapter in his
history.

The poet did not enter the army as a soldier, but when in
1862 word reached him that his brother, who was serving as a
captain of infantry, had been shot in battle, he went at once
to the front to give what aid he could to the wounded man. This
mission accomplished, he devoted himself to nursing, now in the
hospitals at Washington, and again on battlefields and in camps,
and what he saw and did during those heroic days is described
in *Specimen Days* and the *Wound Dresser,* the latter a posthum-
ous volume of letters to his mother, offering pictures of the worst
side of war, which for directness and power have few equals in
our literature. The strain of nursing, however, broke him down
in the summer of 1864, and he was at the family home in North
Portland Avenue, recovering from a long illness, when in April,
1865, the end of the war was followed by Lincoln's assassination.
Lilac bushes were in full bloom when news came of the President's death, and gave the title, *When Lilacs Last in the Door-
yard Bloom'd,* to the poet's tribute to his memory. The house in
which Whitman wrote this poem has given way to a more modern
structure, but in the yard adjoining its site is still to be seen a
clustering bush of lilacs which may have kept him silent and
fragrant company while at work on his moving and noble elegy.

For eight years following 1865, Whitman, now become prematurely "the good gray poet" of his friend O'Connor's spirited
vindication, had his home in Washington where he held a minor
post in the government service; but he often visited his mother
in Brooklyn, and in 1871 built a house for her at 107 North Portland Avenue. Two years later his life underwent a great and
lasting change. A stroke of paralysis which incapacitated him
for labor was followed by the death of his mother, and, reduced
to want through the fault of his publisher, he removed from

Washington to Camden, where he was for a decade a member of his brother's household. Then an increasing income from his books, to which had been added *Drum Taps* and *Democratic Vistas*, supplemented by gifts from friends, enabled him to secure a modest home of his own in Mickle Street, Camden. There he passed the remainder of his life, and there death came to him at the age of seventy-three. Brooklyn, during these last years of recurring illness and stoic waiting—but years also of steadily growing fame, knew him only as an infrequent visitor, nor, when the end came, did it receive the mortal part of him. He lies instead in a massive tomb in Harleigh Cemetery, Camden, which has become a shrine for pilgrims from both the Old World and the New.

The first Brooklyn home of Henry Ward Beecher was a house which stood until 1927 at 126 Columbia Street. Perhaps the most widely known of all the men who in times past claimed Brooklyn as their home, Beecher was but thirty-four years old when he came from the West to enter upon his long pastorate of Plymouth Church. He was then in the first flush of the powers which made him ere long the most famous preacher of his period, and church and congregation, which were in struggling infancy when he came to them, quickly grew under his charge to the largest in America. Regarding Christianity not as a series of unchanging and inflexible dogmas but as a creed broad enough to shape and influence all phases of life, he made his pulpit a forum for the discussion of the great social and political questions of the time, and during the stormy days which ushered in the Civil War, than his no voice was more potent and fearless in its opposition to slavery. Beecher's oratory had always the earnestness of passionate conviction, tempered, however, with a rich vein of humor while, with a sure sense of the needs and understanding of common men, he drew his material from every sphere of life and thought. Thus, though some modern orators have surpassed him in depth and breadth of intellectual power, few, if any, have equalled him in the ability to sway and mould to his own way of thinking great masses of his fellows. And of this gift he made splendid and memorable use when in 1863 he visited England to enlighten its people as to the issues which then separated North and South. The English, or at least a great majority of them, until he went among them, had been strongly in favor of the Confederacy; but his speeches, addressed at first to hostile audiences, helped to work a revolution in popular sentiment; and, perhaps, more than any other single factor, influenced Great Britain's final decisions to refuse recognition to the Richmond government.

When he had been twelve years pastor of Plymouth, Beecher removed to 82 Columbia Street, where he had his home during the busiest and, in many ways, most fruitful period of his career. He long contributed to and for a time edited the New York *Independent,* first publishing in its columns his once widely read *Star Papers,* and later he was for a number of years editor of the *Christian Union,* predecessor of the *Outlook.* The New York *Ledger* also numbered him among the contributors who helped for two decades to make it the weekly journal of largest circulation in America, and through that medium he gave to the public his novel of *Norwood.*

Nor did these activities, which kept company with frequent appearances on the lecture platform and as an orator at public meetings, represent the total of Beecher's literary output. His *Lectures to Young Men* and *Life Thoughts* commanded a numerous audience, while his collected and revised sermons, published under the title of the *Plymouth Pulpit* filled many volumes, and a *Life of Christ,* which ran through successive editions when it first came from the press in 1872, still finds readers. An abode of Beecher's later years was on Columbia Heights, but his home when he died in 1887 was at 124 Hicks Street, in an old-fashioned brick structure now replaced by an apartment house. His grave is in Greenwood Cemetery, and in one of Brooklyn's most frequented quarters Ward's fine statue of him with a kneeling negro girl at its feet, fittingly commemorates his brave and puissant labors in behalf of the slave.

Besides its reminders of Whitman and Beecher, Brooklyn is rich in memories of a lettered past. When in 1837 John Greenleaf Whittier spent a few months in New York as secretary to the American Anti-Slavery Society, he was often the guest at 109 Bridge Street of John Hooper, whose daughter Lucy, early claimed by death, was a devoted and admiring friend of the Quaker poet, and herself a maker of graceful verse. A house at 20 Concord Street now used for a shelter for indigent women, was the birthplace and early home of John Bach McMaster. George Washington Bethune, eminent in his time both as preacher and as author and editor, lived at the corner of Jay and Fulton Streets during his pastorate of the Dutch Reformed Church on the Heights, and at 96 Pineapple Street was the abode of Henry Morford, when in his last days he edited the *Brooklyn Magazine.*

The birthplace of Heywood Broun, who long enjoyed a wide measure of favor as a commentator on men and events, was at 55 Clark Street, and Paul Leicester Ford was born and dwelt during the early part of his life in an old mansion at 97 Clark Street, built by his father to house the library of a hundred thousand volumes which was long the envy and delight of scholars given access to its treasures. One of these was Moncure Daniel Conway, a friend of Carlyle and Emerson, and himself a man of vision and uncommon quality, who while living at 62 Clark Street found in the Ford alcoves much of the material for his exhaustive *Life of Thomas Paine*. Born in Virginia in 1832, and descended from one of the signers of the Declaration of Independence, Conway, true to his ancestry, was from youth to old age, a ready and resolute champion of struggling causes. He early abandoned the law for the ministry and for a time was a Methodist circuit rider in his native state; but soon a change of views took him to Harvard Divinity School, and after his graduation at that institution in 1854, he was in turn the pastor of Unitarian churches in Washington and Cincinnati.

While a student at Cambridge, Conway had become a convert to the anti-slavery movement, and, at a cost of friendships and associations which would have dismayed a less resolute man, he gave it single-minded and unswerving support. He was editing a Boston weekly journal devoted to the cause when the break came between the states, and in 1863 he went to England to speak and write in its behalf; but he had not been long in London when he received an invitation to become pastor of South Place Chapel, a congregation of liberal inclinings, and this post he filled with great ability and steadily growing influence for more than a score of years. During the same period he was a member of the staffs of the London *Daily News* and the *Pall Mall Gazette*, and a regular contributor to English and American magazines.

Thinker and man of action in one, all who sought a broader future were quick to recognize in Conway a kindred and sympathetic influence, and he numbered among the intimates of his English exile most of the finest spirits of the Victorian era. But that exile was broken by frequent visits to America, and in 1885 he returned here to end his days. The literary harvest of his later years included, besides the *Life of Paine*, volumes on Carlyle, Emerson and Hawthorne, which bear the impress of a richly stored and catholic mind, and an *Autobiography*, published shortly before his death in 1907, whose modesty, wealth of incident and unfailing human interest, give it a place apart among modern books of the kind.

Charles Nordhoff dwelt at 56 Willow Street when one of the editors of the New York *Evening Post,* and the home of Lyman Abbott was at 148 Willow Street when he succeeded Beecher as pastor of Plymouth Church. Newell Dwight Hillis lived for many year at 23 Monroe Place as did Edna Dean Proctor who there wrote much of her best verse, while at 21 Monroe Place was the home of St. Clair McKelway, for more than a generation editor of the Brooklyn *Eagle.* A few blocks distant at 80 Pierrepont Street is the former home of Richard Salter Storrs, for upward of two score years pastor of the First Congregational Church of Brooklyn, and for a yet longer period a pulpit orator of learning and power. George Ripley's abode during the Civil War was at 56 Joralemon Street, and Theodore Tilton, when editor of the *Independent* and a brilliant figure in journalism and letters, lived at 136 Livingstone Street. Again at 150 Livingstone Street was the last home of Poe's whilom partner, Charles Farrar Briggs, who was also a co-worker with Tilton on the staff of the Brooklyn *Union,* while during part of the same period Edward Eggleston, then pastor of a Brooklyn church, resided at 298 Schermerhorn Street, and there wrote his best remembered novel, the *Hoosier Schoolmaster.*

Joseph Pennell, rarely gifted both as artist and author, died in the Hotel Margaret on Columbia Heights and at 101 Columbia Heights was the home of burly Thomas Wolfe, whose career has already become a legend, when under discreet guardianship he first won notice as a prolific and often provoking writer of fiction. Again at 204 Columbia Heights was the home of Albion Winegar Tourgee when editor of *Our Continent,* a short-lived weekly journal in which he sunk much of the money brought him by a *Fool's Errand* and other widely read novels dealing with the period of reconstruction in the South, in which, as a Union veteran who in 1868 found a place on the North Carolina bench, he had played a stormy part. Tourgee's pen was an acrid one, and his tales when they appeared provoked angry discussion, but are now a part of the dead and gone era which brought them into being.

The last home of Elizabeth Luther Cary, long a member of the staff of the New York *Times,* whose delightful studies of Tennyson, Browning and other Victorian worthies still claim readers, was at 160 Henry Street. A house numbered 242 Henry

Street has association with another author of pleasant memory, for it was the long-time abode of Alice Morse Earle, whose informing books on colonial life and customs claim a place in every library dealing with our country's past. Not far away at 543 Henry Street was half a century ago the dwelling of James Watson Green, whose daughter, Anna Katherine Green, there won success with the *Lavenworth Case* and a *Strange Disappearance.* Robert William Chambers, another weaver of tales always sure of a welcome from the multitude, was born at 166 Fort Greene Place, and there Robert Lowry, author of *I Need Thee Every Hour* and other famous hymns, lived while serving as pastor of a Baptist church in Hanson Place.

Thomas De Witt Talmage, after Beecher the most widely known preacher of his period, lived during his years of most varied activity at 1 South Oxford Street, and at 176 South Oxford Street, was for more than a generation the abode of another pulpit orator of mark, Theodore Ledyard Cuyler, pastor for thirty years of the Lafayette Avenue Presbyterian Church of Brooklyn. Born in 1822 at Aurora, New York, a town founded by one of his New England ancestors, Cuyler was graduated at Princeton at the age of nineteen, and in 1843 entered the Presbyterian ministry. During the following seventeen years he had charge of churches in Burlington and Trenton, New Jersey and in New York, finally in 1860 settling in Brooklyn, where he passed the remainder of his life, dying in 1909 at the age of eighty-seven years. He was, like Beecher, a man of wide reaching sympathies, who made his pulpit a place for the discussion of every question vitally affecting human welfare. He led in the foundation of the Republican Party, and all forward moving causes won the quick and unwearying support of his tongue and pen. His *Recollections of a Long Life,* written in the well-earned leisure of a hale old age, are rich in intimate glimpses of the eminent men who counted him as a friend, and furnish at the same time a winning portrayal of their author's brave and modest soul.

Leonard Grover, author of many plays, died at 194 South Oxford Street, and five doors removed on the same side of the way was the last home of Edward Cary for upward of a generation one of the editors of the New York *Times* and a sane and tolerant shaper of public opinion in an uncertain, troubled era. Chester Sanders Lord, managing editor for a generation of the New York *Sun* and the incomparable trainer of three generations of newspaper workers of the first-class, lived for many years at

57 South Portland Avenue. The last home of James C. Derby, whose recollections of his experiences as publisher for not a few of the rising authors of his time fill diverting pages, was at 47 Downing Street, and that of Don Carlos Seitz for many years before his death in 1936 at 75 Downing Street. Born in 1862, the son of a Universalist minister who in his long life labored in many fields, Seitz passed his boyhood and obtained his schooling in Norway, Maine, not far from the early home of Charles Farrar Browne, whose biographer he was to become in after years. He left school at an early age to become a printer's apprentice, and as time passed gravitated naturally and inevitably from the management of printing plants to the management of newspapers.

For a number of years Seitz directed with skill and shrewdness the business affairs of the Brooklyn *Eagle* and after that was the right hand of Joseph Pulitzer during the New York *World's* most successful period. But he was much more than one of the ablest newspaper executives of the last fifty years. His leisure hours were devoted, with zestful assiduity and a never satisfied thirst for new and out-of-the-way facts about the great and the near-great, to historical research and writing. The collector of a great library, rich in rare and unusual items, he was an authority on English and American chap-books and broad sheets, and during the last thirty years of his life he wrote nearly as many books on such widely contrasting subjects as Japan, the Mediterranean, Whistler, the buccaneers, William Kidd, John Paul Jones, duelling in America, and the Wyandot Indians. His account of the Wyandots ran to 300,000 words and competes in scope and importance with Morgan's *League of the Iroquois*.

Other works by Seitz included besides the authoritative volume on Artemus Ward already referred to, lives of Pulitzer, Greeley and the Bennetts and of Braxton Bragg, the Confederate general. He was also a lifelong student of the career of Abraham Lincoln, and wrote and published a carefully considered and understanding study of the Civil War President as a politician. Moreover, like Lincoln "he was always doing something for somebody," and the memory of him that abides with those who enjoyed his friendship is that of a generous, kindly man ever ready to minister to the needs of his fellows.

Mary Virginia Terhune, best known as Marion Harland, lived at 166 Bedford Avenue, while her husband was pastor of a church in that part of the town and there wrote a number of the books which bred in their readers a zestful interest in the colonial era.   The last home of Andrew McLean, a runaway Scot who found a career in America, was at 284 Carlton Avenue.   McLean who served as a powder-monkey on Winslow's *Kearsarge* in Civil War days, became at an early age editor of the Brooklyn *Eagle,* but left it in 1886 to found the Brooklyn *Citizen,* which he edited with outstanding ability until his death.   Frederick S. Cozzens died at 301 Carlton Avenue, and the long life of A. Brendan Ford, a Galway Irishman who as a lad set type on Garrison's *Liberator* and later placed to his credit four years of fighting in the Union Army, came to an end in his ninety-fifth year at 432 Carlton Avenue.   Ford who had much to say and was a master of the trenchant phrase, in 1870 joined a brother in founding the *Irish World* and later was for a quarter of a century editor of the New York *Freeman's Journal.*   A militant member of a fighting race Ford knew his enemies and the latter also and always had good reason to remember him.

Again at 626 Carlton Avenue was the last home of John White Chadwick, preacher, author and poet, and for forty years pastor of the Second Unitarian Church of Brooklyn, a post in which he succeeded Samuel Longfellow, brother of the poet. Chadwick was the son of a Marblehead sailor and served as a shoemaker's apprentice before preparing for the ministry.   He was graduated at the Cambridge Divinity School in 1864 at the age of twenty-four, and a trial sermon on Abraham Lincoln, then a candidate for re-election, by its earnestness and force, so impressed his hearers that he was at once called to a pastorate that ended only with his death.   Dr. Chadwick quickly proved himself a master both of the spoken and written word; his sermons never failed to reflect love of truth and deep spiritual insight, while his scholarship and poetic gifts bore fruit in standard lives of Theodore Parker and the elder Channing, and in a long array of volumes of essays and verse.   It was fittingly said of him when he rested from his labors that "God was in his world to him, and that all was well with his world, because of that."

Kate Upson Clark, resolute champion of struggling causes, died at 464 Clinton Avenue.   Robert Burns Wilson, artist and poet, lived in his closing years at 21 Clermont Avenue.   At 658 Lafayette Avenue was the last abode of John Swinton, long a writer in the service of the *Sun,* and a sturdy and individual figure in the journalism of his period, while at 420 Greene Avenue was the home of Will Carleton during his middle and last years. Born on a Michigan farm in 1845, Carleton began to write when little more than a boy, finding congenial subjects for his poems in the joys and sorrows of the plain people about him, and the welcome from the first given the children of his fancy, quickly decided his career. He was for a time an editor in his native state, but soon removed to the East and until his death in 1913 was a resident of Brooklyn. He published in all nearly a dozen volumes, and, though his homespun verse lacks many of the elements critics demand in poetry, its feeling and sincerity never failed to touch the popular heart, so that its author early won and held until the end a larger audience than, perhaps with a single exception, has been commanded by any other American poet of the last century.

The last home of Philip Henry Welch, who made the English-speaking world laugh for years, was at 351 Jefferson Avenue. Newspaper readers of half a century ago have not forgotten the tragic close of that gentle humorist's too brief career—a career which in many ways was that of a typical American. Phil Welch, as he was known to an army of friends, was born in 1849 in Angelica, New York, and, trained for commercial life, for a number of years served a New York hardware house as a traveler in the South and West. Then, quitting New York on account of business changes, he took up his residence in Oil City, and from there sent contributions to the *Petroleum World* and market reports to the Bradstreet agency.

In the autumn of 1882 Welch joined the editorial staff of the Rochester *Post-Express,* and, by the quaint humor and telling shots at the foibles of the day contained in a column which he called the *Present Hour,* quickly won public attention and favor. Before the end of the year the Philadelphia *Call* sought and secured his services, and ere long, his work having caught the shrewd eye of Charles A. Dana, came his transfer to the New York *Sun.* To that journal he contributed the little dialogues styled *Queer Wrinkles* which for many years brightened and enlivened its pages. Each *Queer Wrinkle* consisted of a question and answer, and travestied with keen, terse wit or fine dry humor the fashions and follies of the day. An untiring worker, he wrote and sold more than he turned out for the *Sun* and thus shortly became the most widely quoted and best paid humorist of his time. Then he fell a victim to cancer of the tongue, and after long suffering borne with quiet heroism in 1892 passed from life. Welch's influence while on earth was a joyous one, and he left only gentle memories behind him.

One finds at 25 First Place, a house which seventy years ago was for a time the home of John Godfrey Saxe, a poet as popular with readers of his age as was Carleton, with those of a later generation. Charles B. Lewis, another humorist of other days, lived for many years at 71 Third Place. The last residence of Robert Henry Newell was at 128 First Place, and that of Maurice Francis Egan at 534 Third Street, where he ended his days in the home of a daughter. Egan's career, the story of which is pleasantly told in the volume of recollections he wrote and published just before his death in 1924, touched life at many points. Born in Philadelphia in 1852, he received a classical education at La Salle College and was for some years a professor at Georgetown University before in 1880 he entered journalism first as associate editor and later as editor of the *Catholic Review* in New York.

Dr. Egan quit journalism in 1888 to become for seven years professor of English language and literature at Notre Dame. After that he filled the same post at the Catholic University until in 1907 Theodore Roosevelt appointed him American minister at Copenhagen, where he remained through three administrations. As a diplomat he had much to do with Denmark's cession of the Virgin Islands to the United States as a protection for the Panama Canal, and he adroitly handled the delicate situation produced by the advent in Copenhagen of Dr. Cook as "discoverer" of the North Pole, an incident of which he gives an amusing if discreet account in his recollections. A ready and graceful writer of both prose and verse, Dr. Egan had more than a score of volumes to his credit before he went to Denmark, and after 1918, when ill-health compelled his retirement from the diplomatic service and his return to America, he continued with unabated industry his labors in letters and journalism. His volume of recollections was clearly his best work, perhaps because it told with unfailing tact and admirable regard for others the story of an unusually successful experiment in the art of living. A friend once declared that Dr. Egan led a charmed life because he himself was charming, and it is not too much to say that wherever he went, at home or abroad, he left behind him a trail of affectionate goodwill.

When Edwin Markham came east in 1900, on the morrow of the sudden and worldwide repute as a poet which the *Man With the Hoe* brought him, he lived for a time at 545 Third Street. One of the present writers recalls an hour with him soon after his settlement in unfamiliar surroundings. Sober in his tastes and homely in his habits as befitted one born and reared in the Farthest West he was, both in middle life and extreme old age, a stalwart, upstanding figure of a man, revealing in his ways and speech the freedom and carelessness of a large nature. Books lined the walls of his new home, the beloved books he had brought with him across the continent, and although no longer young he voiced the eager faith of youth in a future made up only of confident and triumphant tomorrows. Hamlin Garland also records a characteristic meeting with the poet during these first days in the East. "Markham and his wife," he writes in his diary, "came to dinner with us, and we had a good, noisy evening. He was a problem so long as we remained in our little suite at the hotel, for he had a resounding voice and his laugh is like that of a sea captain. My wife was somewhat stunned by him, but I assured her that his open-air quality of speech was only a survival of his youth in Oregon."

The home of Anna Katherine Greene Rohlfs during her later years in Brooklyn was at 323 Fourth Street; and the last city abode of William Hamilton Gibson, author and artist in one, at 11 Lincoln Place, while the poet Stoddard and his wife lived for several years at 13 Douglas Street, and there for a shorter period Bayard Taylor was a member of their household. One other old house in this quarter of the town has intimate association with the lettered past—a three-story brick structure at 125 Dean Street, which was once the home of Estelle Anna Lewis, a gifted and beautiful woman whom her friends knew as Stella.

Four score and ten years ago the home of Mrs. Lewis, herself the writer of verse which caused Poe to liken her to Sappho, was a resort for the leading authors of that time. In her drawing-room Irving, Cooper and Willis met kindred spirits; Bryant recited his *Thanatopsis,* and Poe gave one of the first readings of *The Raven.* There came a time, however, when her extravagance led to quarrels with and separation from her husband. She left America and settled in Paris, where her wit and beauty soon made her a brilliant and central figure in social and literary circles. Lamartine and the elder Dumas were numbered among her friends; Rosa Bonheur painted her, and the third Napoleon honored her in many ways. Her last days were passed in London, and when she died in 1880, at the age of fifty-six, a resting place was made for her in Kensal Green Cemetery. But when her will was read it was found to contain a request, duly honored, that her body should be returned to America and buried in a spot she had selected in Greenwood Cemetery, Brooklyn.

The present grave of Stella is marked by a granite block inscribed with her name and the date of her death; but weeds cover the mound and tall grass grows all about it, eloquent witnesses to the neglect and forgetfulness which have claimed the life and work of the woman who there takes her rest. Not far away the mortal part of James Kirke Paulding reposes in one of the underground vaults now in disuse in the cemetery. There is no indication of his burial in this place save the name "Paulding" cut in small letters on a granite gate-post of the plot, while a honeysuckle climbs over the only entrance to the tomb, in summer almost hiding it from view.

Greenwood guards the last sleep of a number of other authors. The grave of McDonald Clarke, as already noted, faces the shore of the little lake called Sylvan Water, and in other parts of the Cemetery are those of the Cary sisters, George Arnold, Fitz-James O'Brien, Horace Greeley and Henry Ward Beecher. A bust made of old type surmounts the Greeley monument, and that which guards Beecher's solemn sleep bears the words "He Thinketh no Evil."

John Russell Young, when Greeley's chief lieutenant on the *Tribune,* lived at 215 Dean Street. Luis P. Senarens, who was born in 1862, the son of a tobacco merchant who had moved to Brooklyn from Cuba; and who lived to the ripe age of seventy-six, wrote the last of more than a thousand dime novels at 269 Martense Street, while a house yet standing at the corner of Fifty-sixth Street and Fourteenth Avenue, in one of the newer parts of the spreading town, was the final abode of Marcus Mills (Brick) Pomeroy, the hero of a career possible only in an America that is now part of the unreturning past. Pomeroy was born in Elmira on Christmas Day in 1833, learned the printer's trade in the neighboring town of Corning where he had David Ross Locke for a fellow apprentice, and in turn founded weekly journals in Corning and Athens, Pennsylvania, both of which came to an early and disastrous end.

Then in 1857 Pomeroy made his way in a well-nigh penniless condition to Wisconsin, at that time a frontier state, and in the town of Horicon founded his third newspaper, the Horicon *Argus.* This he sold at the end of two years for two thousand dollars, and after a short sojourn in Milwaukee as city editor of the *Daily News* in 1860 settled in La Crosse, a growing town on the banks of the Mississippi, where he became half owner and directing spirit of the *Union and Democrat,* a daily journal then in a languishing condition. The stout champion of any cause that enlisted his sympathy and support—some of them of a perverse and eccentric sort—Pomeroy was also a warrior of the printed page with whom, in pleased recognition of his straight-from-the-shoulder utterances and ways, Paine and Cobbett would have clasped hand in cordial fashion.

During and after the Civil War, in which Pomeroy was a persistent and unrelenting critic of the Lincoln administration, with a particular hatred of Ben Butler and his doubtful ways, its editor's trenchant pen brought the La Crosse *Democrat* a national reputation and its weekly edition a circulation of a hundred thousand copies. Money poured into his coffers and at La Crosse he erected the finest building in the town, including an opera house and accommodations for his printing establishment. Then he sought new worlds to conquer, and in August, 1868, in the heat of the Grant-Seymour battle for the Presidency, founded a daily paper in New York.

So keen were people to see and read the new journal that more than thirty thousand copies of it were sold the first day. Pomeroy's forthright editorials, however, while pleasing a fraction of his new constituency gave lasting offense to the greater part of it. Soon his circulation fell to a few thousand copies and no effort however determined sufficed to increase it. At the end of two years its editor gave up the fight, having lost every dollar he had brought with him to New York, and being also deeply in debt. But he found ways to continue the publication of a weekly first in New York, after that in Chicago, Denver and Washington, and finally again in New York. During these years he also made and—lost—new fortunes. When death claimed him in 1896, with ever renewing faith in his own ability to do things, he was seeking another one as promoter of a tunnel through the Rocky Mountains, which he assured the public would "shorten routes, save time and open up rich mining lands." Later a tunnel through the Rockies was brought to completion by other hands.

At 1618 Beverly Road, Brooklyn, was the last home of James Gibbons Huneker, like Pomeroy a typical American, but one moved by widely different aims and purposes. Huneker was born in 1860 in Philadelphia, the home of his family for generations, and was educated there and at the Sorbonne in Paris. Music, painting and the stage were primary interests with him, and he first came into notice in 1891 as musical and dramatic critic for the New York *Recorder*. Later he was in turn a member of the staffs of the *Morning Advertiser,* and of the *Sun, Times* and *World*. He was in the service of the *World* when he died in 1921 after a short illness.

Huneker's first book published in 1899 was a collection of his contributions to the press to which he gave the title *Mezzotints in Modern Music*. This book won him a unique place as an author, for while he wrote with versatile brilliancy of all the arts —music, painting, sculpture, the drama and literature—he especially excelled in the analysis of music and musicians. During the years that followed the publication of his first volume he issued a full score of collections of his random papers, in all of which he employed a rare command of words and facts to reveal to his readers the glorious and beautiful things achieved by men and women of genius. To his later years belonged an art romance, *Painted Veils,* and an autobiography entitled *Steeplejack,* which has already become a source book for students of an interesting period. Huneker detested shams, and was an eager lover of excellence in every form. Moved always by generous impulses, he was also a sensitive and abiding friend, and than he no man of his generation gave to his fellows a fuller measure of delightful and uplifting comradeship.

Returning to the older part of the town one finds at 375 State Street the house in which Major Alfred Ross Calhoun passed his last years. Calhoun, who died in 1912, was the hero of a career possible only in the era of which he was a part. Born in Kentucky, he was a student at Heidelberg when the Civil War began, but hastened home to enlist in the Union Army. Before the war ended he was advanced from the rank of private to that of major, lost a leg in battle and for eight months was confined in Libby Prison. There he wrote the words of *Marching Through Georgia,* and *Tramp, Tramp, Tramp*. An army band-master set them to music, and they quickly won a popularity that long made them prime favorites with Union veterans.

After 1865 Major Calhoun was employed for several years on government surveys in the West, where he had a part in numerous fights with Indians, and became the friend of Kit Carson and other noted plainsmen. Then he returned to the East and for two score years was a prolific producer of tales of adventure, placing to his credit hundreds of titles. He knew also how to make and keep friends, and the writer as a young man passed many delightful hours in his company, one of which

yielded an amusing anecdote of another redoubtable story-teller—
Ned Buntline. "He was writing a story," Calhoun recalled, "for
a weekly journal on which we were both employed when he
elected to take a sudden vacation. It was a way he had, and
nobody thought much about it, but now the publishers were in a
dilemma, for they had in hand only one of Buntline's installments.
I was asked to read the chapters already printed, and then to
finish the story in a couple of installments. When I read what
had been printed I quickly discovered to my dismay that I had
a perplexing job ahead of me. There was a baffling number of
characters in the story, for Judson could easily take care of a
small army while spinning a tale. In fact there were more of
them than I could handle. So I resolved on a method of my own
to get rid of some of them. I put a number of them on an excursion steamer and then exploded its boilers, sending all of them
to watery graves. With the rest I worked out a plot to a climax,
and brought the story to a conclusion. But great was Judson's
wrath when, returning to the office a fortnight later, he was told
what had been done. I explained, of course, that I had acted
under orders, but he refused to be pacified, and was, indeed, a
very angry man. He cared nothing, he declared, about the finishing of the story; but it was to the wholesale and brutal slaughter
of his characters, an inartistic procedure, that he objected. In
the end, however, he saw the thing in its proper light, and we had
many a laugh over it."

Major Calhoun no doubt now and again touched elbows with
another indefatigable spinner of yarns, Harlan Page Halsey,
creator of the Old Sleuth tales which in the last decade of the last
century moved and enthralled successive armies of readers. Halsey, who lived for many years and died at 111 McDonough Street,
took his pen name from the title of a book he wrote in 1870—the
first of hundreds of detective stories in which Old Sleuth was
the central figure. Before that he had been a private in the Union
Army and a writer for the Brooklyn *Eagle*. Before his death in
1898 the sale of his books reached two million copies a year, and,
so insistent were the demands of his publishers, every member
of the author's family had a hand in an output which occasionally
ran to scores of titles in a twelve-month. One of his sons clipped
usable plots from the daily press; his wife made legible a hand-
writing that was the despair of printers, and his daughter carried
the corrected manuscript to the publisher. This daughter, Rena
Isabelle Halsey, became with the years a popular writer of stories

for boys and girls. Her home in old age was at 149 Halsey Street, a thoroughfare named for her family.

Another diligent and prolific craftsman with an appeal, however, to a more discriminating and selective audience than the one commanded by Calhoun and Halsey, was Charles Montgomery Skinner, elder brother of the noted actor of that name, whose home was long in Park Place near Bedford Avenue. The sons of a Universalist minister and born in 1852 at Victor, New York, the brothers attended the schools of Cambridge, Massachusetts, and Hartford, Connecticut, where the family in turn resided, and in 1880 Charles Skinner took up his residence in Brooklyn in order to study medicine, securing at the same time a post on the staff of the Brooklyn *Times*. Ere long he decided to give up medicine for journalism, in 1884 becoming an editorial writer for the Brooklyn *Eagle,* and in the columns of that journal for two-and-twenty years contributed in generous measure, and in terse and telling English, to the shaping of sound public opinion on a great variety of subjects.

Skinner was also a reverent student of history for whom the folklore of his own and other countries had an especial and continuing appeal, and he spent ten years in writing *Legends of Our Own Land,* which, well received when published in 1897, was followed by other volumes dealing in a sympathetic and understanding way with their author's love of nature and a storied past. Stricken with a premature and wasting illness Skinner passed his last months in the Vermont village of Proctorville, and death when it came to him in the Christmastide of 1907 was a merciful relief from suffering borne with patient endurance. He was a lover of beauty in all its phases—the beauty alike of justice and truth, of character and service, as well as of nature; and it was well said of him when he died that for a goodly company of rare and gentle spirits he had helped to make life worth living.

Had length of days been granted this gifted man there is little doubt that he would have admired and praised the poetry of Lola Ridge who died in the May days of 1941 at 111 Montague Street. This maker of verse now and then uneven in quality but nearly always remarkable for its depth and sincerity had a message for a troubled world. Her longest poem, *The Ghetto,* was a vivid and arresting portrayal of the life of Jewish city-dwellers perhaps without an equal in our literature, and other examples of her art proved her right to a place all her own among those charged with unfailing resolve to serve their fellows. Ill-health and a grim struggle for existence were continuing handicaps to the exercise of her talents, but they never failed to shake a spirit that bowed alone to death. For those who knew the woman, Lola Ridge, remains a tenderly cherished memory.

Finally a modest frame house at 2752 Fulton Street in the Highland Park section of Brooklyn, has interest for all lovers of books and their makers for it was long the home of Wilberforce Eames, most learned and indefatigable of American bibliographers. Born in Newark in 1855 his schoolmaster father removed shortly to Brooklyn, where the son in his youth served first as a printer's devil, and then as a postal clerk. His future career was decided when his mother took him at the age of thirteen to the shop of William Gowans in Nassau Street, New York, to purchase a much desired copy of Herodotus. There he came in contact for the first time with a great collection of books and resolved to companion with them for the remainder of his days. For a number of years he found congenial employment with various book-sellers, and in 1885 at the age of thirty became assistant to George Henry Moore, head of the Lenox Library.

In 1893 Dr. Eames succeeded his chief as librarian, and when in 1895 the Lenox was consolidated with the Astor and the Tilden Trust to form the present New York Public Library he became chief bibliographer of the last named institution, serving in that capacity until his death in 1937 at the age of eighty-two. Americana was the chief specialty of Dr. Eames as a bibliographer, but he carried his exact and thorough scholarship into many other fields, and when he died, poor in purse but rich in the things of the spirit, he had long been held in honor by grateful students in all parts of the world.

CHAPTER XI

Through Farther Long Island

Long Island's north shore is rich in memories of poet and story-teller. It was at Ravenswood in the summer home of a friend that Irving gave the finishing touches to his *History of New York*, while Cooper lived for a time in Astoria, and there wrote the *Last of the Mohicans*. Going back to an earlier time a house situated in Flushing's Cedar Grove Cemetery, and now occupied by the caretaker of that ancient burial ground, was identified a few years ago as the summer home of Cadwallader Colden in the closing decades of the colonial period. Born in Ireland of Scotch parentage and educated at the University of Edinburgh, Colden came to the colonies in 1710 at the age of twenty-two, and after an eight years' residence in Philadelphia removed to New York. There in 1720 he was made surveyor-general of the province, and during the remainder of his life of eighty years was almost continuously in public employ, acting as chief adviser to a succession of governors, and from 1760 until his death filling the post of lieutenant-governor.

Colden in the leisure afforded him by his official duties found time to make himself one of the most learned and many-sided men in the colonies. The *History of the Five Indian Nations* which he wrote and published in 1727, and which deals with the Iroquois tribes, remains after the lapse of two centuries a source book held in respectful regard by students of Indian tradition. He was also a capable and painstaking botanist and naturalist, and one of the first to analyze and expound Newton's law of gravitation. This was in 1751 and the book with a many-worded title which he published in that year is prized by collectors so fortunate as to possess copies of it. It was in 1762 that Colden purchased from John and Thomas Willett a tract of 120 acres at Flushing to which he gave the name Spring Hill, and on which he erected the house that was his main abode during his troubled last years. The visitor finds reflected in its construction the thoroughness and sedulous attention to details which marked every important act of its builder's life. Its foundations are solid, thick walls, with the largest of its beams hewn by hand; while the halls and sound-proof rooms are spacious with high ceilings, and solid concrete was encountered when a few years ago the floors were drilled for the installation of electric lights.

As a representative of the royal authority Colden's status in the years immediately preceding the revolt of the colonies was a difficult and trying one. In the end he retired from New York to Spring Hill never again to leave it. There he died in September, 1776, a few weeks after the adoption of the Declaration of Independence by the Continental Congress. In his will he requested that his "body be interred with as little expense as with common decency may be," and so he was buried on his farm. His grave, however, is not in "a certain ancient burying place," still recognizable, which the Willetts reserved in their deed to him, and no one knows his resting place.

Flushing was the boyhood home of Richard Watson Gilder, editor and poet, and 372 Broadway, was long the abode of Manley M. Gillam who in his youth served with gallantry in the Army of the Potomac and then for half a century was eminent as a newspaper worker, and as the creator of a new era in the art of advertising. Albert Bigelow Paine, who first attracted notice as a writer of humorous skits, lived at 136 Delaware Street when Mark Twain chose him as his biographer, with results that ever since have been an occasion for sharp differences of opinion between those who admired the greater man or had knowledge of the unpredictable qualities which placed him apart from his fellows.

Daniel Carter Beard, who in the middle decades of his life of ninety-one years illustrated with sympathetic understanding one of Mark Twain's books, dwelt for upward of a generation at 87 Bowen Avenue, Flushing, in a house to which in 1894 he brought the bride who, when he saw her for the first time, had moved him to remark to a friend: "There goes the future Mrs. Dan Beard." Charles Dana Gibson was best man at the wedding of the Beards, for the husband was already a fellow illustrator held in high regard by magazine editors. Beard was born in Ohio in 1850, the son of an artist, but passed a part of his youth across the river in Kentucky, where he saw at close range much fighting between the Union and Confederate armies, and as a volunteer helped to nurse the wounded who crowded the wards of local hospitals.

The war ended, young Beard studied engineering and practised it with success until he found that editors were ready to buy and pay for the drawings which occupied his leisure hours.

Then he resigned, telling his employers: "These people will give me more money for playing than you do for working, and I am going on a vacation." That "vacation," begun with a period of study at the Art Student's League in New York, lasted for more than sixty years. Soon his drawings were appearing in many magazines, and attracted the attention of Mark Twain, who early in 1889 invited him to illustrate *A Connecticut Yankee at King Arthur's Court*. Thus was born a mutually helpful friendship that lasted until the death of the elder man. "What luck it was to find you!" Clemens wrote Beard when his work was done. "It was a fortunate hour when I went netting for lightning bugs and caught a meteor."

The artist thus praised ere long became an author on his own account, and wrote in quick succession a series of volumes—the *American Boys' Handy Book* was the first of them—which dealt in a practical yet beguiling way with the sports and pastimes dear to the heart of youth, and of which the house of Scribner during three score years have sold more than 250,000 copies. Success as an author also led without delay to Beard's major part in the founding of the Boy Scouts of America of which from 1910 until his death he remained moving and directing force—unnumbered thousands of boys through the years coming to regard him as a modern and inspiring counterpart of Boone and Crockett. He made it his mission to interpret the best in the older to the best in the younger America, and to such effective ends did he shape this mission that when death claimed him he had long been an uplifting and potent influence in the moulding of modern America.

Another lettered dweller in Flushing was Ellis Parker Butler who lived for many years at 144 Thirty-fifth Street, departing in 1934 to end his days in a Berkshire village. Best remembered as the author of *Pigs is Pigs*, Butler, who was born in Iowa on the morrow of the Civil War, began his business career as a bill clerk and salesman in his native town. However, he early became a writer of amusing skits which found acceptance by editors—one of them while its author was still in high school winning a place in the *Century Magazine*—and in 1897 he made his way to New York hoping there to win success as a humorous writer. This hope had surprising fulfilment at the end of eight years, when Ellery Sedgwick, then editor of the *American Magazine,* suggested to him the plot of *Pigs is Pigs*.

There are few oldsters who do not recall with cheerful

chuckles their first reading of this initimable piece of foolery—twice rewritten before its author was satisfied with it—which set forth the story of a literal-minded express agent who contended that guinea pigs were live stock and of the long dispute between the express company and the consignee who angrily insisted they were pets—ending in a victory for the guinea pigs which meanwhile had increased so rapidly that they overran the entire express company office. First published in the *American Magazine*, *Pigs is Pigs* swept the country and promptly reprinted in book form ran through thirty editions in as many years. During these years Butler wrote a total of thirty-two books, and as a resident of Flushing also achieved success as a banker and business man, active in all that concerned the welfare of his community, Butler's quality was not a major one, but no humorist of a generation which included Finley Peter Dunne and George Ade, Gelett Burgess and Oliver Herford, for a longer period amused and delighted a greater number of readers.

It is a short ride from Flushing to Forest Hills where at 51 Wendover Road Don Marquis, another humorist who was also a poet, passed his last days. There he died in 1937 after long and painful illness, during which he was tenderly cared for by two maiden sisters, and the mortal part of him now rests in Cedar Grove Cemetery, Kew Gardens. Donald Robert Perry Marquis, to give him his full name, was born in Illinois, and was a country printer before he became a newspaper worker. He underwent a long and struggling apprenticeship in Atlanta and other cities, but came finally into his own during the course of his thirteen years as a columnist in New York—first as conductor of the *Sun Dial* in the *Sun* and later *The Lantern* in the *Tribune*—which proved him a humorist Rabelais would have claimed as a brother.

Men not yet old zestfully recall how through these mediums Marquis brought into being Pete, the pup, Mehitabel, the cat, and Archy, the cockroach inhabited by the soul of a poet—each a promoter of grins ending in laughter. Out of his columns also came Clem Hawley, who, as *The Old Soak,* brought rich rewards to his creator; along with *Hermione* and her *Little Group of Serious Thinkers* in which was held up to ridicule some of the absurd as well as amusing culture cliques of a period soon to become a part of the past. And it is gratifying to record that through the years the best of the newspaper output of Don Marquis was gathered into volumes which found an army of readers. He also wrote and produced *The Dark Hours,* a drama of com-

pelling excellence while much of his verse has a poignant individuality which assures it unfailing charm for lovers of true
poetry.   The life of Marquis was attended by tragic losses not
of his own making, but faced with courage of the rarest sort.
His head and heart always kept happy company, nor did he fail
to win and until the end hold friends, whose devotion made him
one of the best beloved men of his era.

The long life of Amelia Edith Barr, whose two score tales
written after she was forty were read with zest by the grand-
parents of the present generation, came to an end in 1919 at 454
Bedford Avenue, Richmond Hill; and at 524 North Beach Street
in the same suburban community was the home for many years
of Jacob A. Riis.   Born in Denmark in 1849 and intended by his
father to be a schoolteacher, Riis elected instead to follow the
trade of carpenter, and coming to America in his youth carved
out the career set forth in his admirable *The Making of an
American*—a career which at its close moved his friend Theodore
Roosevelt to pronounce him "the man who came nearest to being
the ideal citizen," adding: "When I preach about decent citizenship I can turn to him and think he has practised just what I
have been preaching."

The first job of Riis in America was in a Pennsylvania coal
mine.   Later in a New Jersey brickyard he slept at night in a
wagon used by day for carting furniture.   In New York he once
secured free lodging in a police station and was robbed of his
only possession of value—a tiny gold locket.   In Buffalo he was
by turns carpenter, lumber yard hand and traveling salesman.
There also, self-reliant and unafraid, he resolved to become a
newspaper reporter, and returning to New York finally found
employment as assistant to the reporter of the *Tribune* at police
headquarters in Mulberry Street.   This proved to be for Riis the
door of opportunity, for in the stress of a reporter's daily round
he learned to write with vigor, directness and simplicity, and also
came to know at first hand social conditions of an evil sort that
called for the mending.   Out of this knowledge in the fullness
of time grew his *How the Other Half Lives, The Battle with the
Slums, The Children of the Poor,* and other books which helped
to effect reforms where reforms were most needed and proved
their author the wise and helpful friend of all sorts and conditions of men.   One who had frequent contact with Riis in his
middle years recalls him as a simple, kindly soul who loved birds
and flowers and children.   Perhaps his best claim to remembrance

lies in the fact that he conceived and brought into being the play-
grounds of the city in which he lived and labored with such
inspiring results.

At Lawrence, close to the sea one comes upon the former
home of another migrant from the Old World to the New who
is now remembered as an American of an unusual and distinguished order. William M. Laffan, who was born in Dublin in 1849
and had a slight but pleasing brogue, studied at the famous university of his native city, and at the age of twenty made his way
to New York and thence to San Francisco, where he became a
member of the staff of the *Chronicle.* Later he was an editor
and newspaper owner in Baltimore, but in 1877 at the invitation
of Charles A. Dana joined the staff of the New York *Sun* with
which, except for brief intervals, until his death in 1909 he had
continuing and intimate association.

When Dana died in 1900 Laffan who was then business
manager of the *Sun,* with the timely aid of friends, became its
owner, thereafter directing it in every detail as well as contributing constantly to its editorial page. Master of an acute and brilliant literary style, sure to be called into effective use by each new
example of sham and pretense, he was also an accomplished critic
of the arts and the drama, held in high regard by collectors and
men of the stage. His books on *American Wood Engravers* and
Chinese Porcelain, the one published in 1883 and the other in
1906, remain authorities on the subjects with which they deal,
and as a trustee of the Metropolitan Museum of Art he long had
an active part in adding new treasures to its collections in various
fields.

Laffan, however, narrowly missed a place among the great
editors of America, for his plain speech and acid wit were always
in evidence; his hatred of humbug too often became bigotry of a
savage and unrelenting sort, and if advertisers objected even
mildly to his methods he was quick to dismiss them from his
presence. Frank O'Malley in his *Story of the Sun,* tells of
Laffan's attacks on a railway magnate, and how as a gesture of
peace the latter's agent visited the business office of the *Sun* to
tender it some thousands of dollars' worth of advertising. A
clerk told Laffan that the agent wished to see him.

"Tell him to see the advertising manager," said Laffan.

"But he insists on seeing you," was the clerk's reply.

"Tell him to get out of here," said Laffan; and on this abrupt
note ended the call of the magnate's agent.

It is a pleasant ride from Lawrence, through a section now given over to the country homes of city workers to Hempstead and to the burial ground adjoining old St. George's Episcopal Church where the wife and daughter of Joseph Rodman Drake take their rest. Mother and child spent the years of the former's brief widowhood in the home of Mrs. Drake's father, Henry Eckford, and after her death the daughter grew to womanhood under the care of her grand-parents. She became in the fulness of time the wife of Commodore de Kay of the navy, and the mother of Charles de Kay; prepared her father's collected verse for the press, and died when only a year short of the century mark. Henry Eckford travelling by stage coach with his family often visited the Bedell homestead at Hempstead, then a village noted for its beauty and quiet charm; and it was in that way that he and his wife, his children and grandchildren eventually found their last home in St. George's churchyard. On each returning Memorial Day a flag is placed on Mrs. Drake's grave by the women of Hempstead to honor through his wife the author of *The American Flag.*

Alice Morse Earle passed her last days in the home of a son in Hempstead, and a stretch of farm land in North Hempstead had a place in the lives of two outstanding men, one of the colonial period and the other of the birth years of the republic —Thomas Dongan and William Cobbett. In 1683, Dongan, later Earl of Limerick, by appointment of James II, became for five years perhaps the most capable of the royal governors of the province of New York. He had not been long in office before he purchased for a county seat a Long Island farm. To this farm about 1724 another owner, George Clarke, also in his time one of the governors of the province, in honor of his wife, who was kin to Edward Hyde, the renowned first Earl of Clarendon, gave the name of Hyde Park.

In 1817 after passing through many hands HYDE PARK FARM became by lease the home of William Cobbett during his second American sojourn. Since the close of his first sojourn in 1800 Cobbett had become in his native England the contentious and foremost champion of the common man. This had brought him the ill-will of those who then governed the British Empire, rulers more concerned with the defeat of Napoleon than the welfare of their humbler fellows. Cobbett's criticisms of their course, couched in the most trenchant English at the command of any writer of his period, led in 1810 to his confinement for two years in Newgate Prison; and when, at the end of a stormy five years, a suspension of the Habeas Corpus Act gave warning that for him another stay in jail was in the making, he resolved to find temporary refuge in America.

Accordingly in the spring of 1817 Cobbett sailed from Liverpool for New York, accompanied by his two oldest sons, but leaving his wife and younger children behind him in England. He at once leased HYDE PARK FARM; and with the aid of his sturdy sons settled down to farming. He also set up an office in New York, and between town and country continued at long range the editorship of his *Political Register,* still making it a thorn in the sides of those who had forced him into exile. Thurlow Weed, then employed as a printer in Greenwich Street, New York, recalls in his *Autobiography* a memorable meeting with Cobbett. "Being anxious to see the great radical," he writes, "I volunteered to carry proof sheets (of his *Register*) to him at a basement in Wall Street which he occupied as a publishing house. I found him quite affable, evincing in conversation, as in his writings, energy and good will."

And there is abundant proof that Cobbett now found much to admire and praise in the America which he had heartily detested in an earlier time. "In the world," he wrote in a *Journal of a Year's Residence in the United States,* published in 1818, "there is not so well behaved, so orderly, so steady a people, a people so obedient to the law." The avowed object of this volume as set forth in the preface to it was to give an account of the United States as a country to live and farm in; but the present-day reader finds it also a full-length portrait of the author, whose mind darts here and there in random fashion, mingling in an ill-balanced yet diverting way, his personal likes and dislikes, and the causes for them. One page records Cobbett's aversion to Shakespeare and Milton and to the potato, which had no place among the crops raised on HYDE PARK FARM, while on another page he takes care to note that Elias Hicks, the Quaker preacher who lived nine miles from him, had at seventy years of age, cradled four acres of rye in a day.

Cobbett on the whole approved of his new neighbors, and when he secured a cook who knew how to make puddings and pies to his liking, he found his Long Island sojourn a satisfying one, despite separation from his wife and younger children. On his first Christmas Day he had a group of English friends as his guests, and entertained them with sirloin of beef, cakes, puddings, and homemade candles, "as handsome," he observes, "as I ever saw, and, I think, the best I ever saw." The light of these candles took the mind of the exile to England, and to its farmers, who, through evil conditions, were forced to waste their produce, and "no more dare to turn their tallow into candles than to rob on the high road."

The failure, however, of Cobbett's Long Island neighbors to adorn their homes with shrubs, flowers and bordered paths greatly distressed him, and to set this matter right he wrote and published the *American Gardener* in which he gave minute directions for the planting and care of flowers and vegetables of every sort—a much needed handbook that in time ran through many editions. In truth, Cobbett's second stay in America, thanks to freedom from unseemly demands on his time, was one of the most productive periods of his career as editor and author. Many of the articles which he sent to his *Political Register* were among the best he ever wrote, while in addition to the books already mentioned, he revised his *French Grammar,* and completed a *Grammar of the English Language,* which published in 1818 long remained a favorite text-book on both sides of the sea.

The desire to end his exile, however, was constantly in Cobbett's mind. In the early summer of 1819 fire destroyed many of the buildings on the HYDE PARK FARM, and, failure of Parliament to renew suspension of the Habeas Corpus Act having removed the threat of another term in prison, he decided to return to England. Before he sailed he secured permission to dig up the remains of Tom Paine, whom he had once savagely assailed, but later had come to revere as a champion of human rights. These he now took with him, planning to give them impressive reburial in Paine's native village. But it speedily developed that aside from Cobbett no one in England had real regard for the bones of Tom Paine. They remained for a lengthy period in the hands of Cobbett and his family; but, as elsewhere recorded, no one knows what in the end became of them.

Back again in England near the end of 1819 Cobbett still had sixteen strenuous years before him. These were made noteworthy by conduct of the *Political Register* and other journals in which he continued his fight for the English laborer, and began another for a queen whom he felt had been the victim of despicable treatment by her husband; by management of Normandy Farm set down in a vale among the Surrey hills; by a somewhat barren term of service in Parliament; by publication of *Rural Rides,* his most famous book in which without design he drew another full-length portrait of himself, and finally by his death in June, 1835 and burial beside his farmer father in Farnham churchyard. All in all one of the outstanding and uncommon careers of the late eighteenth and early nineteenth centuries—a career attended from youth to old age by resolute and unswerving if now and again mistaken battle for what William Cobbett regarded as right and justice.

A few miles north of Hempstead one finds close to Roslyn the lovely nook where for many years William Cullen Bryant had his home. Roslyn has a history running back into the seventeenth century, but was a village of only a few hundred souls when Bryant visited it for the first time in 1843, and, making it his place of summer residence, soon grew to regard it as the most beautiful spot he had ever seen. Love of nature was his absorbing passion, and to this Roslyn ministered with gentle prodigality, furnishing inspiration for many of his poems. There also in old age he completed his stately translation of Homer. He made annual pilgrimage to his New England home at Cummington, in the Hampshire hills, but Roslyn grew to be the place he loved best in all the earth, and in his latter years he hurried to it early in the spring, and lingered there until late in the fall. It is related of him that, an early riser, he passed as many hours in the open air as he did with his books, in the summer mornings cutting paths, tending shrubs and flowers, or plying sickle and scythe. And in addition to his yearly visit to Cummington, he went on long walking trips to the Delaware Water Gap and the Catskills. The artists Cole and Durand now and again kept him company on his Hudson River outings, and one summer he explored the Berkshires with William Gilmore Simms.

The Quaker homestead to which Bryant gave the name of Cedarmere, and in which he dwelt for thirty-five years, was a roomy, rambling structure, in the colonial style, with broad piazzas, quaint extensions and heavy oaken timbers. It stood on a bench in the hillside, flanked on the one hand by a lake and brook, and on the other by a garden teeming with flowers and fruit. Before and below its site, then as now, the waters of the Sound spread their ever changing panorama. Inside Cedarmere were wide open grates, huge throated chimneys, and antique balustrades, while a broad hallway ran the entire length of the house which, carefully guarded by reverent hands until its destruction by fire in 1902, remained as Bryant had known and loved it. The grave of the poet is in the village cemetery on the slope of a neighboring hill. The lot which holds it is large and hemmed in by trees, with a plain granite shaft in the center. On one side the shaft is recorded the death of Fanny Bryant, the poet's wife, "who was the beloved disciple of Christ, exemplary in every relation of life, affectionate, sympathetic, sincere, and ever occupied with the welfare of others." On the other side there are simply the name and birthplace of the poet, and the dates of his birth and death. There is no epitaph, and none is needed.

Not far from the grave of Bryant is that of Frances Hodgson Burnett and at nearby Plandome, facing the Sound, one finds the spacious house and lovely garden, in which old age and death came to her and which was long the center of a generous and gracious hospitality, held in grateful memory by its recipients. Frances Eliza Hodgson was born in Manchester, England in 1849. Her father was a merchant and her grandfather a cotton manufacturer. Financial reverses overtook her father and after his death, her mother decided to take her family to America and in 1865 they emigrated to Knoxville, Tennessee where the family moved into a log cabin which the children named Noah's Ark.

From her earliest years Frances had been fond of scribbling and in the new home resolved to win a reputation as an author. She read the stories she had written in England and selected one called *Miss Carruthers*. She copied this painstakingly intending to submit it to a magazine, but, her task completed, found that she had neither stamps nor money with which to buy them. These a friend provided and her manuscript, sent to *Godey's Lady's Book* was accepted and published, this in her fifteenth year. Successes thereafter were constant. The turning point in her career came with the appearance of *Surly Tim's Trouble*, an English dialect story published by Scribner's.

In 1870 Dr. Swan Moses Burnett, a native of Tennessee who had studied medicine with his father and then had graduated from Bellevue Medical College began practice as an oculist in Knoxville, Tennessee, where he made the acquaintance of Miss Hodgson. This led to mutual affection and they were married in 1873, the year Mrs. Burnett laid the foundation of her literary reputation with her striking picture of the life of a pit girl in the coal regions of England, *That Lass o' Lowries.'* She secured a divorce from Dr. Burnett in 1898 after she had published *The Lady of Quality* and *His Grace of Ormonde,* and afterwards married Stephen Townsend an English author who predeceased her. Thereafter she preferred to use her first married name under which she felt she was best known—and as the mother of her two sons, Lionel and Vivian. Her greatest fame perhaps came, as author of the childhood classic, *Little Lord Fauntleroy* which first was published serially in *St. Nicholas* and appeared in book form in 1886. The book was a literary sensation not only in this country but abroad. England and America were swept by the vogue of Fauntleroy curls, a fashion, imposed on thousands of youngsters of the day.

Mrs. Burnett was early rated as possessing real genius and a "mastery of childhood spirit" when writing in the juvenile field. She literally seemed to go on fairy wings and revelled at the idea of magic transformation. Dramatized by its author *Little Lord Fauntleroy* was played for many years here and abroad. She won a suit against the producers of an unauthorized stage version of the story in England and established in that country for the first time the right of an author to control dramatization of novels, lack of which had cost Charles Dickens and others thousands of pounds. The writers of England gave Mrs. Burnett a diamond bracelet as a token of gratitude for her success in establishing a valuable precedent.

For many years, Mrs. Burnett divided her time between her English country home, Maytham Hall in Kent, and New York, but in her later years she lived principally at the Long Island home she had named for her former estate in England. It was characteristic of Mrs. Burnett that wherever she made her home whether at Maytham Hall, Kent, or on Long Island she planned and planted a garden and her understanding love of flowers shows itself in all her writings. The rose garden of *The Lady of Quality* grew at Maytham. The *Secret Garden* was an enchanted corner of the same domain. Even during her last illness she sat propped up in her den writing a garden story, her last, for *The Country Gentleman,* meanwhile looking out on beds of lingering roses, gorgeous clusters of dahlias, masses of budding chrysanthemums that were said to have "blossomed with unusual luxuriance for her passing." Her often quoted statement was "When you have a garden, you have a future." She died October 29, 1924 in her home surrounded by loving friends, and servants. From there she was borne to God's Acre at Roslyn.

Back again in Roslyn an ancient highway takes one to Locust Valley, and thence a short detour northward leads to Dosoris, long the country home of Charles Anderson Dana, editor of the New York *Sun.* The island of Dosoris is distant from the mainland of Long Island about a hundred yards, and is part of an estate which has borne that name for upward of two centuries. The original title was derived from the Matinecock tribe of Indians, and, in 1668, under a patent granted by Richard Nicholls, first English governor of the province of New York, it passed into private hands. In 1693, "it was owned," runs the record, "by John Taylor, who died seized thereof, leaving his surviving daughter and heir-at-law, Abigail, who subsequently intermarried with the Reverend Benjamin Woolsey, and the title was, therefore, by deed of lease and release, conveyed to him, and the trust from that circumstance acquired the name of Dosoris—dos uxoris."

About 1872 the island was bought by Mr. Dana, who there passed the spring and summer months of the years that remained to him. After 1920 it was the home of the younger John Pierpont Morgan. A bridge connects the island some forty-five acres in extent, with Glen Cove, and around it rises a seawall, draped and festooned with creeping vines. Locusts and red cedars flourish on the banks, while waxberry and peach plum trees, extending down to high-water mark, hide the sand and gravel of the beach with a mantle of luxuriant leafage. The house, with broad, shaded piazzas, stands on high ground near the center of the island, and from one side the prospect is over a stretch of green lawn, with glimpses of the open waters of the Sound between the trees, to give life and light to the picture. On the other side there is an attractive view down a long slope and through a vista of rich foliage toward the bridge which unites island and mainland. One could not imagine a more delightful retreat for a hard-working editor and man of letters.

The old road from Roslyn to Locust Valley extends on to Oyster Bay, home and burial place of Theodore Roosevelt who there wrote most of the books that followed his retirement from the Presidency. Oyster Bay was also the early abode of Miriam Coles Harris, the novelist. Settled in 1653, it has been the scene during its long history of memorable events, and boasts landmarks of interest to the lover of the past. It lost one of these, however, when a dozen or more years ago the Jacob Townsend homestead, in its shaded Main Street, was torn down to make room for a hotel. The builder of this old house was one of two brothers who, in the last days of the colonial period were in business together at Oyster Bay and in New York. They were the owners of a fleet of ships which plied between Oyster Bay and the ports of England and the West Indies, and so handsome were their profits that they were long reckoned among the great merchants of their period.

Almy, daughter of Jacob Townsend, married Thomas Buchanan, then a rising merchant of New York, and it was her fondness for fresh milk that laid the foundations of the Goelet, Gerry and other great landed fortunes of the present time. When they began housekeeping, Mrs. Buchanan insisted that her husband should purchase a farm where Canal Street now stands, and, when she found that thirty-five acres in that neighborhood did not suffice for the herd of cows which she deemed necessary, he bought an additional twenty-six acres north of what is now Forty-second Street. The daughters of the Buchanans found husbands among the Goelets, Gerrys and Winthrops, and the increases in the value of the former pasture lands, which duly passed to them from their parents and are now in the very heart of New York, have brought multiplying millions to their descendants.

The vanished house in which Almy Townsend was born has interest also for the pilgrim. Born at Dosoris, Miriam Coles passed her early womanhood in Oyster Bay, and in the Jacob Townsend homestead wrote *Rutledge* and *The Sutherlands,* two of the most widely read novels of eighty years ago. Miss Coles left the village in 1864, following her marriage to Sidney Harris, a lawyer of New York, and the rest of her many novels were written in other places; but memory of her is still fresh in her old home, and the tradition abides that the original of the hero of *Rutledge* was a merchant of Manhattan who had his summer abode at Oyster Bay. Though the house built by Jacob Townsend is gone, the former home of his brother Samuel, which dates from 1740, yet stands among a thick growth of trees in the center of the village. The Samuel Townsend homestead was during the British occupation of Long Island, the headquarters of Colonal Simcoe and his band of Queen's Rangers, who danced and flirted with the daughters of the house, and carved their names and those of the girls on the window panes. These panes of glass are among the relics cherished by the present occupants of the house, built in such enduring fashion that it promises to outlive the present century, while on the hill to the west of the village one can still trace the fortifications thrown up and then abandoned by the long-gone British troopers.

The north shore of Long Island also has intimate association with the early career of Walt Whitman, who was born at West Hills, midway between the villages of Huntington and Cold Springs. West Hills itself is not a village in the accepted sense of the term. A small country store, which is also the post office and blacksmith shop of West Hills, serves the farmers of the countryside, a silent, reserved race with more of Dutch than English blood in their veins. About the store are grouped a few dwellings, and one of these, an ancient but comfortable farmhouse, with two stories and a lean-to, shingled and set close to the road, was the birthplace of the poet. Embowering oaks give it a wealth of shade, and in summer wild flowers climb halfway to the roof of the lean-to, while in front of it, beside the road, a marble tablet erected in 1905 by the Colonial Society of Huntington, bears witness that here "The good gray poet was born, May 31, 1819." The Whitmans left West Hills when Walt was a child of four, and he seldom visited it in after years, but traditions of his carpenter father still linger in the neighborhood. "He was," one ancient declares, "as obstinate as old Elias Hicks, the Quaker preacher, and that is saying some."

This neighborhood estimate of the elder Whitman recalls the career and sturdy character of an uncommon man—leader in the most serious schism that has marked the history of the Quakers in America. Elias Hicks was born and reared in the town of Hempstead, but in 1771, when he was twenty-three years old, married a Quaker maiden of Jericho, which became and remained his home until his death at the age of eighty-two. His youth, he tells us in his journals, was one of indifference to the faith in which he was born, but his twentieth year witnessed a great change in his thoughts and mode of life. Seven years later he entered the Quaker ministry, and he labored therein with untiring diligence for more than half a century. It is recorded of him that he travelled above 10,000 miles on foot, another 1,500 by carriage after he was eighty, and preached in the open air more than a thousand times. Attended by poverty all his days, he would accept no compensation for his services, and when not preaching labored on his farm in the out-skirts of Jericho. The doctrines which Hicks expounded with vigor and power may have little meaning for a later generation, but the fact lives that this lion-hearted old man early opposed negro slavery, wrote and preached against it, and was chiefly instrumental in securing the passage of the act that on July 4, 1827, gave freedom to every slave within the limits of the State of New York. Walt Whitman when a lad of ten heard Hicks preach, and in *November Boughs* makes moving reference to him.

From West Hills it is a five mile ride over a sandy road to the village of Huntington, where at the age of twenty, with a press and type purchased on credit, Walt Whitman began the publication of a weekly paper called the *Long Islander*. "I had been teaching country school for two or three years," the poet wrote in after days, "but liked printing. I had been at it while a lad, and was encouraged to start a paper in the region where I was born. I went to New York, bought a press and type, hired some little help, but did most of the work myself, including the press-work. Everything seemed turning out well—only my own restlessness prevented my gradually establishing a permanent property there. I bought a good horse, and every week went all around the country serving my papers, devoting one day and night to it. I never had happier jaunts—going over to South Side, to Babylon, down the South Road, across to Smithtown and Comac, and back home. The experiences of those jaunts, the dear old-fashioned farmers and their wives, the stops by the hay-fields, the hospitality, the nice dinners, occasional evenings, the girls, the rides through the brush and the smell from the salt of the South roads, come up in my memory to this day, after more than forty years."

The *Long Islander* is still published, and in the Main Street of Huntington one comes upon the office in which Whitman lived and worked—transformed now into a stable. It was during his sojourn in the village that the poet wrote the first and one of his few attempts at fiction. It was a weird effort called *Death in the School-Room,* and was based on an incident which had occurred while the author was teaching in Babylon. He did not print it in his own paper, but sent it to the *Democratic Review,* then the foremost literary journal published in New York, in which it appeared in August, 1841. Meantime, Whitman had grown weary of his country weekly—there is a tradition that his financial supporters had grown equally weary of his unconventional ways—and he drifted back to New York to become editor of the *Daily Aurora,* and a little later to found another journal of his own in Brooklyn.

In the hamlet of Woodbury, a few miles south of Huntington, yet stands the squat one-story building in which Whitman, at the age of eighteen, aided by a wooden pointer which he had carved himself, was first employed as master of a country school.

Forty years ago an aged farmer in the vicinity recalled his first teacher: "He did not confine himself to books, as most of the teachers then did, but taught orally—yes, had some original ideas all his own. He was not severe with the boys, but had complete discipline in the school. Before and after school and at recess he was a boy among boys, always free, always easy, never stiff. It seemed his object to teach even when he played. He would give quite a good deal of time to any subject that seemed worth while. The very moment he stepped across that door-sill he was master. He had authority, but was not severe. We obeyed and respected him."

Still another pupil recalled him: "He was always musin' an' writin' 'stead of tendin' to his proper dooties; but I guess he was like a good many of us—not very well off and had to do somethin' for a livin.' I remember some times at recess he would go off and find a place in the sun and lie down on his back; then all of a sudden he would sit up and scribble somethin' on a paper restin' on his knee. The folks used ter say he was idlin', but I guess he was workin' with his brain, and thinkin' hard, and puttin' down his thoughts. He kept school for a year and then his sister succeeded him."

It is plain that the youthful master left the imprint of a unique individuality on the least of his pupils, and that his school-teaching days contributed in generous measure to the making of a poet. Whitman himself commenting in later years on his experience in the school-room and in the homes of his pupils, where he was successively a guest, observed: "I consider teaching one of my best experiences and deepest lessons in human nature behind the scenes and in the masses." Thus the Woodbury school-house holds a sure if modest place among our literary landmarks.

The poet, Isaac McClellan, classmate of Willis and friend of Hawthorne, spent his last days and died in Greenport. For a number of years Richard Henry Stoddard and his wife had their summer home in the old whaling port of Sag Harbor, and there, as noted in another place, they are buried beside their son. Whitman, who once declared that, when he wrote poetry, the sea was his favorite companion, composed a part of *Leaves of Grass* during walks along the eastern shore of Long Island, and in an earlier time its remoter reaches were a familiar haunt of his youth. "Summers and falls," he writes, "I used to go off, sometimes for a week at a stretch, down in the country, or to Long Island's seashores. There, in the presence of outdoor influences, I went over thoroughly the Old and New Testaments, and absorbed (probably to better advantage for me than in any library or in-door room—it makes such a difference where you read) Shake-speare, Ossian, the best translated versions I could get of Homer, Aeschylus, Sophocles, the old German Nibelungen, the ancient Hindoo poems, and one or two other masterpieces, Dante's among them. As it happened, I read the latter mostly in an old wood. The *Iliad* I read first thoroughly on the peninsula of Orient, northeast end of Long Island, in a sheltered hollow, of rocks and sand, with the sea on each side. I have wondered since why I was not overwhelmed by those mighty masters. Likely because I read them, as described, in the full presence of Nature, under the sun, with the far-spreading landscape and vistas, or the sea rolling in."

Cooper is said to have laid the opening scenes of his *Sea Lions* near Easthampton. The latter place, which, until a recent period, was one of those fortunate towns out of reach of the railway, has a history dating back to 1649, and its elm-shaded streets abound in reminders of an earlier time. Many of the houses date from the eighteenth century, and in one of them Lyman Beecher, the famous father of famous children, lived for a dozen years while pastor of the village church. A venerable resident of Easthampton was once asked to describe Beecher's methods in the pulpit. "How did Lyman Beecher preach?" was his reply. "I will tell you. He would get up and read a Psalm and a chapter in the Bible, just like other ministers. Then he would take his text, shut up the book and lean over the pulpit, and the way that man would talk was a caution." Beecher was ordained in Easthampton in 1798, and two of his children, Cath-erine and Edward, were born in the village. When he gave up his pastorate it was because his yearly salary of $400 did not suffice for the needs of a growing family.

Another old house fronting Easthampton's main street was the boyhood abode of John Howard Payne, and memory of it is believed by many to have inspired his song of *Home, Sweet Home*. Payne was born in New York City, but was taken in infancy to Easthampton, where his father was for some years principal of Clinton Academy, one of the first institutions of the kind estab-lished in the State of New York. The former home of the Paynes is more than two hundred years old, and, except for the slow changes wrought by time, remains as it was when the future songmaker passed his childhood beneath its sloping roof. It is a modest structure, unpainted like the other old homes of the village, and with shingled sides half hidden by clambering greens. The house within gives evidence of long usage, but an air of comfort pervades its low-ceiling rooms, and it is easy to picture it the center in other days of more than one happy family group. It has been for some years the summer home of a wealthy resident of Brooklyn. The academy in which the elder Payne taught still stands, and in altered form serves the people of Easthampton as a village hall and library.

Easthampton was also the home after 1927 of Ring W. Lardner, perhaps the most widely read story-teller of his period, who died there after long illness in 1933 at the early age of forty-eight. Lardner's was a great talent, but one that challenged definite analysis. It has been said of him that as a humorist he resembled Mark Twain in his hatred of sham, and that as a satirist he resembled Ambrose Bierce in his capacity for acrid and biting utterance. This estimate, however, is only a half-truth, for Lardner had also a vigor, persuasiveness and piquant mastery of the common tongue which placed him in a class by himself.

Lardner, ever and always a delightful companion, after fame had come to him, used to talk to his friends in a whimsical way of the three great ambitions that had helped to shape his life. He had wondered as a lad if he would ever see enough baseball. A little later he longed to be the author of stories that would win acceptance by editors. Last of all he hoped to write and secure production of a successful play. And in time each of these desires had gratifying fulfilment. He was a bookkeeper in his native town of Niles, Michigan, when at the age of twenty he became by lucky chance sporting editor of a newspaper in South Bend, Indiana. That ere long brought like employment for six years in Chicago and also in Boston and St. Louis. After that came the writing of stories for the magazines collected under such titles as *You Know Me, Al, The Big Town* and *The Love Nest,* and residence near or in New York where in 1933 the production of *June Moon* gave happy proof of his ability as a maker of plays.

And in at least two of the fields wherein Lardner aimed to excel he came close to founding a new school of writing. The talk of the ball player Jack Keefe in *You Know Me, Al* proved his mastery of a novel yet natural idiom, his patient searching for the exact word, and the bitter veracity of *How to Write Short*

Stories, perhaps his best work, revealed his perfect knowledge of every day folk and his purpose, for he was always on the side of the common man, to give that knowledge sensitive and sympathetic but also unerring expression. Some set him down as a cynic and others as a pessimist, but it is nearer the truth to say of him that his changing moods and manners had in them the richness and contradictory variety of nature itself. One can only regret and wonder at the tragic extinction of a talent of such rare accomplishment and splendid promise.

Journeying westward from Easthampton along Long Island's low-lying south shore, the pilgrim is sure to halt at Patchogue, the last home and burial-place of Seba Smith, under the pen name of Major Jack Downing, the best known humorist of his time. Smith spent his closing years in Patchogue, and died there in 1868 at the age of seventy-six. His grave is in an abandoned burial ground near the edge of a wood at the back of the village. The storm-worn marble slab above it, tells the passer-by that Smith was the author of *Way Down East* and other works, and that "he was well-beloved," but no stone marks the adjoining grave, where, in 1892, the body of his wife—the once famous and beloved Eliza Oakes Smith—was laid to rest.

The neighborhood of Babylon, another South Shore town, has pleasant association with the early manhood of Walt Whitman, who there served for a second and last time as master of a country school. Local traditions give evidence that both at Woodbury and Babylon the future poet as a teacher was in advance of his era. He made little use of text-books; but instead went with his classes to groves and sands, and learned with them from nature. He was soon on a friendly footing with all sorts and conditions of men and women, and, finding congenial comrades among the fishermen of the bay beside which Babylon nestles, he soon learned to sail a boat with the best of them. Whitman passed two years in and about Babylon, spending his vacations with his parents, who for a time lived on a farm near the village. During his second year of teaching, he was arrested for assaulting one of the large boys, who had broken the rules of the school, but a trial in which he defended his own cause, resulted in his acquittal. The pupil who had been disciplined, a youth named Carman, afterwards became one of Whitman's firm friends.

One other literary shrine of Long Island demands mention —Point o'Woods on Great South Beach, where, in July, 1850, Margaret Fuller met her death. This once celebrated and now half-forgotten woman was born at Cambridge, Massachusetts, in 1810, the daughter of Timothy Fuller, a lawyer and member of Congress, who died in his prime, leaving a large family to struggle for themselves. Margaret was, for a brief period, a teacher in one of Bronson Alcott's schools; but soon began to attract attention by her writings, while at the same time her famous *Conversations* made her widely known. She was associated with Emerson and other leading men of letters in the publication of the *Dial*, of which she finally became the editor. Her's was a period in which all sorts of reforms were widely discussed, but her interest in most of them was that of an attentive observer. The change which she most warmly urged was that American writers should cease to be imitators and find charm in the things of this country. "Let us write of the woodthrush and the bluebird, rather than of the skylark and the nightingale," was one of her utterances. Her first book was *A Summer at the Lakes* describing a trip through Ohio and Michigan. A little later *Woman in the Nineteenth Century* appeared and found many admirers.

An important change in Miss Fuller's life came in 1844 with her removal to New York, and her association with Horace Greeley as a writer for the *Tribune*. Her contributions were signed by a star, and while her personality was thus concealed, the articles attracted wide attention. In 1846 she went to Europe, and, after a brief trip through England and France, reached Rome, then the center of the struggle for Italian freedom led by Mazzini. Margaret was deeply interested in this attempt to establish a republic, and devoted herself to aiding the patriots, and caring for the wounded. While thus employed she met the Marquis Ossoli, who had been cut off by his family because of his devotion to the republican cause, and an attachment sprang up which soon led to marriage. Then the heroic struggled failed, and the marquis found himself without means of support, and his wife cut off in a land of strangers from earning money with her pen.

Accordingly, they decided to go to America, and in May, 1850 with their little son, sailed from Leghorn on a merchant vessel, the *Elizabeth*. When the long voyage was nearly ended and land in sight, a storm arose and the ship grounded in the shoaling waters of Great South Beach. Then a mighty wave struck the deck, sweeping all before it and Margaret, her husband, and child were carried to death in the wild waters. The boy was drowned while one of the crew was trying to bear him to land, and his lifeless body was carried on the beach, still warm from his guardian's arms. The others were never heard of more.

In 1901 a memorial to Margaret Fuller was erected on Fire Island Beach. Julia Ward Howe wrote a finely worded tribute which was put on a bronze tablet. The memorial consisted of a pavilion, the tablet being placed inside. Julia Ward Howe's tribute deserves to be remembered:

To commemorate

MARGARET FULLER

Marchioness Ossoli

Author, Editor, Poet, Orator,

Who with her husband Marquis Ossoli

And their child Angelo

Perished by shipwreck off this shore

July 19th 1850, in the forty-first year of her age.

Noble in thought and in character, eloquent

of tongue and of pen

She was an inspiration to many of her own
time

And her uplifting influence abides with us.

Erected 1901.

CHAPTER XII

A Staten Island Ramble

A ramble about Staten Island yields much of interest to the literary pilgrim. Thus one finds at the junction of the Clove and Richmond roads and close to the village of Concord, the site of a vanished house which had intimate association with Emerson and Thoreau. A century ago William, elder brother of Ralph Waldo Emerson, settled in New York, and, being a man of character and exceptional parts, soon won an honored place at the bar. One day he went with friends for an outing on Staten Island, and so pleased was he with what he saw that he resolved on the instant to make his home among its hills. Accordingly, he found lodging with his family at a small inn at Dutch Farms, later through his efforts to have its name changed to Concord, in honor of his former home. The old inn, which still stands, was also an early abode of Erastus Brooks, one of the eminent editors of his period, and founder with his brother of the New York *Express*.

William Emerson had not long been settled on Staten Island when he purchased a part of what is now the Unger estate, and set to work enlarging the old cottage which stood on it and transforming it into a comfortable and attractive home. And so skillful were the changes wrought that when Ralph Waldo Emerson journeyed to Staten Island to be one of the first guests in his brother's new abode, he at once christened the converted cottage The Snuggery, by which name it was known during the remaining years of its existence. William Emerson became judge of Richmond County in 1841, and when, in 1855, The Snuggery was destroyed by fire, he built a house on a nearby hill, which was his home for a number of years. This house yet stands with little change in outward appearance, but of The Snuggery there remains no trace, a field of grass, half hidden by a high board fence, covering its site. Time has also taken the little church on the adjoining hillside—the first home of the Baptists on Staten Island —where Judge Emerson and his family regularly attended service, and the slabs in the burial ground which recall its existence are moss-grown and neglected. Here, after long and painful illness, a brother of William and Ralph Waldo Emerson was laid to rest, but later a legal question arising, the body was removed to the family plot of the Emersons in Sleepy Hollow Cemetery at Concord.

Ralph Waldo Emerson made The Snuggery his summer home for several years, and his room on the second floor looked out on the winding highway and the broad fields of grain which then formed part of the landscape. Thoreau was also for a time a member of The Snuggery family circle, serving as tutor to the sons of William Emerson. This was in May, 1843, and the future hermit of Walden was then a young man of twenty-five, only a few years out of Harvard. "Concord is my Rome and its people are my Romans," Thoreau had declared to a friend a short time before, and the letters which tell the story of his brief sojourn on Staten Island, show that, while interested in his new surroundings, his heart and its longings centered always in the village of his birth.

"I have already run over no small part of the island, to the highest hill, and some way along the shore," he wrote in his first letter to his mother. "From the pinnacle of one Madame Grimes' house, the other night at sunset, I could see almost round the island. Far in the horizon there was a fleet of sloops bound up the Hudson, which seemed to be going over the edge of the earth. But it is rather derogatory that your dwelling place should be only a neighbourhood to a great city—to live on an inclined plane. I do not like their cities and forts, with their morning and evening guns, and sails flapping in one's eye. I want a whole continent to breathe in, and a good deal of solitude and silence, such as all Wall Street cannot buy, nor Broadway with its wooden pavement. Give me time enough, and I may like it. All my inner man heretofore has been a Concord impression; and here come these Sandy Hook and Coney Island breakers to meet and modify the former; but it will be long before I can make nature look as innocently grand and inspiring as in Concord."

Thoreau's duties as tutor gave him welcome leisure for almost daily rambles in the open, and for occasional trips to the city, where he made the acquaintance of William Henry Channing; of the elder Henry James, meeting whom, he wrote to Emerson, made "humanity seem more erect and respectable," and of Horace Greeley, then in the early morning of his success as editor of the *Tribune*, and who was destined in after years to prove one of the most helpful of the Concord thinker's friends.

The call homeward, however, proved ere long too strong to be resisted, and the end of 1843 found Thoreau back in the familiar haunts which he was never to leave again, except for an occasional journey into the wild.

The grave of George William Curtis is in the Moravian cemetery at New Dorp, and at the corner of Bard and Henderson Avenues, New Brighton, stands the roomy, comfortable house, set amid flowering shrubs and green sweeps, which for more than thirty years was the home of that many-sided man of letters. Born at Providence, Rhode Island, in 1824, Curtis was educated in schools near Boston, and under private tutors in New York. When he was sixteen, his father, a man of large affairs who desired that he should be trained for a business career, placed him as clerk with an importing house. The clerkship, however, was of short duration, and at the end of a year he went with an elder brother to Brook Farm. There he remained for four years, going thence to Concord, where for two years he and his brother lived with a farmer in the outskirts of the village. During this period it was his good fortune to meet and know Ripley, Hawthorne, Emerson, Thoreau and others, whose influence left an enduring impression on his youthful mind.

In the late summer of 1846, young Curtis, then twenty-two, sailed for Europe, where four years of leisurely and delightful wanderings carried him to England, Germany, Italy, Switzerland, Holland, Egypt, Syria and the Holy Land. The fruits of his travels took form soon after his return to America in *Nile Notes* and *The Howadji in Syria,* his first books. Meanwhile, he had joined the staff of the New York *Tribune,* and in the summer of 1851 he wrote to this paper from various watering places a series of letters afterward gathered into a volume to which he gave the title *Lotus Eating.* He was now fairly embarked upon a literary career, and in 1852, as a contributor to *Harper's Monthly,* began an association with the house of Harper which, with a brief interruption, lasted until his death.

The same year, in association with Parke Godwin and Charles F. Briggs, Curtis became editor of *Putnam's New Monthly Magazine,* contributing to its columns his satirical *Potiphar Papers* and his sentimental *Prue and I.* These when issued in book form enhanced his growing repute as an author, but in a business way his first editorship proved a disastrous venture. He sank in it the inheritance he had received from his father and when the magazine finally suspended publication gave instant and sterling proof of his moral caliber. The firm of publishers in which he was a limited partner having failed, he paid to the creditors the full amount for which his association made him liable, and then, refusing to invoke his legal rights, voluntarily assumed, as a personal debt, every obligation his former partners had left unpaid when taking advantage of the bankruptcy laws.

To the accomplishment of this purpose Curtis devoted the profits from his book, a part of his salary as editor of *Harper's Weekly,* which post he assumed in 1863, and all that he received from his lectures. As early as 1853 he had won marked success as a lyceum lecturer, and for many years after he made himself responsible for the debts other men had repudiated, he often delivered more than a hundred lectures a season. Only his most intimate friends knew why he faced the hardships of almost continual travel under trying conditions, and from the day in 1873 that saw final discharge of his self-imposed task he never accepted another lecture engagement.

Mr. Curtis was married in the late autumn of 1856 to Anna Shaw, daughter of Francis George Shaw and sister of Robert Gould Shaw, who a few years later was to command the first colored regiment raised in a free state—the Fifty-fourth Massachusetts, and who was to fall at the head of his men in an assault on Fort Wagner. Thereafter and until his death an ideal family life furnished a restful yet stimulating background for his labors as editor, writer, orator and champion of good causes. Curtis' first political speeches were made in support of John C. Fremont, in 1856 the Republican candidate for President; he was an outstanding figure in the convention which four years later nominated Lincoln, and then for a generation every forward looking movement was sure to enlist his voice and influence. He was one of the first to advocate civil service reform, becoming with the years the recognized leader of that movement, joined in every liberal departure within his party, and in 1884 left it to support Grover Cleveland for President, his puritan conscience compelling him to oppose James G. Blaine, the Republican candidate for that office.

And so it fell out that the Staten Island home of Curtis was for many years a centre for men and women of light and leading, who gathered there from time to time at the bidding of its master. "He had not, as some have," writes one who was often his guest, "a different character at home and abroad, but rather a different manifestation of it. His talk was, on the whole, the best I have ever known. He had great skill as a narrator, a natural skill, the fruit of keen and sympathetic observation and of hearty enjoyment of re-presentation. He had wit at times caustic, but never cruel or unfair, and always bright in itself and illuminating. He had humor of a generous and suave sort; and he was capable of much of that play with the topic or the feeling of the moment which we recognize as 'fun' though we cannot define it. He was at home in all circles, because in all he was true to a nature constantly sincere and kind and simple. The irritation that is bred of vanity, jealousy, envy; the weariness and distrust that are the revulsion from unworthy desires, seemed impossible to him. He invited and won the best, because naturally and without constraint he offered the best. Charm of many sorts he had, but the supreme one was the completeness with which he could render the charm of virtue, and the constant proof he gave that he was himself possessed by it."

And of the unnumbered proofs George William Curtis gave of helpfulness to others one claims a place in this record. To his office in Franklin Square came a woman wholly unknown to the world of letters and also in great need. She brought with her the manuscript of a novel sale of which she hoped would bring her relief. The busy editor listened to his visitor's story, and assuring her that her manuscript would have an immediate reading asked her to call again the following day. It was read before Curtis went to his bed that night, and when its author returned next morning she was told that not only had her novel been accepted for early publication by the house of Harper, but was also handed a check for a generous amount in anticipation of future royalties. This friend of man died in 1892 after long and painful illness. "Continue to love me," were his parting words to a kinsman who called on him a few days before his death, and than he surely few men have deserved in fuller measure the affectionate good-will of their fellows.

Sydney Howard Gay, long managing editor of the New York *Evening Post* was a resident of New Brighton in his latter years, and there wrote the major part of the popular history of the United States in the preparation of which he had the aid and advice of his old chief, William Cullen Bryant. And New Brighton also has intimate and piquant association with Theodore Winthrop who passed much time there in the years preceding the great conflict between the sections in which he was to be one of the first to fall. Sprung from an honored and historic family,

Winthrop was born in 1828 in New Haven. Graduating at Yale at the age of twenty, he then spent two years in Europe, where he met William H. Aspinwall who made him the tutor of his son, and a little later found a place for him in the employ of the Pacific Mail Steamship Company at Panama.

Winthrop did not remain long on the Isthmus but in 1854, after a visit to California and Oregon, returned to his mother's home on Staten Island, and in the following year was admitted to the New York bar. Literature, however, was more attractive to him than the law, and while waiting for clients he toiled faithfully at the novels and sketches which, though he could find no publisher for them at the moment, were later to win him fame.

Then came the firing on Fort Sumter. The day of Lincoln's first call for volunteers, Winthrop enlisted in the Seventh Regiment of New York, and when that command returned home at the end of the thirty days for which it had taken service, he joined the staff of General Benjamin F. Butler. A night attack on Big Bethel was planned, and Winthrop, then stationed at Fort Monroe, sought and secured permission to accompany the expedition. When near the enemy's lines, in the early morning of June 10, 1861, two companies of Union troops fired upon each other through a mistake. This alarmed and aroused the Confederates; the expedition was repulsed and Winthrop, while rallying his men, was shot through the heart. His body was left in the hands of the enemy, but a week later was delivered to his friends under a flag of truce, and, after a military funeral in New York City, was finally laid to rest in New Haven.

Winthrop's gallant and untimely death deeply moved the popular heart, and upon the appearance of two articles which he had contributed a short time before to the *Atlantic Monthly* widespread attention was drawn to his literary ability. Publishers were now quick to recognize the merit of manuscripts which they had previously declined. Winthrop's novel *Cecil Dreeme,* to which his friend George William Curtis prefixed a memoir, was published in the autumn of 1862, and was presently followed by *John Brent* and *Edwin Brothertoft,* and by two volumes of travel sketches—all of which met with wide circulation at the time and still find admiring readers. They deserve them, for they are charged with strength and sincerity and give evidence of a distinct vein of original genius which, one loves to think, needed only the chastening influence of time and experience to have given their author a place among the makers of masterly fiction.

When in the late eighties of the last century Edgar Wilson Nye, better known as Bill Nye, by his droll and diverting writings in the *Boomerang* of Laramie, Wyoming, came east lured by the handsome salary offered hlm by Joseph Pulitzer of the New York *World,* he lived for a time in a rented house at New Brighton. Then he bought a place on Fort Hill at Tompkinsville—a roomy, old-fashioned structure torn down in 1920 to make room for more modern dwellings. There was a veranda running all around it and at one end a tower which at once became the pride and delight of the owner. A spacious plot of ground surrounded the house, which Nye promptly dubbed his "slosh," not with reference to the rainstorms which at certain seasons pour down on Staten Island, but as a play on the German Schloss. "We like our new house better as we investigate it," Nye wrote to a friend, "and shall be glad to put our money there instead of into rent. It is a large, rangy slosh with a view. Toward the south one gets a southern view, and toward the north one gets a northern aspect. Aspects come high here. As I write the sound of the tack hammer can be heard on the floor below, and also the suppressed thud of the whitewash brush in the basement, and the swash of the brush of the man who is oiling the dining room floor. I go back into the country a mile or two and practice with a new plug hat every day so that I will not disgrace my slosh. O, Sir, I am trying very hard to lead such a life that future generations will say: 'There was a slosher who knew his business. He was a haughty politician, with no hair to speak of, but yet he always spoke kindly to the poor'."

Born near Moosehead Lake in Maine, Nye grew up on a Wisconsin farm, and after brief experience as a teacher of country schools became a law student. In 1876 he began practice in Laramie, Wyoming, where he also served as justice of the peace and postmaster of the town. To eke out an uncertain income he contributed letters to local journals and to the Denver *Tribune,* and when the Laramie *Boomerang* was founded wrote for it a series of humorous articles which quickly brought repute and popularity to author and journal. Then came removal to the East. Nye was thirty-seven years of age and in the fulness of his powers as a droll of unique and unmistakable gifts when he found a home on Staten Island, and much of his best writing was done in the vanished house on Fort Hill.

The Nye home also quickly became a gathering place for a group of writers, among them James Whitcomb Riley, the poet, who for a time was profitably associated with Nye on the lecture platform. A son of the humorist who has written a biography of his father recalls that there was much sky-larking and impromptu humor when Nye and Riley met for dinner and a social evening, and there was sure to be a fuller measure of jollity when Henry Guy Carleton, the playwright and author, another fellow of infinite jest, was also a guest. Indeed a score of piquant ancedotes attach to the friendship between humorist and playwright. On one occasion Nye was at table in Carleton's home when its master had provided a feast of pompano for his guests. The fish had been shipped from Florida in a cake of ice, but the ice had melted and the fish, unknown to Carleton, had reached New York in sorry condition. Nye was one of the first to get a taste of the fish, but did not appear to relish it. Carleton, who had not yet tasted it, noted the puzzled look on the face of his guest. "I guess you don't know how I had that fish shipped up here," he remarked, quick to champion so choice an article of food. "From the taste," was Nye's dry retort, "you must have shipped it in a hearse."

Nye found life very comfortable on Staten Island, to which there is frequent and whimsical reference in his writings, but a sea-level climate proved too severe for the Nye children, who had been accustomed to the dry and bracing air of the Laramie plains. Accordingly in March, 1891, following the death of one of the children, the family moved to Asheville, North Carolina. But the commanding feature of the house he built there and which remained his home until his death in 1896 was a replica of his beloved tower on Fort Hill. Nye's reputation is now a fading one, but he was quick to detect and flay social abuses, while his humor was of an individual and fetching sort. A source of zestful diversion for thousands ceased to be when he laid down his pen for the last time.

When Nye lived in New Brighton he had for neighbor across the way William Winter of the New York *Tribune*, for a full half century the most widely known and esteemed dramatic critic on this side of the sea. More than that Winter was one of those writers—rarely a numerous group—who in their personality and point of view sum up in a striking way the salient characteristics of the period in which they are privileged to live and do their work. His love of and devotion to the past and the artists it had produced was without qualification, and by the same token he was seldom indulgent of the present or of those artists who labored in it. And his writings, whether penned in haste for a waiting press or refined with patient care, revealed the man behind them —the master of a copious and easy style in which poetry and sentiment, humor and prudishness, pugnacity and inflexible honesty were blended in an arresting and unmistakable way.

William Winter was born at Gloucester, Massachusetts, in 1836 and on both sides of his family was descended from seafaring folk. His mother whom he once described as a woman of rare beauty of mind and person died at twenty-four when her son was only four years old, and the latter's motherless boyhood was passed first in Gloucester and later in Boston and Cambridge. In 1852 he was graduated at the Cambridge high school, receiving his diploma, as he was fond of recalling, from Edward Everett. Thereafter he studied law at Harvard, receiving his degree in 1857, but he never practiced his profession.

Instead he turned to letters as a career. Indeed, his first book of poems, dedicated to Longfellow, an early and helpful friend, had been published when he was only eighteen. In 1859 he settled in New York, where he became without delay a contributor to *Vanity Fair* and the *Saturday Press,* journals which for a period attracted to their pages a generous amount of budding talent, and at the same time afforded a welcome if not always certain livelihood for the members of a group who gathered nightly at Pfaff's beer cellar on Broadway, and whose free and easy ways led them to be called at the time and to be still remembered as the New York Bohemians.

Young Winter had been less than two years in New York when he met, wooed and married Elizabeth Campbell, a winsome young actress and writer of short stories born in the Highlands of Scotland. She had good looks and talent, but in worldy goods shared the condition of her lover. "We had nothing," said Mr. Winter once, in recalling those days, "and were quite willing to divide the same." At first the little household had many a struggle with poverty, but soon there was a turn in the tide. In 1861 George William Curtis, who a few years earlier had met Winter at the home of Longfellow in Cambridge, brought the young poet to the attention of the publisher of the *Albion,* a weekly journal of quality with discriminating and appreciative readers on both sides of the Atlantic.

Winter was made dramatic critic of the *Albion* and presently became book reviewer and assistant editor. His articles on plays and players, written over the signature of Mercutio, in a manner at once vigorous and poetic, soon commanded wide and admiring attention, and in the summer of 1865 he joined the staff of the New York *Tribune* as dramatic critic, a post he was to hold for two score and four years. Thenceforth his career developed along established lines, but his range was always a wide one. He wrote not only dramatic criticisms, but editorials, book reviews, poems, full-length biographies and volumes of travel of which following his first visit to England in 1877 there was a steadily lengthening list. As a result of differences of opinion with his managing editor as to what subjects he should or should not treat as a dramatic critic his connection with the *Tribune* terminated in 1909, but his labors as author and bookman did not pause until his death after long illness in his eighty-first year, and when he laid down his pen for the last time more than thirty titles, most of them representing work of the first-class, stood to his credit in the library catalogues.

The home of William Winter for more than a generation was a modest house yet standing at 27 Third Avenue, New Brighton, and there through the years master and mistress gave gracious welcome to many of the leaders of the theatre and of letters both of America and England. The master, writes Joseph Bishop, an intimate friend and associate, "was always delightful, original and entertaining. A more gentle, lovable soul never lived, and one more valiant I have never known." He was also rich in intimate and amusing memories of the men and women he had known, one of which, having to do with his old chief, Horace Greeley, deserves a place in the present chronicle. Winter had given to a young reporter for the *Tribune*, at the moment very much in love with a charming girl, tickets for a popular play of the hour, so that enjoyment of it might follow the dinner he planned to give her. A few hours before the anticipated meeting, however, the reporter sought out Winter to tell him with woe-begone face, that he had just been assigned to report a lecture Greeley was to give in Harlem, then a slow journey by street car from the distant town, and was at a loss to devise how he could be in two places at one and the same time.

"What is Uncle Horace going to lecture about?" asked Winter. When told the topic he went on reassuringly: "That is easy. I have heard him talk on that subject many times, and know just what he will say. Take your girl to dinner and the theater, as you have planned to do. Then meet me at Browne's"—a popular eating-place of the period—"and I will dictate a report of his lecture to you."

This program was carried out to the letter, and the next morning's *Tribune* recorded in half a column what Greeley was believed to have said to his Harlem audience. Later in the day, however, the editor of the *Tribune* appeared at the desk of its city editor, and, pointing to the reporter's article which he held in his hand, angrily demanded: "What infernal fool wrote that?"

The supposed author was summoned, to receive one of the caustic dressing downs of which an offended Greeley was a master. When his chief paused for an instant to take breath the object of his wrath timidly interposed: "But you know, Mr. Greeley, you are a difficult man to report."

"Report, . . ." was the tart retort, "I didn't lecture."

The grave of William Winter and those of other members of his family are in Silver Mount Cemetery not far from his old home; but one perhaps comes closest to the life and influence of a rarely gifted man in the Arthur Winter Memorial Library at the Staten Island Academy in St. George founded in 1886 by Mr. and Mrs. Winter in memory of their son Arthur, who died as the result of an accident while still a school-boy. From a small beginning this library, where in his closing years Mr. Winter often studied and wrote, has grown to number more than 10,000 volumes, nearly all of which apart from their contents, have an interest of their own on account of those who added them to the collection. Thus one finds here Edwin Booth's favorite set of Shakespeare with many annotations by its former owner, and a hundred other items with an appeal of a personal sort which make them dear to the collector. The library is in one large room with a lofty ceiling. At one end of the room is a tall fireplace, flanked on either side by a balcony, and at the other end are spacious windows giving a pleasant, even light. The books are in shelves and alcoves standing out a little way from the wall. Above the shelves and in all the free places are photographs and engravings of actors and authors of renown, signed and sent by them, or by equally famous people who owned them. A particularly interesting relic is a panel from the church at Haworth, with an engraving of Charlotte Bronte set in wood, together with a note from Matthew Arnold and a copy in his own hand of two verses from his *Elegy in Haworth Churchyard*.

The life of Henry Parker Willis, editor, author and scholar of wide and varied interests, came to an end at 215 Prospect

Avenue, New Brighton, and a few blocks distant was the last home in an earlier time of Richard Adams Locke, author of one of the boldest and at the moment, by reason of its realistic detail, most convincing hoaxes ever played on readers of the New York press. Locke was a clever young English newspaperman who came to New York when Jackson, whom he greatly admired, was President, and in the summer of 1835 wrote for the *Sun,* then in its infancy, his famous *Moon Story* which set forth in successive chapters and in a manner calculated to persuade even a Doubting Thomas the observations of men and animal life on the moon supposed to have been made through a powerful telescope at the Cape of Good Hope by Sir John Herschel, the British astronomer, and reported by him to the *Edinburgh Journal of Science.*

Aside from its air of perfect honesty and of profound scientific research, the *Moon Story* was also an admirable piece of writing. The curious will find a reprint of it in the life of Henry J. Raymond by Augustus Maverick, who in an after time counted its author among his friends. Another of Locke's admirers was a struggling young author, Edgar Allan Poe by name, who when occasion offered declared him "one of the few men of unquestionable genius whom the country possesses," adding, "I am acquainted with no person possessing so fine a forehead," which for the author of *The Raven,* perhaps atoned for a stout figure and pock-marked face. Another of Locke's achievements was the founding of the *New Era,* a lively sheet in which, being a radical of an outspoken sort, he for a time defended trade-unions and strikes, attacked paper money as a device of the devil, and championed the political fortunes of Martin Van Buren. In the end, however, that and other of Locke's ventures failed to prosper, and his last years were passed in poverty and obscurity.

Edith Matilda Thomas, beloved by a wide circle of admirers, was for a time a resident of West Brighton, where she wrote many of the poems in which a beautiful and unselfish spirit finds uplifting expression. Florence Morse Kingsley, author of *Titus —A Comrade of the Cross,* and other romances of wide if passing popularity, dwelt during her latter years at 116 Kingsley Avenue, Westerleigh, and at 98 Waters Avenue in the same town after 1900 and until his death resided the poet, Edwin Markham. The cottage which for a generation was the home of Markham and his devoted, albeit at times much enduring wife, was an angular, flimsy affair, which never knew how to take on beauty with age. Hamlin Garland in his *Afternoon Neighbors,* describes the rough-and-ready conditions which ruled it when master and mistress were nearing the end of the road. "We found ourselves," he writes, "entering a welter of books piled on chairs, tables and shelves. Even the piano was covered with manuscripts. It was the home of a book lover and scholar. It showed both learning and poverty—a wretched domicile for so great a poet. It resembled a second-hand bookstore, and yet there was a kind of nobility in its suggested indifference to order and beauty."

Markham, however, never fretted over his need for dollars, and the present writers also recall more than one visit to him when he dwelt at length and with manifest satisfaction on the straitened conditions which had kept him company all his days. In truth he loved to tell how when a youthful teacher in a California village he had plowed for a dollar an acre to buy copies of Byron, Moore and Tennyson and learned from them the abiding charm of poetry. The wolf through the years knocked grimly at the door of the Markham cottage, but was never able to effect an entrance, and those who knew Markham, after the added handicap of old age had come to him, hold stoutly to the belief that from first to last, assured that the way he had chosen was the right and inevitable one, he found a fine profit in living.

Edwin Arlington Robinson, another poet, but one who unlike Markham began to write before editors were receptive to his work, who struck from the ancient formula of wine, women and song only the middle term, and whose lot was an uncertain and difficult one until Theodore Roosevelt, impressed by his verse in 1905 saw to it that a place was made for him in the New York customs house, during not a few of his years of struggle and self-denial had his home on Staten Island. "By Jove, it reads like the real thing," Roosevelt is reported to have declared when the poet's *Children of the Night* fell into his hands. By the same token Robinson did not long remain in the sinecure an admiring President had assured him, for he was poet and nothing else, although he yielded with reluctance to his fate. "If I could have done anything else on God's green earth," he once told a friend, "I never would have written poetry. There was nothing else I could do, and I had to justify my existence," adding grimly: "Whatever honors may be mine must come to me when I shall not be here to receive them."

Finally another and very different man of genius, the Russian Maxim Gorky wrote his *Mother* while the guest in 1906 of friends at 37 Howard Avenue, Grymes Hill. And so ends the record of Staten Islands' part in literature.

CHAPTER XIII

Sound Shore to Riverside

Than Westchester County, flanked by the Sound and the Hudson, no section of New York has had a more stirring and eventful history. And for the literary pilgrim it has an appeal that goes back to the birth years of the republic. Thus one of the most interesting of Westchester's many old buildings is the frame house on North Avenue in New Rochelle, which was once the home of Thomas Paine. It is now owned by the Huguenot Society of New Rochelle, and the small plot it occupies was once part of the widespreading farm which had been confiscated from a Tory named De Veau, and which in 1784 the Legislature of New York granted to Paine "in recognition of his distinguished merit and eminent services rendered to the United States in the progress of the late war."

The house which then stood on the farm was burned in 1793 during Paine's absence in France. The one now standing was built by him after his return to America in 1802, broken and enfeebled by his long and unjust confinement in a Paris prison. Now become a shrine for those who honor the memory of a stout apostle of liberty in thought and action, its original site was a short quarter of a mile west of its present one, removal having been effected when the land surrounding it was cut up into building lots. In front of it, and not far from the spot where Paine's body rested for ten years, stands the monument to his memory erected in 1839 by public contributions. This monument was repaired and rededicated in 1881, and in 1889 topped with a bronze bust of Paine. It was again repaired in 1905, and in the same year the Thomas Paine National Museum was opened on the upper floor of his old home. This museum contains a large number of relics, portraits and other memorials of Paine, including a small stove with the inscription: "Presented by Benjamin Franklin to Thomas Paine, author-hero of the Revolution." Paine's study, in the rear, has a small window below which was once a hole large enough for the insertion of a finger. This hole was made by a bullet fired at Paine on Christmas Eve of 1805 by a hoodlum of the town whom his writings on religion had moved to murderous hostility. The would-be assassin was arrested, but went free when his intended victim refused to prosecute him.

The last seven years of Paine's life were mainly divided between New York and New Rochelle. On occasional Sunday
afternoons he preached to small gatherings of his neighbors assembled in a grove on his farm, and one youthful hearer recalled
in old age that his addresses were earnest appeals for right living
that could give no offense even to the strictly orthodox. And
while he continued to be baited by piety and patriotism, many of
the distinguished friends of his earlier years, Thomas Jefferson
and Robert Fulton among them, remained devoted to him, and
until the end he found joy in simple things. "His affection for
children and dogs," we are told, was long remembered. He had
always been the friend of the dumb beast; now he patted every
stray cur in the town and got a friendly wag in response. He
bestowed cookies and bits of sugar on the youngsters, "and,"
to the astonishment of boys who descended on his orchard for a
raid, he "came out and picked the biggest and best apples for
them." He also faced with stoic and steadfast spirit the ills and
increasing feebleness of old age. "I have been preserved through
many dangers," he wrote Samuel Adams as his own life was
nearing the end, "but instead of buffeting the Deity with prayers,
as if I distrusted him, or must dictate to him, I repose myself on
his protection; and you, my friend, will find, even in your last
moment, more consolation in the silence of resignation than in
the murmuring wish of a prayer."

As elsewhere recorded Paine died in New York in the early
summer of 1809, and a few days later was buried close to his
New Rochelle home. It is also a familiar story of how in 1819
his friend and admirer, William Cobbett, had the remains taken
up and transported to England. Financial reverses, however, compelled Cobbett to postpone the funeral exercises he had planned
for Paine in his native country, and in the end Paine's bones came
into possession of those charged with the adjustment of Cobbett's
affairs. Later they were lost sight of and there is no authentic
proof of what became of them. Paine was born and reared a
Quaker, and one tradition has it that members of that sect ob--
tained possession of his remains and gave them secret burial.
The same tradition has it that many years later Moncure D. Conway ferreted out the place of burial but died without revealing
its location.

Margaret Elizabeth Sangster, whose buoyant verse still lifts
the spirits of men and women who first read and prized it
in their youth, was born and passed her girlhood in New Rochelle.

Another resident of the town in other years was John Habberton, whose career proves the fleeting quality of most literary reputations. Habberton was a native of Brooklyn, and in 1861 at the age of eighteen enlisted in the Union Army, rising during four years of service from private to lieutenant. The war between the sections ended he became a newspaper worker and for nearly two decades following 1876 was an editorial writer on the New York *Herald*. During this period also he wrote a number of plays, one of them, *Deacon Crankett* being performed more than five hundred times, and a round score of novels which found favor with the reading public, among them that best seller of an earlier time, *Helen's Babies* of which a quarter million copies were sold in this country. His earnings for a long period were large ones, but a generous nature made it impossible for him to refrain from acts of kindness even when they were beyond his means, and, his popularity behind him, he ended his days in a home for veterans at Kearny, New Jersey. The memories of him which survive in New Rochelle are gracious and tender ones. He adopted and reared several orphan children, and others owed a welcome start in life to his helping hand.

Another resident of New Rochelle in a later time was Augustus Thomas, playwright and many-sided man of affairs, held in kindly recollection for his vigorous habit and cheerful disposition, whose home for a number of years was a roomy house in Thomas Place. The career of Thomas was an unusual one, and the story of it as he told it toward the end in *The Print of My Remembrance,* a friendly and amiable volume which ran to some hundreds of pages, is a tale well worth reading a second time. It begins with his boyhood in St. Louis where he was born in 1857, when Lincoln in nearby Springfield was making ready for his debates with Douglas, and Emerson in his early fifties was lecturing wherever he could find a profitable audience; tells of his first jobs on a local railway and as a page in the House at Washington, and his return to St. Louis, to amateur theatricals and to dreams of poetry and the theatre.

After that the passage of the years brought Thomas adventures with road companies, essays in authorship, settlement in New York, the friendship of a growing company of actors and managers, and finally success as the author of *Arizona, The Earl of Pawtucket, The Witching Hour* and other well remembered plays which proved their maker a man of worthwhile gifts. And if occasional disappointments came to him more often than not they opened the door to new opportunities. "Altogether" he writes, "I read or proposed many plays to Charles Frohman. Some were accepted, many were refused. Charley one day said to me: 'It is always a pleasure to refuse a play of yours, because it seems to get the thing off your mind, and then we have an interesting talk.' The pleasure was not one-sided, because Charley never refused a play or a story without proposing some project for another one." All of which bears witness to a mutual good-will rich in its fruitage. Than Thomas who died in 1934 few gave to their generation a fuller measure of wholesome diversion.

An old house at the corner of Fenimore Road and the Boston Post Road in the outskirts of Mamaroneck, which in recent years has served as a filling station, has abiding interest for the literary pilgrim, for it was within its walls on New Year's Day in 1811 that John Peter Delancey gave his daughter Susan in marriage to James Fenimore Cooper, twenty-one year-old son of Judge William Cooper of Cooperstown. Built in 1792, this house until 1902 topped Heathcote Hill, a high knoll overlooking the Sound, but in the year last named, when it passed out of the possession of the surviving Delancey heirs, its new owner, a local builder, moved the old structure to its present site on the Post Road. There he repaired it, added a verandah and leased it for tavern purposes. In 1925, having again changed hands, it was converted into a gasoline station.

In its original site it had replaced a brick house erected by Caleb Heathcote, lord of Scarsdale, and burned a few years before the Revolution. John Peter Delancey, who had served as a major of Loyalist troops during that struggle, inherited the interest of his mother, Anne Heathcote, in her father's estate, bought out the other heirs, and in 1789 resigned from the British service to make his home in Mamaroneck. A few years later he built the house which now does duty as a gasoline station and lived in it with his family until his death. There his daughter, Susan, was courted by James Fenimore Cooper, then a midshipman in the United States Navy, and there, as just recorded, they were married on the opening day of 1811.

Tradition has it that, the ceremony ended, the young couple with some of their guests sat down to a game of chess in the Delancey drawing-room. A few days later in a gig drawn by two horses, they set out over roads deep with snow for a visit to Cooper's family at Cooperstown. Before the winter's end, however, they were back in Mamaroneck, and for a year and a half lived with the bride's father on Heathcote Hill. Although shorn of much of its ancient splendor, the house in which they passed their honeymoon is still a satisfying example of early republic architecture. One corner has been cut away to accommodate gas pumps and another walled with plate glass to produce a showroom, but the main entrance, second story and attic remain intact, and the dormer windows are today as they were when first built, while four sturdy brick chimneys still rise above the gray roof of slate, eloquent of broad hearths and the generous hospitality of an earlier time. The old house, besides being the home of the bride of Cooper was the birthplace of William Heathcote Delancey, who ended his days as Protestant Episcopal bishop of Western New York and of James Roosevelt Bayley, archbishop of the Roman Catholic see of Baltimore, who passed his boyhood on an adjoining farm.

Cooper, yielding to the persistent pleadings of his young wife, resigned from the navy soon after their marriage, and when they left her father's home on Heathcote Hill it was to set up housekeeping for themselves in a small cottage in Mamaroneck to which the husband gave the name of Closet Hall. Then in 1814 they removed to the shores of Otsego Lake, where Cooper's father had extensive holdings of land, and where the son, who then planned to devote his attention to agriculture, began the building of a large stone farmhouse. However, while it was still in process of construction, his wife, averse to permanent separation from her family, persuaded him to return to Westchester County. Accordingly, in 1817 he settled in the town of Scarsdale. There he purchased the Angevine farm which took its name from a French family that had occupied it for several generations, and on a site in what is now Mamaroneck Road commanding a splendid view of the country about and of Long Island Sound erected a roomy frame house, which, because of its fantastic architecture, was speedily dubbed by its builder's neighbors, Cooper's Folly. It was also put together in such careless fashion that when a few years later Cooper sold it and the surrounding farm, the new owner tore it down and replaced it with the house which, despite the passage of years, in slightly altered form still gives impressive greeting to the visitor.

During his first years on the Angevine farm Cooper's thought and labors were mainly devoted to the care of his growing family and to the betterment of his modest estate. He built fences, drained swamps and planted the trees, now grown to lordly proportions, which surround the present house. He was nearing thirty when, quite by accident, the urge to write came to him. The story goes that one day, after reading an English novel, he remarked to his wife that he was confident he could write a better one. She urged him to put his ability to the test, and the issue of some weeks of rapid composition was his first novel, *Precaution,* which in November 1820, was published anonymously in New York. Depicting scenes its author had never witnessed and a life with which he was wholly unfamiliar, the book failed to win favor with the reading public. Some of his friends, however, finding promise in its pages, besought him to try his hand on an American subject and in the end he gave heed to their advice.

Cooper had made his home in the very heart of the Neutral Ground of the Revolution, had explored its every nook and corner, and had learned from surviving veterans the moving traditions of a region which for half a decade had been fought over by the British forces stationed in New York City and the American army encamped among the Highlands of the Hudson. And so his deep and abiding love of country made inevitable his choice of the scene and period of his projected tale. Already a fitting theme for it had been suggested to him by John Jay, who during a visit of Cooper to his home in Bedford had told the future novelist the story of Enoch Crosby, the spy of Westchester in the Revolution—a patriot, who posing as a royalist and in consequence bitterly persecuted by supporters of the American cause, was actually and often with fruitful results, in the secret service of Washington.

Deeply impressed by Jay's account of Crosby's heroism, Cooper now made him the hero of the tale which he wrote hastily, a large part of it in an out-building on his Angevine farm. Doubtful, however, of the outcome, he took little interest in his task, and it is of record that the first volume, which the author was compelled to issue at his own expense, was in type in New York for several months before he set to work on the second. More than once he was half resolved to abandon it, fearing a pecuniary loss he was in no position to sustain, for the property left him by his father had dwindled, and the support of his family had become a serious problem. "One incident connected with the composition of this work," writes one of his biographers, "marks plainly the despairing attitude of his mind. While the second volume was slowly printing, he received an intimation from his publisher that the work might grow to a length that would endanger the profits. The author thereupon adopted a course which offers proof of how much stranger is fact than fiction. To placate the publisher and set his mind at rest, the last chapter was written, printed and paged, not merely before the intervening chapters had been composed, but before they had been fully conceived."

When *The Spy* finally appeared late in 1821 it won almost instant success, a first and then a second edition quickly finding buyers and readers. A third edition was published in March, 1822, and in the same month a stage version was played before large audiences. It had also a cordial reception in England. Thence its reputation spread to the Continent, and in no long time it was translated into the principal languages of modern Europe.

Assured of success as an author, Cooper in 1822 removed from his farm to New York City, where he became without delay a prominent and forceful figure in the literary and social life of the town, founding the Bread and Cheese Club of pleasant memory, and numbering among his intimates the poets Bryant and Halleck and other congenial spirits. In 1826 he went abroad, and for seven years served as United States consul at Lyons. On his return to America in 1833 he lived for a time on the Angevine farm, but soon sold it and retired to Cooperstown to pass his remaining years in the beautiful region that had been a part of his boyhood and youth. Thereafter Westchester County knew him only as an occasional visitor.

It is a short ride from Mamaroneck to Rye, with its mellow memories of the youth and early manhood of John Jay, whose part in the writing of *The Federalist* gives him a place in our literary annals, and who in 1829 was laid to rest in the family burial ground of the Jays, lying south of the Boston Post Road, and half hidden by a circle of trees. The ancient town of Rye also recalls gentle memories of Charles Baird, who for twenty-six years served as pastor of its Presbyterian Church and during that period worked on the scholarly *History of the Huguenot Emigration to America* which, to the regret of students, he left unfinished when in 1887 death claimed him. A winding ride from Rye overlooking the Sound takes one over broadway highways through Mount Vernon and other towns to Yonkers on the Hudson. William Leete Stone, editor and historian, was long a resident of Mount Vernon and there wrote the biographies of Brant and Sir William Johnson which are his surest claims to remembrance.

Sundry dwellers in Yonkers have been authors of unusual gifts and noteworthy achievement. Henry Martyn Baird, for more than forty years professor of Greek language and letters at the University of New York, lived after 1860 at 219 Palisades Avenue, Yonkers, dying there in 1906 at the age of seventy-four years. His six volumes on the Huguenots, all of which were written in Yonkers, remain a monument of accurate and understanding historical labor. The once widely popular but now forgotten *Sparrowgrass Papers* of Frederick Swartout Cozzens, which first appeared in *Putnam's Magazine* in 1854 described in an amusing and whimsical way the experiences of a city man in setting up a country abode at Chestnut Grove in the suburbs of Yonkers, which after 1853 and until his death in 1869 at the age of fifty-one was the author's summer home. It is noted in another place how *Sparrowgrass Papers* when issued in book form in 1856 passed through many editions and now call for a reprinting which would be sure of a warm welcome from every student of American humor.

Another wit who placed at least one minor masterpiece to his credit was a resident of Yonkers for more than half of his seventy-seven years and until ripe old age was active in the affairs of the town. This was William Allen Butler, for two score years one of the leaders of the New York bar and the founder of a law firm which flourishes down to the present time, but whom a later public remembers, in so far as it remembers him at all, only as the author of a single poem—*Nothing to Wear*, published in *Harper's Magazine* early in 1857 without the author's name. This poem, the first bit of genuinely rhymed satire in our literature, in relating the woes of Miss Flora McFlimsey of Madison Square, satirized the society of that day with such wit and cleverness that it became almost instantly popular in America and across seas. It was published in book form in London, and leaping the British Channel was translated into French and German. Meanwhile an impostor claimed the poem as her work and Mr. Butler in self-defence was compelled to reveal himself as its author. But all it brought him in a material way, for he had failed to copyright it, was a modest check from the Harpers, nor did any of his later efforts either in verse or prose win any substantial measure of popular favor, all of which caused Mr. Butler little regret, for his chief concern throughout a long life was the successful practice of his profession. Round Oak, his Yonkers home, is still owned and tenanted by members of his family.

During her latter years Mrs. Emma D. E. N. Southworth, whose tales moved our grandmothers to tears, was frequently a member of the family of her son, long a leading physician of Yonkers with a home at 103 Warburton Avenue. The career of this now half-forgotten story-teller lent color to three different eras in our history. She was born in Washington in 1819 and at the age of twenty-five was deserted by an unworthy husband and thrown upon her own resources with two infant children to support. For a time she was a teacher in the public schools of Washington, and in her leisure hours wrote stories and sketches for such editors as would buy and pay for them.

The first of the seventy odd novels Mrs. Southworth gave to the world before she ceased to write in 1893, a tale entitled *Retribution,* was published in 1847 in the *National Era* of Washington, an anti-slavery journal which also introduced *Uncle Tom's Cabin* to its earlier readers. She began *Retribution* as a story for one number of the *National Era,* with no idea of making a novel of it, but once begun she was unable to complete it in one, two or three numbers, for new incidents and new characters from week to week demanded places in the tale. The Quaker readers of the *National Era* complained that the story contained too much carnal affection, but they continued to read it, and its author wrote on and on, until *Retribution* ran through a year and became a long novel—the first serial story to be published in any American journal. Until the end of her days Mrs. Southworth preserved a letter from the poet Whittier in which with pardonable enthusiasm he declared *Retribution* the finest piece of fiction he had ever read. After its year in the *National Era* it was published by Harper & Brothers—the first American serial to be reissued in book form. Not, however, until she had written and sold two other novels, did she give up her post as a teacher and rely wholly upon her pen as a means of support.

Mrs. Southworth's early earnings as an author came to her from Henry Peterson of Philadelphia who published her stories in the *Saturday Evening Post* with growing profit for all concerned, but soon came an engagement on better terms with Robert Bonner who had purchased a small commercial journal and renaming it the New York *Ledger* had turned it into a family story paper. She wrote exclusively for the *Ledger* for three decades—

a new novel each year—and thanks in part to her output saw its circulation rise to half a million copies, while her own stories found a greater number of eager and devoted readers than those of any other woman of her time. Perhaps the best remembered of her many tales was *The Hidden Hand,* forty times dramatised on this side of the sea, and for an extended period played in three London theaters with profitable results.

All of Mrs. Southworth's novels had faults a plenty, but there was vigor in her style and strength in her plots; she saw romance in commonplace things, and for more than a generation she put interest and variety into colorless lives. And she has a minor but sure claim to remembrance by every lover of American verse, for it was she who in September, 1863, having been told by a neighbor the story of Barbara Freitchie at her son's suggestion passed it onto Whittier, and that poet without delay made it the subject of his most widely known ballad. Mrs. Southworth's time after 1876 was divided between her son's home in Yonkers, and a picturesque cottage half lost in trees on the heights of Georgetown, commanding a splendid view of the Potomac, which she purchased in 1851 after success came to her as an author. This home was the birthplace of half a hundred of her books, and there she died in the early summer of 1899 in her eightieth year.

Cyrus Townsend Brady, an Episcopal clergyman turned author, passed his last years and died in a house still standing on Edgehill Terrace, Park Hill, Yonkers. Brady's career was in many ways an unusual one. He was born in 1861 at Allegheny, Pennsylvania, and was graduated at Annapolis at the age of twenty-two, but soon resigned from the navy to enter railroad work in the West. While thus employed a clerical career attracted him, and, studying under Bishop Worthington of Nebraska, in 1890 he was ordained a priest of the Protestant Episcopal Church, thereafter filling pastorates in various parts of the Middle West and the East. During the Spanish-American War he was a chaplain of volunteers.

The following year Dr. Brady became rector of a church at Overbrook, Pennsylvania, but soon resigned that post to devote his entire time to literary work. He had begun to write short stories while a student at the Naval Academy, and now on a bantering challenge from his bishop he essayed his first full-length novel, *For Love of Country.* The manuscript was accepted by the publisher to whom it was submitted, and soon Dr. Brady found himself in full career as perhaps the most prolific American author of his period. During the twenty years which preceded his premature death in 1920 he produced, punctuated by occasional returns to the pulpit, more than forty volumes, including novels, stories for boys, biographies and histories. He worked with such effective swiftness that a short story was less than an ordinary day's work, and the composition of a hundred thousand word novel a matter of only a few weeks. And the general average of his work was a high one, so that only in a still remote future will his books fail to find readers.

Melville De Lancey Landon, a humorist of modest gifts best known to the generation before the last as Eli Perkins, passed his closing days and died at 594 Palisade Avenue, Yonkers. Landon's career was typical of his period. Born at Eaton, New York, in 1839 and graduated at Union College, the opening of the Civil War found him a clerk in the Treasury Department at Washington. After the fall of Fort Sumter and before the arrival of Union troops, he served in the ranks of the Clay Battalion, hastily organized by Cassius Marcellus Clay to defend the capital from capture. Then he resigned from the Treasury Department to join the staff of General Alexander L. Chetlain, Grant's early and helpful friend, and in that capacity saw much hard fighting with the Western armies, resigning from service in 1864 with the rank of major.

After that Landon was for two years a cotton planter in Arkansas and Louisiana. Then he made a tour of Europe which ended at St. Petersburg, where he served for a time as secretary of legation nuder his old commander, General Clay. He began to write while in Russia, and after his return to America in 1870 was for a quarter of a century an industrious author and compiler of books of a humorous sort. During the same period he won repute as a lecturer whose travels yearly carried him to every nook and corner of the land, nor did his career on the platform close until with advancing age his health failed him. Landon's humor was of the perishable sort, but it had its appeal for the average man, and his appearances afforded diversion and laughter for audiences sorely needing them in a thousand towns and villages.

Another humorist and lecturer of pleasant memory was a native and most of his days a resident of Yonkers. John Kendrick Bangs was born in 1862, and was educated at Columbia University, later studying law. His inclinations, however, were for a career in letters, and in 1884 he became one of the editors of *Life,* remaining for four years on the staff of that lively journal. After 1888 he was associated for upward of a dozen years with the house of Harper, serving during a part of that period as editor of *Harper's Weekly.* Still later he was for a year or so editor of *Puck,* but after 1905 and until his death he devoted most of his time to bookmaking and to the lecture platform, going to France in 1918 there to address and cheer many thousands of American soldiers.

The first book by Bangs was *Roger Camerden* published in 1886, and during the thirty-six years that followed, being an indefatigable worker, he placed more than two score titles to his credit. It is good to remember old things and there are few gray beards fortunate enough to have read them when they first came from the press who do not recall with a smile *The Idiot, Mr. Bonaparte of Corsica, A House Boat on the Styx, Ghosts I Have Met, The Enchanted Typewriter* and other droll and whimsical volumes which add up a generous total of humor which was never coarse, and which rarely missed its mark. Nor would a lover of good things wish to spare *Three Weeks in Politics* which relates with sunny humor and as no other could tell it the story of the failure of its author's candidacy for mayor of his native town. The last Yonkers home of John Kendrick Bangs was a roomy house he built for his growing family in North Broadway looking out on the Hudson. This he sold about 1906 and thereafter was a resident of the village of Ogonquit on the Maine coast where he built another house commanding a view of the Atlantic to the horizon's edge. He died in an Atlantic City hospital in January, 1922, after painful illness and an operation resorted to in a vain effort to prolong his life. The sunny optimism which was part of the man remained with him to the end; and one of the present writers has cause to gratefully remember him as an unfailing friend and wise counselor of the literary beginner.

Thomas Beer, whom his friend and comrade Lewis Mumford, has aptly described as an aristocrat of letters, although born in Iowa long had his home at 227 Palisade Avenue, Yonkers. The son of a prosperous lawyer, he graduated from Yale in 1911 at the age of twenty-one and later studied at Columbia Law School, but did not complete his course there, preferring authorship as a career. His first published story appeared in the *Century Magazine* in 1917, and in the following year he went to France to do staff duty with the rank of first lieutenant. After the war Beer continued to write short stories, and in 1923 won critical acclaim with a deft and penetrating study of Stephen Crane. During the next six years he wrote and published three other books which are his surest claim to remembrance—a novel of New York in the seventies entitled *Sandoval; The Mauve Decade,* a classic survey of the American scene at the turn of the centuries, and *Hanna,* a life of the famous Republican leader of the nineties, in which its author's individual method and style found ripest expression.

These volumes made up Beer's output of first-rate work. His audience was never a wide one, and all of his books have now retired to library shelves to be rarely called for by current readers. Nevertheless they have had and still have a vitality and influence all their own, for their author was from first to last an exacting craftsman, with poise, balance and a sure sense of precision. A lover of the pleasures of the table, with the instinct of the epicure for the best in food and drink, Beer was also a delightful companion, with an amiable yet insatiable curiosity as to the lives and doings of his fellows—people were always the documents which he preferred as source material—and a talker whose scintillating speech, and urbane give and take, were of the first-class. After 1930, however, ill health dogged his footsteps, and his latter years were practically barren ones. In April, 1940, following a heart attack, he died alone in a New York hotel, and was laid to rest in Sleepy Hollow Cemetery at North Tarrytown, not far from the grave of Irving.

At 11 Greystone Place, Yonkers, was the last home of Dr. Joseph Jacobs, fine scholar and versatile writer, often called by his admirers the Jewish Andrew Lang, while one of the most widely known of living poets has again and again attested lively memories of a brief and not wholly agreeable residence in the town by the Hudson. For a period of two years during a youth of poverty and self-denial, John Masefield, now English poet laureate, labored for wages pitifully small in the carpet factories of Yonkers.

Pushing northward from Yonkers along the Albany Post Road one comes shortly to Greystone, now owned by the heirs of Samuel Untermyer, but in an earlier time the home of Samuel J. Tilden who died there in 1886 at the end of a career in which one of the most acute and self-sufficient intellects of his period saw a great ambition brought to unexpected and ill-starred issues. Again at Hastings one turns from the post road to visit the old stone house which for more than a generation was the home of John William Draper, a scholar and scientist who in his time played many parts and all with usefulness and honor. Born and schooled in England, Dr. Draper came to America in 1832, soon after entering his twenty-second year; in 1836 was graduated in medicine at the University of Pennsylvania, and two years later became professor of chemistry at New York University. Thereafter his career was one of constant and steadily increasing service to his fellows.

Tradition has it that when a boy in England, Dr. Draper had had a dream giving form and substance to the country place he would most desire for a home. In 1846, returning from a trip to the Adirondacks he found in Hastings a place very like the one that had filled the dream of his boyhood. What he came upon and purchased was a stone house of Dutch design dating from the first decade of the eighteenth century. Here he lived until his death in 1882, and here, in addition to the scientific studies which were always his chief concern, he wrote two masterly works which did much to shape the thought and enlarge the mental outlook of the generation which came to maturity in the years immediately following the war between the sections. One of these was *The History of the Intellectual Development of Modern Europe* and the other *The History of the Conflict between Religion and Science,* books of disturbing import which were in turn praised and challenged when they first came from the press, and which, with old controversies now fought out and forgotten, still command appreciative and grateful readers.

Dr. Draper's son Henry was also a scientist of rare gifts and despite his early death, of unusual achievement. Astronomical photography was the younger man's particular field, and in the observatory which he erected near his father's home were taken one of the first photographs of the moon and of the spectrum of a star. When she died Dr. Draper's daughter, Antonia Draper Dixon, gave the thirty acres overlooking the Hudson on which the observatory stood to form John William Draper Memorial Park, and fulfilling her wishes the observatory has now become a public centre for astronomical study. Father and brother could not have a more fitting monument.

Scarsdale and White Plains, a few miles eastward from the Hudson, have appealing memories of Cooper and of his hero, Harvey Birch. The town first named was also the home in a more recent period of James Howard Bridge and Dixon Ryan

Fox. Bridge was a native of Manchester, England, and in early manhood served Herbert Spencer as secretary, transcribing more than one of the volumes of his employer's now out-dated philosophy. In 1884 he came to America where in turn he was literary assistant to Andrew Carnegie and secretary to Henry Clay Frick, helping to assemble the art collection which bears the latter's name. Bridge at other periods of his career on this side of the Atlantic was one of the founders of the Authors Club of New York and editor of the *Overland Monthly* in which, quick to discover merit in beginners, he published a number of the early stories of Jack London, and so helped to start that unusual writer on the way to success. One of his own dozen volumes bore the title *Millionaires and Grub Street* and deals in amusing fashion and without reserve with the comrades and contacts of a career which had its full measure of successes and failures.

Scarsdale was the home of Dixon Ryan Fox after 1911 and during most of his twenty-three years as teacher and professor at Columbia University which he left in 1934 to become president of Union College at Schenectady. It was while a resident of the town that Dr. Fox wrote most of the books which prove him a profound and discriminating student of American history, especially of its political phases. These he treated with authority and charm in such volumes as *The Decline of Aristocracy in the Politics of New York* and *Yankees and Yorkers*. He was also a considerate and inspiring teacher, and students and friends together recall him as a delightful talker with a rich and rare store of anecdote. His death in 1944 almost without warning was a tragic loss to American education in a period of growing need for leaders of courage and vision.

Again in nearby Purchase one finds stately Ophir Hall, so-named by its builder, Ben Holliday, in token of the source of the fortune he had amassed in the gold fields of the West. Ophir Hall became in a later time the country home of Whitelaw Reid, editor, author and diplomat, and is now occupied by members of his family. An easy four miles from Purchase, in the village of Elmsford, known of old as Hall's Four Corners a less imposing but more piquant survival of other days warms the heart of the pilgrim. A building now known as O'Brien's Chateau was in Revolutionary days called Flanagan's Tavern, taking its name from its mistress Betty Flanagan, the widow of a patriot soldier who had been killed in action, and who earned her living by furnishing lodging and food, seasoned by an Irish sense of humor and a ready wit, to officers of the contending armies who now and again marched and camped in this part of the Neutral Ground.

It was from Flanagan's Tavern that Cooper's Harvey Birch, who carried to Washington the information he had picked up when masquerading as a peddler, made his escape on the eve of the day which his British captors had fixed for his execution as a spy. He had been placed in a room under a heavy guard. During the night he dressed in Betty Flanagan's clothes, and, making timely use of a clever imitation of her Irish brogue, successfully passed the troopers who had him in custody and crept away to freedom. It is also to be noted that Flanagan's Tavern was the birthplace of the American cocktail, and thereby hangs a story which, if somewhat out of place in the present chronicle, is clearly worth retelling.

The first cocktail is said to have been a mixture of arresting potency concocted by Betty Flanagan, and into which she thrust the tail feathers of roosters purloined after nightfall from the farmyard of a well-to-do Tory of the countryside, whose unpopularity made theft of his stock little less than a patriotic duty. One night a young officer of Rochambeau's army, lounging in the dining-room of the tavern, with its low ceiling and heavy beams, and curiously alive to his surroundings, caught sight of the feathers of a fowl standing in tall glasses behind the bar. Whereupon, if we are to believe the legend, he sprang to his feet and, raising a just filled goblet to his lips, cried as he sipped its contents: "Long life to the cocktail." And the name thus given to a familiar drink has persisted through the years.

Back again to the banks of the Hudson, Zion Church at Dobb's Ferry, a squat stone structure built in 1833, has pleasant association with Washington Irving who during his first years at Sunnyside served as one of its vestrymen. And in Ashford Avenue, Dobb's Ferry, stands Walston, the last home of Robert G. Ingersoll, renowned orator and champion of free thought, who in the summer of 1899 there came to the end of a life which more often than not was a battle and a march, but which also was rich in good deeds born of unfailing concern for the humble ones of earth. Colonel Ingersoll's old home is now owned by two of his grandchildren.

Again in Clifton Avenue, Dobb's Ferry, one finds Thorwood, a lordly house of brick and stone, which was long the country home of Henry and Fanny Garrison Villard. The union of this gifted pair was one of the romances of the Civil War period. Henry Villard, the son of Gustav Hilgard, a Rhenish Bavarian, came to America in 1853, being then in his eighteenth year; and, a youth of extraordinary endowment, as the sequel proved, he seems never to have had to face a day of small things. Instead, he quickly learned to speak and write English, and before he was twenty-three became a welcome contributor to leading journals of New York and the Middle West. In 1858 as a special correspondent for the New York *Staats-Zeitung* he journeyed to Illinois to report the Lincoln-Douglas debates, and came to know the tall, lank lawyer of Springfield in an intimate and appealing way—"a thoroughly earnest and truthful man inspired by sound convictions in consonance with the true spirit of American institutions. There was nothing," he adds, "in all of Douglas' powerful efforts that appealed to the higher instincts of human nature, while Lincoln always touched sympathetic chords."

Young Villard spent a part of the presidential campaign of 1860 and the first weeks of 1861 in Springfield as correspondent for a chain of newspapers, and early in the following year went to the front for the New York *Tribune*. In April, 1863, he was in New York enjoying a well-earned leave of absence, and, advised so to do by Sidney Howard Gay, then managing editor of the *Tribune,* decided to spend a part of it in Boston. There he had a hearty welcome in the family of William Lloyd Garrison, then reaping the stormy reward of his labors as a lifelong champion of the slave, and there he met the happy fate that some good angel had reserved for him. "It was to this chance visit to Boston," he wrote long after in his *Memoirs,* "that I owe the greatest happiness of my life—my marriage to Miss Fanny Garrison, the only daughter of the great abolitionist, to whose charms of mind and person I surrendered on first acquaintance."

Henry Villard and Fanny Garrison, who as a girl had read proofs for the *Liberator,* were married early in 1866, and at home and abroad wandered for years according to the unexpected but upward course of the husband in journalism and international finance. It was at the zenith of his career as a builder and completer of railroads that contributed mightily to the development of the Farther West that the Villards bought Thorwood, making it through good and evil fortune a center for those who battle bravely for worthy causes the success of which is still an uncertain one. There were completed the negotiations which made Villard and after him his family for more than a generation owners of the *Nation* and the New York *Evening Post;* there welcome was given to Carl Schurz, Horace White, Edwin Lawrence Godkin and other stout apostles of the right as they saw it; and there the master of Thorwood began the delightful *Memoirs* he did not live to finish.

Henry Villard died after wasting illness in November, 1900. Fanny Villard lived to the ripe age of eighty-three, and during all the years of her long widowhood was an active and inspiring leader in wide ranging works of good citizenship. The triumph of woman's suffrage owed much to her devoted efforts; she helped in the establishment of Barnard College, and she founded the Woman's Peace Society, her father's radical tendencies persisting in her championship of peace by non-resistance. Death finally came to this great woman in 1928, and she lies now beside her husband in Sleepy Hollow Cemetery.

CHAPTER XIV

Sunnyside, Sleepy Hollow and Beyond

The Hudson in its middle and lower reaches has a breadth and a slow moving majesty which have made it for ten generations the best loved of American rivers, and by the same token, wedded to the gracious and benignant spirit which this lordly stream reffects on days of summer sunshine and stillness, the hills and vales which flank its eastern shore were in his youth and early manhood favorite resorts of Washington Irving, who in holiday rambles received from the lips of aged and aging men and women the myths and legends which in the fulness of time he made a wistful and inseparable part of our literature. For all students and lovers of the past the Hudson is Irving's river.

And it was altogether fitting and proper that, when long and successful effort had made him on both sides of the sea the most widely known and honored of American authors, Irving chose a house beside the Hudson as the home of his latter days. It was in the summer of 1835, a few years prior to his period of service as American minister to Spain, that he purchased Wolfert's Roost, an old Dutch farmhouse facing the river just beyond Irvington, built in 1656 by Wolfert Ecker, one of whose descendants is today a resident of Tarrytown. The original structure of many gables, modelled, we are told, after Peter Stuyvesant's cocked hat, was rebuilt in more modern style following the Revolution, and so Irving found it, with its ancient walls, when he bought the place. He called in the services of an architect, who made important alterations and gave the cottage back better suited to its new owner's needs, yet no less picturesque than when he first described it as a "stone mansion all made up of gable ends, and as full of angles and corners as an old cocked hat."

After Irving's return from Spain in 1846 the services of the architect were again called in for an addition which should make it more comfortable as a permanent dwelling, with better offices and larger servants' quarters. This work was accomplished as successfully as the first, and when completed the house had a charm quite its own. Then as now a fine growth of English ivy covered its eastern side with a thick mantle of green. This ivy grew with the years from a slip secured at Melrose Abbey and presented to Irving by his friend Mrs. Renwick, the heroine in her youth of Burns' *Blue-eyed Lassie* as well as of another of that poet's songs, *When First I Saw My Jennie's Face.*

At Sunnyside, following his return from Spain, Irving passed the most peaceful, as well as the most fruitful, years of his life. His fame was assured and the reissue of his works by Putnam in 1848 brought him an income more than sufficient for his modest wants—an income supplemented by the returns from the *Life of Washington* and the other master works which he brought to a conclusion during this period.   And it is to be recorded that neither the public honors heaped upon him, nor the belated prosperity that came to reward his labors, could wean him from the simple pleasures of a country life, his old friends, his plain house, his quiet study lined with books, his rambles among familiar hills and lanes, and the vine-trellised piazza where he could sit of an evening and hear the waves of the wide spreading Tappan Sea softly lapping the shore at his feet.

The legend of this broad reach of the Hudson must have been often in Irving's thoughts at such times, and from one of them, had he been so minded, he might have woven an arresting sequel to *The Headless Horseman of Sleepy Hollow.*   Rambout Van Dam, a roistering young Dutchman hailing from Spuyten Duyvil, so the story runs, on a Saturday night crossed the Tappan Sea in his boat to attend a frolic on the western shore.   He danced, drank and caroused until midnight when he entered his boat for the return trip.   He was warned that it was on the verge of Sunday morning, but swore a fearful oath that he would not halt until he reached the landing nearest his home if it took him a month of Sundays.   He pushed from shore and was never seen again, yet by sailors and believing landsmen at midnight he can still be heard plying his oars over the lonely waters in never-ending voyages between the eastern and the western shore—the Flying Dutchman of the Tappan Sea.

The privileged visitor to Sunnyside finds in the library, with its low ceiling and casement windows, many things as Irving left them, and of its treasured possessions none is so eloquent of vanished days as the quill pen browned by the ink left upon it when its tired author laid it aside for the last time.   Over the fireplace is a portrait in oil of Irving; the walls are hung with quaint drawings of the characters to whom he gave life and humor, and on the library shelves the tales of his friend, Sir

Walter Scott, hold a prominent place, while of equal interest is a carefully preserved portfolio beside the desk long used by the master of Sunnyside containing sketches by Washington Allston, Darley's original drawings for his books, and autographed engravings of William Cullen Bryant and other authors who helped to shape thought and letters in the early and middle years of the last century.

Near the point where Sunnyside Lane leads from the Albany Post Road to Irving's old home, now the residence of Du Pont Irving, has stood since 1928 a memorial designed by Daniel Chester French. In its center is a bronze bust of Irving with suitable inscription. On the right a bronze figure represents Boabdid, the last King of Granada and on the left another bronze figure depicts Rip Van Winkle, an inscription tells the passerby, "the dreamer of the Kaatskills." Thence a short and pleasant stroll northward through Tarrytown with its red brick Christ Church, where Irving was once a warden and communicant, and then past the monument which marks the spot where Major Andre, carrying in his boots the plans for West Point he had received from Benedict Arnold, was captured on a fateful September morning in 1780, brings one to North Tarrytown and, facing the Post Road from the west, the stronghouse, once pierced with loopholes for musketry and porthoues for cannon, built full two and a half centuries ago by the first lord of the manor of Philipsburg.

All around are objects made familiar by the author of *The Sketchbook*. Here is Sleepy Hollow, now as of yore a winding cleft amid tree tops with the waters of the Pocantico still finding their way over the dam by the site of the ancient mill, just south of the manor house, to which the Pilipse tenants once brought their grain to be ground. A few rods upstream from the stone bridge which in these days of the hasting automobile carries the Post Road across the Pocantico stood of old the more modest crossing over which Ichabod Crane galloped in his mad flight from the headless horseman, and close at hand on the east side of the way, stands the Old Dutch Church, celebrated in the same legend. This church, reputed the oldest ecclesiastical building in the State of New York, was erected prior to 1699 by the first Frederick Philipse and his second wife, Catherine Van Cortlandt. It still cherishes communion silver that was the gift of its builders, while two lords of the manor, with many of their kin, lie buried beneath its floor.

Not less interesting than the proofs of departed grandeur which the old church offers the visitor is its present guardian, a man who has lived long and who has much to tell to those who come his way. From him one learns that the windows were placed high by the builders so that if prowling Indians shot arrows into the church they would pass over the heads of worshippers seated in the pews; that two odd box pews on each side within the chancel rails are all that remains of the "thrones" upon which the lord of the manor and his lady were accustomed to sit while the rector preached to them and to such of their retainers as occupied the body of the church; that of old the pews were without backs, like the specimen still planted firmly in the centre of the chancel fronting the pulpit, and that on winter Sundays the women of colony times brought with them heated Dutch bricks on which to warm their feet during service.

Old Dutch Church, with its tiny weather-vanes, its bell cast in Amsterdam and its brick and window-trimmings, the former imported from Holland in the ships, tradition has it, owned and operated by the first wife of the first lord of the manor is surrounded by the graves of many generations—those of the pioneers clustering thick about the edifice itself, while newer graves people the rising ground. The burial ground may be entered at the church gate or here and there along the low stone wall that separates it from the Post Road. A little way inside this wall a narrow path climbs the hill and threading it one comes shortly to a broader walk running east and west.

Turning to the right on this path the pilgrim presently faces a tiny cemetery within a cemetery—the burial plot of the Irving family encircled by a thick hedge and shaded by tall trees. A little northeast of the centre of this enclosure, its gate locked against intruders, is the grave in which in 1859 Washington Irving was laid to rest, a grave distinguished from its fellows only by the fact that the white marble stone above it is a bit broader and higher and has a rounded and slightly ornate top. It bears only Irving's name, age and the dates of his birth and death. Around it are two or three score other tombstones each bearing the name of Irving or by its inscription giving evidence that the person commemorated was a member of the family.

Other authors and bookmen take their rest within the shadow of Old Dutch Church. Not far from the Irving plot is that of the Badeau family, whose most conspicous member General Adam Badeau, served on Grant's staff during the Civil War and later was the capable and sympathetic biographer of his great commander both as soldier and civilian. Here also one finds the graves of Colonel William Conant Church, who with his gifted brother, Francis Pharcellus Church in turn founded and edited the *Army and Navy Journal,* and the *Galaxy Magazine,* and whom John Ericsson, engineer and inventor, chose for the chronicler of his memorable and unusual career; and of Andrew C. Wheeler, in his early and middle life an incisive and penetrating critic of the stage and its people, and in latter years of self-sought seclusion, under the pen name of J. P. Mowbray, a sympathetic and popular writer about nature and country life. Both Badeau and Wheeler passed a part of their boyhood in the Tarrytown neighborhood, and so did Hamilton Wright Mabie, critic and essayist, who sleeps not far from them.

Two other graves in the burial ground of the Old Dutch Church are silent reminders of one of the tragedies of our literary annals—the untimely death of Paul Leicester Ford at the hands of a half-mad brother in an hour when, with worthwhile things already achieved despite grievous handicaps, years of sustained and fruitful effort promised to be stretching before him. A huge brown boulder separates the grave of Paul Ford from that of Malcolm Ford, who slaying his brother for imaginary wrongs in the same instant ended his own life. When Whitelaw Reid died in London in 1912 while serving as ambassador to Great Britain his remains, in fulfilment of an often expressed wish, were brought back to America for burial in Sleepy Hollow.

Six years earlier and also in fulfilment of an earnestly expressed desire all that was mortal of Carl Schurz, stout and ever ready fighter for what he believed to be right, and friend of and fellow worker with Reid during eventful years, had been laid to rest in the same place. Another gifted German, Henry Villard, has his grave in Sleepy Hollow, with his wife beside him. And here also was journey's end for the Scotch lad who found America the doorway to an unexampled career. It is interesting to record that Andrew Carnegie who when selecting a burial plot on this storied hillside framed the following inscription for his tombstone: "Here lies a man who knew how to enlist in his service better men than himself." Nor will anyone deny his claim to a place among the lettered dwellers in Sleepy Hollow for no man of his period did more than he to spread love and knowledge of books among the people both of the United States and of England and her overseas dominions, or found keener delight in the companionship of men for whom learning was the chief concern.

Henry Villard during some of the crowded years of a career attended by sharp turns of good and ill fortunes had a country home in Pocantico Hills to the north and east of Sleepy Hollow. Carl Schurz in the closing years of the last century was also a dweller in this lovely section and here, with a great library at his command wrote a part of his *Reminiscences,* and planned the history of the Civil War period which he did not live to put on paper. Solitude was the name Schurz gave to his Pocantico Hills retreat, but his desire to be free from unseemly interruptions did not blunt his will to further the well-being of those about him. One of his neighbors recalls that when it was planned to establish a kindergarten for the children of the workmen on the large estates of the region, "Schurz attended the meeting, told how his wife had been the first person to introduce the kindergarten in the United States, and subscribed liberally to put the plan into operation."

Again at North Tarrytown an easy detour to the right from the Post Road leads through Hawthorne, Chappaqua and Mount Kisco to Bedford House the last home of John Jay. The hamlet of Hawthorne takes its name from the romancer's gifted and devoted daughter, Rose Hawthorne Lathrop, known in her latter years as Mother Alphonsa, and links the name of both to a story of beauty and self-sacrifice that will never be forgotten, "until," as Mark Twain once said of it, "pity fails in the hearts of men, and that will never be." It was in 1897 that Mrs. Lathrop, who had won an enviable place in the literary and social life of her period, left the circle to which she belonged, took up her abode in a two-room tenement in Water Street, New York, and there set to work nursing such cases of incurable cancer as she could find among the most destitute in that section of the city. The first influence to take up this work, she wrote in after years, "came from the attitude of my father's mind toward both moral and physical deformity," and she cited the chapter on English Poverty in *Our Old Home* as showing "how far his practical pity reached down, both in observing the exterior aspects of the lowest class and the inner misery out of which they spring."

Mrs. Lathrop was also moved to a great mission by the cruel fate which had overtaken a devoted and gifted friend. A poet of rare endowment, Emma Lazarus died of cancer while still in the bloom of early womanhood. Those who knew and loved her were shocked by her passing, but ere long the shock merged into mild regret, except in the case of her sister Josephine, and of Mrs.

Rose Hawthorne Lathrop who resolved to devote their lives to the care and nursing of the twin victims of poverty and cancer. After a period of hospital training Mrs. Lathrop began her self-appointed labors. She was alone with only a few dollars in her purse, and the patients she picked up she cared for in her restricted Water Street quarters.

Friends predicted failure, but patience, cheerfulness, courage, faith and an amazing personality helped to success, and slowly yet surely her effort grew in scope and usefulness. A few years earlier Mrs. Lathrop and her husband had left the Unitarian faith of their New England fathers and joined the Roman Catholic Church. When George Parsons Lathrop died in 1898 his widow at once underwent training for the Dominican Order, and a year later took the veil. Then in due process the Servants of Relief for Incurable Cancer, a sisterhood of limited membership, became a part of the Dominican Order and Sister Rose, round of face and figure, became Mother Alphonsa.

Soon it was necessary to move from Water Street to larger quarters in Cherry Street, where Mother Alphonsa and four other nuns gave an asylum and care to a growing number of patients who had aroused their interest and sympathy. There were only two requirements for admission: The patient must be incurable and must be poor. Race, creed and color did not matter. Rarely with cash resources in hand, dependent upon voluntary contributions, but always finding money when needed, the work expanded with the years into two large institutions, one in Jackson Street, New York, and the other in Hawthorne, with an average total of 160 patients. And they were granted all that their gracious founder had to give of love and labor until on a July morning in 1926 and at the ripe age of seventy-five death, gentle in its approach, came to her in her sleep. Can anyone who reads this record be permitted to doubt that the daughter of Nathaniel Hawthorne, with no desire except to serve those who most needed her services, won for herself an inspiring and imperishable place in the annals of humanity?

Chappaqua, founded by the Quakers in 1730 was for many years the home best loved by Horace Greeley, founder of the New York *Tribune*. "And so I, in the sober afternoon of life," the famous editor wrote on the morrow of his settlement in 1853, in Chappaqua which the years have transformed into a popular residential community, "when its sun, if not high, is still warm, have bought a few acres of land in the broad, still country, and, bearing thither my household treasures, have resolved to steal from the city's labors and anxieties at least one day each week, wherein to revive, as a farmer, the memories of my childhood's humble home."

In another place Mr. Greeley sets down the consideration that decided his purchase of the Chappaqua farm. "The choice," he writes, "was substantially directed by my wife, who said that she insisted on but three requisites—1. A peerless spring of pure, soft, living water; 2. A cascade of brawling brook; 3. Woods largely composed of evergreens. These may seem light matters; yet I was some time in finding them grouped on the same small plot, within reasonable distance from the city. I did find them, however; and those who object to my taste in choosing for my home a rocky, wooded hillside, sloping to the north of west, cannot judge me fairly, unless they consider the above requirements."

Soon after buying his farm, Mr. Greeley built him a home in the woods which covered a third of his seventy-five acres. This, however, was in due time discarded for a house in the open —a large, plain mansion, with wide piazzas extending along its entire front and with few trees to shut out the sun, so that it gave out an air of cheerfulness unknown to the earlier dwelling in the woods. Mr. Greeley also built a fine barn on his farm, wholly of stone gathered or blasted from the slope which near its summit furnished a site for the structure. Thus the walls were nearly solid rock, the roof being of Vermont slate. "I drive," wrote Mr. Greeley, "into three stories—a basement for manures, a stable for animals, and a story above this for hay, while grain is pitched into the loft, from whose floor rises the roof to a height of sixteen or eighteen feet. There should have been more windows for light and air, but my barn is convenient, while impervious to frost . . . . I calculate that this barn shall be abidingly useful long after I shall have been utterly forgotten; and that, had I chosen to have my name lettered on its front, it would have remained there to honor me as a builder, long after it had ceased to have any other significance."

And in later years this belief of its builder had strange fulfilment. When in 1890, seventeen years after Mr. Greeley's death, his old home was destroyed by fire, his youngest and only surviving daughter, Gabrielle, who later became the wife of Frank M. Clendenin, Episcopal rector of Chappaqua, converted the barn into a residence. Here she lived until her death, and here are preserved many intimate reminders of her father's colorful career. In the reception room of the massive stone structure, to which its last owner gave the name Rehoboth, stands the aged-darkened desk on which its builder penned his editorials and the printer's case from which he set type as a young man, the latter affording a shelf for a copy of the *Northern Spectator* of February 6, 1826, the Poultney, Vermont, newspaper on which he served his apprenticeship. Close at hand are the flag which flew over the *Tribune* Building in New York during the Civil War and Hart's marble bust of Greeley at the age of thirty. Chappaqua also takes pride in a statue of Greeley which since 1900 has stood in its main street.

For nearly a score of years Mr. Greeley, when not absent from New York on some one of his frequent journeys to all parts of the land, made it a custom not to be broken to spend his week-ends at his Chappaqua farm. There he found needed diversion and—ever recurring demands for fresh outlays of money, draining his bog and his purse at the same time. In his twenty-five acres of standing timber he loved to whack about with an ax, lopping off useless limbs and felling trees which crowded their more vigorous neighbors. And here he found inspiration for *What I Know About Farming,* perhaps the most widely read book to come from his pen. Nevertheless his success as a farmer was an indifferent one, turnips being now and then the only crop to yield a profit. Dishonest foremen and lazy hands added to his troubles, but did not diminish his love for his farm. "As yet," he wrote, "I am a horse in a bark-mill, and tread his monotonous round, never finding time to do today what can be postponed to the morrow." However, through crowded years he continued to look hopefully forward to the time when he could gather his treasures at Chappaqua and in retirement there know days of ease and mellow thought.

Such days never came to Horace Greeley. His contest for the presidency in 1872 was still three weeks from its ill-starred conclusion when he was called to the bedside of his wife, who, after long illness, was facing the end. Here for a fortnight of anxious and sleepless hours he watched and waited until on October 30 death came to her relief. Six days later fell the election and the husband's defeat. After that followed the treachery of associates and threatened loss of the journal he had made a power in the land. On November 13 he made his last visit to the office of the *Tribune*. Then he broke under the strain of loss and threatened disaster; his weary brain flamed into fever, and November 29 his soul fled its burned-out tenement. Five days later, mourned by multitudes and escorted by a great procession, his body was laid to rest in Greenwood Cemetery, Brooklyn.

But, with two generations now come and gone, Horace Greeley is still a living presence in Chappaqua, and so is his wife whose uncertain temper and unpredictable ways often afforded amusement both for her friends, and those who were not her friends. Amos Jay Cummings used to tell how when a member of the staff of the *Tribune* he had occasion to call on his chief at Chappaqua. He carefully deposited his hat, gloves and cane on a marble-topped center table which graced the room in which Mr. Greeley received him, and was engaged in earnest discussion of the matter which had brought him from the city, when Mrs. Greeley appeared unheralded, threw hat, gloves and cane through an open window and without a word to her husband or his visitor left the room. "Never mind, Amos," said Greeley, "she thinks they are mine." But Cummings always doubted the truthfulness of this reassuring injunction.

Mrs. Greeley was also when occasion demanded a woman of stout-hearted courage, one memorable proof of which must claim a place in this chronicle. When in the summer of 1863 the Draft Riots of shameful memory startled New York and shocked the country the editor of the *Tribune* through days and nights of mounting horror went quietly about his accustomed tasks, indifferent to the threats from which he scorned to flee. And at Chappaqua his wife gave equal proof of fortitude in the face of danger. When warned that a drunken mob had set out from Ossining to attack her and her children she made ready to blow up her home with gun-powder. Whereupon, its members harangued by a Quaker, who warned them that Horace Greeley was a man of peace, but that Mary Greeley would fight to the last, the mob beat a retreat. And Mary Greeley went to bed to sleep the sleep of one who fears not the empty threats of violent men.

An ancient farmhouse yet standing midway between Chappaqua and the village of Pleasantville was one of the country homes selected in turn by Ray Stannard Baker before he began his long residence in Amherst, Massachusetts. Baker was then in the early years of an unusual career as a recorder of the American scene and a commentator on men and events that in another time would have won the hearty approval of Horace

Greeley. A native of Michigan and in 1892 at the age of twenty-one a graduate of the University of that state, he began his writing career as a reporter in Chicago, but soon established an association with *McClure's Magazine* and for nine years following 1898 was a member of its staff. Then with John S. Phillips, Ida M. Tarbell and others he purchased the *American Magazine* for which during the next few years he wrote a series of articles which aroused the nation. To the *American* under the pen name of David Grayson he also contributed the first of a series of essays dealing in an individual way with every-day life which quickly won and retained enduring popularity.

Deeply concerned with the right exercise of democratic processes, Mr. Baker early came in friendly contact with Theodore Roosevelt, approving with reservations the latter's course as President. In 1910 he met Woodrow Wilson for the first time and soon came to regard him as one of the great men of the centuries. In turn he quickly won favor with the President and in 1918, at the latter's instance, was sent to Europe to report on war-time conditions. Later he organized the press department at the Peace Conference, and still later, his career becoming more closely linked with that of Wilson, he edited the latter's papers and wrote his life in a series of imposing volumes. His last years were quiet ones given over to writing and study in his Amherst home. In addition to other noteworthy qualities Mr. Baker had a nearly infallible understanding of other men and was rich in the number and variety of his friendships. His autobiography published under the title of *American Chronicle* in 1945, shortly before his death, is an indispensable source for students of the new America that was in the making half a century ago.

Cross Roads Farm, an inviting country place six miles from Mount Kisco, was the last home of Richard Harding Davis, author and war correspondent. Davis is now half-forgotten, but those who recall the turn of the century remember him as one of the romantic figures of his period. Born in Philadelphia, the son of L. Clarke Davis, long editor of the *Public Ledger,* and of Rebecca Harding Davis, a novelist of gifts and repute, he left college to become a reporter, in his native city at the outset and later in New York. He first won the favor of discriminating readers with *Gallagher,* a short story which had for its hero an office boy of the Philadelphia *Press.* A little later his Van Bibber stories appeared as special articles in the New York *Evening Sun* and were welcomed by critics as work of charm and quality.

Thus before he was thirty Davis found himself fairly launched on a career which made him one of the most popular and generously rewarded authors of his time. He left the *Evening Sun* for *Harper's Weekly* and for three years was managing editor of that journal. Thereafter he gave all of his time to the writing of novels, stories and plays broken after 1897 by occasional labors as a war correspondent in Cuba, Mexico, South America, South Africa and the Near and Far East. His earnings in his latter years enabled him to lead the life of a country gentleman at Cross Roads Farm, and there in the spring of 1916, following a late return from services as a correspondent in Greece and Serbia, death claimed him almost without warning in his fifty-second year.

Two years later Charles Belmont Davis, himself an admirable literary craftsman, told the story of his brother's life and gathered some of his letters in a volume which throws interesting light on its subject, and also on certain standards and ideals which may be said to have come to an end with the first world war. One may not take seriously some of the things regarded as of first importance by Richard Harding Davis and the circle of admirers whom he drew about him, but the fact remains that he was a loyal friend, a genuine American, and a first-class reporter with an unfailing zest for life in all its phases which remained with him until the end. One who touched elbows with him when for both the world was still in the Golden Age gladly pays this tribute to the memory of an uncommon man.

A short ride from Cross Roads Farm brings the pilgrim to Bedford House, the last home of one of the great figures of the Revolutionary era. John Jay's active part in public affairs was behind him when in 1801 at the early age of fifty-six he built stately Bedford House which, except for the addition of a stone wing, retains its original form. It was his home until his death in 1829 and is still occupied by his descendants. The house, furnished as it was in Jay's time, contains paintings by Peale and Stuart and other mementoes of its builder's career, and to visit it is a privilege to be gratefully remembered by anyone for whom the builders of the republic have a meaning. Than Jay not one of them, if we except Washington and Franklin, had for a long span of years a higher claim upon popular respect and confidence. Nor in an age of change and transition can any lover of our lettered past forget that as one of the authors of *The Federalist*, after nearly eight score years still read and honored by students of our federal beginnings, he wrought mightily for the adoption of the Constitution.

John Jay in his old age at Bedford House frequently exchanged visits with Gouverneur Morris, then living in retirement at Morrisiana. They had served together in the Continental Congress. Later Morris, another able man with a mind of his own, had helped to frame the Federal Constitution, and had represented the infant republic in Paris when France in turn faced a violent and bloody remaking of its institutions. Thus lively and some times racy must have been the talk of the two veterans when in their meetings they recalled old days and those who had had a part in them. The story goes that at one of these meetings the Continental Congress and the dubious methods of some of its members were the subjects of lengthy discussion. At last there was silence and then, as a sober after thought, Morris remarked to his visitor: "There were a lot of infernal rascals in that Congress, weren't there Jay?" A question to which historians have since returned more than one specific and confirming answer.

William Jay, who succeeded his father as master of Bedford House, was an able lawyer and writer who helped to give effective shaping to the abolition movement, when it still had need for leaders of breadth and vision; and in the old burial ground of Bedford Village is the grave of a later descendant of John Jay, who dying in 1935, is remembered as a stout champion of unpopular, and, if vagrant impulses chanced to grip him. perverse causes. Born in 1863, John Jay Chapman was the son of a New York lawyer who sprang from a New England family of liberal inclinings, and of a mother descended from the Jays. He was graduated from Harvard at the age of twenty-three, studied law and practiced it for a decade, but then, being a man of fortune, quit the bar for authorship, and between 1898 and 1927 published more than a score of volumes of essays, plays and verse. The subjects of these volumes ranged from Dante through Shakespeare to Emerson, and, utterly independent in their point of view—an independence enforced by boldness, insight and a style of signal beauty and charm—some of them will long remain as brilliant examples of literary criticism as ever has been written by an American. Their author was also one of the great letter writers of his age, made so by his individual, intimate and searching comments on men and affairs, and no student resolved to know his country at the century's turn can afford to neglect them.

Nor does this tell the full story of a many-sided career. The writers have occasion to recall Chapman as an active, heavily-built, and, in his later years, deeply bearded man, while the record represents him as from youth to age governed by a drastic sense of personal justice, and a consciousness of civic responsibility so strong that he was led more than once into what appeared to be oddly contradictory acts and utterances. The same processes made him the unrelenting foe of conditions which other men accepted without protest or patiently endured rather than openly quarrel with them. Once he went from New York to a Pennsylvania town on the anniversary of a brutal lynching there, to conduct a public prayer meeting, with only two curious residents of the place to keep him company, and so bring a measure of peace to his own soul; and, although he never sought or held public office, he was rampant in a dozen reform movements which borrowed new interest and piquancy from the support he gave them. Lovers of truth, even when it takes disturbing forms, must wonder and regret that fate fails to produce more than one John Jay Chapman in a generation.

Another Bedford landmark is the house known as the Old Parsonage which was the last home of Jacob Gould Schurman for nearly thirty years president of Cornell University and also eminent in other fields. A native of Prince Edward Island, born in 1854, Dr. Schurman studied first at the University of London, and then in Paris, Edinburgh and Heidelberg, and for six years was Sage professor of philosophy at Cornell before at the early age of thirty-eight he became its president. A man of action as well as a philosopher, he greatly enlarged Cornell's scope and usefulness, and during occasional leaves of absence served as head of the commission which following 1899 brought a measure of law and order to the Philippines, and as minister to Greece and China.

Dr. Schurman, who in 1921 resigned the presidency of Cornell, began his last period of service as a diplomat in 1925 when President Coolidge appointed him minister to Germany, retiring at the end of five years to make his home in the Old Parsonage, Bedford, surrounded by reminders of his career as educator and diplomat. One or another helpful task, however, continued to engage him, and at an age when most men are content to rest from their labors he was the directing spirit of a successful movement to raise among Americans a fund of half a million dollars for the erection of a new building at the University of Heidelberg.

The facade of Schurman Hall as it was named had to submit under Hitler to an odd and melancholy transformation. Then an original inscription To the Eternal Spirit gave way to The German Spirit surmounted by a golden swastika and an eagle. How Dr. Schurman regarded this change was never in evidence; but time brings in its revenges; and Cornell now numbers among its students hundreds of young men who in trying weeks and months, when the future of civilization hung in the balance, fought in Germany to put an end to Hitlerism. Although the author of many books, Dr. Schurman, a man of reserves, was never moved to put on paper the story of his own long and useful life. That life ended in 1942 and his grave is near that of John Jay Chapman in Bedford cemetery.

The pilgrimage here recorded had its conclusion at Katonah, a pleasant hamlet a few miles north of Bedford, where stands the house Clyde Fitch bought and remade, but was permitted to occupy only for a brief period. It was in 1907 that Fitch, then at the apex of his career as the most popular playmaker of his generation, during a ride over Westchester roads came upon a rolling plot of ground graced by an ancient farm home set amid deep hills and near a chain of lakes, which he purchased, christened The Other House, and with loving care for detail but small regard for expense, enlarged and remodeled aginst the time when he could build there the place of his dreams—Quiet Hills. He moved into it in October, and passed his week-ends there until late June of 1909, when, warned by his physician, he departed for Europe to seek much needed strength for another stretch of hard labor. A short three months later while resting in a quiet French village death came without warning to Clyde Fitch, and The Other House, empty and forlorn, passed shortly into other hands—an arresting example of the irony which now and then drops the curtain on the hopes and plans of short lived men and women.

CHAPTER XV

ALBANY AND THE WAY THERE

Back again on the Albany Post Road and with Tarrytown a scant half-mile behind him the pilgrim comes upon a roomy stone house surrounded by pines in Sleepy Hollow Manor which were it able to speak could relate a long and varied history. In 1680 the land on which it stands was sold by the Indian sachem Sho-harius to Frederick Phillipse. After the Revolution, in which many of the great landlords of this region were Royalists, the land and the house Phillipse had built on it were conveyed by the commissioner of forfeitures to General Gerard G. Beekman, whose family retained it until 1845, when it was purchased by General James Watson Webb, long editor of the New York *Courier and Inquirer* and an outstanding and contentious figure in a period when journalists fought one another with ruthless energy both in and out of their columns.

Webb, who had been a soldier in early manhood and who took complacent pride in his own good looks and fastidious garb, found occasion on the morrow of Horace Greeley's struggle with hard conditions to sneer editorially at the latter's ill-worn and sometimes shabby clothes. Fresh in the public mind were Webb's conviction and sentence for leaving the state to fight a duel with Thomas F. Marshall of Kentucky. He had been condemned to pass two years in Sing Sing, but William H. Seward, then governor of New York, had pardoned him before he went behind the bars. The pardon incident gave Greeley an opening of which he made effective use in the columns of the *Tribune*. He had worn, he tartly commented, better clothes than Webb could wear if he paid his debts, adding, "That he ever affected eccentricity is most untrue; and certainly no costume he ever appeared in would create such a sensation in Broadway as that which James Watson Webb would have worn but for the clemency of Governor Seward." And that ended the matter.

General Webb, who had gained his title by service in the state militia of New York, was a publisher of energy and vision and the innovations which he effected in news-gathering led in no long time to the organization of the Associated Press. Bennett of the *Herald* was once in his employ and Raymond ended an association with him to become the founder of the *Times*. He gave a name to the Whig Party and later helped by voice and pen and with his usual ardor to call the Republican Party into being. A majority of the leading men of his period were either General Webb's friends or his enemies, and of the former many were now and again guests in his home here by the Hudson. One of these was Commodore Matthew C. Perry, who on his return from the Mexican War presented his host with four bombshells that were used to cap the gate-posts of the estate. These shells played a part in a stirring incident for they were fired from the Castle of San Juan d Ulloa at Vera Cruz when Perry landed the army of General Scott on the beach south of that city. They struck within a few feet of where Perry was standing, but for some reason failed to explode. The commodore picked them up and on his return home presented them to General Webb as ornaments for the latter's gateposts.

In 1861, the redoubtable editor, having sold his newspaper, by appointment of President Lincoln departed for a long period of service as American minister to Brazil, and in 1865 his home passed into the possession of General John C. Fremont and his wife, Jessie Benton Fremont, who gave it the Indian name of Pocaho. Here the West's greatest adventurer, as one of his biographers calls him, and the gracious woman who shared with steadfast heart the good and evil fortunes of a dramatic and unusual career, for a period all too brief kept open house for their friends, who included choice spirits from many lands. Here also a spacious room was set aside for General Fremont's literary treasurers, which included copies of the reports of his western journeys, reports which for a time made him the most widely read of American authors, first editions of Audubon's books on birds, and the library of Alexander Humboldt, purchased and brought from Germany soon after the great scientist's death.

Soon, however, the fortune Fremont had made in mining took wings; at the end of trying months Pocaho passed into other hands, and its late owners, forced to part with their most prized belongings, found refuge in a modest apartment in New York. But threatened poverty did not cloud Mrs. Fremont's sunny outlook on life and the world. A friend relates that on one of her last mornings at Pocaho a caller, who had asked to see the dismantled house with a view to purchase, praised the beauty and size of the rooms. "Yes," was the reply, "they are large. They have held much happiness, and newcomers will find few shadows on the walls." Here spoke the stout-hearted daughter of Benton and wife of Fremont.

From Tarrytown the Post Road runs northward through Scarborough and Ossining, and past Croton Point, with its memories of Andre and other Revolutionary figures, to Peekskill, gateway to the Highlands of the Hudson, and the country home for upward of a generation of Henry Ward Beecher. In the many roomed house at the corner of Main Street and Grant Avenue, Peekskill, which the famous preacher built in 1875 and called Boscobel, he found time, while giving welcome to an ever-growing throng of visitors, to write his novel of *Norwood* and other once widely read and now half-forgotten books. In another part of Main Street is an earlier home of Beecher which in Civil War days had an ample acreage as a setting. This acreage for several battle summers was turned into a produce garden from which heaping car-loads of supplies were shipped to the Army of the Potomac, and so, in other forms than his well remembered series of speeches in England, the pastor of Plymouth Church made helpful contribution to the Union cause. Both of Beecher's old homes are now occupied and kept in repair by lovers of the past who delight in divers ways to pay honor to the career and memory of their former owner.

Again a short detour from Peekskill takes one to an old farm-house near the Putnam County hamlet of East River which was the birthplace and girlhood home of Fanny Crosby, perhaps the best known of American hymn writers. This gifted woman's story has to do with one whose ninety-four years were lived graciously and bravely under hard conditions. Christened Frances Janet Crosby at her birth in 1820, through the negligence of an attendant she became totally blind when she was six weeks old, and at the age of fifteen was put to school at the Institution for the Blind in New York. Here she received an education which enabled her to teach grammar, rhetoric and history in the institution until at the age of thirty-eight she was married to Alexander Van Alstyne, a blind teacher in the same school, a union which until the husband's death in 1902 gave to both a full measure of content and happiness.

Although Fanny Crosby early began to put her thoughts into verse she was forty-five years of age when she wrote her first hymn, but so full a measure of success attended her efforts in a field to which she was a late comer that in the half century that preceded her death in 1915, when she was nearing the age of ninety-five, she composed more than a thousand hymns, many of which enjoyed abounding popularity in their author's lifetime, and not a few of which are still sung in Protestant churches throughout the world. Indeed since the days of Watts and the Wesleys no single individual has won larger space in Gospel songbooks. She belonged to the era of the great revivals of Moody and Sankey and other evangelists, and for them she wrote not a few of her most widely known songs. Popular tastes are subject to change, but *Safe in the Arms of Jesus, Close to Thee, Blessed Assurance* and *Rescue the Perishing* are titles that have an intimate and cherished meaning for uncounted numbers of devout men and women.

Miss Crosby's method of work was unique for a blind person, and also interesting in an unusual degree. It was her custom when composing to hold a small open book closely over her eyes. When a piece was finished to her satisfaction she would dictate it to an amanuensis who wrote it out for the printer. The music, as a rule, was composed in each case after the stanzas were written, but at intervals she was called upon to supply verses for tunes both new and old. It is credibly related that Phillips Brooks once gave her seventy-five topics with a request that she should write verses based on them; and she composed all of the hymns before a line of any of them was given final form by an assistant. Nor, despite her amazing facility, was it given her to write a line that lacked the lyric lilt, while all that she did was charged with the sincerity of a radiant and unquestioning faith. "My hymns," she was wont to declare, "sing themselves, and I cannot rest until they are on paper."

Miss Crosby's last home was in Bridgeport, Connecticut, where, when extreme old age came to her, she was tenderly cared for by relatives and friends. A cheerful spirit remained with her until the end. "I do not know," she said to a visitor just before her death, "but that on the whole it has been a good thing that I have been blind. How could I have lived such a helpful life as I have were it not that I am blind? I would not have it otherwise."

Back once more on the Post Road a short drive northward and a detour westward to the banks of the Hudson take the traveller to Beacon, the Fishkill Landing of an earlier time, with its memories of Andrew Jackson Downing, who wrote on the art of landscape gardening with abounding profit and growing

fame and who met an untimely and tragic end in the *Henry Clay*
steamboat disaster in the summer of 1852 when had fate been
kinder to him, a long future of usefulness was still before him,
and of Christopher Pearce Cranch, who in early manhood was a
clergyman in the village, but who gave up preaching to write
verses and paint pictures. A center of Fishkill Landing hospitality in the early decades of the last century was Locust Grove,
the many-gabled Dutch homestead of John Peter De Windt,
which took its name from the great trees shading the approach
to it. De Windt, a West India trader, who kept slaves and helped
to develop a port beside the Hudson, won the heart and hand of
a grand-daughter of John Adams, second president of the United
States, and of the eleven children born of this union Caroline, the
eldest, became in 1838 the wife of Downing, while a few years
later her younger sister, Elizabeth, was led to the altar by Cranch.
Surely those were days worthy of remembrance.

A mile north of Beacon stone gate posts and a great white
oak tree mark the entrance to Mount Gulian, an estate which for
more than two and a half centuries has never been owned by any
other than a Verplanck. On a knoll rising perhaps a hundred
feet above the Hudson stand the charred walls of a mansion,
which, built in 1740 and destroyed by fire in 1931, for nearly two
centuries had a Verplanck for its master. The mansion has other
claims to remembrance, for in the last days of the Revolution it
was the headquarters of Baron von Steuben, and there in 1783
was organized the Society of the Cincinnati. Gulian Cromelin
Verplanck, lawyer, publicist and critic, occupied the old house
for many years prior to his death in 1870, and its walls were
silent witnesses to the long and patient labors which attended the
preparation of his edition of Shakespeare—hailed as an outstanding achievement when it first came from the press, and still regarded as one of the landmarks of American scholarship.

A more august name than that of Verplanck has abiding
association with Beacon, for in the burial ground of St. Luke's
Episcopal Church, which covers both sides of a rocky knoll to the
north of that ivy-clad structure, one comes upon the grave of
James Kent, jurist and author, whose *Commentaries on the
American Law* for more than a century have caused his learning
and rare ability to be honored on both sides of the sea. Kent's
middle and later years, as elsewhere recorded, were passed in
New York City, but when death came to him at the age of eighty-
four he elected to take his long rest in this quiet hamlet beside

the Hudson, only a little way removed from his birthplace at what is now Doanesburg in Putnam County.

On the Post Road, four and a half miles east of Beacon, lies Fishkill Village, which also has its appeal for the lover of letters and of a storied past. When the Revolution broke in 1776 Fishkill, then a hamlet of a few score souls, but lying on the only practical military route through the Highlands of the Hudson, as well as upon the most direct route from the Hudson Valley to New England, quickly became a military base and supply depot. By the same token Trinity Episcopal Church, known locally as the English Church, a frame structure erected in 1769, which the present-day visitor finds little altered by the years, quickly became a hospital where care was given to the victims of smallpox, then raging in the patriot ranks and to the men wounded in the battle of White Plains. At the same time the Dutch Reformed Church, dating from 1731 and today, after the passage of more than ten score years, still giving ample proof of the tastes and inclinings of its builders, was converted into a prison for Tories, deserters and British troopers captured by Washington's men.

The Dutch Church figures also in Cooper's *The Spy*, for Enoch Crosby, now believed, as hinted in another place, to be the original of Harvey Birch, the hero of that absorbing tale, was once a prisoner within its walls. Cooper wrought wisely in choosing a hero, for Crosby's career, shorn of all save its matter-of-fact details, affords material for a romance such as Scott or Dumas, each an elder brother of the New World story-teller, would have found delight in putting on paper. When the Revolution opened he was a young man of twenty-five, living on a farm in what is now Putnam County, a member of the family from which in a later generation descended Fanny Crosby. Resolving to enter the service of his country, he shouldered his musket and set out to join the patriot army. On the Westchester border he fell in with a Tory, who, supposing him to be of like mind, warned him of the danger of the way, "as the rebels were on the alert."

Crosby, with seeming concern, asked the best course to follow, and was advised to go with the Tory to his home and join a company then forming in support of the British cause. He accepted the invitation and was in due course introduced to a number of rabid Tories. Before a week was ended he had made himself master of all the information they could impart, and, affecting impatience to join the enemy, despite many warnings, he took his leave, and was soon on the road to New York. His journey ended, he sought the house of a patriot friend, and together they secured an audience with the Committee of Safety, then sitting at White Plains. The mission of this body, headed by John Jay, was to ferret out and counteract the intrigues of the Tories, who included many men of standing and influence. Jay and his associates, having heard Crosby's story, requested him to go as guide to a company of rangers, and the result was the arrest of the entire Tory group.

Impressed by this proof of Crosby's peculiar ability, Jay now urged him to serve his country as a secret agent, and to this he agreed, only stipulating that in case of his death justice should be done his memory. Before a fortnight had elapsed Crosby unearthed and resolved to join another company of Tories about to enter the British service. Winning the confidence of its leader, he was led to the hiding-place of the company—the interior of an immense haystack. While the others slept he hastened to White Plains, and, informing the committee, returned before his comrades had discovered his absence. Quickly followed the capture of the entire company including Crosby. After examination they were conducted to the Dutch Church in Fishkill, where word that one of the windows had been left unfastened was secretly conveyed to Crosby. When night fell he leaped from this window, and, eluding the sentinels, was again at large. Captain Townsend, commander of the patriot troop that had captured him, keenly bewailed his escape, for all except the committee counted him a dangerous Tory.

Crosby had not been long at liberty when he discovered another company of Tories with a hiding place in the Highlands on the west side of the Hudson. Again he sent word to Jay and his committee, who dispatched Townsend and his rangers. The whole band surrendered at the end of the skirmish that ensued, and great was Townsend's joy to find among them the prisoner who had escaped from him at Fishkill. The Dutch Church became the prison of all of the captured men except Crosby, who, to make assurance against his possible escape doubly sure, was led to the house where Townsend had his headquarters and confined in a securely locked room with a guard at the door. The committee was at first perplexed as to how his escape could best be effected, but in the end a quantity of laudanum was mixed with rum and molasses, and a trusted agent treated the thirsty guard to the mixture. A quarter hour later, with the guard in a deep stupor, the door was unlocked and Crosby once more at large. His later adventures would fill a volume much longer than the novel that purports to relate them.   The war ended, he purchased a farm in Putnam County, where he passed the remainder of his days a much respected citizen, serving in turn as justice of the peace and as one of the judges of the court of common pleas, It was John Jay who in old age told the story of Crosby's exploits to Cooper then at the outset of his career as an author, and so made possible the writing of a romance that has given delight to four generations of readers.

Fishkill cherishes other memories of its part in the Revolution.   The New York Provincial Convention, compelled in the last days of August, 1776, to flee New York before the threatened invasion of the British, found refuge in Fishkill, where it held its sessions until February of the following year when it removed to Kingston.   Like conditions brought to Fishkill the patriot printer Samuel Loudon, who set up his press in a house the site of which in Main Street is pointed out to visitors, and on October 1, 1776, reviving the journal he had published in New York, founded the New York *Packet and American,* the first newspaper to be published in Dutchess County.   Here he also printed many of Washington's military orders and the first copies of the Constitution of New York drawn up by John Jay.   Loudon continued his paper until the end of the war when he returned to New York to become in 1786 in association with Noah Webster founder and editor of the first American magazine.

Poughkeepsie, fifteen miles northward from Fishkill on the Post Road may well be regarded as a daughter of what in these parts is a smooth and shaded thoroughfare for it came into being soon after the Provincial Legislature in 1703 voted the construction of a King's Highway from New York to Albany.   The opening of the Revolution found it a hamlet of a few hundred souls, some of whom were slaves, and, while it played a less active part than Fishkill in that long struggle, dwellers in the present city take pride in the fact that in its modest courthouse, serving as a meeting-place for the Provincial Legislature, were staged the debate and final vote which assured ratification by the needed number of colonies of the Federal Constitution.   These took place in the fateful July days of 1788, and it is a part of history that the great and winning arguments in support of the proposed Constitution put forth by Alexander Hamilton, then in his thirty-second year, in opposition to stubborn George Clinton and the latter's followers, proved him a statesman of the first rank.

One of the admiring and quickly persuaded listeners to Hamilton's stirring pleas was then youthful James Kent who seven years before, lately graduated at Yale, youngest of his class, had come from his native Putnam County to Poughkeepsie to study law under Egbert Benson, attorney-general of New York. In 1788 he had been three years a lawyer, and, although his clients were few and his fees pitifully small, he already had begun the assembling of the library dealing with the law and history, diligent use of which was to make him one of the learned men of his time. Kent removed to New York in 1793, and, at the end of a brief period of struggle, won the standing as a lawyer which in turn made him a Master of Chancery, first a member and then Chief Justice of the Supreme Court of the State, and finally in 1814 its Chancellor.

In 1823 an ill-judged provision of New York's Constitution forced Chancellor Kent's retirement from the bench at the arbitrary age of sixty, but that retirement gave Columbia College for a memorable period her most famous teacher of law and the United States a set of *Commentaries* quickly accorded an equal place beside those written a half century earlier by Blackstone. Kent's biographer tells us that he did not at first plan to publish his lectures at Columbia and when his son persuaded him to do so had to hazard a considerable part of his savings to meet the demands of printer and binder. The work, which he intended to complete in two volumes, in the end required four, and it would be difficult to estimate their abiding influence on American law. Every lawyer and judge, no matter what his place or rank, at once profited by the precision, clarity and comprehensiveness of these *Commentaries*. Their author made repeated revisions until 1841, a few years before his death. In later times more than a dozen editions have been required and after the passage of five and a half score years the original work remains, what Charles Sumner called it, "the manual of the practitioner and the institute of the student."

Time has spared us a droll anecdote of how Kent was regarded by one of his famous contemporaries. From their first meeting, in Poughkeepsie Alexander Hamilton won and held a warm place in Kent's affections, and when the great Federalist was killed in a duel with Aaron Burr, Kent became his slayer's implacable enemy. One day long afterwards when on Nassau

Street, New York, the Chancellor espied Burr on the opposite side, he crossed with such haste as his years would permit, and, shaking his cane in Burr's face, shouted: "You're a scoundrel, sir! a scoundrel! a scoundrel!" But Burr, as usual, was equal to an unwelcome emergency. He raised his hat and, bowing to the ground, replied in his calmest professional tone: "The opinions of the learned Chancellor are always entitled to the highest consideration." After which, apparently undisturbed, he continued serenely on his way.

Kent's own quaint account of the cardinal event of his years in Poughkeepsie, revealing as it does that not all of his thoughts were devoted to the law, merits a place in this chronicle. On the morrow of his admission to the bar he fell in love with and married Elizabeth Bailey, daughter of his landlord. "At the age of twenty-one," he records in his diary, "I married without one cent of property. Why did I marry? I answer that at the farmer's house where I boarded one of his daughters, a little, modest, lovely girl of fourteen, gradually caught my attention and insensibly stole my affections, and before I thought of love or knew what it was, I was most violently affected. I was twenty-one when we married, and my wife sixteen, and that lovely girl has always been the idol and solace of my life." Nor did the wife ever have cause to regret their union. Thus, while the husband was hospitable to a fault, she was ever devising ways to prevent his yielding to occasions for extravagance, especially in the purchase of books, when in the first days of married life there was no money with which to pay for them and the wolf was at the door. And after prosperity came it was his frequent practice on the receipt of a large fee to retain a few dollars for his own use and send the remainder home to his wife "to keep for her gratification."

Five years after the Kents left Poughkeepsie there came to live in the town a man who holds a secure if modest place in our literary annals. The newcomer was Isaac Mitchell. When in 1798 John Woods, to preach the principles of Jefferson to the worthy voters of the Valley of the Hudson, founded in Poughkeepsie, the *American Farmer and Dutchess County Advertiser,* a weekly newspaper with a long name, he employed Mitchell, a writer of parts, to edit it. The *Farmer* failed after a year or two and in 1802 Mitchell became part owner and editor of another Jeffersonian journal, the *Guardian,* the name of which he changed to the *Political Barometer.* Another turn of the wheel made him editor of a third Jeffersonian organ, the *Republican Crisis,* published in Albany and later removed to Hudson with its name changed to the *Balance and New York State Journal;* but ere long a political upset cost him this post, and he returned to Poughkeepsie there to write and in 1811 to publish in two volumes his once amazingly popular and now more than half-forgotten romance, *The Asylum, or Alonzo and Melissa,* described by the bookseller who first pushed its sale as "an American tale founded in fact."

One of the journals which Mitchell had edited in announcing the promised publication of his tale took occasion to add: "From the known talents of the author, and the pains he has bestowed on this work we have reason to expect a well-finished and interesting tale." The editor of the *Balance and State Journal,* which then enlightened the citizens of Albany, was not disappointed in his expectations. When Mitchell's book appeared the American press was filled with accounts of Bonaparte's campaigns, and the minds of their readers were mainly turned to our approaching war with England and its probable outcome. Thus, *Alonzo and Melissa* was at first favored with few reviews. Moreover, it had its faults, undue length and episodes that had nothing to do with the main plot being among them.

From the first, however, it found readers, for it was an interesting tale; and when, a second edition being called for, a new publisher by prudent excisions reduced the tale to a single volume and changed the title to *Alonzo and Melissa, or The Unfeeling Father,* it won a new and ever-growing measure of favor which made it for a full half century one of the most popular novels ever published in America. It was reprinted in every section of the country—North, South and Middle West; it was read by all classes and conditions of people, and tradition has it that for many years in Dutchess County, the country of its birth, fond parents named their children for its leading characters. And yet it is now so completely forgotten that historians of our literature rarely give it passing reference. The visitor can find nothing about its author in the Poughkeepsie Public Library, and nothing is known of how and where Isaac Mitchell ended his days.

The present writers like to think that in the days when *Alonzo and Melissa* was still required reading in most households its pages were thumbed by another Poughkeepsie author to whom time has accorded a fuller measure of remembrance—Henry Wheeler Shaw, cracker-barrel humorist and philosopher best known to three generations of readers as Josh Billings. Born in 1818 in the hill country of Western Massachusetts, the son and grandson of men who had served in Congress, Shaw, after long rovings in the West, in 1854 settled in Poughkeepsie where he followed the vocation of real estate agent and auctioneer, at the same time taking an active interest in civic affairs and serving in turn as an alderman of the town and as a member of the county board of supervisors. He united a rare knowledge of human nature to a keen sense of humor, so that the droll and pithy stories which he soon began to tell from the auction block and around the court-house won him quick and growing favor with his fellows.

Thus encouraged Shaw under the pen name of Josh Billings began to write first for the local and then for the city press. At the outset he spelled correctly, but noting that too often his wise and witty sayings failed to score he shrewdly followed the example of Artemus Ward and began a systematic course of phonetic spelling which instantly caught the popular fancy and in a period of time comparatively brief made Josh Billings a household name. After that he took to lecturing, sure of a welcome wherever his appointments carried him, and then to almanac making, his *Farmer's Allminax,* first published in 1873, reaching a sale of 130,000 copies in its second year, and yielding him a generous income during the remainder of his life.

And now and again Shaw published a thin volume made up of brief essays, charged with homely and telling common-sense like the one on *The Mule,* which Abraham Lincoln upon reading at once accorded a leading place in his selected repertory of good things. It is said that the President, when opportunity offered, delighted to read parts of this essay to his cabinet, much to the disgust of his irascible secretary of war, Edwin M. Stanton, who had little time for laughter or its sources. Old men recall Josh Billings as in private life a delightful companion whose tart remarks were often charged with a grim humor that caused them to be remembered long after the occasion which prompted them had passed from mind. A chance companion once asked him if he was not going to hear Ingersoll lecture, to which he returned a negative answer. "I would not," said he, "give half a dollar to hear Bob Ingersoll lecture on *The Mistakes of Moses,* but I would give ten dollars to hear Moses lecture on *The Mistakes of Bob Ingersoll.*" Josh Billings died in October, 1885, at Monterey, California, where he had gone to fill a lecture engagement, and his body was brought back for burial among his native hills. His homely philosophy, charged with the worth of common things, has helped many a man to plain living and straight thinking, and his best writings well deserve reprinting.

The faculty of Vassar College, during the years in which that institution, founded by a Poughkeepsie worthy who had gained wealth as a brewer, has played an outstanding part in the training of the American woman, has included many gifted teachers among its members, perhaps the one best remembered being Maria Mitchell, who for longer than the average lifetime, was its professor of astronomy, and whose bust was early placed in the Hall of Fame in New York, the first of her sex to receive that honor. And among the graduates of Vassar, now numbering many thousands, note must be made of Adelaide Crapsey, all too early enrolled in the army of the silent, and of Edna St. Vincent Millay and Constance Rourke—each with a record of rare accomplishment in her field—the first named still living and at work.

Alfred Billings Street, whose verse dealing in the main with colony times and frontier folk still finds a place in the anthologies and who for more than thirty years served as state librarian at Albany, was born and passed his boyhood in Pougskeepsie. There too Dr. Nathaniel Scudder Prime, who wrote books and sired a gifted family, once conducted a female academy, having for an assistant his son, Samuel Irenaeus Prime, who in after years as editor of the New York *Observer* and as an essayist under the pen name of Irenaeus gave sound advice to Presbyterian households in all parts of the land.

Another lettered resident of Poughkeepsie in the early decades of the last century was Benson John Lossing, a name deserving of honor by every lover of our history. The son of a Dutchess County farmer and largely self-taught, Lossing was only a year past his majority when in 1835 he became an editor in Poughkeepsie, first of the *Telegraph* and then of the *Casket*. From one J. A. Adams, who drew illustrations for the *Casket*, Lossing learned the elements of engraving on wood, and in 1838 removed to New York to follow that vocation. There after a period of struggle he became associated with the house of Harper, and with the financial support thus assured him he devoted five years of labor and more than 8000 miles of travel to collecting material for and writing and illustrating his *Field Book of the Revolution* which published in parts between 1850 and 1852 gave him a wide reputation.

When Lossing went his rounds in search of material he found at every turn surviving veterans of the Revolution eager to give him first-hand information of the events in which they had played a part, and this sympathetic use of sources which death soon closed to later inquirers, wedded to a facile handling of pen and pencil, makes his volumes after three generations an indispensable aid to the student and writer of history. He followed his first success with another *Fieldbook* dealing in like manner with the Second War with England. Thereafter his career was one of such steady and fruitful labor in his chosen field that when he died in 1891 more than forty titles stood to his credit in the library lists. Of one of these, a volume which tells in a beguiling way the story of the Hudson and its shores from source to sea, the present writers have made frequent and appreciative use.

It is a pleasant ride through Dover Plains, Wassaic and Amenia and thence back to Poughkeepsie. Near Dover Plains, a house which crowns a high hill and so commands a sixty-mile view of the country lying between the Shawangunk and Catskill Mountains, was built by Lossing for a dwelling-place in old age. He named it Chestnut Ridge and there securely housed the great and varied historical collection which he had assembled through the years and which sold and dispersed after his death yielded his heirs a modest fortune. The quiet village of Wassaic was for a time the home of Agnes Laut, who there wrote not a few of the stirring books which promise to long afford congenial hours to readers who love the story of the making of the Farther West.

And in Amenia Joel Benton, by turns farmer, editor, author and man of affairs, was born and passed the greater part of his life. Benton's place in American letters is a minor but pleasantly remembered one. His writings prove that he had humor and gift of phrase, and that he was a close observer of out-of-door life and of his fellows, but the part he best liked to fill was that of friend and confidant of older and greater men. He was early on an intimate footing with Emerson and Greeley, and wrote books about them which have a value of their own because filled with revealing facts concerning widely different shapers of thought. Benton was of imposing mien, and it pleased him, as he grew older, to be told by his friends that he bore a close resemblance to the poet Tennyson. After 1885 he made his home in Poughkeepsie, where he died in 1911 in his eightieth year and where he now takes his rest.

From Poughkeepsie the Post Road runs northward through or past Hyde Park, Red Hook, Rhinebeck and Claverack to Kinderhook, each rich in memories of a mellow past. Hyde Park, which takes its name from Edward Hyde, Lord Cornbury, sometime governor of the colony of New York, and which, long the home and now the resting place of a President, has another claim to notice in the fact that here in his closing years resided James Kirke Paulding, the friend and early associate of Irving, and himself an author of mark in the early and middle decades of the last century. Paulding's fame has been dimmed by the years, but it was envied by less fortunate men in the days when he joined hands with Irving in the publication of the *Salmagundi Papers* or later wrote the *Dutchman's Fireside*, a veracious and amusing chronicle of the life led by the Dutch of the countryside when New York was still a British colony. At the end of a long and prosperous career in business and as a public official he served as Secretary of the Navy under Van Buren, this as prelude to his retirement to the home, which attracted, perhaps, by its early associations and ancient Dutch traditions, he bought at Hyde Park in 1846 and gave the name Placentia. Here toward the end he shaped for a friend an appealing picture of serene and sunny old age. "I smoke a little," he wrote, "read a little, grumble a little and sleep a great deal. I was once great at pulling up weeds to which I have a mortal antipathy . . . but my working days are almost over. I find that carrying seventy-five years on my shoulders is pretty nearly equal to the same number of pounds; and instead of laboring myself, I sit in the shade watching the labors of others which I find quite sufficient exercise." Paulding died in 1860, at the age of eighty-two, when, although a lifelong Democrat, he was preparing to vote for Lincoln, and, as recorded in another place, found a grave in Greenwood Cemetery, Brooklyn.

Red Hook was the birthplace of James Gordon Brooks, who studied law in Poughkeepsie and later was an editor in New York and Albany, where he died after winning a measure of success as a poet which has not survived the test of time. Northward from Red Hook the Post Road is for the most part level, delightful to walk or motor over, winding, first to the right and then to the left through a land of quaint houses and steep-roofed barns, and abounding in legends and tokens of its first Dutch settlers. It also has its appeal for the literary pilgrim. Claverack, a sleepy village on a creek of the same name, where of old the Van Rensselaer tenants came to pay their dues to the lord of the manor, was the birthplace of James Watson Webb; and a little way to the south of Kinderhook is Lindenwald, the pleasant country place in which Martin Van Buren spent his last years, there working at intervals on the engaging if not always candid autobiography, the finished portions of which waited upward of seventy years to find their way into print. Van Buren's grave is in the village cemetery. A plain granite shaft surmounts it, and the inscription contains in addition to his name, and the date of his birth and death only the words, "Eighth President of the United States."

The mansion which Van Buren bought and called Lindenwald had been known in an earlier time as the Van Ness house, after its builder, Peter Van Ness, who served as a colonel in the Continental Army, and had a hand in the capture of Burgoyne at Saratoga. The three sons of Van Ness were all men of mark. William P. Van Ness, the youngest, read law in the office of Aaron Burr, and acted as his tutor's second in the duel with Hamilton. Another of his friends was Washington Irving, who in early manhood spent much time at Lindenwald. There Irving is said to have written *Rip Van Winkle* and in the region thereabout found material for *A Legend of Sleepy Hollow* and other of the writings which first gave him fame. The scenes of the *Legend* were laid in Kinderhook, and Jesse Merwin, a local schoolmaster of Irving's day and the author's lifetime friend, suggested the character of Ichabod Crane, although his personality was in sharp contrast to that of the hapless pedagogue of Irving's tale. Tradition also has it that Katrina Van Alen, a buxom maiden of Kinderhook, furnished an original for Kathleen Van Tassel to whom Crane paid unlucky court.

One more interesting reminder of the past claims the attention of the visitor as he puts behind him the few miles which separate Kinderhook from Albany. Fort Crailo, in other days the manor house of the Upper (Eastern) Manor of the Van Rensselaers, whose holdings stretched for miles on both sides of the Hudson, stands on the banks of the river in what was once known as Greenbush but is now the city of Rensselaer. It is one of the oldest houses in the United States, its most ancient part dating from 1642, and until it fell into decay two generations ago was continuously owned and occupied by Van Rensselaers. It has been restored in recent years, and is now owned and cared for by the state.

In colony times and during the Revolution commanders of passing troops were now and again guests of the Van Rensselaer who chanced to be in residence at Fort Crailo. Thus in 1758 General James Abercrombie and his staff made a long halt here on their way to Ticonderoga and defeat by Montcalm. Richard Shuckburgh, a young surgeon on Abercrombie's staff, was vastly amused by the garb and bearing of the raw Yankee recruits who came straggling in from the countryside, and, so the story runs, seated on the curb of Fort Crailo's old garden well, scribbled the lines of *Yankee Doodle,* which became in the Revolution the rallying song of these same Yankees, and so saved from forgetfulness their author's name.

Albany at present journey's end also has its memories of the poets and story tellers of other times. Ray Palmer, the hymn writer, for nearly a score of years occupied an Albany pulpit. John Godfrey Saxe, wit and punster, whose appeal was to the average man, wrote and published some of his merriest verse during an early residence in the capital city, and there also, devotedly cared for in the house of a son, he dwelt in broken and clouded age and passed from life. Harold Frederic for a brief period in early manhood was editor of the Albany *Evening Journal,* going thence to larger fame and influence as a correspondent and author in London. And finally the name and stories of Philander Deming are things held in wistful memory by many an aging man and woman.

Born in 1829 in Schoharie County, New York, the son of a Presbyterian minister, Deming was graduated in turn from the University of Vermont and the Albany Law School, and, self-taught in a difficult art, was for a score of years a legislative and court stenographer in the capital city. In odd hours he wrote short stories which reveal keen yet tender insight into the workings of the human heart and the pathos which is a part of human lives. In 1873 William Dean Howells, then editor of the *Atlantic Monthly,* accepted and printed one of these tales, and thereafter Deming was long an occasional but welcome contributor to that magazine. And as time passed the best of his work was gathered into two thin volumes—*Adirondack Stories* and *Tompkins and Other Folks*—which so long as there are readers who recognize and cherish minor masterpieces will hold a secure place on library shelves. Their author survived for a generation his retirement from active labor; and in old age—he died in 1915 at the age of eighty-six—his abundant white hair and deeply lined face made him a striking figure on the streets of Albany. A meeting and speech with a man who could have posed for a portrait of Liszt are abiding memories of one of the present writer's first visit to the old town in which Deming lived and died. His grave is in the town of Burke, the home of his youth and early manhood.

No Albany writer of the last century, however, exercised a longer or wider measure of influence than did Thurlow Weed in the columns of the *Evening Journal* of which he was owner and for upward of thirty years years editor. In the *Autobiography* which he began in 1845 during a winter stay in the West Indies and worked at through the years, this remarkable man tells that he was born in 1797, at Cairo, Greene County, New York, the son of a hard-working father whom ill-luck persistently pursued from one to another village. Thus the Weeds lived for a time in the town of Catskill, and the son was wont in old age to recall how with other lads he swam out to a small island a little way from shore, and with mingled wonder and delight watched Fulton's *Clermont* noisily puffing up the Hudson on its first trip to Albany.

Weed in his teens mastered the printer's trade in Herkimer, and other towns, worked at it in Albany and New York and in 1817 at the age of twenty bought his first newspaper, the Norwich *Journal*. A few years later another turn of the wheel made him a resident of Rochester, where he secured election to the Legislature—the only office he ever held; began his long friendship with William Henry Seward, and in 1827 founding the *Anti-Masonic Inquirer,* became one of the leaders of a movement which, prompted by the disappearance the previous year of William Morgan, who had threatened to disclose the secrets of Masonry, swept the country, made William Wirt its candidate for the Presidency, and winning the support of men of future mark and influence, for a time played havoc with the Democratic Party.

Three years later Weed assumed the editorship of the Albany *Evening Journal,* and became for many years first a state and then a national leader of the Whigs, and of their successor, the Republican Party. He was rarely moved to write lengthy editorials, but was a master of the short, pithy paragraph, and knew how in divers ways to make it effectively serve his purposes. Thus, when rising young lawyers and politicians from other parts of the state had occasion to visit Albany he was sure in the *Evening Journal* to predict a brilliant future for each of them, and so add another devoted recruit to his personal following. He was a directing spirit in the choice and election of two Whig Presidents —Harrison and Taylor, and was largely responsible for the nomination of Clay and Scott to the Presidency.

Defeat finally came to Weed in 1860 when the Republican national convention, at the end of a strenuous contest, rejected Seward and made Lincoln its candidate. Twelve years earlier Lincoln, soon to end his only term in Congress, when passing through Albany on his way back to Illinois, had met Weed for the first time. Then neither could have dreamed of the august career destiny was to allot the younger man, or of how the elder was to serve him in noteworthy ways. Be it recorded in closing that in addition to his ability as an editor and party leader Weed knew how to win and hold friends, and also how to convince former enemies that he had a heart full of generous impulses. When Edwin Croswell, editor of the Albany *Argus,* fell on evil times, Weed, who had had many bitter battles with him, quickly secured from old friends and enemies, a fund of generous proportions; and this fund, conveyed to Croswell in a most considerate way, made his last days smooth and pleasant ones. Kindness of heart atoned in a measure for Weed's numerous and manifest shortcomings as a political leader.

CHAPTER XVI

North Jersey and Its Bookmen

Not a few of the towns and cities of North Jersey once gave homes or welcome to men and women the record of whose lives and work must be regarded as part of any account of New York in literature. Thus the Cockloft Hall of the *Salmagundi Papers,* now replaced by a red brick factory building, stood for nearly two hundred years on the banks of the Passaic at Gouverneur Street and Mount Pleasant Avenue in the city of Newark. In other days this old mansion, with its unobstructed view of blue miles of river and green acres of meadows, and of the then quiet hamlet of Newark a mile or more to the south of it, was the manor house of a large plantation which on one side extended to the Passaic and on the other touched the road that led to Belleville or Second River.

A typical mansion of its period, its builder was Nicholas Gouverneur, head of a wealthy New York family of Huguenot extraction, and during the Revolution Washington and other patriotic leaders had welcome at its hospitable table. It descended when the last century was young to Gouverneur Kemble, then a jolly New York bachelor, who became a friend and crony of Washington Irving, soon after the latter's return from his first sojourn in Europe, and who delighted to entertain congenial guests at his country place. It was in this manner that Irving came to know the mansion to which a little later in the *Salmagundi Papers* he was to give the name of Cockloft Hall. It was already old when Irving was first entertained within its walls. "It has become so patched up and repaired," he wrote in 1807, "that it has become as full of whims and oddities as its tenants, and requires to be nursed and humored like a gouty old codger of an alderman. Whenever the wind blows the mansion makes a most perilous groaning, and every storm is sure to make a day's work for the carpenter who attends upon it as regularly as the family physician."

But Irving who always loved old things early formed an attachment for the ancient house with its spacious grounds and noble setting of trees; and he and other young men of his period counted it a rare delight to journey from New York across the Jersey marshes for a week-end on the banks of the Passaic. Besides Irving and his host this convivial circle included Irving's elder brother, James Kirke Paulding, Peter Kemble, Henry Ogden and Henry Brevoort. Lively blades all of them, they figure in *Salmagundi* as the Nine Worthies, but in familiar converse it was Irving's wont to call them the Kilkenny Boys. In their meetings wit was matched against wit, and letters and topics of the time were discussed by men who knew how to mix mirth and sound sense in the opinions to which they gave expression.

Kemble and his guests rode, hunted and swam, and fished not only in the Passaic, but also in the private pond of the estate which was so liberally stocked that the most awkward fisherman could not fail of a catch. "Although the river," wrote Irving, "runs at about one hundred yards from the house, and is well stocked with fish, there is nothing like having things to one's self." There was a summer house fronting the river with a cellar under it in which the Nine Worthies held some of their most jovial feasts. The punch bowl used on such occasions is now in the keeping of the New York Historical Society, given to it by a Kemble of a later time, and its size tells its own story to the seeker after facts. Small wonder that Irving writing at the age of sixty-tree to Kemble and recalling the bouts of their youth marvelled "that we should ever have lived to be two such respectable old gentlemen."

Again on the banks of the Passaic between Newark and Belleville, and in a cottage of Tudor design to which its builder gave the name of The Cedars, ninety odd years ago lived Henry William Herbert, honored by a small but devoted group of admirers as the author, who under the pen name of Frank Forrester, gave sportsmen the first important books on hunting, fishing and horsemanship to be published on this side of the sea. He still finds readers, for at a time when in America sport in forest, field and river was confined chiefly to frontier folk and to people of the back country, Herbert, born an English aristocrat, fished and hunted in the states of New Jersey and New York, and by his writings, which he illustrated himself, won a large following among city dwellers.

Born in London in 1807, the son of the dean of Manchester and grandson of the Earl of Pembroke, Herbert was graduated at Cambridge at the age of twenty. In 1829, having become involved in debt, he migrated to New York, where for eight years he was a teacher in a private school for boys, also serving during a part of that period as one of the editors of the *American Monthly Magazine*. In 1834 he began his career as a sporting writer under the pen name of Frank Forrester, suggested to him by the friendly editor of the *American Turf Register*. Success quickly came to him in his new field, and with money sent him by his English father he built The Cedars in what was at the time the outskirts of Newark.

When Herbert took up his abode on the Passaic and for long after that stream, now sadly fallen from its virgin state, furnished the best of fishing, while the country between Newark and Warwick in New York teemed with game birds and wild life of all kinds. Herbert not only wrote books inspired by his congenial surroundings but made himself an authority on fishing and hunting in the United States and Canada. One of his works bore the title *Field Sports of the United States and the British Provinces of North America,* and two other widely read books of the same period were *My Shooting Box* and *American Game in its Season.* Present day collectors also seek and prize his *Warwick Woodlands,* contributed in 1839 to the *American Turf Register,* and *Horse and Horsemanship,* which published in two volumes in 1856 remains after more than four score years in many respects the best work ever written on the American turf and trotting and the trotting horse.

Herbert was not without vanity of a harmless sort, and after success as a sporting writer had come to him he affected at all times the dress of a sportsman. Tall and erect and of military bearing, when he appeared on the streets of Newark clad in moleskin with thick shooting boots on his feet, a stalking cap on his head and followed as a rule by a pack of dogs, he never failed to attract a measure of attention that was as food and drink to him. His life was one of hard and constant labor, but he found time to be a generous and considerate host, and never permitted a caller, no matter what his rank, to go from him without food and drink. Sportsmen were his favorite companions, and he was never so happy as when surrounded by them.

Herbert's writings on sport have charm and quality, heightened by loving regard for the life that called them into being, but they represent only a part of his literary output. He wrote a score of historical romances, and he was also a poet and translator of merit. But high strung and sensitive he was dogged all his days by lack of money, and then as he grew older belief that he was neglected and estrangement from his wife drove him farther into the shadows. He took his own life on a May night in 1858 after a dinner at a New York hotel to which he had bidden many friends only one ot whom attended. He was buried in Mount Pleasant Cemetery, Newark, not far from the site of his home, The Cedars, of which in these days no sign remains. Eighteen years after his death a small stone was placed at his grave by the Forrester Association of Newark. The visitor finds the low mound overgrown with English ivy, planted no doubt by some friend who has now been claimed by the years.

Dr. Thomas Dunn English, author of *Ben Bolt* and in early life an associate of Poe, was long a resident of Newark, his last home being at 57 State Street, where he died in 1902 at the age of eighty-three. English in his time played many parts. Born in Philadelphia, at twenty he was graduated in medicine at the University of Pennsylvania. After that he studied law and was admitted to the bar, but ere long turned again to medicine, and was engaged in practice at Fort Lee, New Jersey, when in 1843 he wrote the song which remains his strongest claim to remembrance. Fond of books and their makers he had begun in his teens to write for the press, and coming under the favorable notice of Nathaniel P. Willis, then one of the editors of the *New Mirror* in New York, was asked to write some verses for that publication. The result was the poem now known as *Ben Bolt*.

This song when first published won instant popularity. Set to music by an actor and singer in a Pittsburgh theater it went around the world, and half a century after Willis printed and praised it, a new lease of life was given it by its inclusion in Du Maurier's *Trilby*. In the years between Dr. English was a practicing physician and editor in Newark, served in the Legislature of New Jersey and the lower branch of Congress, and never ceased to be an indefatigable and prolific maker of prose and verse. His range was a wide one, but perhaps he took most satisfaction in the stirring ballads and lyrics for boys which he wrote in his middle years. His collected works would fill many volumes, but of his fifty plays only one, *The Mormons,* was ever published, while his novels, *Jacob Schuyler's Millions* and the rest, which failed because of lack of warmth in their heroes and heroines, long since ceased to find readers. Dr. English's breadwinning efforts, owing perhaps to their conflicting diversity, were not always happy ones, and sharp financial ups and down attended his journey through life. Happily in old age he found himself able to liquidate all of his obligations, and did not rest content until he had paid to the last penny debts outlawed or forgotten by his creditors. A little later he went out of life at peace with himself and his fellows.

When Dr. English settled in Newark John Burroughs, was a youthful and passing resident of the town, on the way to government service in Washington and to later fame as an observer of and writer about nature. Ray Palmer, preacher and hymn writer, died in 1889 at 107 Academy Street in a house now replaced by a filling station. And Noah Brooks during the years in which he served as editor of the Newark *Advertiser* lived at 2 Lombardy Street, in what was the town's first elevator apartment house and has now given way to a twenty-story office building. This gifted and kindly man demands a place in the present chronicle. He was born in 1830 at Castine, Maine, and before he was thirty had been a merchant in Illinois, a farmer in Kansas, and in California one of the founders of the Marysville *Appeal*.

From 1862 to 1865 Brooks served as the Washington correspondent of the Sacramento *Union* and the letters he wrote for that journal are an intimate and arresting history of a fateful period. At the same time he won the friendship and confidence of President Lincoln, whom he had first known in Illinois and whom during his second term he was to have served as secretary had not death intervened to prevent it. Instead he returned to the Pacific Coast to serve as naval officer of the port of San Francisco and as editor of the *Alta California,* in which post he gave timely encouragement to the first writings of a modest, red-haired compositor, one Henry George, who a few years later was to become the author of *Progress and Poverty*. During the same period he became the friend and comrade of Mark Twain and Bret Harte, and at the latter's invitation a contributor to the *Overland Monthly*.

Another turn of the wheel found Brooks a member of the staff of the New York *Tribune,* from which he shortly withdrew to enter the service of the New York *Times*. And then for a decade following 1884 he was the editor and guiding genius of the Newark *Advertiser*. It was while thus employed that he began short stories and reminiscent articles for the magazines, and books of adventure which not only won the favor of the youthful readers of his own day, but continue to give delight to those of a later generation. He also made time for more serious works, among them an admirable life of Lincoln and an account of the federal capital in war-time which contains many an informing detail students would not willingly spare from the record. His last years were passed in New York and his native Castine. He died in 1903 at Pasadena, California, where he had gone in what proved a vain search for health. Men whose faces are no longer turned toward the morning recall him as a faithful friend and a rare and delightful companion.

A house which stood aforetime at 14 Mulberry Place in what has now become one of Newark's drab neighborhoods, and which not long ago was leveled to furnish a site for a skating rink, was the birthplace of Stephen Crane. Born in 1871, the youngest of the fourteen children of a presiding elder of the Methodist faith, Crane, as the father shifted stations, had uncertain schooling in Bound Brook, Paterson, Port Jervis and finally Asbury Park. He was also for brief periods a student at Lafayette and Syracuse. In Asbury Park when he was eighteen he began to serve as correspondent for the New York *Tribune* and other papers, and before he was twenty-one, although he had never heard the report of a cannon or smelled powder smoke, wrote the *Red Badge of Courage*, a moving tale of battle and death, based on the emotions of an individual soldier, which he never surpassed in after years.

This early masterpiece was preceded by *Maggie: A Girl of the Streets*, a grim story of the New York slums, which won Crane, who had then become a free-lance in New York, the admiring friendship first of Hamlin Garland and then of William Dean Howells, both of whom gave him sound advice and a helping hand. A vivid memory of one of the present writer's early days in New York has to do with an evening at the walk-up flat Garland shared with his actor brother when their host read *Maggie* to a little group of visitors, pausing now and again to stress the stark yet compelling veracity of the narrative. Crane was also present, boyish, and ill at ease, a reluctant listener to his own work and Garland's comment on it. There and then began a friendship which helped to the removal of a few unwelcome stones from the path Crane was following, led to meetings which have now taken on the pathos of distance and ended only with his too-early death, for he was lovable to a degree, compelling genuine affection from those who best knew him.

Soon after that evening in the flat of the Garlands, Crane made a long tour of the South and West for the newspaper syndicate then conducted by Irving Bacheller. In 1897, on the strength of the *Red Badge of Courage,* a London journal engaged him to report the war between Greece and Turkey. The same year he joined a fillibustering expedition to Cuba. The steamer on which he travelled was wrecked, and he was one of three men who before their rescue were compelled to spend several days in an open boat—an experience which gave him a title for one of his books, and material for a noteworthy bit of writing. In 1898 during our war with Spain he was a correspondent for the New York *World* in Cuba and Puerto Rico.

This service behind him Crane spent some time in New York, and then went to England. There editors made haste to buy his wares and Henry James and Joseph Conrad gave him their friendship. But soon a wasting illness seized him and on a June morning in 1900 at Baden-Weller in the Black Forest, still under thirty, he passed from life, leaving behind him as his legacy to posterity, nine thin volumes of prose and verse. One can but surmise what measure of achievement would now stand to his credit had a longer span of years been granted him. One only knows that he had imagination and an unerring instinct for the inevitable word, so that in his short existence he was able to portray numerous and varying phases of American life with exceptional clarity and power. "He loved horses and the sea," Conrad wrote of Crane twenty years after his death; "and his passage on this earth was like that of a horseman riding swiftly in the dawn of a day fated to be short and without sunshine."

Roselle, an Elizabeth suburb, was for a time the home of Frank Norris, who there meditated and began to write a series of novels which he planned should tell in an epic way the story of the growth, distribution and final use of wheat, but which he left unfinished when he died in 1902 at the age of thirty-two. Not far away at 206 North Union Avenue, Cranford, was the last home of Edwin Martin Kingsbury, for three score years a brilliant writer first for the *Sun* and then for the New York *Times.* Youngest of the ten children of a well-to-do and unbending abolitionist who in the town of Sutton, Massachusetts, long conducted an important station on the Underground Railroad, he was graduated at Harvard in the class of 1875, studied law and won admission to the bar, but soon turned to newspaper work. Settling in New York in 1882 he was given by Charles A. Dana a place on the staff of the *Sun,* and quickly helped to make the style of that journal one of the most distinctive in the country. An untiring student of thought and achievement in many fields, both for the *Sun* and later for the *Times* Kingsbury wrote with wit and easy command of the right phrase on any subject assigned him, and when he died in 1944 in his ninetieth year, had he not been all his days a modest man, he could have claimed, with no one to contradict him, that he had influenced with his pen as many readers as any writer of his generation.

Had Kingsbury, who delighted to consort with other out-of-the-common men, lived in an earlier generation he would have found a congenial and inspiring companion in Albert Brisbane, who long had his home at Fanwood, a few miles from Cranford, where his son, Arthur Brisbane, passed his boyhood. Born at Batavia, New York, in 1809, with no need to earn his daily bread, Albert Brisbane early became a militant figure in a period of ferment—a period bent on reforming both men and society, and which was to bequeath to the republic some of its greatest names, Channing, Emerson, and Thoreau among them. Its dreams and visions appealed to young Brisbane, and, with his father's purse to make things easy for him, he went to Europe at eighteen, and studied for a time in Paris and Berlin, in the latter city having Hegel for a teacher and the poet Heine for a fellow student.

When Brisbane, after a later sojourn in the British Isles, returned to America in 1834 it was as the preacher of a social gospel in the shaping of which Hegel and the Frenchmen, Saint Simon and Fourier had each had a part. Fourier, however, contributed in fullest measure to this gospel and his contention that labor could be made attractive, Brisbane in 1841, after a long period of invalidism, set forth in a book the *Social Destiny of Man* which made its author an important figure in American life —and the country's first socialist. Among others it won favor with Horace Greeley, who gave much space to its doctrines in his lately established *Tribune,* and it had a major part in the founding of Brook Farm and other communities which took as their guide the creed of Fourier as reported by Brisbane. Most of these communities in no long time ended in failure, but not before they had given an exalted and continuing purpose to the lives of a goodly company of great-souled men and women.

The rest is a familiar story. Albert Brisbane during the long span of life that remained to him—he died in 1890 at the age of eighty-one—dwelt sometimes in Fanwood and New York, and again in London and Paris. He was twice married and the father of many children, one of whom, Arthur Brisbane, was in time to command a wider audience and a larger fortune than were ever the lot of his father. The latter was more than once compelled to sail on troubled waters; but he faced with light heart cares of every sort, and remained until the end a reformer whose chief concern was a right answer to the question, "What is the social destiny of man?" He also cared in an occasional and somewhat different way for the education of his children, and one of Arthur Brisbane's tutors in his boyhood at Fanwood was a young man named Dunning who later was to win renown as a professor of political science at Columbia.

Henry Mills Alden, editor and mystic, long had his home at Metuchen a few miles from Fanwood. Born in Vermont in 1836, Alden as a growing lad was employed in a cotton mill, and until he was fourteen found no time for schooling, but after that worked his way through Williams College, graduating in 1857 as member of a class which included James A. Garfield and John J. Ingalls. He had been three years a student at Andover Theological Seminary, preparing for the ministry, when the *Atlantic Monthly* accepted and printed two papers he had written, and this, with the failure of his voice to meet oratorical demands, turned his thoughts from the pulpit to a career of letters in New York.

Coming to the city in 1861 Alden, after a brief period of labor as a free lance, joined the staff of Harper & Brothers, serving first as assistant editor of *Harper's Weekly* and as one of the authors of an illustrated history of the Civil War. Then, in 1869, he succeeded Alfred H. Guernsey as editor of *Harper's Magazine,* which position he filled with rare insight and discrimination to the day of his death half a century later at the age of eighty-three years. He delighted in and took pride in the discovery of new talent and the writers nearest his heart were Owen Wister, Mary E. Wilkins, George Du Maurier, James Lane Allen and others to whose writings he had first assured publication. For more than a generation Alden read every manuscript submitted to him, and visitors to Franklin Square at the meeting of the centuries will recall him seated in a corner of the editorial floor of Harper & Brothers, his battered black walnut desk covered with the proferred contributions the morning's mail had brought him, and at his side a pine bin of accepted articles. The most diffident beginner was sure of a fatherly welcome from him and a measure of timely advice perhaps so softly spoken as to be half lost in the noise of an elevated train thundering by only a few feet from the editor's head.

During his middle and most of his later years Alden had his home in Metuchen where, reasonably free from time-consuming intruders and the city's social demands, he found leisure to write, in addition to the *Editor's Study* which was his monthly contribution to his magazine, a number of books, two of which are to be counted among his sure claims to remembrance. These were *God in His World* and *Study of Death* both written with a beauty of phrasing in harmony with their theme, and both charged with quiet, unswerving faith in an unseen yet beneficent power, a power that shapes the flight of the sky-lark and man's upward course through the ages, which in hours of suffering and loss give ease and comfort to lonely and troubled hearts. His was the gospel of quietude and its exercise in daily life made him from youth to age a self-effacing but influential friend and helper of men.

During a part of his years in Metuchen Mr. Alden had for neighbor a gifted woman whose success in letters he had helped to make an early and easy one. It was in 1901 that Mary Wilkins Freeman came as a bride to the town, and she lived there in the old and roomy house her husband at their marriage had purchased for her until her death in 1930 in her seventy-eighth year. The greater part of the work which gives Mrs. Freeman, a leading place among American writers of the short story had been accomplished before she made her home in Metuchen, but her pen remained a busy one until the end, and in her last as in her first years her tales of the New England life, austere in its simplicity and its modesty of mind, and charged with painful tenderness, which had been a part of her girlhood and early womanhood, maintained the easy, almost flawless mastery of subject and method which gave their author fame as a veracious chronicler of the social history of her time.

Summit was for nearly a generation the home of Hamilton Wright Mabie, never a major figure but long the right hand of Lyman Abbott in the conduct first of the *Christian Union* and then of the *Outlook,* and at the same time a popular and stimulating commentator on letters, and the trend of events. During the same period Margaret Elizabeth Sangster, first at Glen Ridge and later at Maplewood, where she died in 1912 at the age of seventy-four, wrote verse and in prose gave sound counsel to her sister women, her product in both mediums finding favor alike with editors and readers, and helping to right thought and living. And at 325 Ridgewood Avenue, Glen Ridge, was for many years preceding 1920 the home of Edward Page Mitchell, long a writer for and at the end of his career editor of the New York *Sun*. Mitchell was born in Bath, Maine, in 1852, was graduated at Bowdoin at the age of nineteen and four years later joined the staff of the *Sun*. Thereafter for more than half a century he shaped in larger measure than any other man—Dana alone excepted—the history of that journal. "Both the range," he once declared, "of a newspaper and the power of the writer for it depend upon the breadth of sympathy with human affairs and the diversity of things in which he takes a genuine personal interest." And fidelity to this standard made him perhaps the greatest editorial writer of his generation, always with something pertinent to say on the subject in hand, and an individual way of saying it.

The twenty thousand articles Mitchell contributed to the *Sun,* sharing the fate of most writings of the kind, are buried past recovery in the files of that journal, but the autobiography, *Memoirs of an Editor* which he published in 1924, after his retirement to a Rhode Island farm, will long claim a devoted audience, for its every page holds things "as interesting to read as it was for the author to remember." Witness his droll account of a meeting with Lincoln when at the age of ten he was permitted to accompany to Washington an uncle by marriage intent on discussing with the President better ways of caring for the Union wounded. Came the appointed morning for the interview and uncle and nephew walked from Willard's to the White House.

Let the future editor of the *Sun* tell the rest of the story. "The negro doorman," he records, "must have been new to his job, for he led us through what seemed an endless row of apartments, threw a door open and stood aside. It was a small room," and at a "table in the middle of it sat Mr. Lincoln all alone, facing us and eating his breakfast. At the opening of the door he raised his eyes and gazed at the unexpected comers. The large hand holding the fork that carried a considerable cargo of baked beans remained suspended for several seconds between plate and half open mouth. His expression, rather sad at first, changed quickly to surprise and then to mild annoyance. Of course there was . . . a hurried withdrawal of the intruders. We were conducted to the proper antechamber and in due time and form Uncle Henry was summoned . . . for a conference in which it was not my fortune to participate. I have seen since then hundreds of representations, graphic and plastic, depicting Abraham Lincoln," but "the print from that instantaneous exposure has never faded. Whenever I think of the greatest American, it is first as an extremely tall man with a sad, surprised countenance, seated at breakfast, with beans half-way between starting-point and destination."

Parke Godwin, Bryant's successor as editor of the New York *Evening Post,* and all his long life the ready advocate of struggling causes, was born, passed his boyhood and studied law in Paterson, while Wendell Phillips Garrison, son and biographer of another stout defender of human rights, was for upward of forty years a resident of the Llewellyn Park section of Orange. Garrison claims honored remembrance not only as a poet and reviewer, but as the founder with Godkin of the *Nation* and for forty years one of the editors of that organ of liberal and enlightened opinion. Paul Elmer Moore, in another period one of the editors of the *Nation,* was for several years following 1908 a resident of East Orange, while nearby Madison was the home in his middle and latter years of William Osborn Stoddard, who as a youthful editor in Illinois was one of the first to urge the nomination and election of Abraham Lincoln to the Presidency; who although John Hay did not like him, became in due course one of Lincoln's secretaries, and who lived to put on paper his memories of his great chief and also to write nearly four score books for boys.

Stoddard's output for growing lads, however, was a modest one compared with that of Edward Sylvester Ellis, a schoolteacher turned author, whose home during his busiest years, and until his death in 1916 at the age of seventy-six, was at 85 Norwood Avenue in Upper Montclair. When a school teacher still in his teens, Ellis delighted to spin yarns for his pupils, hanging up as a reward of merit for them the privilege of listening to stories on Friday afternoons. Soon the quality of these stories was bruited about, and parents of pupils came also of a Friday afternoon to listen to them. When Ellis found his tales being circulated through the countryside he decided to put them on paper. His first book was published in the later fifties of the last century, and, never lacking readers, thereafter and until his death he was one of the most prolific of American authors. He began in the age of the dime novel, an age which called for swift production, and the tales he wrote streamed forth in series and in such volume that a catalogue of *Books in Print,* published the year that he died credited him with three full columns of stories,

title after title, publisher after publisher, prices varying with different stories, and stories altering as new tastes claimed the
interest of the boy world.

Ellis was teacher in a high school for boys at Paterson and
later superintendent of schools in Trenton before he settled in
Montclair and gave all of his time to authorship. He came of
pioneer stock and from first to last kept in close touch with
frontier folk and their ways. These furnished subjects and color
for his first stories, written in the heyday of the ten-cent novel,
and so rapidly did he rise in favor that soon he was writing for
half a dozen publishers under as many pen names. To the boys
of seventy years ago, Colonel H. R. Gordon and Lieutenant R. H.
Jayne—two of these pen names—were very real persons, and
more than one youthful reader now grown old pleasurably recalls
the exploits of their heroes. Some of the latter had lengthy series
devoted to them, and, for the author was ever on the alert for
new subjects and new material, each addition to a series was
sure of a warm welcome from an army of readers. There came
a time, however, when the writing of juveniles was a side issue
with Ellis, and his last years were mainly and profitably devoted
to text-book making and to historical work for adult readers.
Thus his *Standard History of the United States* in eight volumes
is still read and treasured in many a household.

An author of another and very different caliber made his
home in New Jersey during his most productive years. Born in
Philadelphia in 1837 Francis Richard Stockton was first an engraver and draughtsman, but soon turned to literary effort, and
after holding minor posts in Boston and New York, when *St.
Nicholas* was established in 1873 became its assistant editor. He
and his wife were then living in a house yet standing in Rutherford. Needing household help Mrs. Stockton went to New York
and procured from an asylum a girl of fourteen whom the husband afterward described as "a middle-sized orphan." The newcomer's spare time was devoted to the reading of books, mostly
of a blood-curdling sort; and she read them aloud to herself in
the kitchen in a sing-song fashion which at first amused her employers, but soon became a diversion of a very different sort.

The Stocktons never knew their maid's real name, but she
had three or four romantic ones borrowed from sentimental
novels. Stockton dubbed her Pomona and wrote a paper about
her entitled *Rudder Grange* which in 1874 was published in
Scribner's Magazine. It attracted much attention, and, although

at first the author had not planned to further celebrate Pomona's beguiling qualities, he now made her the heroine of a series of papers which were issued at irregular intervals. These he collected in a book *Rudder Grange,* for which he at first found difficulty in finding a publisher, but which with its mirth-compelling adventures of a young couple who kept house in a canal boat and took a boarder, met with great and instant success, winning its author national fame as master of a droll and whimsical vein of humor. All this was in 1879, and thereafter there was a ready market and eager readers for whatever he offered them.

Five years later came *The Lady or the Tiger,* the most famous of all Stockton's stories. Written to be read before a literary society of which he was a member, it caused so much discussion in the society that he recast it and published it in the *Century Magazine.* There followed a reception by the public that startled both editor and author. The little tale with its intriguing and unanswered question was translated into a dozen languages; public readers expounded it to their audiences; it made without delay the circuit of the globe, and as an English friend told Stockton that in India he had heard the problem it presented gravely discussed by a group of Hindus. In 1884 was published *The Late Mrs. Null,* Stockton's first long story, and this was followed by nearly a score of titles of varying quality but unfailing charm.

Many of these were written in the wooded seclusion afforded by a fine old country house at Convent Station, whence he removed from Rutherford, and where he lived for more than a dozen years, with Frost, the artist, a neighbor and kindred spirit. He died in Washington in 1902, having passed his last days in the Shenandoah Valley, not far from Jefferson's Monticello. And he is sure of readers through the long future, for he was a gentle purveyor of good cheer to mankind, with a gift of invention at once playful and all his own, and an insight into the workings of the human heart as real and tender as that of Lamb in an earlier day.

About the time that Stockton was introducing Pomona to an appreciative audience, in 1877 to be exact, a young man of twenty-two succeeded to the editorship of the humorous journal *Puck,* and soon gave proof that he had wit and spirit, could produce verse diverse in mood and easy in its range, and was a master of a limpid and quick moving prose style. Henry Cuyler Bunner was born in Oswego, and had been a clerk in a Beaver Street, New York, counting-house before he became first a contributor to and then editor of *Puck*. He was a rapid and facile writer, and for a long period there were weeks when he supplied more than half of the matter printed in that journal, this without impairment of quality or any sign of strain.

Part of Bunner's work for *Puck* was collected into books, and as time went on he produced many independent works including poems, short stories and magazine articles, and plays in the writing of which Brander Matthews had a part. His *Airs from Arcady*, published in 1884 had an unusual sale for a volume of verse, and as a short story writer his work ranks with the best produced by the men of his period. In this field he had a poet's instinct for selection and compression, wedded to a love of nature and a whimsical fancy which rarely if ever made demands on the reader's sense of reality. Who fails to recall with delight *The Nice People* and the other tales included in *Short Sixes*, which reveal at their best the author's engaging qualities or *The Love Letters of Smith*, which claim zestful rereadings by many a man and woman who in youth first made acquaintance with them?

Bunner did not suffer fools gladly, but those of whom he was fond cherish memories of his rare qualities as comrade and friend, and of the home he set up in Nutley soon after his marriage to the sister of Walter Learned, a fellow poet. In his New Jersey retreat, with a plot of a couple of acres about the house which he shared with the gracious woman to whom after their marriage he dedicated each and all of his books, he bred pigs and chickens, and surrounded himself with domestic animals to some of whom in his quaint way he gave more than local fame. One of these was a donkey named Joy, used by the Bunner children as a saddle animal and by its master as a pack animal when he took his family into the woods for summer picnics. There were, alas, too few of these outings. Bunner died in 1896 at the early age of forty-one after a long struggle with tuberculosis and was buried by the side of his wife's kinsfolk in New London.

When in the spring of 1871 Bred Harte's first stories of the California Argonauts, written at the age of thirty-one, published in the *Overland Monthly* of which he was then the editor, and never again equalled by him in three after decades of literary effort, gave him an international reputation, he left California for the East in order to have closer contact with editors and publishers, and until 1878 made his home in Morristown where not less than three houses still standing are pointed out to visitors as successive abodes of the author of *The Luck of Roaring Camp.* During his residence in Morristown, broken by occasional tours as a lecturer, he produced half a dozen volumes of prose and verse, including *Gabriel Conroy* and *Thankful Blossom,* the latter a romance of the Revolution.

Harte's outgo, however, due in part to extravagant ways of living, always ran ahead of his income, and when the glamor of his first success grew dim and editors manifested a growing inclination to drive hard bargains with him, he was glad to accept the United States consulship at Crefeld, Germany. In 1880 he was transferred to a like post in Glasgow, where he remained until Cleveland came into power and his resignation was requested of him. Thereafter he made his home in London, because he could earn more money there than in America, and there he pushed his pen with such diligence that when death came to him in 1902 his published volumes numbered nearly two score, while the list of his stories had risen into the hundreds. But the title of Harte's final volume, *Openings in Old Trails,* best tells the tale of his closing years. He drew first and last from the same rich yet narrow bed of California gold, but never again did it yield the rare and coveted nuggets with which it had favored him in fortunate youth.

The North Jersey rambles here recorded came to an end at Pompton Lakes and Sunnybank, long the home of Albert Payson Terhune, a pioneer in the field of stories about dogs. Terhune was born in Newark in 1872, the son of a preacher father and of an author mother, Marion Harland, who in turn wrote popular novels and informing books on the colonial period and its landmarks. The younger Terhune was graduated at Columbia in 1893, and, following a period of travel in the Orient, was until 1916 a member of the staff of the *Evening World* in New York. Then he retired to Pompton Lakes to breed dogs and write about them, at the suggestion of Ray Long, then editor of the *Cosmopolitan.* And, being a capable craftsman as well as a keen lover of dogs, he did both so acceptably that when he died in 1941 his novels and stories had long commanded a goodly company of devoted readers who shared his liking for dogs of every sort.

Terhune loved his Pompton Lakes home with a compelling passion, and there he and his family lived a happy life, with friends and kin, and an ever changing group of dogs to keep them company. A powerful man above six feet in height, he retained until the end the high spirits of his youth, and an unquenchable zest for life and dogs and open fields. He never laid claim to greatness, but he was a royal comrade good to know and worthy to be held in kindly remembrance.

CHAPTER XVII

WALT WHITMAN AND OTHER WORTHIES

Henry Mills Alden had among other qualities a keen if quiet sense of humor which now and again found unexpected expression. Ada Foster Murray, an attractive and talented widow hailing from Norfolk, who had come to New York hoping to win a hearing from editors and publishers, was by a common friend given a note of introduction to Mr. Alden. Some months later the writer of this note and Mr. Alden met at lunch. "What did you do for that young woman whom I sent you?" was asked during the leisurely chat that followed food. "Why, I persuaded her to marry me," was the answer returned with a twinkle of the eyes.

And through this union, Mr. Alden, who a few years earlier had lost the beloved companion of his early and middle life, became also the step-father of Arline Murray, a charming and gifted girl who is now the widow of the poet, Joyce Kilmer, the first American man of letters to fall in the First World War. One finds at 17 Codwise Avenue in the town of New Brunswick the house in which Kilmer was born and passed his early years. He was graduated at Rutgers College in 1904, at the age of eighteen and four years later at Columbia University. After that he was for a brief period a teacher of Latin in the Morristown high school, and then for a decade an editor and newspaper worker most of the period a member of the staff of the New York *Times*.

Kilmer early won favor as a gifted writer both of prose and verse. The delicate and lovely lines *Trees,* which gave a title to one of his three thin volumes of lyrics, brought him extensive repute, and he reached a higher and sterner level in *The White Ships and the Red,* a memorable and powerful poem prompted by the torpedoing of the *Lusitania.* And it was this tragic circumstance that led Kilmer, when the United States entered the First World War, to join the army and as a sergeant of the Rainbow Division meet in his thirty-second year a hero's death in the Marne advance. He was buried near where he fell, and the memory of him that endures is that of one of the heirs of unfulfilled renown—a fine, intrepid spirit to whom "all kindly things were brother."

It is a pleasant cross-country ride of a May morning from New Brunswick to the Freehold neighborhood where Philip Freneau, the poet of the Revolution who best gave a voice to the spirit which shaped that struggle, passed most of his years. Born in New York in 1752, "that rascal Freneau," as Washington not without reason called him, was reared in Monmouth County, whence when he was ten his family removed from the city, and in 1771 was graduated at Princeton, where he had James Madison and Aaron Burr for fellow students. From earliest childhood Freneau composed rhymes and verses, and during a prolonged stay in the West Indies in 1776, following brief experience as a teacher and law student, he wrote several ambitious poems which proved that their author had real creative power.

News of the Declaration of Independence caused the young poet to hasten home, and, armed with letters of marque and reprisal issued by the Continental Congress, he took command of a privateer which captured and destroyed a large number of British merchantmen. Attempting a second trip to the West Indies in 1780, he was captured by the British and confined in one of the prison ships in New York harbor. Thence sprang an experience and a hatred which found bitter, trenchant expression in *The British Prison Ship* and other verse, and helped to stiffen patriot determination in the closing years of the Revolution. Freneau had studied to good purpose the great English satirists —Dryden, Pope and Churchill—and it has been aptly said that his writings "furnish an almost complete commentary on the whole revolutionary struggle, nearly every important phase of which is photographed in his keen, merciless and often brilliant lines."

Independence assured Freneau until 1790, when he married, was an editor in Philadelphia and New York, broken by six years of service at sea as captain of a merchantman. After that came his association with Jefferson and his vigorous editorship in Philadelphia of the *National Gazette,* organ of the anti-Federal party, an editorship which made him a thorn in the side of Washington. When Jefferson retired from Washington's cabinet Freneau returned to Mount Pleasant, the thousand-acre estate he had inherited from his father, and until late middle age alternated service at sea with half-hearted attempts at farming. After 1808 he seldom left Mount Pleasant except to visit old friends in New

York and Philadelphia. Until the end he was alert and active and fond of the society of his neighbors.

On a December night in 1832 the white-haired poet tarried overlong at the village library in nearby Freehold where he was in the habit of meeting his friends. Homeward bound he was caught in a snowstorm, and falling benumbed died by the roadside in the eighty-first year of his age. His grave tops a knoll on his former farm, and at the base of the marble shaft which marks it the visitor finds graven these words: "His upright and benevolent character is in the memory of many and will remain when this inscription is no longer legible." And Freneau's claim to remembrance as a poet is a sure if modest one. Not a few of his earlier lyrics have a freedom and spontaneity otherwise unknown to Colonial literature. Nor should we forget that his *The Wild Honeysuckle,* dear to the hearts of nature lovers, preceded by a dozen years the *Lyrical Ballads* of Coleridge and Wordsworth; that Scott knew by heart his *Eutaw Springs;* that Campbell took over word for word the closing lines of his *Indian Burying Ground,* and that Keats, perhaps without ever having heard of author or poem, used a like motive of Freneau's in his *Ode to a Grecian Urn.*

In Freneau's youth the journey from his father's home in Monmouth County to Princeton was a difficult and tiring one. Now it is made over well-kept roads in little more than an hour of comfortable wheeling. And Princeton reached the lover of the past is sure to first make his way to the ancient cemetery, sometimes called America's Westminister, where are buried many of the men who through three centuries have added to the town's renown. There sleeps the elder Aaron Burr, son-in-law of Jonathan Edwards and president of Princeton, and at his feet, fulfilling an oft expressed wish, his son and namesake takes his long rest. Close at hand is the grave of Jonathan Edwards, the plain marble stone which marks it much mutilated by relic hunters.

Princeton knew Edwards only at the close of his career. He was in charge of the Indian Mission at Stockbridge and busy with the writings which proclaim him one of the master minds of his era when the death of the elder Aaron Burr left vacant the presidency of Princeton College and in September, 1757, at the age of fifty-four he was chosen to succeed his son-in-law. He agreed with reluctance, should the council so decide, to accept this call. When the council, meeting early in January, 1758 elected that he should go his biographer tells us that, feeling triumphing over will, he burst into tears. He went, leaving his family behind in Stockbridge, only to die of smallpox before the end of winter and find a grave in Princeton Cemetery.

About him now, with their wives keeping them silent company, lie more than a full score of his successors as president of Princeton. One of these graves is that of John Witherspoon, the Scotch preacher who crossed the seas in 1768 to become president of Princeton and to help it to larger usefulness, and who a few years later championed the cause of the colonies and as a member of the Continental Congress signed the Declaration of Independence. A later grave is that of James McCosh, one of the founders of the Free Church of Scotland, who as president of Princeton for the twenty years following 1868 taught successive generations of students and made the institution over which he presided in the widest sense of the phrase a real center of learning. Two other graves regarded as shrines by Princeton graduates are those of Archibald Alexander and Samuel Miller.

A native of Virginia, Alexander was at twenty-six the president of Hampden-Sydney College and at forty the first professor in Princeton Theological Seminary. When he died in 1851 at the age of seventy-nine he was by laborers in his chosen field held in honor as the most influential theologian not only in his own church but in all America. Samuel Miller, born in Delaware in 1769, was for twenty-one years pastor of the First Presbyterian Church of New York, and then for thirty-six years, and until his death at the age of eighty-one, professor of ecclesiastical history and church government in Princeton Theological Seminary. And upon all who came in intimate contact with him he stamped the impress of a masterful and uplifting personality. In the early days of the railway a gentleman travelling from New York to Philadelphia had as seat companion one whom conversation disclosed as a recent Princeton graduate. As the train halted at Princeton Junction the young man pointed towards Princeton, and remarked with quiet conviction: "The greatest man in the United States lives over there in Princeton." He was asked whom he had in mind. "Samuel Miller," was the prompt and confident reply. And it is the verdict of the years that Samuel Miller had few equals among teachers of his era and in his chosen branches of study.

Another name held in honor at Princeton is that of Joseph Henry, whose old home erected for him in 1837 now occupies a site on the campus not far from the building of the School of Science. Born in Albany, New York, and in the main self-educated, Henry had already won standing as a scientist when in 1832 at the age of thirty-three he came to Princeton as professor of natural philosophy. He held that chair for fourteen years, as a teacher with profit to his students and as a scientist with increasing benefit to mankind by reason of researches and discoveries which made him a leader in electricity and kindred fields.

In 1846 he was called to Washington as secretary of the Smithsonian Institution, and in that post until his death in 1878 labored with distinction and success to make James Smithson's bequest to the American people a boon world-wide in its scope and beneficent results. Blessed with a rare gift for friendship, he was also the valued and welcome counselor of men in widely varied walks of life, and during the years of conflict between the sections from no man did Abraham Lincoln in critical hours more frequently seek and accept advice than from Joseph Henry, shrewd weigher of affairs as well as scientist and student. Models of apparatus perfected by Dr. Henry are preserved at Princeton, and the story of his long and useful life is set forth in a *Memorial* prepared by men who had been his associates at the Smithsonian Institution, and who could justly yet gratefully measure his worth.

It was during his twenty years association with Princeton which began in 1890 that Woodrow Wilson wrote most of the books which gave him distinction as an author. These included *Division and Reunion, An Old Master and Other Political Essays, George Washington, Mere Literature, Constitutional Government in the United States,* and, what was perhaps his most important and widely read work, the history to which he gave the title *The American People*. The essays which at intervals Dr. Wilson assembled into volumes stood for voluntary and congenial exercise in the use of words, but all of his historical works were the result of urgings by insistent editors.

Thus his *George Washington* was undertaken at the suggestion of Henry M. Alden of *Harper's Magazine,* and the same editor was the begetter of *The American People* to which, using the earlier work of John Richard Green as a model, Dr. Wilson devoted much hard labor in his last years of service as a Princeton professor. An amusing story attaches to the compensation received for this particular task. The author thought he was to be paid $1,000 for each of two parts of a serial consisting of a total of twelve chapters. The first chapter completed and delivered, he was surprised to received a check for $1,000. When he sent it back, saying a mistake had been made, it was promptly returned to him with a note stating he was to be paid $1,000 for each chapter, not each part—a total of $12,000 instead of $2,000. On receipt of this unexpected but pleasing bit of information the Wilsons at once planned a trip to Europe.

The final proofs of *The American People* were lying on Dr. Wilson's desk when in June, 1902, without dissent and somewhat to his surprise, he was elected to the presidency of Princeton University. That election ended his literary work. In after years many of his addresses, articles and messages were assembled into volumes, but he never wrote another book. Time and opportunity were denied him for *The Philosophy of Politics,* the theme and substance of which he had long meditated and which he planned should be his masterpiece. Henceforth and until disabling illness seized him action took the place of admonition and interpretation.

The first Princeton residence of the Wilsons was a roomy frame house yet standing at 48 Library Place, a short walk from the University buildings, but at the end of six years they built a home of their own on the adjoining property at 50 Library Place, a house in the English style standing back from the street among trees. Here, in a study especially designed for him, "the orderly workshop of a scholarly professor," and secure from interruption in his hours of labor, Dr. Wilson wrote all of his later books. Here also, as the reflection of a charming and delightful home life, was dispensed a gracious hospitality the memory of which is cherished by those who enjoyed and profited by it.

The inner circle of Dr. Wilson's friends in these years included John Grier Hibben, who was to follow him as president of Princeton; Bliss Perry, whose career as professor ran parallel with that of his brilliant associate, and Dr. Henry Van Dyke who in 1900 succeeded Perry in the chair of English literature at the University. Dr. Van Dyke was forty-eight years of age when he became a member of the Princeton faculty, and, except for the years during which he was United States minister to the Netherlands under Wilson, there was no break in his long period of service until in 1923 he became professor emeritus. His Princeton home was a comfortable house at 59 Bayard Lane, only a step from the town's main thoroughfare, a structure of colonial design and date set in an ample acreage. A great elm, now more than a century old, fronts and shades the house, which Dr. Van Dyke remodeled and named Avalon. "I watch that elm closely," he once told a visitor, "for the first touch of spring. I can see the first buds that burst through their rough winter covering, and I know that spring is abroad in the mountains, and that fish are running in a hundred clear streams. It is hard, then, to stay at home, and I generally manage to get out now and again for a day close to nature's heart." But he also spent many hours in his study at Avalon, and there wrote *The Poetry of the Psalms, The School of Life, Out of Doors in the Holy Land* and other well-remembered volumes in prose and verse. There in his eighty-second year death ended a serene and useful life.

Dr. Van Dyck during his Princeton days had for a congenial neighbor and friend Katherine Fullerton Gerould, wife of another university professor, and herself the author of short stories and essays of signal excellence. Mrs. Gerould was a native of Massachusetts and a graduate at Radcliffe, who, before her marriage taught English at Bryn Mawr. Her career as a writer began in 1914 with the publication of a collection of short stories, some of them written while she was still a student at Radcliffe, to which she gave the title *Vain Oblations* This volume met with a hearty welcome, and so did later collections of short stories and two or three novels. Some reviewers and not a few of her readers, however, regard with especial favor the essays, witty, penetrating and always mournfully alive to the faults and waywardness of her own and a younger generation, which she wrote for the magazines. During the period which ended in 1837 Mrs. Fullerton, with a steadily growing audience, published a dozen volumes of essays, fiction and travel. Then ill-health put an end to her literary labors, and her last years—she died in 1944 at the age of sixty-five—were silent ones.

William Milligan Sloane was professor of history at Princeton when he brought to conclusion his massive biography of Napoleon, Laurence Hutton, a direct descendant through his father of Scott's *Old Mortality*, and an engaging if modest figure in the literary life of his period, was after 1898 a resident of Princeton, and a lecturer on English literature at the university. It was in the home which he called Peep O'Day that Hutton dictated to an amanuensis *The Talks in a Library*, the chronicle of a happy life of friendship and work, which published after his death in 1904 still finds appreciative readers. And finally Princeton was the last home of Paul Elmer More, who served in turn as literary editor of the New York *Independent* and *Evening Post*, as an editor of the *Nation*, and whose legacy to posterity consists in part of the eleven volumes of acute and stimulating criticism, faithful at every turn to what is best in letters, to which he gave the title *Shelburne Essays*. But held in higher honor by many scholars is his mellow and reverent work on the *Greek Tradition,* a narrative spanning nine centuries of human thought before and after Christ, which he wrote in ripe age at Princeton.

The journey southward from Princeton to Camden lies, if one so shapes it, through Trenton, Bordentown, Burlington and Mt. Holly each with its memories for the literary pilgrim. Charles Conrad Abbott, the naturalist, was born and passed his life in the Trenton neighborhood, his home for many years being at Three Beeches, an estate long in the possession of his family which faces the Delaware a few miles south of the city. Born in 1843, Abbott, a graduate physician who never practiced, was all his life a devoted and keenly observant student of nature and her ways, and his *Rambles About Home, Days Out of Doors* and other volumes made up of his magazine articles prove him a worthy disciple of White of Selborne. He was also a lifelong student of Indian history, and a reading of his *Ten Years Digging in Lanape Land,* an autobiography of an uncommon sort, offers rich diversion for the lover of out-of-the-way things. Abbott died in 1919 in the ancient town of Bristol, on the Pennsylvania side of the Delaware, the home of his old age.

Thomas Paine after his return in 1802 from his ill-starred sojourn in France lived for several years in Bordentown which was also the birthplace of Richard Watson Gilder, for nearly thirty years editor of the *Century Magazine,* and of the latter's elder brother, William H. Gilder, journalist and Arctic explorer. Thomas Dunn English for a part of his boyhood attended a Quaker boarding school in Burlington, and one of the founders of that town was the first American ancestor of Francis Richard Stockton. But Burlington's chief interest for the present day visitor lies in the fact that it was the birthplace of James Fenimore Cooper and of James Lawrence, whose dying words as captain of the Chesapeake defeated by the British frigate Shannon, "Don't give up the ship" gave him an heroic and enduring place in our naval annals.

Lawrence and Cooper were born next door to each other in South High Street, Burlington, and the houses which once sheltered them still stand in an excellent state of preservation. Cooper, Lawrence's junior by a number of years, was a sailor before he became an author, and only his bride's aversion to the sea caused him to resign from the navy in 1811 and so to miss participation in the War of 1812 in which his gallant townsmen lost his life. When Cooper was still an infant his father left Burlington to found on what was then the wilderness shores of Lake Otsego the town which bears his name. The son in after years rarely visited the place of his birth, but through the years the people of Burlington have cherished the Cooper homestead as a shrine, and in general appearance the house remains much as it was in 1789 when the novelist entered life. Since 1923 it has been the property of the Burlington County Historical Society and now performs fitting service as a public museum charged with interest for students of an earlier time.

A farm at Rancocas not far from Mt. Holly, which for the better part of three centuries yearly has yielded abundant harvests to its successive owners, has reverent meaning for every lover of what is noblest in our country's past, for it was the birthplace and early home of John Woolman, stout-hearted, God-fearing Quaker, who was one of the very first in America to protest and denounce human slavery. Born in 1720, Woolman became a Quaker preacher at the age of twenty-three and for nearly thirty years his life was one of constant pleading for the slave and of travels which once and again carried him to all parts of the colonies and across seas.

He had the serene, steadfast faith of his creed that in the end the right will triumph, and a quiet gift of speech that, based on truth and justice, rarely failed to move and persuade his hearers. To the impatient the seed he planted seemed overlong in bearing fruit, but the ultimate harvest changed the course of millions of lives. And all that Woolman did, said and thought was recorded with simple and beautiful devotion in the *Journal*, which first published in 1774 has since passed through forty editions, one of which was supervised by the poet Whittier, a fellow Quaker. "Get the writings of John Woolman by heart" was Charles Lamb's advice to his friends, and through the years they have been an unfailing source of cheer and comfort to modest folk who lead kindly lives. He died in 1772 at York, during the last of many visits to England, and his grave is in one of the burial grounds of that ancient city.

Present journey's end carried the pilgrims to Camden and to the last home and grave of Walt Whitman. The house is a few blocks from the Federal Street ferries from Philadelphia. You walk or ride three blocks along Federal Street, then turn to the right for two blocks, and midway of another block at 328 Mickle Street, come upon a dull gray frame building wedged in between two of brick. When Whitman bought this house in 1873 he was still in the shadow of the paralytic stroke which had felled him while a clerk in the Treasury Department at Washington and which, in a very real sense, was to make the rest of his days, a patient and self-reliant waiting for the end.

A college student who called on him in 1876 has recorded his impressions of the poet during his first years in Camden, when, as a matter of fact, he was still an object of ridicule in some quarters, and as yet only held in high regard by a limited group here and in England. "We found him seated," we are told, "in the ground floor front room of the little house in Mickle Street. The room was of good size and cheerful with sunshine which fell in at the window upon the figure of Whitman as he sat in his shirt sleeves surrounded by newly printed copies of *Two Rivulets,* his latest book, into each of which he was pasting a portrait of himself as frontispiece. I understood that most of these copies were to be sent to friends and brother poets here and abroad. He was then still under sixty, but to the eyes of youth he looked an old man, and indeed he was far older in appearance than his years warranted, with hair deeply grayed and face lined, though the complexion was clear and ruddy. As ever he was neat in dress and agreeably unconventional. We youngsters, recently out of college, and full of ill digested good reading, talked with Whitman of books and writers, and to our talk he responded with patient good nature. I feared we asked impertinent questions, but Whitman kept on with his pastebrush industry in the sunlight, and possibly did not listen to our chatter."

Whitman's first years in Camden were years of broadening recognition and of steadily growing fame. By the middle eighties he had been definitely accepted by the major part of literary America, and in steadily increasing numbers letters and visits from new friends came to him from all parts of our own land and from every corner of the Seven Seas. Now and again a new contact had unforseen and delightful issue. The alert and keen minded daughter of a Philadelphia business man, a junior at Smith with a mind of her own, at breakfast one morning calmly announced, to the dismay of the elder members of her family, that a few days hence she planned a trip to Camden and a call on Whitman, whose greatness as a poet, a college lecturer, alive to new trends in literature, had lately made known to members of her class.

The rest of the story has been told by the young woman's brother in his own inimitable way. "My father," writes Logan Pearsall Smith, "well aware that if my sister meant to go on Thursday, on Thursday she would go, wisely decided that the best thing under the circumstances was to accompany her and thus lend an air of propriety to this visit. I was invited to join the party, and on Thursday afternoon we started from our home in Germantown, behind a pair of my father's fine horses. The poet's elderly sister, who answered the doorbell, ushered us into a little parlor, and shouted upstairs, 'Walt, here's some carriage folk to see you.' We heard a stirring above us as of a slow and unwieldly person, and soon through the open door we saw two large feet in carpet slippers slowly descending the stairs, and then the bulky form of the old man appeared before us.

"Walt Whitman greeted us with friendly simplicity; he had no notion who we were, and we had no introduction to him, but our appearance did not surprise him in the least. My sister informed him that our name was Smith, that she had read his *Leaves of Grass,* and had come to express her immense admiration for that volume. This explanation was received with great complacency; we were all invited to follow him upstairs to his den, where we sat down on what chairs could be hastily provided, and were soon engaged in lively talk. My father, who at first held himself aloof in the most disapproving manner, soon, to the surprise of my sister and myself, began to join in this friendly conversation, and we were still more surprised, when we got up to take our departure, to hear our impulsive parent invite the object of his grave disapprobation to drive back with us to Germantown and spend the night.

"The afternoon was, he urged a fine one, the drive would be pleasant, and it would be a pity to bring to a premature end so agreeable a confabulation. 'No, Mr. Smith, I think I won't come,' the poet answered; but when he saw my father's equipage waiting in the street outside, he said that he thought he might as well come after all, and, hastily putting a night shirt and a few other objects in a little bag, he hobbled downstairs and we all drove off together. It was, as my father had said, a pleasant afternoon; we crossed again the ferry, we drove through Philadelphia and the park to our home in Germantown, where Walt Whitman remained with us for a month, and whither he would often afterward return. His arrivals were always unannounced; he would appear when he liked, stay as long as he liked; and then one morning we would find at breakfast a penciled note to say that he had departed early, having had for the present enough of our society."

By slow degrees Whitman made partial recovery from the stroke that had sentenced him to retirement in Mickle Street. Individual in dress, his slow moving pace always aided by a cane, he became in time a familiar figure in the streets of Camden and Philadelphia and on the ferry between the two cities. He was also able to make occasional visits to New York and to the home of his old and ever faithful friend, John Burroughs at Riverby on the Hudson, and to make infrequent platform appearances as reader and lecturer. He further found time and strength to revise much of his early work and to put on paper his grave and uplifting meditations on old age and death.

And in the years between 1876 and 1879 Whitman was many times and for long periods a guest in the Philadelphia home of Anne Gilchrist, the rarely gifted English woman who had been one of his first admirers across seas, and who, when an exchange of letters had developed an understanding friendship, came to America in order to be near the poet and to educate her growing children in a country whose democratic principles strongly appealed to her. Much has been written, not all of it in good taste, regarding the relations of Walt Whitman and Anne Gilchrist. Suffice it to say in this place that if, when she left England she cherished thoughts of becoming the poet's wife and the guardian of his old age, these thoughts after their first meeting were gently and permanently put aside for an intimate and tender companionship, which first in the flesh and later by letter, was maintained until her death. "My noblest woman friend, now buried in an English grave," Whitman wrote of her in one of his latest and finest bits of verse, and others should not seek to alter or add to so touching a tribute.

For at least a dozen years before Whitman's death a front room which took up much of the second story of the little house in Mickle Street became his sleeping-room and workshop, and there more often than not he gave welcome to friends new and old and to admirers who sought a first meeting with him. The floor of this room was covered to the depth of a foot or so with a sea of papers, and now and then to divert a caller he would prod this pool with his cane and fish up a letter from an English admirer—Tennyson or Symonds or Dowden, or some newspaper article about the Good Grey Poet. Boards strung on trestles made a long table such as paper hangers use, and this afforded a resting-place for other heaps of letters, documents and junk. And through months and years in this cheerless habitat Whitman calmly and with steadfast heart awaited the end.

Another devoted friend of Whitman in his last years was Horace Traubel whose series of imposing volumes entitled *With Walt Whitman in Camden,* record almost daily conversations had with the poet from March, 1888, until the latter's death, and constitute as a whole one of the most unusual biographies in the English language. The son of a Jewish father and a Christian mother, Traubel was born in Camden and spent most of his life in the town. He was a lad of fifteen when through his father he first met and knew Whitman, and their comradeship, growing steadily closer, lasted nearly a score of years. Towards the close it was to young Traubel that the poet instinctively turned for help when there was need for it. This constant, long continued contact of a sensitive mind with a greater one left its mark, and now that Traubel is gone—he died in 1919 at the age of sixty-one—it is difficult to consider him apart from Whitman.

After Whitman entered his seventy-first year there was an increased and inevitable weakening of his hold on life. William Roscoe Thayer has left us a moving account of his last call in Mickle Street. "Stretched out," he writes, "in a long chair, propped with pillows and with a gray wolfskin thrown over his knees, lay Walt, a broken, helpless, pathetic figure. We talked little, mindful of his condition. When I arose to leave his 'Goodby, come again,' was uttered feebly, because of his physical weakness, but with no suggestion that he had lost courage or was even surprised at the defection of life. Neither that day or earlier did I hear him whisper a complaint against the weariness which old age and disease had laid upon him."

Death came to Whitman in the early evening of March 26, 1892, and four days later in the presence of a great multitude he was laid to rest with impressive ceremonies. "Look upon Walt's face long and long," Burroughs wrote in his journal during the solemn pause between death and burial. "Cannot be satisfied—it is not Walt—a beautiful, serene old man, but not Walt." The house in Mickle Street in 1922 was purchased and restored by the city of Camden, and within its walls are now assembled under a careful guardian all available Whitman relics there to be preserved through the long future. The tomb of the poet is in Harleigh Cemetery, near Camden, set in a side hill under a gnarled oak. It is of massive blocks of Quincy granite, fashioned after the walls of King Solomon's Temple. Whitman occasionally drove out to see this tomb while it was building, and the singular fact must be recorded that to pay for it, being a bit uncertain as to what posterity might do for him, he diligently and persistently saved through a long period. In most matters Whitman had the carelessness of a large nature, but in other and more intimate things he did not fail to exercise the frugality and foresight of his Dutch ancestors.

CHAPTER XVIII

The West Bank of the Hudson

Although its west bank used to be called, and with good reason, the poor man's side of the Hudson, it has through the years brought forth or furnished homes for more than one man and woman of mark, and so has much to interest and hold the literary pilgrim. The last home of Arthur Willis Colton, a skilled guardian of books who also wrote much pleasing verse, was at Palisades, over-looking upper New York City and the Hudson, while John C. Fremont and his wife spent several summers in the village of Piermont. There in their impoverished latter years Mrs. Fremont wrote with unresting pen and there they are buried near the brink of a bluff looking out over the Tappan Sea. Lewis Gaylord Clark, for nearly a generation editor of the once widely known and popular *Knickerbocker Magazine,* and the helpful friend of many a struggling writer, passed his closing years at Piermont, and his grave is in the village cemetery of nearby Nyack. And it is a short ride from Piermont to Tappan where John Andre's life had its tragic ending. The old Dutch farmhouse of graystone in which the British major passed his last hours still stands in the outskirts of Tappan. The room in which Andre spent his waking hours is in the front of the house. Back of it is a smaller apartment in which he slept and through its one window facing the west, tradition has it, he saw them rear the scaffold for his execution—a melancholy yet inevitable incident which the reader finds retold with sympathy and understanding in Dr. Weir Mitchell's fine tale of the Revolution, *Hugh Wynne, Free Quaker.*

The American Winston Churchill had his home in South Nyack when in 1898 his first novel, *The Celebrity* came from the press. A native of St. Louis, Churchill had graduated four years earlier near the top of his class at Annapolis, but promptly resigned from the navy to take up writing as a career. He had brief service in New York as an editor first of the *Army and Navy Journal* and then of the *Cosmopolitan Magazine,* but at the end of a year resigned from the latter periodical and retired to South Nyack to become a writer of fiction. His first novel, *The*

Celebrity, found readers, and in 1899 *Richard Carvel* brought his fame at twenty-eight. The latter, a tale of the Revolutionary period, Churchill rewrote five times before it went to the printer, and it sold 750,000 copies.

Two years later a full measure of success attended *The Crisis,* marked by a range and an accuracy of detail, which assured it a sale of more than a million copies and made it for long the outstanding novel of the Civil War period. Between 1904 and 1917 Churchill wrote half a dozen other novels—among them *The Crossing, Mr. Crewe's Career, A Modern Chronicle, The Inside of the Cup, A Far Country* and finally *The Dwelling Place of Light,* which closed his labors as a maker of fiction. He was seventy-five when he died in March, 1947, in Florida, and he had not written a novel in thirty years. He had ceased to write, he declared, because "it was no longer fun," but his novels dealing with sure and careful touch with memorable periods of our history, have given instruction and delight to millions of readers. The last half of Mr. Churchill's life was passed in happy retirement in New Hampshire, where he found diversion as an amateur farmer and painter, and from time to time made the role of political reformer a congenial and more than once an effective one. The affairs of his adopted state profited by his stern efforts for their mending.

The hamlet of Monsey in another part of Rockland County was the last home of Andrew C. Wheeler, whose career, because of its sharp contrasts, remains one of the minor romances of American letters. Wheeler, long best known by his pen name of Nym Crinkle, was born in New York and in early manhood led an adventurous life in the Farther West, and as a correspondent with the Union armies during the Civil War and as an editor in Milwaukee and Chicago. Another turn of the wheel brought him back to New York and in no long time to brilliant service first on the *World* and then on the *Sun* which made him, William Winter alone excepted, the best known dramatic critic of his period. When nearing sixty Wheeler quit journalism and sought the retirement and privacy afforded by a country home at Monsey. There his first wife died and after a time he married a young woman of the neighborhood, Jennie P. Mowbray by name and in age many years his junior.

It was soon after this second union that he broke a long silence, and again began to write, using "J. P. Mowbray," a part of his second wife's maiden name as a pen name. The first articles to attract attention and win favor over the initials "J.P.M." were a series of papers entitled *A Journey to Nature,* published in the *Evening Post* of New York and later issued in book form. Gathered between covers they met with instant favor. The reading public accepted their author as a new writer who was an intent and loving observer of Nature with a rare gift for depicting its forms and moods, and hastened to purchase and proclaim the merits of three other volumes which he wrote without delay—the *Making of a Country Home,* another Nature book, and two novels, *Tangled Up in Beulah Land* and *The Conquering of Kate.* But Wheeler was not permitted to long enjoy this cordial recognition of a late flowering in new fields. He died in 1902 after long illness in his seventieth year. There is a hint in his last letter to an old friend that he was ready for departure. "The weather here," he wrote, "is insufferably gray and moody, and from my prison window the old world looks outworn."

It was during a summer sojourn near the village of Highland Falls that in 1819 Joseph Rodman Drake wrote his best known poem, *The Culprit Fay.* The story runs that in the course of a stroll with friends one of them remarked to the poet that with human characters eliminated it would be difficult to write a purely imaginative fairy poem. Drake accepted this as a challenge and within a few days read to his companions the first draft of the work which is now his strongest claim to remembrance. A dozen years later and in another part of the Highlands a far more gifted poet, Edgar Allan Poe, during a brief and stormy cadetship at West Point which ended in expulsion, wrote some of the best of his early verse.

James Gates Percival, whose place among our early poets is a secure if modest one, was for a time a teacher at the Military Academy, and, approaching West Point from the south, one finds in a house set on an island in the river, a bit of ground bearing the imposing name of Constitution Island, another of the literary landmarks of the Hudson. Henry Warner, a New York lawyer, in the early years of the last century bought Constitution Island for a summer residence, but soon thereafter losing his fortune through no fault of his own, he retired to the island homestead, a low, straggling structure with small windows and smaller panes of glass, in which as the years passed his elder daughter Susan wrote *The Wide, Wide World, Queechy* and other tales which for a time made her the most widely read and popular author of her period. Her first novel ran into upward of three score and five editions, and her *Queechy* into thirty, while both were published with success in other countries.

Susan Warner continued to write until near the end of her life, and her younger sister Anna was also the author under the pen name of Amy Lothrop of several books of a religious nature, all of which found reverent readers eighty years ago. The sisters never married, and the life they shared in their island home was in all ways a charming one. They were in close and constant touch with West Point, and through a long stretch of years the cadets prized invitations to tea and Sunday afternoons at the Warner home. Through several decades the sisters, and after Susan's death in 1885, Anna alone, conducted a Sunday Bible class, always well attended, for the cadets. "As she sat in her chair in the orchard," a former member of this class long afterward wrote in affectionate memory of Susan, "with the boys in a semi-circle around her on the grass she looked like a print from *Godey's Lady's Book* of half a century before."

Standing beside the grave of Susan Warner one cannot fail to muse upon the forgetfulness which surely and swiftly overtakes all but the greatest names. It is in the military cemetery, where in a spot she herself had selected close by the Cadet's Monument, she was buried with military honors, army officers serving as pall bearers. Her sister Anna, who died in 1915, now rests beside her, and the flowers that in summer bloom above their graves, tell the West Point visitor that the name of a once famous author has not wholly passed from memory. Constitution Island, through the generosity of the late Mrs. Russell Sage, is now the property of the government, and, as part of the West Point reservation sedulously cared for, is visited every summer by hundreds of pilgrims.

A drive of a few miles northward from West Point, over a road disclosing vistas of a beauty and charm all their own, leads to the village of Cornwall closely associated with the closing years of Nathaniel Parker Willis, poseur and poet, city dandy and country gentleman. The house to which he gave the name of Idlewild stands a little way from the village. Since the death of Willis the place has passed in turn into various hands, until now it is the home of a New York business man of means. Here and there in the grounds remain suggestions of the time of Willis. The pine drive leading to the house along which of old passed many of the literary workers of the Knickerbocker period, remains intact, the dense growth of the trees only making the road the more picturesque, and the brook by which Willis often sat still runs through the grounds as of yore; but within the house has undergone many changes. The room from whose windows Willis used to look out on the Hudson, and where he did most of his writing, is now a bedchamber, suggesting its age only by its high ceiling and antique mantel.

When Willis lived at Idlewild his long-time associate George Pope Morris, the "Dear Morris" of so many of his partner's letters and *Hurrygraphs,* had his summer home near Cold Spring, on the east bank of the Hudson, and, at the cost of a short row across the river, there was much visiting between the two places. General Morris, a title gained by service in the state militia, was one of the best known song writers of his period, and it will be long before his *Woodman, Spare That Tree,* fails of a place in American anthologies. The home of Morris was at the base of a branch of Mount Taurus known as Cloud's Rest and this prompted its owner to name it Undercliff. Here men and women of mark had welcome in other days, but now the house has fallen into sad decay and the unkempt grounds about it are overgrown with trees. It is to be noted in passing that Hamilton Wright Mabie was born in Cold Spring and that when Morris lived at Undercliff he had Gouverneur Kemble for a friend and neighbor, and as a guest at the latter's Saturday night dinners long famous up and down the Hudson must often have drunk from the punch bowl celebrated by Irving in his stories of Cockloft Hall, its first home.

Back again in Cornwall one contacts other literary memories than those associated with Willis. Thus, only a few blocks from Idlewild, is the house in which Edward Payson Roe lived and wrote most of his novels. Roe's first book came into being in an unexpected way. He was born at New Windsor not far from Cornwall, served as a Union chaplain in the Civil War, and in 1871, at the age of thirty-three, was pastor of a Presbyterian church at Highland Falls. An engagement to preach called him to New York on the day in October that the great fire broke out in Chicago. The newspaper reports thrilled him, and moved by an impulse to witness what he felt would be the event of a lifetime, he bought a ticket and boarded the first train for the West.

The fire had been extinguished when Roe reached Chicago, but he spent much time walking about the ruins, viewing with his own eyes the suffering of the homeless people, and listening with sympathetic ear to the stories of distress and loss that passed from mouth to mouth. While thus occupied the inspiration came to him to write a story based upon what he had seen and heard. He returned home and set to work on *Barriers Burned Away*, which, published a few months later, in a single year yielded its author a royalty of twenty-five thousand dollars. It never had occurred to him that he could write a book, least of all one that would prove a source of wealth, but he now discovered, to his great surprise, that he was a born story-teller.

Accordingly, Roe gave up his pulpit at Highland Falls, and moving in 1874 to Cornwall devoted the rest of his days to novel writing, with fruit growing a congenial and profitable diversion for his leisure hours. During a period of seventeen years, aside from several books about fruit growing he wrote a dozen novels not one of which failed of welcome from an eager public. His talents were of the second-order, but he had rare kindness of heart and he wrote with sympathetic knowledge both about and for the great middle class. And so he was heard gladly by men and women who liked nothing better than to hear about themselves. Roe died suddenly in 1888 and his grave is in the little Presbyterian cemetery at Cornwall, close to the bank of the Hudson— a spot of great beauty and just the nook in a noble country where a lover of Nature should take his rest.

During his last years in Cornwall Roe had for a neighbor Amelia Edith Barr, another teller of tales whose appeal was to the multitude. Mrs. Barr was born in Lancashire, England, in 1831, came to America as a bride of twenty-two, and, early left a widow, in 1868 with only a few dollars in her purse journeyed from Texas, where she had been a teacher in the family of Sam Houston, to seek as a writer in New York a livelihood for herself and her three small daughters. The struggle at first was a difficult and doubtful one, yet she was always confident of the outcome. In later middle life, a full measure of success had long been hers, but an abounding energy that never balked at obstacles still drove her forward, an energy ennobled by a deep and abiding faith in spiritual values and their power to elevate and shape human lives. "The woman within," she once wrote, "if she be of noble strain, is never content with what she has attained; she presses forward in the lively hope of some better way, or some more tangible truth. I write mainly for the kindly race of women. I am their sister, and have drunk the cup of their limitations to the dregs . . . If my experiences can help any sad or doubtful woman to outleap her own shadows, and to stand bravely in the sunshine, to meet her destiny whatever it may be, I shall have done well."

During her three and thirty active years as an author, the greater number passed at Cherry Croft, the hillside home at Cornwall which she bought with her first savings, Mrs. Barr wrote more than sixty novels; for a long period, although she did not consider herself a poetess, she made more than a thousand dollars a year from her verse alone, and she turned out so many essays, short stories and social papers that in later life she forgot the titles of many of them. One of her novels she wrote in five weeks, producing during the same period a dozen newspaper and magazine articles. Nor did she ever have reason to forget the titles of her longer stories or make excuses for their quality. No other woman writer of her time had a surer instinct for pure narrative, and, writing as she did in a simple, unaffected style for the hearts of men and women, its exercise won her the love and admiration of a great army of readers in all parts of the English speaking world. Mrs. Barr died in 1919 at Richmond Hill, Long Island, the home of her last years at the great age of eighty-seven.

Another and later lettered dweller in Cornwall lived also for four score and seven years. This was Lyman Abbott, lawyer and preacher, author and editor, and for more than half a century a vital force and influence for light and truth. He was one of the four sons of Jacob Abbott, a Congregational minister who turned author and wrote the *Rollo* books beloved by the boys of two and three generations ago. Lyman Abbott was born in Roxbury, Massachusetts in 1835, was graduated from the University of the City of New York at the age of eighteen, after which he studied law and practiced for a time with his two elder brothers; but the ministry called him, and for six years following 1860 he filled a Congregational pulpit in Terre Haute, Indiana. Then he returned to New York where in succession he was pastor of the New England Congregational Church, editor of the *Illustrated Christian Weekly* and associate editor under his friend Henry Ward Beecher of the *Christian Union*. He was successor to Beecher as pastor of Plymouth Church, Brooklyn, from 1888 to 1899, when he took the editorship of the *Outlook,* the *Christian Union* under a new name—a position of power and responsibility which gave him a nation-wide audience and which he held until his death.

In 1870 Dr. Abbott bought a plot of land and built a house at Cornwall overlooking the Hudson which was his home for half a century. There he wrote most of his many books. Among these were a biography of Beecher, *Christianity and Social Problems, Life and Letters of Paul, The Rights of Man,* and his *Reminiscences.* Many, if not all, of the chapters of the book last named appeared first in the *Outlook* and they reflect on every page the serene, forward-looking spirit of their author. They reflect also his belief in God as the immediate and ultimate force governing the lives and conduct of men and shaping their social and political institutions. He was in the best sense a prophet of the brotherhood of man, charged with a gentle yet persuasive message. In his last years, a patriarch who lingered because the people needed him, he continued to exercise an effective and unflagging industry until in 1922 death finally halted his pen.

A short drive westward from Cornwall brings one to the village of Blooming Grove in Orange County, and, on a road leading thence to Chester, to the former home and farm of St. John de Crevecoeur, hero of a long life of change and adventure and author of *Letters from an American Farmer,* perhaps the best known book produced on this side of the Atlantic in the years that immediately preceded the Revolution. Crevecoeur was born in France in 1735, came to America at three and twenty, and, having gained a knowledge of the craft in England, was a surveyor in Vermont and New York City, where he laid out the lands of Trinity Church, before in 1769, having wed a young woman of the section, one Mehitable Tippet, he bought an Orange County farm and built the house which, although much altered, the visitor finds affording a comfortable home for its present owners. It is a house of two stories, and overlooks undulating fields watered by a brook.

There Crevecoeur became the father of numerous children, planted an orchard, gathered successive harvests and wrote the *Letters,* which, first published in England in 1782 by their appealing portrayal of country life and scene, charmed Byron, Lamb, Hazlitt, and other gentle or eager spirits, and carried their author's name all over Europe. Meanwhile with Crevecoeur now a widower, the uncertain conditions of the Revolution had caused his confinement for a time in New York by the British authorities who regarded him as a secret supporter of the patriot cause, and in 1780 prompted his return to France, where he was welcomed by Buffon, Marmontel and Grimm, and gained the friendship first of Franklin and later of Jefferson. He came again to America in 1783 to serve for a brief period as French consul in New York and to win the goodwill of Washington; but he soon went back to France, and there and in Bavaria, where his son-in-law was long French envoy, passed the remainder of his seventy-eight years. The last edition of his *Letters* was published at Paris in 1787 and is now an item sought for and prized by collectors.

If the record can be trusted Crevecoeur was a winning and delightful comrade, described by one of his biographers as "modest even to humility," and faithful in his many friendships. These included a number of Quakers of mark and steadfast purpose, among them stout-hearted Anthony Benezet, one of the first abolitionists in America. He was also a close and loving student of Nature in all of its phases and described what he saw with a zest and artlessness which made him an admirable writer, and, after eight score years, still assures him readers. True, he enlarged at times on the truth of things, but that is a fault he shared with greater men, and should not stand against him in the final count. Instead his lively pages, first and last caused many of his countrymen to settle in America, and, only with sincere and unfeigned regret could the English translation of them be denied a place in our literary heritage.

Timothy Shay Arthur, whose name deserves to be held in honored memory, was born in 1809 on a farm near Newburgh, the son of a veteran of the Revolution. His childhood was passed on another farm in the neighborhood of West Point and in Baltimore, where he mastered the trade of watchmaker but owing to weak eyesight did not follow it. Instead he became an editor and writer first in Baltimore and later in Philadelphia, where he was a prolific contributor to *Godey's Lady's Book* and other magazines of the period. In 1851 he founded and until his death in 1885 edited *Arthur's Home Magazine*.

Arthur as an author was seldom idle and before he reached old age the total of his books mounted to more than eighty titles. Many of these had to do with temperance of which he early became an earnest even fiery advocate, his influence with his pen for a long period equalling that of John B. Gough on the platform. His most effective effort in this field was his somber romance, *Ten Nights in a Barroom and What I Saw There* which first published in 1854 in the years preceding the Civil War commanded sales second only to those of *Uncle Tom's Cabin*. It was not literature, but it deeply stirred the popular heart, and when, like Mrs. Stowe's tale turned into a drama, it shared that poignant portrayal of slavery and its evils, and enjoyed a new and longer lease of life. A now thinning army of country-bred boys and girls recall first attendance at a performance of *Ten Nights in a Barroom* as one of the moving and memorable experiences of a long vanished youth.

Another author who once won and held great numbers of readers has pleasant association with the old town of Newburgh. Joel Tyler Headley, born in 1813 at Walton in Delaware County, was trained for the ministry, but, his health proving unequal to the demands of the pulpit, he was early compelled to resort to other sources of livelihood. He wrote letters of a popular sort from Italy and the Adirondacks, and when opportunity offered succeeded Henry J. Raymond as associate editor under Greeley of the New York *Tribune*. His home after 1850 was in Newburgh, where he led a life of unresting and profitable industry, turning out as the years passed more than thirty biographies, histories and books of travel. Headley's *Napoleon and His Marshals* ran through more than half a hundred editions, and there was a time when his *Washington and His Generals,* its every page colored with pride of country, claimed an undisputed place on most American book shelves. Eager, however, to profit by the ebb and flow of changing literary fashions his style was not always a happy one, and caused Poe, made impatient by his staccato sentences and his search for the obvious, to dub him The Autocrat of the Quacks—a harsh classification which might have been saved for a less innocent offender against good taste and the conventions. Headley died at the age of eighty-four and was buried at Newburgh.

A few miles from Newburgh the pilgrim northward bound passes the site of the house which Andrew Jackson Downing in the golden days of easily won success built for his bride from across the Hudson, and at Rondout, now a suburb of Kingston, he has pointed out to him the old home of Henry Abbey, a native and lifetime resident of the town, who gave to verse making of modest quality the leisure afforded by his duties as a country banker and merchant. And not far from the railway station at West Park one finds the graystone house which John Burroughs reared in early middle age, giving it the name of Riverby, and in which after 1875 he passed the remainder of his long life of eighty-four years.

What was the life led by John Burroughs at Riverby? "It is mainly," he wrote towards the end of it, "the life of a countryman and a rather obscure man of letters, lived in eventful times indeed, but largely lived apart from the men and events that have given character to the last three-quarters of a century. Like tens of thousands of others, I have been a spectator of, rather than a participator in, the activities of the times in which I have lived. I have known but few great men and have played no part in any public event." But this tells only part of a story of quiet yet splendid achievement, for it was at Riverby or in the hillside study which he called Slabsides that John Burroughs wrote most of the long series of essays, successively gathered into volumes, which began with *Wake Robin* and ended with *Under the Apple Trees,* wherein landscape, animals and birds are treated with a combination of scientific accuracy and literary charm equalled by few other writers. The quiet, genial Nature that he knew and loved; the daily life of bird, bee and ant; the animals of the countryside—woodchuck, muskrat and squirrel; the experiences of a farmer and fruit-grower in the valley of the Hudson, of a tramper in the Catskills and of a fisher along the upper waters of the Susquehanna, these he describes with a skill and sympathy which win added admiration with each rereading.

Burroughs was born on a farm near Roxbury in Delaware County and in the village school had a boy named Jay Gould for a schoolmate. Visits to the library of the Military Academy at West Point gave him his first acquaintance with Audubon's *Birds of America* and fired him with a resolve to become a naturalist. Then he escaped from the hard lot of a farmer's hired hand by becoming master of country schools, first near home and later in Illinois and New Jersey. Between classes he studied Emerson, Thoreau, Whitman, Wordsworth and other writers, and began to write essays some of which were accepted in due course by the *Atlantic Monthly,* then edited by James Russell Lowell. After that fresh tosses on the fork of good luck made him in turn a government clerk in Washington and a national bank examiner, which latter position he held for a dozen years. Meanwhile, he won the friendship of Emerson and during a trip to England in 1871 was taken by Moncure D. Conway to call on Carlyle.

Meanwhile also, this time in 1873, Burroughs bought a tract of land at West Park, which he improved from year to year and to which, having built a house, soon after its purchase, he retired in 1884 for a life of study and writing. It was his later boast that from the first he made his Riverby acres yield a profit. He relied at first on berries and peaches, but in 1884 began grape-raising on a substantial scale. Proud of his ability to grow grapes of the right flavor, he took it much to heart when one season a hail storm ruined his crop and in other seasons the invasion of California grapes caused disastrous falls in prices. There were compensations, however, for these drawbacks. Such was the steady increase in the sale of his books and with it his royalties that in no long time his publishers were able to settle on him an annuity in quarterly instalments. The end of twenty years at Riverby found him with some thousands of dollars in bank and a yearly income more than sufficient for his modest needs.

Burroughs had married the maiden of his heart's choice when he was twenty and had hardly more dollars than years; but as time passed the wife's mental growth did not keep pace with that of the husband, while her over-anxious housekeeping became a persistent if minor thorn-in-the-flesh of her helpmeet. So, for these and other reasons, on the hillside a mile or so from Riverby, in a hollow on the edge of a peat bog, in the summer of 1895 Burroughs built Slabsides, a substantial two-story shack of bark-covered boards, the first cuttings off the log, and made it both study and summer camp. The growing fame as a naturalist and writer which came to him as the years rolled on brought an ever lengthening line of visitors to Riverby and Slabsides, where a cordial greeting and talk of the best sort were given them; but for none was there so warm and sure a welcome as waited Walt Whitman when he came now and then from his Camden home.

Poet and naturalist met in Washington where the latter, a minor clerk, in working hours sat in a cellar watching the doors of a safe in the Treasury Department guarding millions of the nation's money for a wage that would now be scorned by a carpenter or bricklayer, and at the same time finding leisure to write the essays which now make up *Wake Robin,* his first book. Burroughs saw Whitman for the first time when one day on Pennsylvania Avenue some of the soldiers of a Pennsylvania regiment broke ranks to grasp the poet's hand and call him Walt. The young Treasury clerk followed their example and thus began a friendship which ripened and strengthened until in Whitman's last days Burroughs became one of the little group to which he instinctively turned for aid and comfort in periods of trial and discouragement.

In Washington Whitman soon fell into the habit of making his way on Sunday mornings to the Burroughs home not far from the present site of the Library of Congress, arriving there "always late" to enjoy the wife's delicious pancakes and the vegetables and berries raised by the husband on the acre of ground which formed a part of his modest leasehold. Now and again the two passed the Sunday evenings of spring and autumn on the steps of the Capitol watching the birds, and talking of flowers and the art of simple living. And it was accepted as a part of the natural of order of things that, three years after the Burroughs family settled on the west bank of the Hudson, Whitman, now ailing and feeble of limb, should find his way to Riverby. In fact for a time Burroughs cherished a plan of building Whitman a hermitage not far from his own home, but nothing was born of it. "Oh, if that dream could have come true!" Burroughs wrote after Whitman's death. "But Walt, with all of his love of country, was more at home in a city, among many people."

There is an engaging record in Whitman's *Specimen Days* of his second visit to Burroughs at Riverby. "Here I am," he wrote, "on the west bank of the Hudson, eighty miles north of New York, at the handsome, roomy, honeysuckle—and rose-embowered cottage of John Burroughs. The place, the perfect June days and nights, the air, the fruit, the room I occupy at night, the perfect bed, the window giving an ample view of the Hudson and the opposite shores, so wonderful toward sunset—the peaceful rest, the early Venus heralded dawn—the noiseless splash of sunrise— all inspiring my invalid frame with new life for the day." Whitman writes further of his drives with Burroughs along the country roads; of the stone fences, the brawling runs, the shrubs and wild flowers, and the "eloquent hemlocks—plenty of locusts and fine maples, and the balm of Gilead giving out aroma."

Burroughs in his *Journal* gives an account of Whitman's last visit to Riverby. "These days I am happy," he writes. "The days are perfection—sweet, bright, uncloying April days—and then Walt Whitman is here. He sits in the open bay window, reading, writing, musing, and looking down on Smith and me grafting the trees or ploughing among the currants, or upon me alone wheeling baby Julian about the grounds. His white beard and ruddy pace make a picture that I delight to see. Occasionally he comes out and strolls about, or sits on the wall on the brink of the hill, and looks out upon the scene. Presently I join him and we have much talk." These lines were written on April 26, 1879.

A week later Whitman left for his Camden home, and during the thirteen years of life that remained to him he did not come again to Riverby.

John Burroughs, alert and active in the "white winter of his age," spent the early weeks of 1921 in Southern California. Eastward bound he died without warning on a railway train near Kingsville, Ohio, in the early morning of March 29, his last words being, "How far are we from home?" When the train reached Poughkeepsie his body was received by his son and other waiting friends, and on his eighty-fourth birthday given back to Mother Earth. "I shall not be imprisoned," he had written in 1915, "in that grave where you are to bury my body. I shall be diffused in Great Nature, in the soil, in the air, in the sunshine, in the hearts of those who love me, in all living and flowing currents of the world." Riverby is now the home of Julian Burroughs, son of its builder, and the visitor finds Slabsides carefully tended by reverent hands.

Saugerties, a few miles north of West Park, was the birthplace of John Romeyn Brodhead, patient and indefatigable antiquarian, who ransacked the libraries of London and of The Hague for documents relating to the early history of New York, and who came home to assemble his findings in ten great tomes which are one of the monuments of American scholarship. And finally at Malden, the Bristol of an earlier time, a river hamlet not far from Saugerties, John Bigelow, both maker and writer of history, was born and passed many of his ninety-four years, Bigelow was first a lawyer in New York and then an associate of William Cullen Bryant in the conduct of the *Evening Post*. A by-product of his career as an editor was a part in giving final shape to a book which has remained for a century one of the classic accounts of western travel and adventure. Josiah Gregg, a lawyer and schoolmaster, who, when his health failed, had entered the Santa Fe trade, and who was also a keen observer of men and things, appeared in New York in 1845 intent on preparing for print the journals he had kept for a decade. He needed an assistant; Bryant recommended Bigelow for the place, and out of their joint efforts in 1845 issued *Commerce of the Prairies,* which has fairly earned many reprintings for it deals in an arresting and unforgetable way with the varied and colorful life of the Southwest. Bigelow in truth has few better claims to remembrance than his association with Gregg.

It was followed by other and weighty labors both at home and abroad, and it was not until 1867 that Bigelow again took up his residence at Malden. There he wrote his life of Samuel J. Tilden, of whom he had been the friend and trusted adviser: prepared for the press the edition of the *Works of Benjamin Franklin,* for which he had gathered material while serving as minister to France under Lincoln, and a few years before his death brought to a conclusion the five stately volumes to which he gave the title *Retrospections of an Active Life* and which remain required reading for serious students of the stormy period that saw the downfall and end of slavery. John Bigelow lived his life out in the fullest sense, a shining example of old-fashioned culture and accomplishment, and the plaque that now marks his birthplace might well declare that in a very real sense he was greater than anything he ever wrote or did.

CHAPTER XIX

Where Legend and History Meet

This is the record of a leisurely journey, over a winding trail and through a region where legend and history meet, which from Dunham's Landing on the shores of Lake George, carried the chroniclers south to the Catskills, then west and north to Cooperstown and Syracuse, and again south through Auburn and the Finger Lakes country to Ithaca and Owego. And it was a journey holding at every turn interest and instruction for lovers of our literary history and its makers.

A rambling house on the west side of Dunham's Bay, perhaps the most beautiful spot on the shores of beautiful Lake George, was the last home of its builder, Edward Eggleston, who there did his ripest and best remembered work. Born in Vevay, Indiana in 1837 of Virginia ancestry, Eggleston's first essay in authorship was largely an accidental one. After boyhood on a farm he had become at nineteen a Methodist circuit rider first in his native state and later in Minnesota, but at thirty had ceased to preach, and, a lover of books and letters, had turned to journalism in Chicago. In 1870 he settled in New York to become in turn literary editor and, as successor to Theodore Tilton, managing editor of the *Independent*.

For a period in 1871 Eggleston also served as editor of *Hearth and Home,* later absorbed by the *Century Magazine;* and it was while holding this post that unsought opportunity came to him. One of his story writers failed to forward manuscript, for a certain amount of space that needed to be devoted to original fiction. At the eleventh hour the editor filled the gap with the first chapters of *The Hoosier Schoolmaster,* a tale which, mindful of Taine's injunction that men should write only of places and people with which they are familiar, he founded on his experiences as a circuit rider, depicting the life, hopes and quaint dialect of the early Indiana settlers. He finished it in a few numbers, and was surprised at the welcome, both as a serial and in book form, which it received from readers alive to new and distinctive ventures in America fiction. Purely from want of copy honor and acclaim had been thrust upon its author. Few books of its period won a larger circulation and later tales by Eggleston met with a steadily increasing measure of favor. Among these were *The Circuit Rider* and *Roxy*, and, after a long interval, *The Graysons*, wherein a memorable incident in the life of Lawyer Abraham Lincoln figured for the first time in the pages of a novel.

In 1872 Dr. Eggleston returned to the ministry as pastor of a church in Brooklyn, but resigned that post at the end of seven years to give himself wholly to writing and research, carried forward in the winter in New York and in the summer at Lake George, where on Dunham's Bay in 1889 he built Owl's Nest, a house in three distinct buildings, one a library. There he gathered the thousands of volumes which were his work tools, and there, through years broken by visits to the great libraries of the land, he gave study, labor and unending revision to what he planned should be his master work, a *History of American Life*, designed to tell in a new and delightful way the story of the beginning of a nation.

At the same time he made leisure for long rambles in the hills about his home, and for inspiring converse—he was one of the great talkers of his period—with his family and intimate friends, among them his gifted younger brother, George Cary Eggleston, who formed a summer colony at Dunham's Bay. But to the deep and lasting regret of students he had finished only two volumes of his history when in the early autumn of 1902 death came to him practically without warning. When he was gone his brother wrote of him that he was the best man he had ever known. His old home, Owl's Nest, is now owned by the son of one of his daughters.

Bolton Landing, also on Lake George, was for a time the summer abode of Carl Schurz and the last home of an author of another and very different caliber—James Roberts Gilmore, whose earlier books were written under the pen name of Edmund Kirke. Born at Boston in 1823 Gilmore entered a counting-room when a lad just entering his teens and before he reached his majority was a partner in the business. At twenty-five he became head of a firm of cotton shippers in New York from which he retired with a competency on the eve of the Civil War. That struggle made him an editor and author and won him the friendship of Abraham Lincoln and Horace Greeley. To support the former's war policy and shape northern opinion in favor of emancipation he established the *Continental Monthly*, with Charles Godfrey Leland as its editor, and for it wrote a series of sketches of southern life entitled *Among the Pines,* which when published as a book in 1862 had a wide sale and won repute for its author. Like success attended Gilmore's second book, *My Southern Friends,* which grew also out of contributions to his magazine.

Gilmore withdrew from the *Continental Monthly* when the issuance of the Emancipation Proclamation accomplished the purpose which had brought it into being, and became a member of the editorial staff of the New York *Tribune* with liberty to go and come at his pleasure. In this capacity he witnessed the Draft Riots in the summer of 1863 and later wrote a graphic and moving account of them. During the later stages of the war he was in close and friendly touch with Lincoln, who in July, 1864, entrusted him and Colonel James F. Jaquess, an Illinois preacher turned soldier, with an unofficial mission to the Confederate Government. It was the hopeful belief of the two envoys—a belief shared only in part, if at all, by Lincoln—that they could arrange terms of peace. All they succeeded in securing from Jefferson Davis was a declaration that he would consent to peace only on the basis of the independence of the Southern States. Their errand, however, was not without result, for its failure, when it became known, helped to destroy the peace party in the North.

Having lost his fortune as one of the minor results of the war, Gilmore, with his usual energy once more engaged in business. That was in 1873, and at the end of ten years he again retired to apply himself anew to literature. After 1888 his home was a fine old place at Bolton Landing, which had come to him through his wife, daughter of John W. Edmonds, a well-known New York jurist. There, among other noteworthy books, he wrote the *Rear Guard of the Revolution,* a spirited account of the settlement of Tennessee and the patriotic services of John Sevier, and *Personal Recollections of Lincoln and the Civil War* which in some of its parts must be accepted with liberal grains of allowance but which as a whole remains a valued and informing contribution to the inner history of the struggle between the states. Gilmore died in Glens Falls in 1903 after a slow, pathetic failure of both mind and body.

It is a delightful drive of a June morning from the shores of Lake George down the valleys of the Upper Hudson and the Mohawk to the village of Broadalbin—long home of Robert William Chambers, who, giving up the city for country quiet, there wrote the greater number of his seventy-two novels. A descendant of Roger Williams, Chambers was born in 1865, in Brooklyn, and, his school days ended, persuaded his father, a lawyer of large practice, to supply funds for a period of art study in Paris. For seven years he was a pupil at Julien's, exhibiting toward the end in the Salon, and then returned to this country to draw illustrations for *Life, Truth, Vogue,* and other periodicals of the period.

Meanwhile young Chambers had begun to write to amuse himself, and he soon gave up art to make authorship a life vocation. In 1893 his first volume, *The King in Yellow* was brought out by a Chicago publisher to be followed at brief intervals by *The Red Republic, The Maker of Moons, A King and a Few Dukes* and many another tale, some of which did not meet with favor from the critics, but all of which by reason of his gift for clever plot and swift and enthralling narrative won their author a growing army of readers. This army grew in numbers when Chambers turned to the writing of *Cardigan, The Maid-at-Arms* and other historical romances, each based on painstaking study of the period with which it dealt and constant use of the great library assembled by their author through the years. Be it noted in passing that one shelf in this library was given over to books about Captain Kidd, whom, their owner's tale *The Man They Hanged,* sought to prove that the hero had never turned pirate.

When a full measure of popular success had come to him, Chambers left the city, bought an 800-acre farm at Broadalbin, and built on it a house designed by an architect brother which became his home for the rest of his days—the home also of the master's rare and costly butterfly, armor and Japanese art collections. Moreover, Chambers was a lover of trees, and caused many thousand of them to be planted on his widespreading acres His fertility and iron industry as an author knew no abatement with the years, and he was still busy with his pen when seized with a fatal illness. He died in a New York hospital in the winter of 1933, but was buried near his Broadalbin home which the visitor finds reverently cared for by members of his family. Chambers was ever a man of good-will, and a numerous company to whom he held out a helping hand or gave timely counsel when they had need for it hold him in kindly memory.

It is also pleasant summer wheeling from Broadalbin to the hamlet of Leeds which, lovely with its accumulation of years and traditions, lies four miles back from the town of Catskill and upon the right bank of the river of that name. Known in an earlier time as Madison, Leeds stands on a low plain which was once the dwelling-place of a tribe of Algonquins. In and all about it, Time and Nature have touched things with gentle hand, and, embosomed by hills and dales, the little village remains a well-nigh perfect relic of a past lived and shared by the men and women of six generations ago. And for the literary pilgrim Leeds has interest as the home of Irving's Rip Van Winkle, the luckless wight driven from home by a scolding wife to watch Henry Hudson's men bowling noisily among the hills, and to help himself stealthily to the brew which brought him dreamless sleep through twenty years of changing seasons. Most of the dwellers in present-day Leeds are prompt in their denials that such a man as Rip Van Winkle ever lived in the town, but there is one wrinkled veteran, far spent in years who, if discreetly questioned, will tell you in confidence that were he again a lad he would lead you to the rock, a little way this side of Palenville, where Rip used to camp and sleep on his hunting trips. Let us believe with this Ancient of Days that not all real things have form and substance, and that the legend of Rip Van Winkle—"Are we so soon forgot when we are gone?"—is one of them.

Westward from Catskill a road of easy grades leads through Tannersville to Arkville and thence to Roxbury and Stamford. Tannersville's most active resident in the closing years of the last century was Mrs. Candace Wheeler, an able woman of affairs, who founded the Onteora Club and then managed it, to the eminent satisfaction of all concerned, through a long span of successive summers. The Onteora Club, it is proper to state, was the name given to a congenial colony of authors and artists gathered in a number of cottages, with a comfortable inn for the care of transient guests. Mark Twain, with his wife and growing daughters, passed the summer of 1890 at this picturesque nook in the Catskills, with Mrs. Mary Mapes Dodge, Laurence Hutton, Brander Matthews and the widow of General Custer as fellow cottagers. From this retreat the humorist by invitation addressed to the editor of *Free Russia* a letter not published at the time, but which remains a devastating arraignment of the abuses of a now dead era. At Onteora Mark Twain also began and worked upon a sequel to *Huckleberry Finn—Huck Finn and Tom Sawyer Among the Indians*—which he planned should first have publication in a syndicate of newspapers, but in the ninth chapter runing into difficulties with his heroes, for which at the moment there appeared no solution, the manuscript was laid aside and a later will to finish it never came to its author.

Mrs. Dodge, for a generation editor of *St. Nicholas* which she named, and author of tales the memory of which is cherished by men and women who read them sixty years ago, passed many seasons at Onteora, and there in the summer of 1905 her long and helpful life came to an end. In later years Hamlin Garland, with the wife and daughters he acquired when success had come to him as the austere recorder in *Prairie Folks* and other tales of the scenes and the lives of the men and women he had known in his youth, passed several seasons at the Onteora Club. There during the summers of the First World War and those which followed he worked upon *A Daughter of the Middle Border* and other volumes of a series by many regarded as his best gift to posterity; and there he now and again had as guests John Burroughs, Henry B. Fuller and other fellow craftsmen. He has left an account, one would not willingly spare of the last visit of Burroughs to Onteora a year or so before his death. "We spent the evening before the fire," writes Garland, "talking quietly. He made a great picture as he sat in the firelight, listening while we sang our old songs. Then a young girl, the friend of one of my daughters, played the violin from a dusky corner of the room, while Uncle John, a majestic figure, sat like some old saint, the radiance of the chimney creating about his head a nimbus of gold-colored light. He was like a piece of granite sculpture as he dreamed in the glow of the embers. It was a sweet and noble hour, one we shall long remember."

Two miles from Roxbury, as one approaches that village from the south, is the mountain-side farm where Burroughs was born, and the house which he restored and naming it Woodchuck Lodge, spent there the last summers of his life. Woodchuck Lodge is an humble place, plain to the point of bareness, but it commands a noble sweep of the valley of the Delaware far below, and the high range of hills on the eastern horizon, and it is easy to believe the old friend of Burroughs who asserts that "not at Riverby nor Slabsides was he so thrilled as at Woodchuck Lodge with sheer joy of living, or so responsive to the silent influences of Nature bearing in upon him from every side. There he seemed most in his native element, and there he found its fullest expression. His talk, as one walked with him at evening along roads lined with rough stones, had in it a cheer and mental stimulus not to be forgotten. 'Here I am,' he once remarked, 'and these mountains stand in place of father and mother to me'."

Not far from Woodchuck Lodge when John Burroughs died
a grave was blasted for him from solid rock in the center of a
plot now known as Memorial Field. A boulder on which Burroughs played as a boy surmounts it. Rocks native to the region
and built into pillars have been placed about it, and between them
have been set limbs of birch, maple and other trees intertwined
to form a rustic fence. A bronze plaque imbedded in the stone
records its significance. Back of the grave and rising to the tip
of a mountain named for Burroughs is a clump of woods where
he hunted the fox and watched the birds both in youth and age.
To the right over a low knoll can be seen the house in which he
was born, and farther away another house which was the birthplace of Jay Gould, and the stone school-house built in 1813
where both men obtained their first knowledge of books. All in
all a fitting last home for a man who never lost his love for the
simple and familiar things of his youth.

Stamford, another Delaware County town, has a meaning
all its own for men whose favorite books in boyhood were rugged
and thrilling tales of the West, for it was the birthplace and last
home and now holds the grave of the best known and most redoubtable of the first writers of the dime novel. Edward Zane
Carroll Judson, or, to call him by his better known pen name,
Ned Buntline, was born in Stamford in 1823, the son of a country
school-teacher turned lawyer, and at the age of eleven ran briskly
away from home to begin a career perhaps without parallel in
the literary annals of his own or any other country. He became
a sailor and then a midshipman, and at fifteen fought duels with
seven of his mates—he had challenged thirteen—who had refused to mess with him as a man who formerly had served before
the mast.

Four years later young Judson, having resigned from the
navy, served with distinction in the Seminole War, this as a prelude to mighty deeds as a hunter in the Everglades. Then he
hurried off to the Rockies to enter the employ of the Northwest
Fur Company. The next turn of the wheel carried him to the
Southwest, where he discovered that he had the story-teller's gift,
and—fought more duels. In one of these he killed his man, and
as a consequence was tried for murder in Nashville and lynched
by a mob, but cut down in time to be restored to life. After this
episode New York claimed him. There he became a mainstay of
the *Knickerbocker Magazine,* which in 1838 had published his
first story, *The Captain's Pig,* and with Marcus Cicero Stanley,

another picturesque adventurer, founded a weekly periodical called *Ned Buntline's Own*. For it he wrote some of the tumultuous tales which made him the father of the dime novel, preceding Beadle and Adams in this field by a dozen years. It is interesting to note in passing that one of the compositors on *Ned Buntline's Own* was a young Scotchman, Robert Bonner by name who later was to become owner and editor of the New York *Ledger*.

Judson, however, needed other outlets than story-telling for the full expression of his urge for action. He found one not wholly to his liking in 1849 when he led the Astor Place riots against the English actor, Macready, and, with a heavy fine added, was sent to cool for a year in the penitentiary on Blackwell's Island. On his release he was escorted from prison by a procession of his admirers, and ere long again proved himself a furious patriot as one of the leaders of the short-lived Know Nothing Party. Then came the Civil War and Judson's enlistment in the Union Army as lieutenant in a New York regiment; but he had long been given to drinking bouts of a limitless sort, and indulging in one of these affairs while on duty in Baltimore he was stripped of his uniform and discharged from service.

This episode, however, did not bar Judson from claiming in after years that he had been chief of scouts in the Army of the Potomac or from assuming the self-bestowed title of colonel which he bore with complacency for the rest of his days. At the moment he was hunted up by friends and taken back to New York to resume his writings and to spend periods in the Adirondacks, where he built himself a house of logs at the foot of Blue Mountain and helped with his pen to make the region classic ground for sportsmen. In 1869 during a trip to the West he met William Frederick Cody and, bestowing on him the name Buffalo Bill, wrote a series of dime novels about his career. Five years later in St. Louis he brought Buffalo Bill on the stage in a play, *The Scout of the Plains,* which he began on a Wednesday, rehearsed over the week-end and produced the following Monday.

Judson and Cody, however, soon parted company, and the latter, retiring to a home in his native Stamford which he called Eagle's Nest, found content and peace of mind in hunting and fishing, and in the writing of tales, a pursuit which he followed with an industry so fruitful that his income often exceeded $20,000 a year. It is told of him that he once earned $12,000 in six weeks, and that at another time, under pressure, wrote a novel of upward of six hundred pages in sixty-two hours, scarcely pausing for sleep or food during the time. It was in 1883 that a lad not yet out of his teens, made his way to Eagle's Nest to receive a hearty welcome from its master and to listen with youthful zest to first-hand accounts of a hundred incidents in an astonishing career. Judson was then hale and hearty at sixty, but he died three years afterward, briefly mourned by the last of his four legal wives—he had been a great lover, catholic in his tastes and eager in the pursuit of his quarry—and leaving to his credit more than four hundred tales, each long enough to fill a book. These are now forgotten, and nothing perhaps can revive them, but the saga of their author remains in a class by itself, and promises to long survive both time and changing taste.

The pilgrim at Stamford is on the border of the old land of the Six Nations. When he reaches Cooperstown, at the outlet of Lake Otsego, at the end of a thirty-mile ride through a lovely stretch of country he finds himself in the heart of it. This is as it should be for the noblest monument to the memory of the Iroquois are the romances of James Fenimore Cooper, and Cooper dwelt, wrote and died in the town called after his father's name. The novelist was not born in Cooperstown, but he was carried there when a child in arms, and the village and the region about it were always very dear to him. In 1838 he wrote a history of the village, under the title the *Chronicles of Cooperstown,* a slender volume marred here and there by expression of some of its author's peculiar views, but on the whole full of interest and charm. And the third of Cooper's novels, written he declares in the preface "to please himself," was intended to be a description of frontier life as he saw it in his boyhood at Cooperstown. Its scenes and charcters were all real and apparent through the thin disguise of names and the modifications of a plot.

When in 1833 after long sojourn in Europe, Cooper returned to Cooperstown to pass the remainder of his days he wrote *The Deerslayer,* the scene of which is laid on Otsego Lake and around its borders in 1745 when all the country west of Albany was an unbroken wilderness. He had already written three of the Leatherstocking Tales and in the last of the three, *The Prairie,* had brought the life of the old trapper, Natty Bumpo, to an end. Now, however, came a desire to revive him and present him in early manhood on his first war-path. This tale Cooper wrote with his heart in his work. He loved the locality, his theme was a congenial one, and the result is a novel well-nigh perfect of its kind. And no one today has real reason to question the order of creation. The Leatherstocking series is now a complete and rounded whole, and *The Deerslayer* a guide to the incidents of the tale.

Otsego Hall, the home built by the founder of Cooperstown on a rise above the lake, was the original of the residence of Marmaduke Temple in *The Pioneers,* and in Judge Temple himself the novelist drew his own father. The original of Natty Bumpo, if that mighty hunter ever had existence except in the imagination of his creator, was an old hunter named Shipman, who used to offer his game at Judge Cooper's door, "and whose rude equipment, dogs and rifle," we are told, "had much attraction for the lads of the house." In 1834, after his return from Europe, Cooper restored and improved Otsego Hall, using plans prepared by his friend, Samuel F. B. Morse, who resided for a time in Cooperstown; and in a room opening off the hall, at the southwest corner of the house, he wrote the books which came into being during the last seventeen years of his life.

Otsego Hall, where Cooper long kept open house, passed into other hands shortly after his death. It was transformed into a hotel, and later was partially burned, falling at last into complete and utter decay. A generation ago the spacious site of the hall was converted into an attractive little park known as the Cooper Grounds, entered from the main street of the town, and now attracting the visitor by a bronze replica of *The Indian Hunter,* which first brought fame to the sculptor, Ward. Close at hand is Christ Church, a brick structure, with spire and buttresses and long Gothic stained windows, in whose remodelling Cooper interested himself after his return from Europe. In its auditory he was baptized and confirmed in September, 1851, a few months before his death. The Cooper burial plot lies in the shadow of Christ Church. Here rest the novelist, his parents, brother, wife, son and daughter.

Cooper's grave is marked only by a low, weather-greyed stone, without other inscription than his name and the dates of his birth and death; but not far away is an imposing monument to his memory. The novelist in his later years owned a farm on the ledge of a steep hill above the east bank of Lake Otsego a mile or so from his home. As on pleasant spring and autumn days he walked to and fro between village and farm, one of his biographers tells us, many of the scenes later given a place in his tales, took form in his mind ready for transcription to the written page. Then as now a road from village to farm ran along the base of an eminence called Mount Vision, because of the far-reaching view to be had from it—a view in which Cooper found never-ceasing delight. "Nothing is wanting," he wrote, "but ruined castles and recollections to raise it to the level of the scenery of the Rhine."

Lakewood Cemetery today covers the hillside below Mount Vision. There, just beyond the spot where in *The Pioneers* stood the cabin of Natty Bumpo and where he saved Elizabeth from the panther, stands a monument to Cooper's memory erected in 1859 by a committee, which had Washington Irving for its chairman. This monument, a graceful shaft of Italian marble, is topped by a figure of Natty Bumpo, who, his faithful hound Hector crouching at his feet, is represented in the act of loading his rifle, with gaze fixed on the waters of the Haunted Lake.

All about th old home of Cooper, now grown into a thriving town much frequented by summer visitors, are points of interest and great natural beauty. About a mile from the town a path leads from the road along the east side of the lake to Leatherstocking Cave which pierces the cliff forming the upper part of a ridge. The path is steep the latter part of the way, but the cave is well worth a visit. Leatherstocking Falls, on the west side of the lake, is a pretty cascade in a leafy dell; and near the outlet, where the Susquehanna begins its journey to Chesapeake Bay, Otsego Rock rises out of the water a few feet from shore, its size and shape recalling a haycock. Tradition says it was a council rock for the Iroquois, and Cooper makes it the place where Deerslayer met Chingachook, the young chief of the Delawares, who had come up from the hunting grounds of his tribe to rescue his promised bride held captive by the Hurons.

The outlet is another interesting spot. Cooper, in *The Deerslayer*, represents it as well-nigh concealed by overhanging trees, which now have wholly disappeared from the west shore, although along the eastern side there is still a margin of shade. It was here that Hutter's lumbering ark, slowly pushed up-stream from its leafy ambush below and about to emerge into the lake, had a narrow escape from capture by Indians, who had been lying in wait on a huge tree which hung over the outlet, and leaping too late, as the ark warned of danger was poled to safety, tumbled one after another into the water. There they lie until this day, but they live again in Cooper's pages, and perhaps on nights when the moon fails to shine, their harmless wraiths come once more to the shores of the Haunted Lake.

Cooperstown has other associations which make it dear to the hearts of boyhood and youth: it was the birthplace of base-ball, America's national game, while Erastus F. Beadle, descen-dant of pioneers and soldiers, was born on an Otsego County farm, and in a Cooperstown shop learned the trades of printer and binder to such good purpose that over a period of nearly two score years he furnished reading matter to a wider public than was commanded by any other publisher of his time. Born in 1821, Beadle as a boy worked on a farm and then as apprentice to a miller. Finding need one day for letters of some sort to label the bags of grain, he cut them from blocks of hardwood, as had been done by the men who preceded Gutenburg.

This experience interested young Beadle in printing, and in 1852, five years after he had mastered the art in Cooperstown, he had a shop of his own in the growing town of Buffalo. Thence he moved in 1858 to New York and forming the firm of Beadle & Adams put to the test an idea that had been long taking shape in his mind—the publication of books to be sold at ten cents a copy. He began with song-books and joke-books, and in 1860 issued his first dime novel in orange colors. He found his writers among men who knew pioneer life at first hand, and chose for his editor, Orville J. Victor, a really remarkable figure in the history of American letters. During a period of more than thirty years Victor read and edited the thousands of tales published by the house of Beadle, selecting his authors with care, and insisting that their narratives should faithfully reflect the spirit of the times and people with which they dealt.

Among Beadle's authors were Captain Mayne Reid, Ned Buntline, Edward S. Ellis, Colonel Prentiss Ingraham, "Bruin" Adams and Edward L. Wheeler, and from the first his output had welcome from a devoted and steadily widening constituency. *Seth Jones*, a tale of the New York frontier by Edward S. Ellis, sold more than 450,000 copies, and a like measure of success attended Mrs. Victor's *Maum Guinea*, a portrayal of slavery, which Henry Ward Beecher took with him when he went to England to win support for the Union cause from the British public, and which President Lincoln is said to have preferred to *Uncle Tom's Cabin* as a compelling account of a great evil. In the trenches during the Civil War the soldiers absorbed Beadle's dime novels by the million. That struggle ended publisher and editor turned their attention mainly to the Far West, and Beadle made a trip across the plains to study at first hand the life in those regions. Tales of city life also found an army of readers, but with the passage of time the competition of rivals steadily and sadly reduced the profits of the house of Beadle and in 1889 it closed its doors. The founder retired to Cooperstown, and dying in 1894 was laid to rest in Lakewood Cemetery, where Natty Bumpo and his hound Hector watch over his grave.

It is a morning ride from Cooperstown through Cazenovia, with its memories of sturdy Jan Von Linklaen and his part in the settlement of the Genesee country to Syracuse, where at 990 James Street one finds the house in which Edward Noyes Westcott finished *David Harum*. Westcott's single success as an author had an unusual and pathetic story behind it. He was born in Syracuse in 1846, the son of a leading physician who later served as mayor of that city, and after leaving school held various posts in one of its banks. Later he founded a banking house of his own, but soon his health failed, and he turned to authorship as a possible means of livelihood. He began *David Harum* in the summer of 1895 while living at Lake Meacham in the Adirondacks. Finished and repeatedly revised at his home in Syracuse, this diverting story of a shrewd country trader and cracker-box philosopher, was rejected by one publisher after another until it finally reached Ripley Hitchcock, literary adviser to the house of Appleton. Hitchcock discovered merit of an unusual sort in the manuscript which had passed through so many unfavorable readings and, whipped into final shape by his experienced hand, it was published late in 1898, six months after its author's death of tuberculosis. Barely had it issued from the presses when *David Harum* became the best seller of its period. After the lapse of more than two score years it still finds readers—an impressive example of the belated recognition that now and then attends literary effort of an unusual sort.

If one pushes southward from Syracuse into the Finger Lakes country, he will have pointed out to him in the older part of Auburn, a town proud of its famous sons, the roomy house, still occupied by his descendants, which was the home of William Henry Seward before, during and after his services as governor, senator and secretary of state. There, aided by his admiring and devoted friend, Thurlow Weed, he advanced by steady and even step to leadership in state and nation first of the Whig and then of the Republican Party. There he meditated and gave final shape to many of the great addresses which in the Senate and in political campaigns had a fateful share in shaping the later history of the anti-slavery contest. There in 1860, an eager and confident aspirant for the Republican nomination for the Presidency, he saw that honor at the eleventh hour snatched from him by an angular Illinois lawyer who six years earlier had been practically unknown outside of his own state. And there in the opening days of 1861 he accepted the post offered him by a successful rival to whom he was to be through four troubled and anxious years the potent and devoted right hand.

A book dealer whom one of the writers knew when a young man used to talk of a business call made on Seward at Auburn after his public career had come to an end, and how in the course of a reminiscent hour his host, pointing to a sheaf of books on a library shelf made up of his letters and papers as secretary of state declared with quiet conviction: "Those are my best claim to a place in history." Had further length of days been granted him he might have revised this estimate. His retirement as secretary of state in 1869 was followed by a leisurely trip around the world, and in October, 1871 he sat down in his Auburn library to dictate his memoirs to an adopted daughter. He had covered the first thirty-three years of his life when he turned to the writing of an account of his trip around the world, and did not again take up his autobiography before his death in October, 1872. But a reading of the finished part of it proves that the unusual mind of its author was still clear and vigorous, and had he brought it to an end we should now have an inside story of the Civil War period by one of its greatest figures, which would be treasured by students as a source document of the first order.

Andrew Dickson White was born in 1832 at Homer, a town midway between Syracuse and Ithaca, and first in one and later in the other of these cities had as teacher, university president, diplomat and author a career of exceptional and enduring achievement. The son of a wealthy father who after 1839 made his home in Syracuse, he was graduated at Yale in the famous class of 1853 which included Edmund Clarence Stedman, Isaac Hill Bromley and George Washburn Smalley. For five years following 1857 he was professor of history at the University of Michigan. Then he returned to Syracuse to take charge of his dead father's large estate, and in 1863 was elected to the first of two terms in the Senate of the State of New York. One of his fellow members in that body was Ezra Cornell of Ithaca, "a stern shrewd old man of Quaker birth and breeding," who had made a great fortune by helping to spread the electric telegraph, and who was now casting about for a worthy public use for his wealth.

To the million acres of land allotted to the State of New York by the Morrill Agricultural College Act of 1862 White persuaded Cornell to add an initial endowment of half a million dollars; and in 1865 on the hill overlooking Ithaca and the waters of Cayuga Lake the two men laid the foundation stone of Cornell University. When in 1866 a head was sought for the new institution Cornell insisted that White accept its presidency. Dr. White held that post until 1885, when ill health compelled his resignation, and during this long period built it into one of the nation's great centers of learning with a cordial, impartial welcome for students of both sexes. In 1879 he was granted a leave of absence in order that by appointment of President Hayes he might serve for two years as American minister to Germany, and after his retirement from the presidency he served as minister to Russia under Harrison and again as our representative at Berlin under McKinley.

A great executive, Dr. White was likewise a student who from youth to extreme old age took all knowledge for his province, and his *History of the Warfare of Science with Theology in Christendom,* begun and finished during his active years at Cornell, remains one of the monuments of American scholarship. Occasional sojourns in other lands excepted, Ithaca after his retirement remained Dr. White's home, and the fine house he built on the campus and deeded to the university for ultimate use by its presidents was long the center of a hospitality held in grateful memory by those who were fortunate enough to enjoy it. There he wrote his admirable *Seven Great Statesmen* and the account of his long life which is also one of the most delightful of American autobiographies. There in November, 1918, he passed from life, and on the eighty-seventh anniversary of his birth was laid to rest in the Founders' Chapel at Cornell.

Dr. White from the first insisted that Cornell students should be instructed only by trained and mature minds devoted to the subject in hand: tutors were sternly denied a place in his plans. Thus from the earliest days the faculty he gathered about him included men of light and leading. Goldwin Smith Hall on the Cornell campus recalls the devoted and helpful service that eminent English historian and writer gave without money and without price when the future of the new university was still a doubtful one. It was while a member of the Cornell faculty that Moses Coit Tyler, who was to end his days in Ithaca, wrote his classic *History of American Literature* during the Colonial and Revolutionary periods, and Henry Morse Stephens had like employment when he published what is regarded by scholars as the most satisfactory account we have in English of the course of the French Revolution prior to the reign of terror. And Hiram Corson, a unique personality who oddly united a profound knowledge of Shakespeare and his period to a firm belief in spiritualism, was during his long association with Cornell an undisputed leader in the modern teaching of English.

Yet another unusual man was an early member of the Cornell faculty. Born in Southern Norway in 1848 of sea-going stock Hjalmar Hjorth Boyesen came to America in early manhood and was first an editor in Chicago and then a tutor in a college at Urbana, Ohio. Having been carefully educated in Norway, in these posts he quickly learned to speak and write English, and in the summer of 1872 made a journey to Boston carrying with him the manuscript of a romance to which he had given the title of *Gunnar,* and for which he hoped to find a publisher. In Boston by happy chance he won the friendship of Francis James Child of Harvard, one of the kindliest and most helpful of men, who secured acceptance of his manuscript by William Dean Howells of the *Atlantic Monthly* and placed him in touch with Dr. White, then building a faculty for Cornell University.

Thus favored by fortune young Boyesen in the fall of 1873 after a period of study in France and Germany came to Cornell as assistant professor of northern languages, later being made in addition full professor of German. He remained at Cornell until 1880 and in quarters in South Building, which afforded a wonderful view over Cayuga, taught his classes, making, as one of his former students has phrased it, "grammar secondary to the poetry of speech." His *Gunnar* began to appear as a serial in the *Atlantic* early in 1873 and when issued a year later in book form was received with acclaim both by reviewers and the reading public. During the decade of the seventies, with success assured, he wrote two other novels *A Norseman's Pilgrimage* and *Falconberg* and *Tales of Two Hemispheres,* a group of short stories— all three Norwegian in content. To the same period belonged *Idylls of Norway,* a volume of verse which proved him a poet of more than common quality.

Boyesen left Cornell as already noted in 1880, and from 1881 until his sudden death in 1895 at the early age of forty-seven was a member of the faculty of Columbia University in New York. During a little more than a score of years he had with unflagging industry written and published twenty-four volumes of novels, short stories, essays, history and verse. Many of these in an era of changing tastes no longer find readers, but the memory of their author cherished by many an aging man recalls a true son of the Vikings, virile in bearing, thought and speech, who was always ready to battle for the faith that was in him; a stout-hearted fighter for any cause that appealed to him, but who rarely failed to blend tenderness with courage, and who often accorded but never asked clemency from a foe.

Francis Miles Finch holds an honored place in the early history of Cornell University, for, in the intervals of weighty service on the bench, he attended to its legal interests and during the last years of a long life was the head of its law faculty The world, however, best remembers him as the author of *The Blue and the Gray,* a poem read and recited wherever the English language is in use. In 1867, when the fires of hate were still aflame both North and South, a little group of women at Columbus, Mississippi, strewed flowers alike on the graves of the Confederate and Union dead in their local burial-ground.

An item in the New York *Tribune* recording this moving proof of renewed amity between the sections was read by Judge Finch, then a lawyer of forty in his native Ithaca, and, convinced that the time had come when the North should clasp the friendly hand held out by the South, he wrote *The Blue and the Gray,* voicing the equality and the serene forgetfulness of old wrongs that lie in death. His poem, published in the *Atlantic Monthly* for September, 1867, at first attracted little attention; but breathing the spirit of Memorial Day then on the way to general observance, and keeping time also to a needed and welcome change in public opinion, it slowly yet surely won its way to a place all its own in the popular heart. Moved by a profound conviction shared by millions of his countrymen its author had again proved the truth of the saying that the writer of a nation's songs is elder brother to the man who shapes its laws.

When Judge Finch was a growing lad in Ithaca on a farm not far from the nearby town of Owego, Nathaniel Parker Willis was writing one of the colorful chapters in an unusual career. In 1836, Willis, then one of the most widely known of New World authors, returned from a long sojourn abroad bringing with him a commission from an English publisher to prepare the text for an illustrated volume on American scenery. The following summer he set forth with William H. Bartlett, an English artist, to gather material for this book, and in the course of their wanderings he chanced upon a lovely spot on the banks of Owego Creek near its junction with the Susquehanna which so pleased him that he resolved on the instant to there make his home. "Owego Creek," he wrote in one of his letters to the New York *Mirror*, "should have a prettier name, for its small vale is the soul and essence of loveliness. A meadow of a mile in breadth sprinkled with stately trees, furnishes a bed for its swift windings; and on the southern side rise three steppes or natural terraces, over the highest of which the forest rears its head, and looks in upon the meeting of the rivers; while down the sides leap the small streamlets from the mountain springs. Here I would have a home! Give me a cottage by one of these shining streamlets, and let me ramble over these mountain sides, while my flowers are growing, and my head silvering in tranquil happiness."

In fulfilment of these desires Willis bought from an old college friend a farm of some two hundred acres on the banks of Owego Creek which he named Glenmary in honor of his wife, and there in the fall of 1837 he began the five years residence which he was to regard in retrospect as one of the happiest periods of his life. There he wrote for the *Mirror* his light hearted yet mellow *Letters from Under a Bridge* to which when gathered into a volume he gave the title *A l' Abri, or the Tent Pitched*. There also among other things he wrote his *Reverie at Glenmary*, the most joyous as it is also the most seriously devout of all his religious poems. But ere long Willis, facing unforseen reverses, found there was need for him to be nearer to a market for his literary wares, and late in the summer of 1842 he with heavy heart broke up his home at Glenmary, which soon found another owner, and returned to New York to resume an active career in journalism, which with one brief interruption was to continue until his death. The present-day visitor finds only one visible reminder of his days at Glenmary—the tiny plot of ground reserved from purchase by his successor where, on a gray December day in 1840, with his own hands he broke the snow and frozen earth to make a grave for his first child, a daughter born dead. A second daughter, who came into life at Glenmary in June, 1842, survived to become the comfort of her father in his ailing and broken old age at Idlewild.

CHAPTER XX

Mark Twain's Days in Elmira

It was on a late afternoon in August, 1868, that young Charles Langdon with one of his chums to keep him company, journeyed to Waverly, a pleasant town on the line of the Erie railway midway between Owego and Elmira, where he planned to meet his new friend, Sam Clemens, westward bound from New York for a first visit to the city which, by Destiny's planning, was to play so large a part in his after life. Clemens, soon to become best known by his pen name Mark Twain, was then three months short of thirty-three, and already had behind him his days as wandering printer and Mississippi River pilot, and as prospector, miner, newspaper reporter and budding lecturer in Nevada and California.

Late in 1866 Clemens came east intent on a trip around the world, in the course of which it had been arranged he should send letters to the *Alta California* of San Francisco. However, in April, 1867, while on a visit to his mother and sister in St. Louis, he read an announcement of the excursion the steamer Quaker City sailing from New York soon was to make to the Holy Land. Fired by this new prospect, he gave up the longer journey he had planned, and, with the financial support promptly pledged by the owners of the *Alta California* enrolled as a member of "the refined party that was to sail for a long summer journey to the most romantic of all lands and seas, the shores of the Mediterranean." There were sixty-seven in the party when the Quaker City left New York on June 8, 1867, and what they saw and did Clemens recorded in three score letters to the *Alta California* and the New York *Tribune* which later gathered into a book entitled *The Innocents Abroad* were to make their author the most famous humorist of his time.

Not least among the voyagers on the Quaker City as the sequel proved was Charles Langdon, the eighteen-year-old son of Jervis Langdon, a wealthy coal dealer and mine owner of Elmira. Despite the difference in their ages a friendship quickly developed between Clemens and Langdon. The latter had two sisters at home, and of Olivia, the younger, a lovely girl, he had brought with him a miniature done on ivory. On a fateful September day in the beautiful Bay of Smyrna, Clemens, lounging in Langdon's cabin, was shown this portrait. He studied it with manifest admiration, and each time he came after that he asked to see the picture. He had fallen in love with a face, and "as long as he lived he never saw another woman."

The Quaker City returned to New York on November 19, 1867, and four weeks later there was a lively reunion of some of the party at the New York home of one of them. Clemens had a part in this reunion and so did young Charles Langdon. More important to the purposes of the present record two days before Christmas Clemens was invited to dine at their hotel with Langdon's father and sister who were passing the holiday season in the city. And at this dinner Clemens met his future wife for the first time. Olivia Langdon was then twenty-two years of age, and had lately recovered from a long period of invalidism, the result of a fall on the ice. Gentle, winning and lovable, the heart of the man from the West was in her keeping from the first moment of their meeting. The young couple saw much of each other during the next few days, and when they parted it was with an invitation from the father and son, for Clemens to visit Elmira in the early future—an invitation which had prompt acceptance.

There unexpectedly intervened, however, need for a business trip to the Pacific Coast and Clemens did not see Elmira for the better part of a year. When at last he was able to make the journey he took by mistake a slow train instead of a fast one, and it was a series of telegrams announcing his belated progress that on that August afternoon in 1868 moved young Langdon to go down the line as far as Waverly to meet him. When the New York train arrived Langdon and his chum found Clemens in the smoking-car, clad in nondescript fashion, for the humorist had not yet acquired the neatness of dress which was habitual with him in his later years, and also somewhat the worse for wear at the end of long hours of travel on a hot summer day. The greeting given Clemens was a cordial one, but was followed by a hesitant inquiry as to whether or not he had brought with him other clothes than those he was wearing.

"Oh yes," was the cheerful reply. "I have a fine new outfit in this bag, all but a hat. I won't see anyone tonight, for it will be late when we get in, and in the morning we'll go out early and get a hat."

True to promise the guest appeared at daylight correctly clad, and an early trip to the nearest haberdasher secured the needed hat. There followed three gay and happy weeks in the stately Langdon home which stood until late in 1939 at the corner of Main and Church Streets in Elmira. Before they were ended Clemens was more than ever alive to the fact that there was only one woman in the world for him. At the outset, however, his courtship was not in all ways a smooth one. Olivia Langdon was not easily won, and, while her brother found much to admire in his friend from the West, he could not see him as the life companion of his adored and precious sister. On the other hand and from the first Jervis Langdon had faith in the essential manliness of his daughter's suitor, and, after other visits and the inquiries it behooved a careful father to make, on February 4, 1869, gave his approval to a formal engagement. Olivia's mother and elder sister, aware that she now knew her own mind, seconded this approval, and so did the latter's husband, Theodore Crane, who, long before had read Mark Twain's sketches and now endorsed him without reserve.

The happy lover hastened to pass the glad news on to his mother. "She is only a little body," he wrote from Elmira, "but she hasn't her peer in Christendom. I gave her only a plain gold engagement ring, when fashion imperatively demands a two-hundred dollar diamond one, and told her it was typical of her future life—namely that she would have to flourish on substance, rather than luxuries (but you see I knew the girl—she don't care anything about luxuries) . . . She spends no money but her usual year's allowance; spends nearly every cent of that on other people. She will be a good sensible little wife, without any airs about her. I don't make intercession for her beforehand, and ask you to love her, for there isn't any use in that—you couldn't help it if you were to try. I warn you that whoever comes within the fatal influence of her beautiful nature is her willing slave forevermore."

A few days after the return of the Quaker City Clemens received from Elisha Bliss, Jr., the shrewd and enterprising head of a subscription book concern at Hartford, a proposition to publish a volume of the letters he had written in the course of that good ship's voyage. In due time an understanding was reached by author and publisher, and in the spare hours of a trip to the Pacific Coast already referred to and of a successful and profitable lecture tour in the fall and winter of 1868-69 the manuscript was made ready for the printer. At the suggestion of Bliss it was given the title of *The Innocents Abroad, or The New Pilgrim's Progress*. The lecture tour closed in March, and the lecturer, abandoning a proposed spring tour to California in order to be with his future wife, went at once to Elmira.

There the final proofs of his book came to him, and in the Langdon home he and Olivia read them together, she with an instinctive sense for what was fine and true that was to make her until her death her husband's keenest and most helpful critic. In more ways than one Sam Clemens was still a diamond in the rough, and the processes to which he now submitted were salutary as well as gentle ones. Nor was proof-reading the major concern of those April and May days. "I feel ashamed of myself," Clemens wrote his mother, "and yet I have had really no inclination to do anything but court Livy. I haven't any other inclination yet."

And so, in a beguiling alternation of work and play, the big book was at last completed and in July, 1869, published in a first edition of 20,000 copies, which was but a harbinger of the immediate and long continued favor to be won by what perhaps remains the greatest book of travel ever written by an American. Not yet, however, was its author convinced that he could safely count on his writings as his sole or main means of support. Instead, with the aid of his future wife's father he purchased a third interest in *The Express* of Buffalo, and in the late summer of 1869 began his labors as one of its editors, making time also for frequent week-ends in Elmira, and for occasional lecture tours. On February 2, 1870, in the presence of five score guests Samuel Clemens and Olivia Langdon were married in the parlors of the Langdon home in Elmira—stately rooms which in future years were to witness so much of primal joy and sorrow for both husband and wife. A source of delight at the moment was the receipt by Clemens on his wedding-day of a check from his publishers for upward of $4,000, royalty from the sales in recent months of *The Innocents Abroad*, nearly 100,000 copies of which were sold before the end of the third year.

The day after their wedding the young couple set out for Buffalo to take up their residence in a house which, to the husband's bewildered and pleased surprise, the bride's father had purchased and furnished for them. But their days in Buffalo were to prove brief and troubled ones. Jervis Langdon fell ill in May, and in the following month, his condition having become critical, Clemens and his wife were summoned to Elmira to join in the work of caring for him until the end came in August. Then a baby boy, Langdon Clemens, was born prematurely in November, and there followed months of invalidism for the mother. Sickness and loss gave the husband a distaste for his Buffalo surroundings, and as soon as he could he found a buyer at a sacrifice for this interest in *The Express*, placed on sale the house Jervis Langdon had bought for him and his wife, and in April, 1871, they left Buffalo and their home never to return to them.

During the previous summer while Jervis Langdon lay dying Bliss, the publisher, had visited Elmira and contracted with Clemens to write a book dealing with his western experiences. In Elmira, on July 15, 1870, work was begun on what was to prove one of its author's masterpieces, but for a time, owing to distracting conditions, little progress was made on it. Early in May, 1871, their Buffalo days behind them and his wife and baby finally able to travel, Clemens took them to Elmira and to Quarry Farm, for the first of what was to prove many restful and fruitful summers in rarely beautiful surroundings. Quarry Farm, then the home of Mrs. Theodore Crane, the sister of Mrs. Clemens, is a hilltop house overlooking Elmira and the Chemung River with a lovely vista of distant hills. Mr. and Mrs Jervis Langdon found and fell in love with it in the course of an evening drive, and the husband made haste to purchase it as a summer retreat for his family and kinfolk. There was an abandoned quarry a littleway up the hill from the house, and at the suggestion of Thomas K. Beecher, then best beloved of Elmira ministers, the place became and remains Quarry Farm, being now the home of Jervis Langdon, who bears worthily the name of his honored grand-father.

Mother and baby showed early improvement at Quarry Farm, and with ease of mind the husband, with fresh zeal, resumed work on the manuscript he had begun and laid aside the previous year. "I am writing with a red-hot interest," ran a letter to Bliss before the end of May. "Nothing grieves me now, nothing bothers me or gets my attention. I don't think of anything but the book, and I don't have an hour's unhappiness about anything and don't care two cents whether school keeps or not. It will be a bully book. I have twelve hundred pages of manuscript already written, and am now writing two hundred a week —more than that in fact; during the past week wrote twenty-three one day, then thirty, thirty-three, thirty-five, fifty-two and sixty-five. How's that?" The title finally given it was *Roughing It,* and when it appeared early in 1872 it sold abundantly, widening and confirming the fame of its author as a humorist and as an unsurpassed chronicler of the life he had known in remote places.

In October, 1871, in order to be near his publisher, Clemens arranged for a residence in Hartford, which at first regarded as temporary soon became a permanent one. But the family did not lose its touch with Elmira. On March 19, 1872, in the old Langdon home, a second child, a little girl whom they named Olivia Susan, was born to them. A few weeks later, little Langdon, who had been from the first a delicate child, died in the new home in Hartford, and was laid to rest in the burial plot of the Langdons in Woodlawn Cemetery, Elmira. The blow was a heavy one for the mother, and, with seaside sojourns and a long stay in England and Scotland in 1873, it was not until early May of 1874 that the family came again to Quarry Farm.

The summer that followed was an eventful one. A new baby, a second girl, was born in June, and on the hillside near the old quarry Mrs. Crane built a study for Mark Twain, still standing after more than three and seventy years, where, free from interruptions of every sort, he began *The Adventures of Tom Sawyer,* and completed the dramatization of *The Gilded Age,* the novel he had written in 1873 in collaboration with Charles Dudley Warner. "It is the loveliest study you ever saw," he reported to his Hartford friend, Twichell. "It is . . . a cosy nest, and just room in it for a sofa, table and three or four chairs, and when the storm sweeps down the remote valley, and the lightning flashes behind the hills beyond, and the rain beats on the roof over my head, imagine the luxury of it." A later letter to Dr. John Brown of Edinburgh adds a few details to this picture. "The study," he tells his Scotch friend, "is built on top of a tumbled rock-heap that has morning-glories climbing about it and a stone stairway leading down through and dividing it. On hot days I spread the study door wide open, anchor my papers down with brickbats and write in the midst of the hurricanes, clothed in the same thin linen we make shirts of."

Some days in this secluded nook Mark Twain put on paper as much as fifty pages of the manuscript of *The Adventures of Tom Sawyer.* There were other days when he did not work at all, but, their portable hammocks placed side by side on the lawn, with his brother-in-law, Theodore Crane, read and discussed favorite books through lazy summer afternoons. These included *Two Years Before the Mast, The Mutineers of the Bounty* and *Pepys Diary,* volumes Mark Twain was sure to call for and reread on each return to Quarry Farm. To anticipate the issue of Mark Twain's labors in the summer of 1874: He finished *Tom Sawyer* at Hartford in July, 1875—the family did not go that summer to Quarry Farm—and it was published in December, 1876, to at once take and hold first place among American stories of boy life. The play which he made from *The Gilded Age* was given in Hartford in January, 1875, with John T. Raymond in the role of Colonel Sellers, and for a long period yielded golden returns to authors and actor.

Another product of the summer of 1874 demands a word. Auntie Cord, the colored cook at Quarry Farm, was a Virginian negress who took pride in the fact that in her youth she had been twice sold as a slave. In the long ago a barbarous system had parted her from all her children, but at sixty she was rotund and jolly and plainly without a care in the world. She had told the strange story of her life to Mrs. Crane, and the latter in turn had passed it on to her sister's husband. One evening, with the family gathered on the front veranda in the moonlight, Auntie Card paused to say goodnight. A tactful question or two won her confidence, and a moment later she was seated at Mark Twain's feet repeating the story she had told Mrs. Crane.

The author wrote it out next morning in thought and idiom exactly as she had told it to him and under the title *A True Story, Repeated Word for Word as I Heard It* the article was published in the November, 1874, issue of the *Atlantic Monthly*—Mark Twain's first contribution to that magazine. It is now included in *Sketches New and Old,* and the latter-day reader who comes upon it there will vote it a rare and fine example of its author's gift of transcription and portrayal. William Dean Howells, then editor of the *Atlantic,* described it as "one of those noble pieces of humanity with which the South has . . . atoned for all its despite to the negro," and few there are who will deny Auntie Cord's story a place among minor masterpieces.

The summer of 1876 was another happy period for the Clemens family again at Quarry Farm, where they had gone, ran a letter to Dr. John Brown, to be "hermits that eschew caves and live in the sun." For Mark Twain the season was one of steady industry, and before its end he had written several hundred pages of *The Adventures of Huckleberry Finn,* designed as a sequel to

Tom Sawyer. It was at this time also that, borrowing the manner and methods of his favorite Pepys, he wrote the sketch to which he later gave the title *1601.* Another minor masterpiece, this rollicking and wholly frank report of an imaginary conversation at the court of Queen Elizabeth will not be found in its author's collected works, but it is better than Rabelais and in some future time, for men change and tastes change with them —may find a welcome from those who now read *The Decameron* and *Droll Tales* without a qualm.

In the course of his reading at Quarry Farm in the summer of 1877 Mark Twain came upon and conned with delight an English tale of the thirteenth century written by Charlotte M. Yonge and entitled *The Prince and the Page.* The story of a submerged personality there set forth fired Mark Twain's fancy, and during the summer he wrote some four hundred manuscript pages of the tale later published as *The Prince and the Pauper.* Then he laid it aside until a new period of inspiration should come to him.

The summer of 1877 at Quarry Farm had one tense quarter hour in which John Lewis, colored man-of-all-work, played a hero's part. Mark Twain told the story at length in letters to Dr. John Brown and William Dean Howells. The young wife of Charles Langdon with her little daughter Julia and the latter's nursemaid, were in a buggy and their runaway horse was speeding down East Hill toward Elmira and what seemed fatal disaster, when Lewis, homeward bound with a loaded wagon, discovered their plight. He turned his team across the road and leaping from his seat seized the bridle of the frightened horse and, "mighty of frame and muscle," brought it to a standstill.

When the Clemens and Crane families, who had seen the alarming start from the farm gate, arrived on the scene with fear in their hearts they found that no harm had befallen the supposed victims. Lewis was promptly rewarded for his bravery. He was given fifteen hundred dollars in money and a variety of presents. Most important of these in the hero's estimation was an inscribed stem-winding gold watch, splendid and welcome fulfilment of his long cherished desire to own a silver timepiece "costing at least thirty dollars." Lewis lived on at Quarry Farm for nearly thirty years, his old age, when he was no longer able to work, made one of peace and comfort by a monthly pension to which Mark Twain and Henry H. Rogers were contributors.

The Clemens family sailed early in April, 1878, for the sojourn in Europe which was to furnish material for *A Tramp Abroad*. When they returned in the first days of September, 1879, they went at once to Quarry Farm, where at his accustomed study-table Mark Twain resumed with renewed interest work on the manuscript of this book which he had begun in Paris. Both husband and wife were weary of travel and glad to be back at Quarry Farm. Twichell of Hartford for six weeks had shared Mark Twain's tramps of the previous year through the Black Forest and other parts of Europe. "You have run about a good deal, Joe," Clemens now wrote him, "but you have never seen any place that was so divine as the farm. Why don't you come here and take a foretaste of heaven?"

In March, 1880, *A Tramp Abroad*, which Mark Twain had finished in Hartford early in January, came from the press and was received by the reviewers as a singular blending of its author's best and—worst. But Howells praised it without reserve, and the right word from that friend was always food and drink to Clemens. At Elmira in July, 1880, a third daughter was born to the author and his wife, a robust example of babyhood whom they named Jane Lampton in honor of her grandmother, but who was always called Jean. That summer Mark Twain worked by turns on *Huckleberry Finn* and *The Prince and the Pauper*. The latter, which he brought to an end on September 15, was published in December of the following year, dedicated to the author's daughters, Susy and Clara. It contained some of Mark Twain's best writing, and through the years has won and held the favor of young and old.

The stay at Quarry Farm in the summer of 1881 was a long one. The early part of the summer of 1882 Mark Twain devoted to a trip to his old haunts on the Mississippi. In the opening months of 1875 the *Atlantic Monthly* had published seven articles dealing in a masterly way with his experiences as a pilot. These he now decided with added material to expand into a volume, but first there was need for a freshening of old memories by trips down the river to New Orleans and up the river to St. Paul. These journeys were duly accomplished, with a halt of three days at his native Hannibal. Then he posted eastward to Quarry Farm, where he began work on the book that was to be called *Life on the Mississippi*. He finished it at Hartford before the end of the year and it was published in May, 1883 to at once take its place, by reason particularly of its masterly first chapters, as one of the finest of his many books.

A month later the Clemens family were again at Quarry Farmy, and, rereading the first chapters of a manuscript long on the stocks, Mark Twain found his inspiration renewed, and set out to work with fresh zeal on *The Adventures of Huckleberry Finn*. "I haven't piled up manuscript so in years," he wrote Howells late in July, "as I have done since we came here to the farm three weeks and a half ago. I wrote four thousand words today and I touch three thousand and upward pretty often, and don't fall below twenty-six hundred any working day. And when I get fagged out, I lie abed a couple of days and read and smoke, and then go it again for six or seven days." The book "I half-finished two or three years ago I expect to complete in a month or . . . two months more. And I shall like it whether anybody else does or not."

In this instance Mark Twain had good reason to be proud of the child of his fancy. When, after long labor with the proofs in the summer of 1884, a labor in which Mrs. Clemens with careful regard for the conventions took a critical and by no means minor part, *Huckleberry Finn* came from the press in the last days of that year it was accepted on the instant as a worthy sequel to *Tom Sawyer* and its ragged and homeless yet care-free hero as one of the immortal lads of fiction. It was published, it should be noted in passing, by the firm Mark Twain had established in association with Charles L. Webster, who had married the daughter of his sister Pamela, and which shortly was to win immense prestige as publishers of the *Memoirs* of General Grant.

The summer of 1885 at Quarry Farm, to which the Clemens family came at the end of June, was for Mark Twain one of anxious thought for the success of these *Memoirs* which the slowly dying author was bringing to a painful conclusion at Mount McGregor. A day or two after his arrival at Quarry Farm, he was summoned to Mount McGregor by General Grant, and was able to carry with him the cheering news that there were already in hand advance orders for upward of one hundred thousand sets of the *Memoirs*. General Grant died on July 23, and on February 27, 1886, a little more than seven months later, Charles L. Webster & Company handed his widow a check for two hundred thousand dollars, up to that time the largest single royalty check in history. Later checks made up a total of four hundred and forty thousand dollars paid Mrs. Grant.

The summers of 1886 and 1887 at Quarry Farm do not seem to have been attended by labor on any of Mark Twain's major books, but during the summer of 1888 he took up and worked with fresh inspiration and energy on a story he had begun a few years before after a reading of a copy of Malory given him by George W. Cable—*A Connecticut Yankee at King Arthur's Court.* "As I read those quaint and curious legends," he recalled at a later time, "I naturally contrasted those days with ours, and it made me curious to fancy what might be the result if we could dump the nineteenth century down into the sixth century and observe the consequences." His attempt to do this was now attended by tart expression of his unrelenting hatred of abuses and inequalities pardoned by time; and the book when published in 1889, with apt illustrations by Daniel Carter Beard, gave grave and lasting offense in England; but Mark Twain never did more delightful writing than in the opening pages of *A Connecticut Yankee,* and present readers find it what its author intended it should be—a stern protest against injustice and man's inhumanity to his fellows.

In the summer of 1888 one of the present writers was a youthful reporter in Elmira and an indelible memory of that now faraway time attaches to the occasional appearances of Mark Twain in the streets of the town, clad usually in white and revealing beneath a wide brimmed hat of straw a shock of iron-gray hair soon to become not unlike a silver crown—an unmistakable and unforgetable figure. A second and pleasant memory of those distant times has to do with advice and help given to another reporter who travelling from India to England by way of the United States in the summer of 1889 halted at Elmira in quest of the interview with Mark Twain he desired to procure for his Allahabad newspaper.

Twenty-four year old Rudyard Kipling was then unknown outside of a narrow circle, but in no long time was to claim attention as a star of the first magnitude in the literary firmament. A mid-morning call at the office of *The Telegram,* and a drive to Quarry Farm disclosed the fact that Mark Twain was at the home of Charles Langdon in the city. Thus on an early August afternoon the Langdon homestead became the first meeting-place of the two most widely known authors of their period. Both later recorded characteristic accounts of this contact of kindred spirits and the birth of a friendship which was to end only with the death of the elder man. "I am not a lover of all poetry," Mark Twain more than once declared in after years; "but there is something in Kipling that appeals to me. I guess he is about my level."

Theodore Crane, friend and beloved comrade of Mark Twain, after long illness died at Quarry Farm in July, 1889. Late in the following year the mothers of both Mr. and Mrs. Clemens passed from life—the one at Keokuk, Iowa, at the ripe age of eighty-seven, and the other at Elmira in the home which for more than half a century she had helped to make a center of gracious and beautiful living. Grave presages these of the tragic part death was thereafter and in ever increasing measure to play in the life of Mark Twain. The Clemens family did not spend the summer of 1890 at Quarry Farm, but instead, as related in an earlier chapter, took for the season a cottage at the Onteora Club at Tannersville in the Catskills.

There followed a period of anxiety and trial for the Clemens family. Ill-starred investments in the development of a type-setting machine which had enlisted Mark Twain's interest and support, and an evil turn in the affairs of his publishing house, the latter made more acute by the death of Webster, the managing partner, had now not only made heavy inroads into the husband's available resources, but had also seriously impaired the wife's patrimony. No longer able to afford the expense of the home they had built in Hartford, they closed it after seventeen happy years, and seeking a more modest scale of living, in June, 1891, departed for a long sojourn in Germany, the south of France and Italy. Quarry Farm did not see them again until May, 1895.

During this period Mark Twain made business trips of varying length to America, but none of them helped to restore order and hope to his muddled affairs, and in April, 1894, the firm of Webster & Company made an assignment for the benefit of its creditors and closed its doors, owing more than two hundred thousand dollars, nearly a third of which represented money supplied by Mrs. Clemens. The remainder of the year and the early months of 1895 Mark Twain rested with his family in France or worked on the final chapters of what some regard as the finest expression of his genius, *Personal Recollections of Joan of Arc*. While thus engaged, although loathing the platform and all that went with it, he resolved upon a tour that should compass the globe, in the course of which, by readings from his works, he hoped to earn the money needed to pay his debts in full.

With this purpose in mind the Clemens family sailed for

America on May 11 and a few days later were once more at Quarry Farm. There during the weeks that followed arrangements were completed for the series of readings about to begin, and Mark Twain did almost the last writing he was ever to do in his hilltop study. There also it was decided that Mrs. Clemens and their daughter Clara should accompany him in his long tour, while Susy and Jean Clemens remained with their aunt, Mrs. Crane, at Quarry Farm. They left Elmira on the night of July 14, 1895, and their last sight, as the train got under way, was of Susy, standing with others on the station platform, and waving them good-by.

From the outset, Mark Twain's readings proved a complete success. Their purpose had become a matter of common knowledge, and great audiences greeted him at each appearance. When the party reached the Pacific Coast he was able to forward five thousand dollars to New York to place against his debt account. They left Vancouver on August 23, beginning the long pilgrimage that was to carry them to Australia, New Zealand, India, the Island of Mauritius and South Africa, whence on July 14, 1896, they sailed for England, where it had been planned that Susy and Jean, companioned by Katie Leary, an old and trusted servant, should join them. The last leg of their voyagings was a restful and happy one, for Mark Twain had earned money enough to pay his creditors dollar for dollar, and leave him a free man.

Husband, wife and daughter reached Southampton on the last day of July, and in preparation for the expected arrival on August 12 of Susy and her sister, leased for the summer a house at Guilford. But on August 12, instead of Katie and the girls, came a letter saying that Susy was ill, and that there would be a delay in their sailing. A cabled request for later news brought a reply that the sick girl was facing a slow recovery, and the same day Mrs. Clemens and Clara sailed for America to nurse her. This was on August 15, and three days later when they were in mid-ocean Susy Clemens died of cerebral fever in the old home at Hartford. She had been ailing for a time at Quarry Farm; seeking change and relief had gone for a visit with Mrs. Charles Dudley Warner at Hartford, and by a physician's orders removed to the quiet of her own home there to face an untimely end.

Alone in the hired house at Guilford, despairing and hopeless, Mark Twain received the cabled news of her passing. Mother and sister, arriving three days later in New York, were greeted

with the same sad tidings and that afternoon caught a through
train to Elmira. There Susy had already been taken, and the
following day, after a service in the great house where she was
born, they buried her by the side of her little brother, and or-
dered a headstone inscribed with these lines which they had found
in Australia:

Warm summer sun shine kindly here:

Warm southern wind blow softly here;

Green sod above lie light, lie light—

Good night, dear heart, good night, good night.

Only parts of the after history of the Clemens family and of
the conditions under which Mark Twain's last books were written claim a place in the present chronicle. There were periods of
residence and labor in England, Germany and Italy and in and
about New York. They were living at Riverdale on the Hudson
when, early in 1903, the failing health of Mrs. Clemens prompted
plans for another indefinite stay in Italy. Not, however, before
a final summer at Quarry Farm. They reached that beloved place
on July first, and remained there three peaceful months, in the
course of which Mark Twain did what was probably the very last
of his writings in his old study, his pathetic *A Dog's Tale*. They
sailed for Italy on October 24, and early in November were settled in a fine old palace near Florence. But this last quest for
health proved a vain one. Mrs. Clemens died in her sleep on
the afternoon of June 5, and on July 14, after services in the
Elmira home of her girlhood and young womanhood, was laid to
rest by the side of Susy and little Langdon. "Imagine," the husband had written his old friend Twichell from Florence, "a man
worth a hundred millions who finds himself penniless and fifty
millions in debt in his old age. I was richer than any other person in the world, and now I am that pauper without peer."

Mark Twain passed no more summers at Quarry Farm. For
him there was now only sadness in its beautiful and tender associations. His home for the brief measure of living that remained
to him after July 18, 1908, was a house which had been built for
him on a hilltop near to Redding, Connecticut and to which he
gave the name of Stormfield. A year and a half later this new
home was witness to his last great sorrow. His youngest daughter, Jean, had been long subject to sudden and serious illness, and
on the morning before Christmas in 1909 death came to her in

her bath.   Three days later, the father unable to make the winter journey, she was buried at Elmira.

After that, with the steadily failing strength of age, there was only quiet waiting for the end by a desolate and lonely old man.   Mark Twain died at Stormfield at the sunset hour of April 21, 1910, and was duly borne to Elmira to sleep by the side of his wife and those others who had preceded him.   His grave, now marked by a tall shaft of marble, has become a shrine for summer pilgrims from a hundred lands.

INDEX

NOTE TO THE READER

The text of this book is set in Old Style Roman, a Linotype face which belongs to the family of printing types called "modern face" by printers—a term used to mark the change in style of type-letters that occurred in the opening years of the last century. The book was designed, composed and printed by Barber-Doane-Mosher, Inc., of Elmira, New York, and bound by Moore & Company, Inc., of Baltimore, Maryland.

DATE DUE

GAYLORD

PRINTED IN U.S.A.